TENNIS

GIANNI CLERICI

OCTOPUS

Editor: Enzo de Michele

Design by: Guido Regazzoni

Photo Editors: Laura Gerosa, Antonino Armata, and the author, who researched most of the photographs himself.

Color plates: Paolo Guidotti

Statistics: Rino Tommasi

Credits: In memory of Rosetta Gagliardi Prouse, Herman David, Placido Gaslini, Coco Gentien, Luigi Orsini, and D. H. Sweet.

For patient and persistent help, the author thanks Professor Gabrieli of the University of Rome, Professor Pigato of the Catholic University of Milan, and Dr. Dennis Rhodes of the British Museum in London.

The author also expresses sincere thanks to the following friends and fans who provided information and documents as needed: Russ Adams, Alain Bernard, Federico Billour, Ron Bookman, Toto Brugnon, Jorge Cela Trulok, Santiago Coca Fernandez, Arthur Cole, Bud Collins, Max Décugis, Carlo della Vida, José Maria du Camp, Alfonso Fumarola, France Gay, Pierre Geelhand, Simon Giordano, David Gray, Paul Haedens, Matts Hasselquist, Gladys Heldman, Pat Hughes, Heather and Jimmy Jones, Eiichi Kawatei, Gil de Kermadec, Jack Kramer, Wolfgang Lencer, Alan Little, Thomas Lynch, Dan Maskel, Olivier Merlin, Giulio Marchesano, Umberto Mezzanotte, George Prouse, Fernando Olozaga, Augusto Serventi, Nico Slotemaker, Giorgio de Stefani, Elizabeth Stevenson, Lance Tingay, Teddy Tinling, Tom Todd, Rino Tommasi, Torben Ulrich, Jimmy Van Alen, Hans Wiesner, Lilly Wollerner, Helen and Harold Zimman, Henri Zalzal.

For help in researching photographs the author is very grateful to the editorial staffs of *Il Tennis Italiano, Lawn Tennis, Tennis Club, Tennis de France, Tennis World, World Tennis* and the National Tennis Hall of Fame of Newport.

This edition first published 1976 by
Octopus Books Limited
59 Grosvenor Street
London W1

ISBN 7064 0523 4

Originally published in Italian by
Arnoldo Mondadori Editore

Printed in Italy by Arnoldo Mondadori, Verona

Preface

Dedicated to don Antonio Scaino da Salò

Ah! que nos coeurs sont frais
sous nos chemises blanches!

How pure are our hearts
Beneath our white shirts!

Louis Codet

In order to go to the British Broadcasting Corporation, my friend thought it would be easier to meet me at Lord's, at the old Club. I found him waiting in an old, overstuffed leather chair, deep in thought.

"I want to show you something," he smiled and took me to a wall where a painting stood out from its surroundings. I observed a court scene to the left of a lofty castle, and then, as the panorama of an immense park caught my eye, I could not help but exclaim: "Why, they're playing tennis!"

When my friend confirmed it. I was ready to admit: "It seems authentic, at first glance. And in a big way."

He looked at me with an amused look in his eye.

"It *is* authentic," he finally stated, "and dates from the early sixteenth century. It seems," he continued, "that there are other versions of this work. At least two of them are in England. Well then, shall we be on our way?"

Some days later, as I watched the matches on Centre Court at Wimbledon, I couldn't get my mind off those two men sending a ball back and forth with their rackets, not unlike the champions that I had before my eyes. Tennis suddenly seemed less dramatic and important, and, at the same time, much more heartfelt and justifiable. The dust of time had settled upon it, and I sensed that there was another way of looking at the sport: as a work of art. I had always thought of tennis, from the very moment in my childhood when I chose it as my game, as something different. The conditions that it imposed were rugged individualism and total silence. Its method of scoring had no limits, and theoretically at least, could last for days on end and not even come to an end then. The players had to wear the same pure and spotless white. The awareness of the existence of a similar game at the beginning of the sixteenth century spurred me to search out the other paintings. I was finally able to track down eight of them, scattered from Lisbon to Connecticut, from the Elizabeth Stewart Gardner Museum in Boston to the Louvre. I was convinced that at least one version must be found in my native Italy. And there it was, in the city of Como, only three hundred metres from the club where I had learned to play. Painted by Lucas Gassel, the painting belonging to the Restelli Collection is assuredly the most beautiful of the nine versions, so similar among themselves as to raise doubts concerning the experts' view that each was the work of a different artist. And, once I had located the works themselves, it was not difficult for me to track down the book which gave birth to them all, the splendid technical manual written by Antonio Scaino da Salò in 1555. This philosopher's stone of the sport has afforded me a long although rather labyrinthlike exploration of its Greek and Roman, Arabic, and medieval beginnings. Having brought together the data concerning handball, I again made brief stops at courts and castles, Amboise, Windsor, the Louvre, and Milan. The Renaissance rackets, "modeled on the zither", with "strings like those of a viola", took on the beauty of the racket so tastefully brushed in by the Venetian master Giovanni Battista Tiepolo (1696–1770). Royal tennis, the predecessor of lawn tennis, recapitulated and carried on the tradition of the *jeu de paume* and of rackets, brought the sport to refined gentility, and then declined, phoenixlike, to be born again of its own ashes.

Major Wingfield, always thought of as the inventor of lawn tennis, was unmasked and seen in proper perspective: a pleasant old codger, always ready to smell out the commercial possibilities of a new game, delightfully practical, confused by a thousand rules in a thousand back yards. From then on, the successes and triumphs of the most candid of sports are those of social progress.

The captains of the industrial revolution, the women suffragettes of the gay nineties, and the American investors have all profited from participation in the game. However, I should not want these last words of mine to deter the tennis buff from purchasing the book because of its sociological implications. *Tennis* could (and should) be called *A Cup of Tea in the Afternoon*, *not* as a play on the great Ernest Hemingway's title *Death in the Afternoon*, but because of one of the many cups of tea taken after one of the many games of tennis played any afternoon.

In the color plate on the facing page, the famous mosaic of young women in the Villa of the Piazza Armerina and the less known young men from the fresco of the Via Portuense are the only Roman mural paintings from the Christian era that shed any light on the ball games of the period. Also instructive is the bas-relief of the small juggler from the Castle of Mantua. The women's game that we view here is certainly not follis, *played with a larger ball, or* trigon, *which would require a third player. By the process of elimination, it seems we are witnessing a game of* pila paganica, *played with a ball filled with feathers and occasionally played in the gymnasiums.*

On the following two pages, in the trecento manuscript of the Lancelot of the Lake legend, we see the medieval descendant of the same game, now called paume. *The ball is sewn in segments as was the one from the Villa of the Piazza Armerina. The scorekeeper and the gentlemen at their play seem more expert in the game than the page and the fine lady from the Latin book of hours in the lower right. This manuscript is among the treasures of the British Museum.*

In one version of the Alexander Romance *the little friar is about to hit the ball thrown by the nun. The painting emphasizes that at that time the players were already using instruments other than the palm of the hand.*

The last color plate shows an ethereal young woman, painted perhaps by a follower of Pisanello, or perhaps by the master himself. The work was executed in Borromeo's Palace in the first half of the Quattrocento. The bat is rounded and polished, but this may well represent the refined technique of the painter as compared to that of the unknown French miniaturist who illuminated the Alexander Romance.

5760

spres · li rois nestoit mie en la
e acelle eure ains se siet en un
r praiel ki estoit desous la gnt
r · 7 aud ec lui estoient li pluisor
es hommes · La damoisiele des

i la mort abatu lame li estuet rendre
ses vaches garder ne porra mes entendre

mam de biele coulte amie ghmet
saues vous ke lams est vis. Da
me fait elle oil le vous dirai
bien. Lors li conte comment il
auoit le chlr trouue ki sa serour

ui timent te uidebūt
et letabunt: quia in
iniuste iniquitatē fec
runt in me: ego autem

Contents

THE ANCIENTS

Romans and Greeks. Ovid's Racket. Eclipse of the Game.
Renaissance among the Arabs and the Spaniards.
The Tennis-playing Kings of France and England.
The Origin of the Word *Tennis*.
Lucas Gassel's Early Painting.
Quotations from the Great Writers.
Antonio Scaino da Salò, the Creator of the Game's Manual of Style.
Greatness and Decline of the Sport of Kings.

Toward the middle of the sixteenth century, two books important to the history of tennis begin to circulate in Venetian typography. In 1555 appears the Trattato del Gioco della Palla (Treatise on the Ball Game) *by Antonio Scaino da Salò, and in 1573 comes out Mercurialis's* De Arte Gymnastica (Gymnastics). *Scaino, who will become one of the most important commentators on Aristotle in his day, dedicates the book to Alfonso II of Este, with whom he*

TRATTATO
DEL GIVOCO DELLA PALLA DI MESSER ANTONIO SCAINO DA SALO', DIVISO IN TRE PARTI.
CON DVE TAVOLE, L'VNA DE' Capitoli, l'altra delle cose piu notabili, che in esso si contengono.
CON PRIVILEGIO.
IN VINEGIA APPRESSO GABRIEL GIOLITO DE' FERRARI, ET FRATELLI. M D LV.

had had a technical argument during a game of tennis. His book is one of the most important works on the theory of the sport and the first not to slavishly imitate its predecessors. We see here a copy of the title page of the original edition. To the right is an illustration from the chapter "De sphaeristica" in Mercurialis's work, the most important source of information on the Greek and Roman versions of the sport. Some historians believe that the original for this piece of art work came from an old Roman coin, but its meaning is still obscure.
To the left is a figure of Antoninus Pius on a coin, holding the cosmos with a star superimposed upon it. Avoiding the religious symbolism, some have chosen rather to envision there a ball ready for play.

1 Romans, Greeks, and Archaic Ball Games

The athletes from the wall of Themistocles (B.C. 500) above and the tiny statue to the right are certainly meant to show ball players. It is difficult to tell if this marble effigy of a flesh-and-blood game is an ancestor of the ball games played with the hand (faininda *or* episciro) *or of the more aggressive* sferomachia *(a forerunner of Italian* calcio *and modern soccer).*

The baths opened toward ten o'clock in the morning, but Martial suggested that people of means not put in an appearance before one in the afternoon.

When the marble reflected the sun's rays in a blinding glare and dust darkened the bodies of the ballplayers, even Horace would cease playing. Intimidated by Maecenas's youthful vigor, he found a nap more pleasant for Virgil and himself, for they both were rather frail, their digestion not the best, and their eyes accustomed to the semidarkness of a study.

The exotic appearance of the spectators at the baths often distracted the attention of the players. The audience included farmers from Thrace, half-savage Sarmatians nourished on the blood of horses, and Egyptians used to the yellowish waters of the Nile, who stared in disbelief at the clear-running fountains in the baths. There were citizens from Cilicia, their skin powdered with yellow saffron; Arabs the color of pale olives; and Ethiopians the color of black ones.

How were these ball games played, and how did they resemble court tennis, rackets, not to speak of modern tennis itself? Don Antonio Scaino, the first to write a technical account of the sport, refuses to probe the subject in depth, which he could not hope to master as he did topics like the divine Aristotle, music, the Court of Este, and the delightful game of *rachetta* (racket).

Mercurialis, one of Scaino's contemporaries also interested in the leisure activities of the fifteenth and sixteenth centuries, published a very important treatise, *De Arte Gymnastica* (Gymnastics), in Venice, where Don Scaino had brought out his work. With polished elegance, Mercurialis details for us four different games played by the Romans: *follis, pila trigonalis, pila paganica*, and *harpastum*. The *follis* was made of cured skins filled with air, and when the ball was large in size, according to Mercurialis, it was put into play by using the whole arm.

The *pila trigonalis*, the author continues, ironically enough, did not receive its name from its form, but rather from the triangular playing field, the three players, or the fact that they positioned themselves in the shape of a triangle.

The *pila paganica*, as the name suggests, was played in the countryside as well as in the gymnasiums, that is in enclosed places. Larger than the *trigon* used for *pila trigonalis*, and smaller than the *follis*, the ball for *pila paganica* was filled with feathers.

Lastly, the *harpastum*, from the Greek verb *harpazein*, "to seize or snatch," was the smallest of the four, made of leather, and was probably grabbed by one player from another on a playing field bathed in a cloud of dust.

Referring again to the Greek origin of *harpastum*, Mercurialis fails to mention, perhaps because he considers the point too obvious, that the *pila trigonalis* also is derived from *trigonon*, a Greek word meaning "triangle." This omission is very likely due to the fact that in his day the classics were quoted in the same way that we mouth television commercials at the present time, and he glosses over his references with a quotation from Plautus and an allusion from Martial.

In order to get a clearer picture, it will be worthwhile to glance at the sources themselves.

Among these references we owe the richest ones to Martial because his sense of humor was a constant companion on the playgrounds, on the massage tables, and in the swimming pools. Six of the many epigrams that he dedicated to sport provide us with the answers to some questions as well as with some further questions of our own:

Non pila, non follis, non te paganica thermis
praeparat aut nudi stipitis ictus hebes,
vara nec in lento ceromate brachia tendis,
non harpasta vagus pulverulenta rapis Bk. VII, Ep. 32

Neither *pila trigonalis* nor *follis* nor *pila paganica*
Nor weak blows against the bare posts will get you in shape for the warm baths.
Do not twist your arms wrestling on the mat
Nor half-heartedly seize the *harpasta's* dusty form.

Sic palmam tibi de trigone nudo
unctae det favor arbiter coronae
nec laudet Polybi magis sinistras Bk. VII, Ep. 72

Let the obvious support of the freshly showered fans
Help you win the game of *pila trigonalis* played in the buff
And let them not praise Polybius's left-hand strokes more than your own.

Si me mobilibus scis expulsare sinistras
sum tua. Tu nescis? Rustice, redde pilam. Bk. XIV, Ep. 46

If you know how to return my shots with a speedy left hand, I am yours.
You do not? Then give up the ball, you awkward clown.

Capitabit tepidum dextra, laevaque trigonem
imputet acceptas ut tibi saepe pilas. Bk. XII, Ep. 82

He will receive the warm *trigon* with either the left or right hand,
Often giving away to you the points that he himself should have earned.

Seu lentum ceroma teris tepidumque trigona
sive arpasta manu pulverulenta rapis
plumea seu laxi partiris pondera follis Bk. IV, Ep. 19

You may wear out the soft mat with wrestling or the warm *trigon* in play,
You may snatch dusty *harpasta*,
Or you may send back the featherlike weight of the soft *follis*.

Haec quae difficili turget paganica pluma,
folle minus laxast et minus arta pila. Bk. IV, Ep. 45

This *pila paganica*, which is chock full of feathers,
Is not as soft as a *follis* and less compact than a *trigon*.

Fainында was a game that stressed the element of deception, and in episciro *a point was scored by sending the ball beyond the equivalent of the base line of the field. The descendant of* sferomachia *is still played in the Piazza della Signoria in Florence, Italy, to the delight of native Florentines and tourists alike. To the right, the mysterious and lovely Etruscan lady does her exercises while calmly seated in a representation from a tomb at Vulci.*

The first epigram contains a simple listing of the various games available at the baths. Notice that Martial always uses the shortened term *pila* when referring to the *pila trigonalis,* both for poetic and personal reasons.

From the second epigram we learn that the players often worked out in the nude. Also among women the customs were often relaxed, and we see that one of Martial's characters, Philaenis, the temptress of young men and the perennial moral destruction of young women, had the habit of flouncing her skirts provocatively against her own thighs.

Both in the second and the third epigrams there is a reference to the return of the ball executed at least twice with the left hand. Was there such an abundance of left-handed players among the Romans? Probably not, and we conclude from the poetry, though we cannot state it categorically, that the ball could be returned with the left fist or palm. Even more likely, as in tennis, the poorer player found himself in trouble when he had to return a shot aimed to his left side, and thus the mark of a really fine player was to be able to use the left hand well.

One of the most unusual images that has come down to us is the mosaic in the Villa of the Piazza Armerina in Sicily, where two young girls in their brown bikinis are shown throwing back and forth a small ball divided into blue, green, gold, and reddish sections.

The girl to the right of the mosaic, with her hair worn down, is ready to hit the ball (unless she has just hit it) and is positioned like a left-handed tennis player. Thus her weight rests squarely above her right foot.

The fourth epigram, which speaks of an old cadger always ready for a game, even after having showered and dressed, does not contradict my speculations concerning the use of the left hand. In fact, it seems that this Menogenes has caught the ball with either his left or right hand, and has, as a result, lost a point to his opponent and future amphitryon, with the flattery of some old coaches of today who let their students win so that they can cadge a cocktail.

Twice Martial uses the adjective "warm" to describe the *trigon.* In this case I find Mercurialis's explanation highly acceptable: either the game heated up the players, or, which is more likely, the touch of the players' sweaty hands warmed up the ball.

The last of the six epigrams takes us back to Mercurialis's classification of the sport.

Saleius Bassus, among other authors, gives a beautiful description of some difficult shots, but he is not of great help to us on the whole. He rather creates some doubt as to whether or not the ball could be hit twice in the air, as seems the case in the confused and untutored play of the youngsters in the Portuense fresco.

Plautus often refers to *pila,* applying the meaning of the game to the business of everyday living, as an indication that *trigon* and *follis* were not less popular than the other sports about which we have more detailed information. On one occasion the famous writer of comedies uses two technical terms. In his *Curculio* he calls two rather disreputable troupes of people batters and catchers, who are playing in the streets.

As concerns Ovid, two lines of the *Ars Amatoria* startled me when I first saw them, and I still find them fascinating:

Reticuloque pilae leves fundantur aperto,
nec, nisi quam tolles, ulla movenda pilast.

Almost all the serious Latinists, and Professor Pigato in particular, use the term "racket" in their translations:

The glossy balls rebound from the large racket,
And the only ball in play will be the one that you will return.

We could assume that the Romans already knew the use of the racket, and with good reason, because one of the two etymons that are given by the philologists as the source of the word *rachetta*

1

1. Here is a woodcut illustration of three players from Mercurialis's work. Arm and hand protectors fashioned from leather thongs are typical of Renaissance games like pallone, paume *and other modern ball games. The players are three in number, reminding us of the Roman* pila trigonalis.

(racket) is precisely *reticulum* (small *rete* or "net"). Then it becomes *retichetta* and, finally, *rachetta*.

Could balls that fell to the ground be replayed? They would, of course, put the chase, the point to be replayed, in doubt. We don't know if the Romans had yet invented this rule, which became fundamental in the Renaissance ball games and later in royal tennis.

Ovid himself dampens my enthusiasm with his advice a few lines later when he discourages his lovely women readers from taking part in rough male exercises like javelin throwing, swimming in icy water, and playing the *pila* itself. The gentle and easygoing nature of the fascinating Roman women, he says, is more suited to the games of *astragalus*, dice, and dominoes. It is truly a shame for a young lady not to know how to play these three, for she may well find the love of her life in this way.

What was the fate of ricochets that rebounded from the surface of the large rackets?

We shall never know it unless an inscription comes to light, some bit of mosaic, a mural painting, or even a coin like those from which it is claimed that Mercurialis procured the two classical scenes that introduce this chapter. Caught in motion on copper, in the act of hitting the ball, three big hairy fellows, their wrists and fists wrapped in wood and leather, reinforce the belief that *trigon* was the ancestor of the Renaissance games.

This was no game for sissies, for poor Filimazio, a bishop friend of Sidonius Apollinaris, was completely overwhelmed by it, due to his stubborn insistence on matching his ability with younger men. Sidonius himself, grudgingly but with a certain *noblesse oblige*, went out to the playing field to help his bruised and beaten friend, whose liver was also giving him pain, so that "the suffering of my friend not bring shame upon him."

Not only did they play outdoors on the village green or the town square and in the open areas around the baths, with their bodies powdered from head to foot, but there were also elegant covered playing fields. Pliny, the proprietor of several beautiful villas, described two of them in the region of Tuscany. Trimalchio, certainly not less wealthy, took pleasure in training outdoors, probably because Campania was favored with a milder climate.

This selection from the *Satyricon* is recounted not only for its charm but also for its uniqueness:

". . . We caught sight of a bald-headed old man in a reddish tunic, playing ball with a trio of long-haired youths. We didn't pay as much attention to the boys, though that might have been pleasant, as to the old gentleman in his slippers, busily engaged in hitting a dun-colored ball whizzing his way. He never returned the balls that fell to the ground, and a servant with a full bag replenished the players. We noticed some unusual sidelights as well: two eunuchs stood at opposite ends of the playing circle, one holding a silver chamber pot and the other counting the balls—not the ones that the players were hitting back and forth but the ones that fell to the ground."

We can see that the game was played in the round and that the balls that fell to the ground were not put back into play. Should we assume that some sort of "chase" (as in court tennis) was involved? Or should we rather think that the "unusual sidelights" were the product of Trimalchio's typical snobbish reactions? Or that the author Petronius is struck by the novelty of the chamber pot or, better, by the monetary value of that vessel?

2

3

Despite his eccentricities, perhaps Trimalchio did respect the rules. Precise as a notary, Seneca tells us that the ball itself should retain its momentum in the ball game, as it is skillfully thrown from one player to the other—the good player throws it differently to a tall teammate and a short one. The philosopher then mentions another typical detail that seems to be derived from the Greek game called *faininda,* a word that contains the idea of "deception" in its etymology. The purpose of the evil-intended player, he writes, is to confuse his partner, and to slow the progress of the game so that it cannot be continued until the matter is resolved.

It would seem, after all, that the most important element of the game was not the besting of one's opponent by making a point, but rather the precision of the play itself, such as we see today in our training drills. The game that Seneca compares so wisely to the benefits to be derived from a life of proper actions is not the same one that troubled Maecenas and Menogenes, that failed to enthuse the

2. The two gentlemen come from a nineteenth-century copy preserved in Hobart, Tasmania.
3. The three caricatures from the fancy of the Frenchman A. Guillaume show games played by a cave dweller, by Homer's Nausicaä, and lastly by the elder statesmen Socrates and Plato.

sedentary Virgil and Horace, or that sent poor Bishop Filimazio's liver into spasms.

Nor is it *trigon,* and the size of the ball described makes one doubt that it is *follis* either. Once again Martial laughs down the centuries at our ignorance and complicates the situation even more by asserting that *follis* is a proper pastime for children and old men.

It is unwise to waste too much time in speculation on the matter because the rules may never have been that precise, at least until 1555, when Don Antonio Scaino attempted to give his patron a lesson in technique and good manners and thereby began to standardize the rules.

The many attempts that have been made to establish a Greek origin for the Latin games have all been too optimistic if not altogether foolhardy, and they all bring us gratefully back to that trove of information on the period, Mercurialis.

The historian of the game is aided by lexicographers of the second and third centuries, Atheneus and Pollux, and by Eusthatius of Thessalonica from the twelfth. These worthy writers quote and then interpret texts of greater or lesser antiquity that link the episode of Nausicaä in Homer, the tales of Alexander as a ballplayer in Plutarch, and Galen's ideas on sports medicine.

Mercurialis describes four different sorts of balls. The one he called "larger" is played with hands and arms above one's head as a kind of volleyball, while the other three small ones vary in size.

One of the three, the *faininda,* is likened by Atheneus to the *harpastum,* and this rather vague description leads into more substantial information concerning the *episciro. Skuros* was the name of the line that divided the opposing teams of players who were obliged to hit the ball over one of two goal lines parallel to the midline.

This information makes us think of the similar Renaissance ball games, but we can locate no detailed descriptions, no clear outline of the rules, and no actual family tree of the game in the literature extant.

From a natural and primitive sort of ball game, the athletes probably developed a more sophisticated one, and then another which was a real test of strength, in which the ball was sent beyond the goal line of a field divided down the middle by a line traced in the earth with a stone. This second game then developed into a contest involving body contact, in which the ball was not only thrown but also carried beyond the goal lines.

It is obvious that the refined Greeks had brought with them into Latium not only their arts but also their recreations. "If Roman sports tire you," Horace will state plainly, "and you enjoy the Greek games, play ball!"

I do not possess the erudition necessary to speak further on the topic, but according to the few original documents that we possess, the game enjoyed some popularity and rules were drawn up for its play.

The nude athletes smile down from the walls of Themistocles, and the ball master of Alexander, Aristonicos Caristos, must have smiled down from his marble perch when his Athenian admirers erected a statue in his honor.

On many Roman coins, be they from the days of Hadrian, Gordian III, Aurelianus, or Antoninus, the emperor holds a globe in his hand, a symbol of his power. It is not hard to imagine this as an early symbol of the Game of Kings as well.

2 Arabs and Spaniards

The decadence of the Roman Empire, the invasions, the Dark Ages, all conspired against a light-hearted game consisting of propelling a small ball with the palm of one's hand, the clenched fist, a smooth or carved bat, or diverse kinds of gloves or arm coverings held together with leather thongs. Such frivolity had no place in those gloomy times!

The last news of the sport's survival is hidden away in Saint Isidore of Seville's massive compendium the *Summa*, written soon before the Arab invasion of his country. In his *Etimologiae*, Isidore speaks of the *pila*, explains to the reader that it must be filled with hair, preferably from a stag, and tells how much the ball ought to weigh. He then distinguishes the *trigondria*, played by three persons, from the *arenata*. With new names, the *pila trigonalis* and the *harpastum* have still not passed from the scene. Nevertheless, for centuries thereafter, we find no further references to the sport, and some authorities believe that it was altogether forgotten. Perhaps this theory has not taken into account that the invaders preferred violent recreation, being warlike in nature, and that those who held on to the culture of the land were far more interested in preserving the joy of the game than in writing down its virtues.

As soon as we approach a period of higher culture, of less barbaric customs, we hear the gentle thud of the ball once again.

Seventy years after the completion of Saint Isidore's labors, Seville is occupied by the Arabs. It would indeed be strange if they did not know the Greco-Roman games at least as well as Saint Isidore.

Many writers, from Omar Khayyám to Avicenna, speak of a ball that is hit back and forth in such a dangerous way that it sometimes costs the lives of some of the participants. In one account, a one-eyed emir is deeply mistrustful of his vizier—what would happen if the ball were to knock out his remaining eye?

It is a dangerous sport for the simple reason that it is played on horseback. Not the Persian game brought back from India with the Tibetan name of *pulu*, but a distant cousin, also played centaur-like, that is on horseback, and making use of a kind of racket instead of a mallet.

An Englishman writes in *The Field* of 1927 that "in Persia there were two types of ball games: one was called *savlajan*, played with a long baton carved at one end, evidently the origin of polo. The other, *ciogan* or *tchigan*, was played with a shorter, stringed racket and must have been the origin of the French game *chicane*, or of the *jeu de paume* (ball hit with the palm of the hand) in the same country. Avicenna writes that there were two types of *kora* or *ciogan*, the large and the small, which again seem to correspond to the French games *longue paume* (long *paume* played mostly in the open air) and *courte paume* (short *paume* played in a court)."

This testimony is corroborated not only by Albert de Luze, the most important modern French authority on court tennis, but also by Cinnamus, who writes, soon after the middle of the twelfth century: "Young gentlemen, divided into two teams, sat in the saddle at the two ends of the arena. Suddenly a leather ball the size of an apple was thrown into the center of the playing area. The horsemen of both teams went galloping toward the ball, each one holding a narrow baton which was gently curved at one end, the central part of which was crosshatched with dry animal gut in the form of a net."

Toward 800 A.D. this sort of racket polo was taken right into a closed arena in the palace of Harun al-Rashid, if we are to believe the account of Messaoudi written a century and a half later.

Certainly the arena was no garden, for the walls that surrounded the playing area were painted black as were those in the combat area where the sultans Kamel and El Ashraf did daily battle in 1274, and Nureddin himself, the arch enemy of the crusaders, trained at night by the light of the braziers.

Black provided the proper background against which the ball was easier to see, and I should not be at all surprised if, in the tight quarters of combat, the knights would often come down from their horses, still availing themselves of their rackets. I would never have gotten on the track of this sport, had I not run across the suggestion, and had it confirmed for me by Professor Gabrieli, that *ráhat* in Arabic means "rest" and "amusement" as well as "palm of the hand," that is to say *paume* in French. In the fifteenth and

Upper left: Is the horseman holding a scimitar or a piece of equipment similar to the cesta *used in contemporary Basque* pelota*? The game is probably* ciogan, *like polo played on horseback but not to be confused with it, though further research is needed to shed light on the matter.*

Lower left: This bit of parchment comes to us from the Etimologiae *of Saint Isidore of Seville, the only document we possess pertaining to the game from the period between the decline of the Roman Empire and the Arab invasion of Spain.*

sixteenth centuries, *jeu de paume* is played more and more not only with the hand but with an object held in it. "Racket" began to mean the perfected object, the almost symbolic extension of the palm of the hand itself, carrying the day over less refined methods of propulsion like the French *battoir* and the Spanish *palo*.

The introduction of the term "racket," first in Italy and then in France, does not seem to be an isolated phenomenon. In fact, the word *hazard*, which in court tennis is a winning shot that goes into one of the openings in the enclosure, originally meant "die" (for games) in Arabic. All things considered, it is tempting to speculate that either the word or the instrument or both may have arrived to us mixed with precious silks, perfumes, and ostrich plumes in the sea chest of some crusader, again following the course of the sun, like the journey from Greece to Rome.

It is difficult to maintain, and it is even more difficult to demonstrate, as some historians try to do, that the most highly valued balls arrived from the city of Tinnis, built at the mouth of the Nile and submerged together with its cotton looms by the rising of the sea. Like a mirage, tennis appears and disappears among the Arabs as a word derivation and an assumption.

The first news of the reappearance of the sport in the West comes to us from Spain before the final expulsion of the Moors. The author of the *Libro de Apollonio* (Book of Apollonius), written between 1230 and 1250, is not known by name, but he certainly was a *mester de clerecía*, a learned man capable of combining a Byzantine novel, the *Gesta Romanorum*, Homer and Ovid, and the German version of the *Gesta Apollonii* of the tenth century into a pleasing whole. The protagonist, King Apollonius, forced to flee a menacing situation in Antioch, sets sail, is shipwrecked, and according to the very best novel-of-chivalry tradition, finds himself a ragged beggar in front of the palace of the king Arquitrastes.

The poem, put into modern Spanish by the historian Miguel Piernavieja, goes as follows, bilingually:

Aún no había llegado la hora de comer
salieron los jóvenes afuera a divertirse;
empezaron entonces a jugar a la pelota,
pues tenían costumbre de jugarla a esa hora.
Apolonio se puso, aunque mal vestido,
a jugar con ellos, con su manto abrochado
y jugaba tan preparado
como si de niño se lo hubieran enseñado.
La hacía ir recta al golpearla con el palo,
cuando la recibía no se la iba de la mano,
era en el deporte esperto y ligero.
Cualquiera comprendería que no era un villano.

It was not yet time to go to dinner
When the young men decided to go out for amusement;
They began to play ball
As was their custom at that hour.
Apollonius, although poorly garbed,
Began to play with them, with his cloak buttoned about him,
And he played as well
As if he had been taught the game as a small child.
When he struck it with his staff, he made it go straight,
When he received it, it never got out of hand.
He was quick and expert in the sport.
Anyone could see that he was not a man of low estate.

At that moment the king arrives with his retinue to watch the game:

El rey Arquitrastes, cuerpo de buenas mañas,
salió también a deportarse con buena compañía,
todos traían consigo sus vergas y sus cañas,
iguales y bien hechas, derechas y extrañas.
Se puso a mirar cómo jugaba cada uno,
cómo golpeaba la pelota y cómo la recobraba.

King Arquitrastes, himself a fine athlete,
With good company went out to amuse himself.
They all carried their staffs and clubs with them,
All well made, straight, and exotic to look upon.
He set himself to watching each of them play,
How each hit the ball and received it.

And seeing that Apollonius, despite his pitiable appearance, did not miss one shot, Arquitrastes:

Mandó parara todos y detener el juego,
ordenó que les dejasen a ellos solos la pelota;
el caudillo de Tiro, con toda su pobreza
bien se limpiaba los ojos de la gota.

He ordered all the others to stop their play
And requested that the ball be left to them alone.
The chieftan of Tyre with his poor raiment
Wiped a bitter tear from out his eye.

The game between the two is not described in clear enough terms to help our understanding of the sport, but it ends with a banquet set before the poor king by the rich one. Apollonius is then recognized for what he really is and highly honored.

Nevertheless, let us take a look at an illuminated page which illustrates the *Cantigas* by King Alfonso X (the Wise) of Castile. The miniature was prepared soon after the middle of the same thirteenth century. If we compare King Alfonso's suggestions for the sport with those of the *Libro de Apollonio*, we find, once again, some constant elements in its composition.

Of the five elegant young men in the miniature, the first to the left, with his red tunic slipped down around his waist to have more freedom of movement, has a staff some seventy centimeters (2 ft. 3⁹⁄₁₆ in.) in length and four (1⁹⁄₁₆ in.) in width. This staff reminds us of the bat held in the tiny hand of the lovely girl painted two centuries later in Milan by the master of the games, Borromeo.

In the *Libro de Apollonio* we are told that the players used *palos*, *vergas*, and *cañas*, and were all this equipment the same, the writer would not have felt the need for a different term to describe each. It follows, therefore, that competition was possible with different staffs and bats in the same game, and this fact will be confirmed at several points hereafter.

The second young man, in the violet tunic on the illuminated page, is holding up the ball with two fingers. He reminds us vividly of the *mandarino* (ball server) of medieval Italian *pallone* (ball game), with his arm protector, ready to pitch the ball to the batter. The three other players in the illuminated miniature are positioned to

The illustration at the top of the page is from the Egyptian Beni Hasan fresco. To the left, we see three jugglers, and to the right, a game in which the participant who lost control of the ball played the role of a mount for his partner until he in turn made a fault. According to Plato, this game was also well known in Greece. Bottom right: *The three lightly-clad women are copies of an ivory of the second century found in the Museum of Kabul in Afghanistan. Arm held high above her head, the stance of the woman to the left is typical of many illustrations of* paume *in the Western countries. The woman crouching down is rubbing the ball with something sticky so that it will not slip from her hand.*
Above: Two Chinese women play shuttlecock. The game, which was common in all the countries of the Orient, was renamed badminton in 1873 for the country house of the Duke of Beaufort.
Opposite page, top left: *This painting by Ortega shows the most exciting moment of a game of* tlatchli, *when the winning player demonstrates his joy at his success in passing the ball through the center of the large sculptured stone disk.*

This Toltec game had religious and symbolic elements, and the ball was hit with buttocks and thighs. Upper right: *A Toltec votive statue.* Lower four pictures: *Here we see scenes from the Iroquois sport of baggataway, renamed crosse (lacrosse) by the European invaders. This game, practiced by entire tribes, led to the massacre of the English garrison in 1763. George Catlin, the artist who painted the three scenes, was both an ethnologist and avid historian of the sport. The piece of equipment of the Choctaw used in baggataway, about 1.2 m (4 ft.) long, was made of hickory wood and leather.*

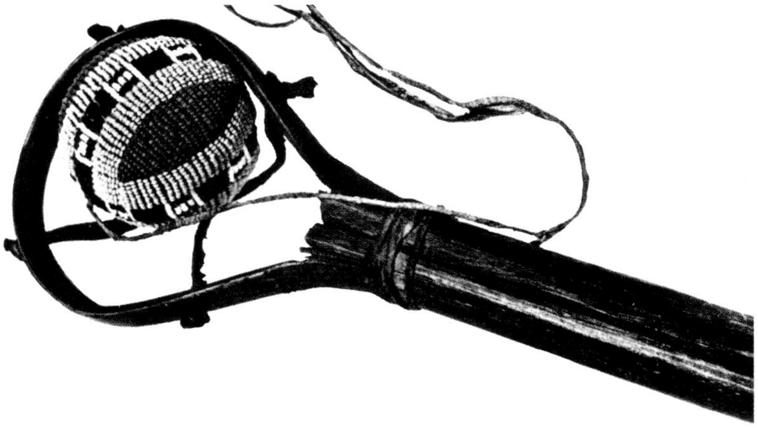

These miniatures from the fourteenth and fifteenth centuries, some of which are obviously later copies show the development of the game from the placement with the hand, through the use of the bat, to an attempt at a volley. The texts inform us that it was very common for games to take place between a player with a racket and an individual using only his hand. The latter player sometimes received a handicap.

receive a ball being thrown to them. They may be playing with the batters, or they may rather be engaged in a game of *pila trigonalis*.

Apollonius's poem tells us that the two kings are playing alone, but a few moments ago the players were absorbed in a game made up of teams of two or three men each. A fundamental rule is quite clear: the ball was struck with bat or staff and received in the hand. As was the case earlier with the Romans, to let the ball fall to the ground was to lose a point.

With such simple equipment it was obviously difficult to maintain rallies of any duration. The balls themselves were very crude: observing the ones in the miniature under a magnifying glass, we can see the points where the hide was sewn together. The seam made them dangerous on contact. One of King Alfonso's decrees promulgated in 1255 shows how dangerous the game could be: Whoever has killed a passerby on a busy thoroughfare, . . . *porque fue a jugar en lugar donde no debía* (because he went to play in a place where he ought not to have been), is guilty of murder with no extenuating circumstances.

In the *Siete Partidas* (1265), Alfonso sets down a stern warning to the clerics, who are not to play ball, under threat of suspension for three years. They are also prohibited from stopping to watch such games or from speaking with the players.

These prohibitions make clear that these ball games were *not* the exclusive province of the aristocracy as has been claimed by some highly authoritative scholars.

It is all very well and good for the anonymous *mester de clerecía* to write that one can see from Apollonius's ability in the game that he is not a person of low estate. But even King Alfonso, in one of the *Cantigas*, speaks to his readers saying:

En aquela praç' auia / un prado mui verd'assaz
en que as gentes da terra / Yan têer seu solaz;
et iogauan a pelota, / que e jogo de que praz
muit' o omêes mancebos / màis que outro iog'atal.

(The passage is from the original Galician, a language akin to Spanish and spoken in northwestern Spain in the province of Galicia. TRANSLATOR.)

There was in that square a deep-green lawn
Where the country folk really enjoyed themselves
Playing ball, the game that pleases
Mighty young men, and more than any other.

It is worthwhile to recall that the Galician *Cantigas* were accompanied by Arabic-Andalusian music, and their line meter is the *jarcha*, happily borrowed from Arabic poetry.

It would be strange to think that two societies so mutually interdependent should not also exchange their games.

3 France: The Sport of Kings, the King of Sports

Louis X le Hutin se trouvait au bois de Vincennes en 1316,
là il avait joué à un jeu qu'il savait, à la paume . . .
Il joua avec la dernière violence, en hutin qu'il était,
fut se reposer en une cave, but un plein hanap d'eau.
Si but trop et froid se bouta.
La fiövre se déclara, il dut se mettre au lit;
Là il perdait plumes et pennes,
autrement dit il trépassa.

Louis X, the quarrelsome, was in the wood of Vincennes in 1316,
They had been playing a game that he knew, playing at *paume* . . .
He played with his last ounce of strength, such a stubborn type was he,
Then went to rest in a cave, where he drank a full dipper of water.
He drank so much that he took a chill.
A fever gripped him, and he took to his bed,
Where he lost both quills and feathers,
In other words, he left this mortal coil.

This miniature of two players is important for the emphasis given to the players' white gloves, used to protect the hands from the blow of the hard leather ball. The low sloping roof around the court and under which the chess game is on will be an important element of court and royal tennis. Below, the men painted by Meissner are pleasant to look upon, but they have nothing to do with our games.

The sad end of the king, who obviously had not followed the precepts of Galen and Avicenna, is not the first record of the game of *paume* or tennis in France. One of the earliest illustrations that I have found of the sport, from the beginning of the fourteenth century, decorates the bottom of the parchment of the *Histoire du Lancelot ou San Graal* (*History of Lancelot or the Holy Grail*). A small hooded man with pointed slippers, perhaps the umpire, watches a shot executed with the open hand on a ball sewn into four sections, like the one used by the young girls in the mosaic of the Piazza Armerina.

The division of the two pages of the manuscript leads us to believe that the playing field was divided into two sections by a cord, or simply, as in this imaginary projection, by a line drawn on the ground. On the page at the right, two other players are posed in anticipation of the ball, ready to hit it back. The fact that the game is played two against one is not surprising, for the same thing happens today in Spanish *pelota* (ball, also a game played with a ball) and in some training matches in tennis.

Church documents from the twelfth to the fourteenth centuries speak only of seminarians, priests, monks, parish priests, abbots, and even bishops, all playing *longue paume* or *courte paume*, either indoors or out in the open, depending on the type of game. Rules in the documents specified when the game could be played and forbade the clergy from playing with the laity. Woe to him who played in shirt sleeves and without his trunk hose.

Jeu de paume continues to be played by the nobility, even if the others are refused the right to play. Sixteen years after his edict against *paume* and other corrupting games, Philip the Fair will acquire the Castle of Nesle, the site of the court where one day Benvenuto Cellini will play.

In the midst of the Hundred Years War, Charles V (the Wise) unleashes new broadsides against *paume*, likening it to "all the games that do nothing to teach the manly art of bearing arms." These prohibitions will be followed by others, but none of them can stop the game from being played on Sundays. Surprisingly enough, the avalanche of bets placed with the royal exchequer will demonstrate the enormous popularity of the game. And, more to

1

2

3

4

5

6

7

8

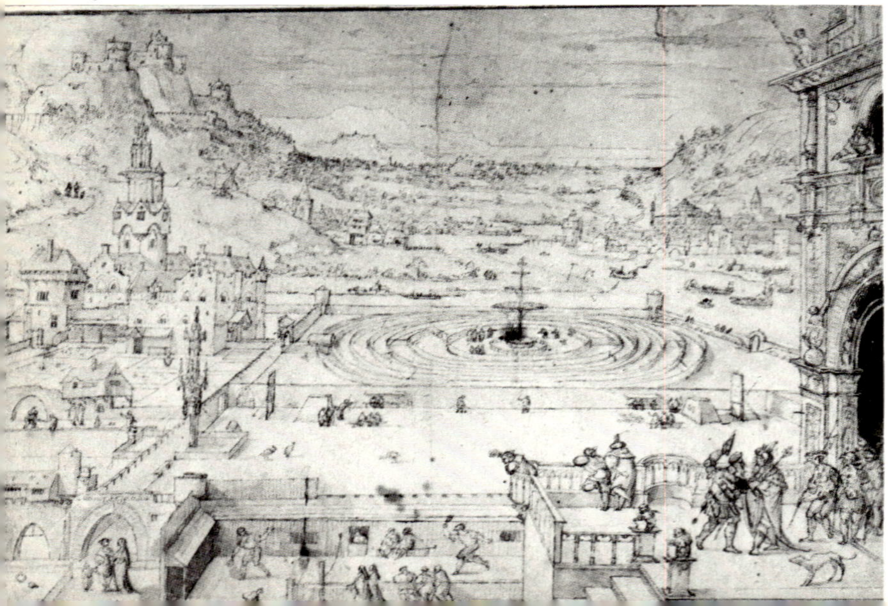

the point, a certain woman by the name of Margot, *qui estoit du pais de Henault, vint a Paris, en cet an 1427* (who was from the countryside at Henault, came to Paris in 1427). The chronicler continues that "Margot was young, between twenty-eight and thirty, and played *paume* better than anyone had ever seen before, with both her palm and the back of her hand. She played vigorously, dishonestly, and ably, exactly like any man. There were only a few men that she could not beat, and these were the very strongest players."

While Margot was fascinating the Parisian fans, Duke Charles of Orléans, who had been taken hostage at the battle of Agincourt, relieved the monotony of the prison routine by playing *paume*. His jailer, from the Castle of Wingfield in Norfolk, was a forefather of the inventor of lawn tennis, Walter Clopton Wingfield.

Set free after more than twenty years, Charles dedicated some delightful verses to *paume*, through which his sorrow for his lost youth shines through, and his adversary, Worry, appears in French as *Soussy* (the old orthography of modern *souci*, worry, care).

J'ai tant joué avec Aage
À la paume, que maintenant
J'ai quarante cinq; sur bon gage
Nous jouons, non pas pour néant;
Assez me sens fort et puissant
De garder mon jeu jusqu'à cy;
Ne je crains riens que Soussy

Car Soussy tant me descourage

1. Chateau at Amboise. The black star in the upper left marks the covered gallery of the court where Charles VIII hit his head against an overhead beam, dying soon thereafter in 1498.

11

10

3, 7, 9. The area of the Louvre closest to the Seine was built by Francis I, who embellished it with statues of satyrs and nymphs. Henry II of Valois ordered the adjoining section of the palace built, according to Scaino, "in the grand style and worthy of a king." 5. Henry played in the courts at Fontainebleau under the watchful eyes of Catherine de Medici, as shown in this sketch by the Florentine Alessandro Francini. The roof of the court is extremely high, as is the one at St-Germain-en-Laye (4), whereas at Périgueux (10) it must have been more difficult to master the lob in 1576 due to cramped quarters. 6. The playing area at the famous Hampton Court is also covered and serves today as a mecca for tourists who are sports-minded. It is shown here as rebuilt by Henry VIII, who dismissed the owner. 8. This sixteenth-century version, perhaps by Lucas van Leyden, of the original court design from Van Gassel, has an uncovered playing area as does the "Tennys Courte" of Windsor, a detail of which is shown here (2). Designed by John Norden in 1607, the playing field was already in existence at the beginning of the sixteenth century, when rackets were still strung diagonally. 11, 12, 13. These are more modern courts, respectively dating from 1676 at Old Hawes (St. Albans Lodge); from the reign of Louis XV at Compiègne; and from 1850, the Royal Tennis Court at Haymarket.

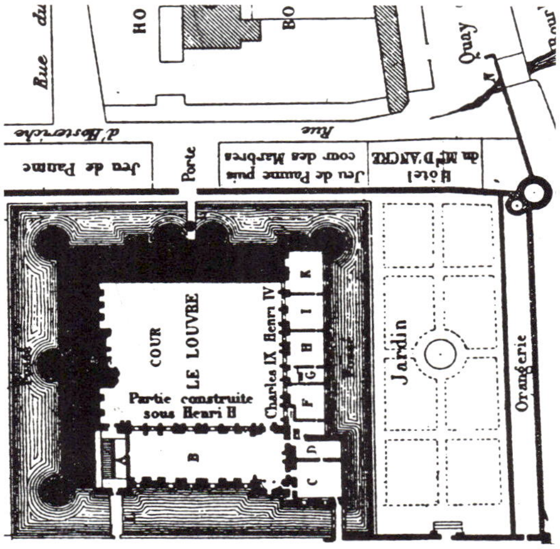

9

de jouer, et va estouppant
le coup, que fier à l'avantage
trop seurement est rachassant;
Fortune si lui est aidant:
Mais Espoir est mon bon amy;
Ne je crains riens que Soussy

Vieillesse de douleur enrage
De ce que le jeu dure tant,
et dit en son felon langage
Que les chasses dorénavant
Merchera pour m'estre nuisant;
mais je m'en chault, je la deffy:
Ne je crains riens que Soussy

Si bon Eur me tient convenant,
Je ne doubte ne tant ne quant,
Tout mon adversaire party
Ne je crains riens que Soussy

I have so long played with Age
At *Paume*, that here I am
At the ripe old age of forty-five;
We played for high stakes, we two,
And I am still strong enough
To keep my game in trim:
For I fear no one but Old Dame Worry.

For Old Dame Worry discourages me so
From playing, and thwarts my shots;
Getting the better of me,

12

13

From the period of the court designed after the style of Van Gassel (about 1540), the various features of the game of rachetta and paume are almost standardized. There is always a spectators' gallery, a penthouse roof above, from which the ball rebounds, the cord that has developed into a net, the square openings of the grille and the round ones of the lunes used to score a hazard, the baskets for balls, the scorekeepers, and the balls left lying on the floor to mark the chases.

2

1. A detail from the painting in Lord's described in the introduction and found in color in the picture section between pages 40 and 41.

1

3

2. The first tennis lesson from the Emblemata *by* Sambucus, *1576. 3. A nineteenth-century copy of Komensky's 1658 original, showing the improvement of the game as played with rackets over the game of* paume *played out-of-doors. 4. A woodcut by Crebierre, frontispiece to the famous Hulpeau's book published in 1632. 5. The German game as played in Tübingen. 6. From the first novel dedicated to tennis, the* Mèmoires de Monsieur le Marquis de Montbrun (Memoirs of the Marquis of Montbrun). *The Marquis himself stands leaning in the doorway. 7. Artist unknown. 8. The game as played at Strasbourg, woodcut by Crispin de Pass in 1608.*

She drives me hard when
Old Dame Fortune gives her a hand.
But Hope is my good friend,
I fear no one except Old Dame Worry.

Old age, made angry by pain,
And by the fact that the game still goes on,
Says, in her thieves' cant
That the chases from here on in
Will be a great deal worse;
But then I get my dander up and defy Old Age,
For I fear no one except Old Dame Worry.
If Happiness keeps me company,
I have no doubts from any quarter;
All my adversaries set to rout,
For I fear no one except Old Dame Worry!

November, 1439

After the poetry of Charles, the princely references to the *paume* become more numerous, and the fine thread of the game was woven into a tapestry in which all the kings appear. Louis XI suggests to his court physician that he prescribe his daughter as a worthy tonic for the reluctant Louis of Orléans. But the son-in-law is decidedly in favor of the game over the lady, and shouts an oath at Madame de Beaujeau, Anne of France, when she misjudges one of his shots.

Deeply hurt, Anne calls upon her cousin, the Duke of Lorraine, *qui frappa au dit Duc un grand coup sur la face* (who struck the duke fully upon the face). The princes in attendance leaped to their feet and separated the two, but from that day on the duke harbored a deep resentment against his counterpart from Lorraine, calling him into account for it later when he was crowned king.

Meanwhile, as Commines tells us, Charles VIII, while escorting Anne of Brittany to see court tennis played for the first time at the Palace of Amboise, struck his forehead on the beam of the doorway and died soon thereafter.

Francis I is the *plus robuste jouer de son temps* (strongest player of his time), and the day that his partner, a monk, beats him with an especially fine shot, Francis quips: "That was a truly priestly shot!" to which his partner retorted: "It's your majesty's privilege to turn it into an abbot's!" No sooner said than done!

It seems that Henry II was the strongest of the tennis-playing kings. Among other things, they were almost all from the branch of Orléans. Brantôme describes Henry II for the reader as playing on the courts that were completed under his reign: "During the great games at the Louvre, dressed all in white, wearing his doublet, a straw hat on his head, he smashes the ball heatedly but without any pomp, except when his servants lift the cord for him. And again: "When he was not riding, he played at *paume*, and indeed very well for all that, for he hated to remain on the base line and enjoyed playing second or third, which are the two most difficult and dangerous spots. He was a good second and the best third in the whole kingdom. He took to the sport not for gain, for he always settled matters in favor of the other players when he won; when he lost, on the other hand, he paid all the costs himself."

Henry II was a modern player who often rushed the net, making himself the target of a leather ball that could hit him full in the nose, a ball stuffed with dog's hair, as specified by a decree of Louis XI in 1480.

4

7

8

Even Rabelais had included *paume* in his Great Catalogue of sports. When Pantagruel arrives in Orléans, he runs into "a large crowd of strapping fellows, who show him a grand time. He learns to play *paume* so quickly that he is soon their master, and as a result, the students in that city go wild about him." So much so, that Pantagruel creates an emblem and a motto for the graduates, when his friend takes a law degree. The friend is not gifted in science, but possesses great dancing and playing skills as told in Pantagruel's story:

Un esteuf en la braguette
En la main une raquette
Une loi en la cornette
Une basse dance au talon
Voy vous là passé Coquillon

A ball in one's breeches,
A racket in one's hand,
A law degree on one's beret,
A merry dance underfoot,
That's the way a doctor is made nowadays!

5

6

At the same time that Rabelais's Pantagruel was studying for his degree, there were at Orléans about forty *paume* courts. At Paris, where Gargantua plays *ez Bracque*, at the Square of the Estrapade, Lippomano, the Venetian ambassador, raised the count to some 1,800, probably exaggerating the facts somewhat. Gargantua played not only *paume*, but also *pila trigonalis*. Though outmoded by its descendants, the old game of the Romans still existed. As far as I know, this is the last time that the Roman game is even mentioned. *Paume* also begins to contradict its own name (palm in French), for it is more and more often played with a racket than with the palm of the hand. Though still costly, rackets are not hard to find: the infant Charles IX can already grip one in his tiny hand at the advanced age of two in 1552.

Toward the middle of the sixteenth century, at the very high point of the game, the need was felt for some kind of standardization of the rules to explain the developing literature that had begun to flourish. But first we shall quickly span the English Channel, where it so often happened in those days that players became citizen soldiers and then players again. In fact, as Sir Braquemont wisely put it, *toujours ne peut on pas jouer, ni toujours armoyer* (you can't always play tennis, and you can't always bear arms), his philosophical rejoinder to the news that a shipment of tennis balls from France had been detained by the outbreak of war.

4 The English and the Word *Tennis*

The scene is laid in the throne room in the first act of *Henry V* by Shakespeare. King Henry, sitting upon the throne, and the Duke of Exeter are listening to the prepared speech of the French ambassadors:

He therefore sends you, meeter for your spirit,
This tun of treasure; and, in lieu of this,
Desires you let the dukedoms that you claim
Hear no more of you. This the Dauphin speaks.
What treasure, uncle?
Tennis balls, my liege.
We are glad that the dauphin is so pleasant with us.
His present and your pains we thank you for.
When we have match'd our rackets to these balls,

1, 2. These two illustrations, from the Art du Paumier Raquetier et de la Paume *by the encyclopedist Garsault, show the two most common courts for play. Above is a* jeu carré, *the older of the two, and below a* jeu à dedans, *named thus for its large opening at which a lady and a gentleman sit observing the game in progress. To the right of the above illustration we see a player executing a vigorous forehand.*
4. On this piece of porcelain from 1757, we observe a strong backhand, executed with the reverse side of the racket, the first pictorial representation that we know of this modern technique. The court has lines on the playing surface used in marking chases to avoid referees and arguments, and the diagonal netting reaches to the ground.

5. A century later at the royal court in St. Petersburg the rules are exactly the same, only the players' wearing apparel has changed.
3. We see in this German eighteenth-century canvas that paume *was often played in buildings that were also used as legitimate theaters.*
6. Here paume, *as played in the days of the French Revolution, has become a game played out-of-doors and has added* longue *to its name.*
7. A photograph showing how ardent conservatives still play the sport of kings in our day. The London Times *never fails to devote at least a few lines to their little publicized championships.*

6

We will in France, by God's grace, play
a set
Shall strike his father's crown into
the hazard.
Tell him he hath made a match with such a
wrangler
That all the courts of France will be
disturb'd
With chaces.

Thus it is that in the repertory of the poetry of the Bard of Avon, we suddenly find "tennis ball" and other more technical terms, such as "chase" and "hazard."

The problem that tennis enthusiasts have set themselves, and I count myself among them, is the following:

Did the period spoken of by Shakespeare, that is the beginning of the fifteenth century, know the refinements of keeping score as well as the complicated method of keeping score with chases? And, moreover, was that ball game already called tennis? Or was Shakespeare using the terms of his own seventeenth-century idiom?

It has always been maintained that *jeu de paume* was exported across the Channel toward the middle of the fourteenth century by the knights who escorted Marie de Couci, the daughter of Enguerand of Picardy. The knights were sent by her husband, Alexander III, king of Scotland.

We may assume that the game was played at that time if we refer to a chivalric poem of the fourteenth century, the *Romance of the Three Kings' Sons and the King of Sicily*, where it is said of the hero that "No man did so wele as he yn rennyng, playng at the *pame*, etc."

Chaucer, who himself had been prisoner in France, has Troilus say to Pandar: "But canstow playen *racket* to and fro." It indicates that the English already knew the use of the racket in 1380.

John Gower, in his poem *In Prise of Peace*, which dates from 1399, says "Of the *tenetz* to winne or lose a chase / mai no lif wite er that the ball be ronne (cannot be decided until the ball has come to a stop)." Thus for the very first time a word similar to "tennis" appears. These two lines of poetry have given birth to endless speculation not only by tennis fans but also by philologists.

If we limit ourselves to other texts that refer to the famous mission of the French ambassadors, we can see the slow evolvement of the spelling of the original term *tenetz*. At the beginning of the fifteenth century it becomes *tynes*, then in 1482 *tenyse*, and finally, in 1548, we read "The Dolphin . . . sent to hym a tunne of *tennis* balles."

The problem, nevertheless, is not only to follow the development of the word, which has some eighteen different spellings in the *New English Dictionary*. We would also like to know precisely why the English even thought it necessary to rename a sport that already had a name, *paume*. They complicated the matter by mixing the variant forms of this word, *paune, pawme, pame*, with the numerous forms of *tenetz*. Since *tenetz* means "take" and is not found even once in the French documents, the researchers have been forced to go back to the Latin word *teneo*.

In a magnificent description of a match by Erasmus of Rotterdam, the server alerts his partner of the act by saying "Ea accipe igitur,"

5

7

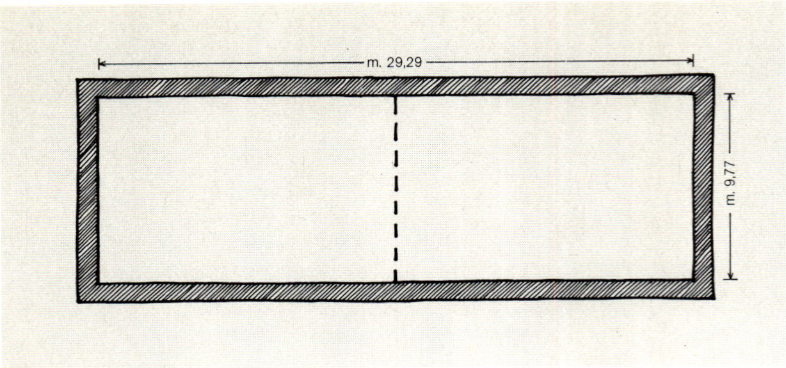

HAMPTON COURT 1529

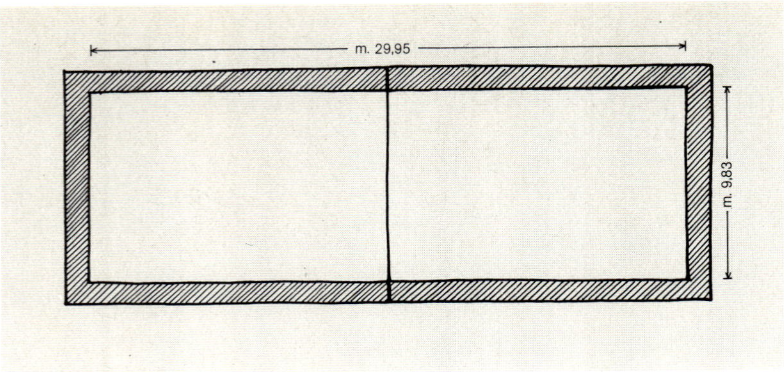

FONTAINEBLEAU 1732

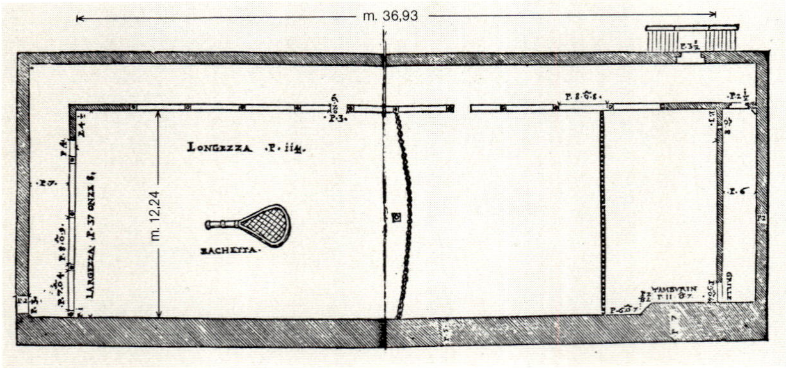

LOUVRE 1555

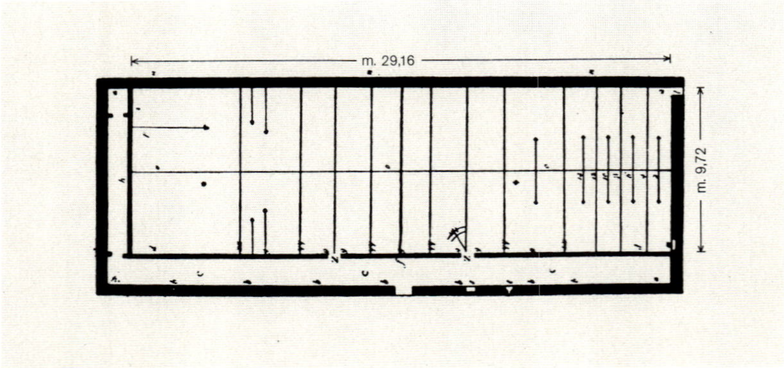

GARSAULT 1767

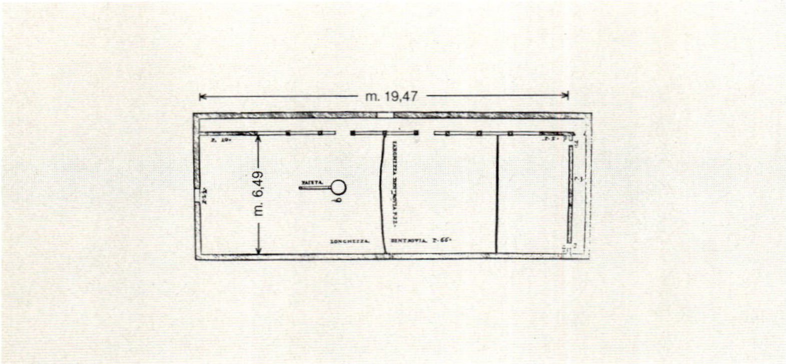

SCAINO 1555

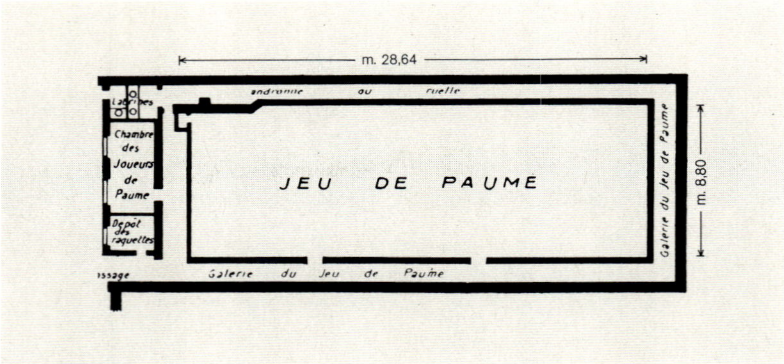

BORDEAUX 1822

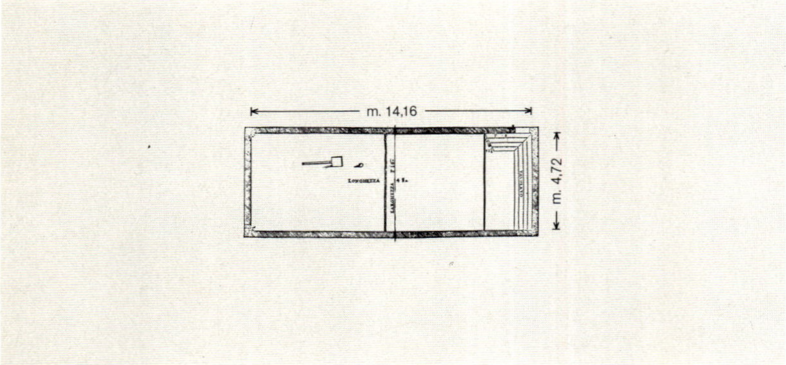

SCAINO 1555

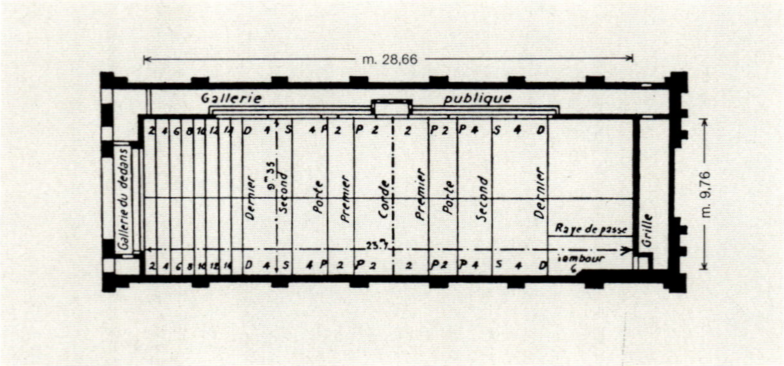

TUILERIES 1862

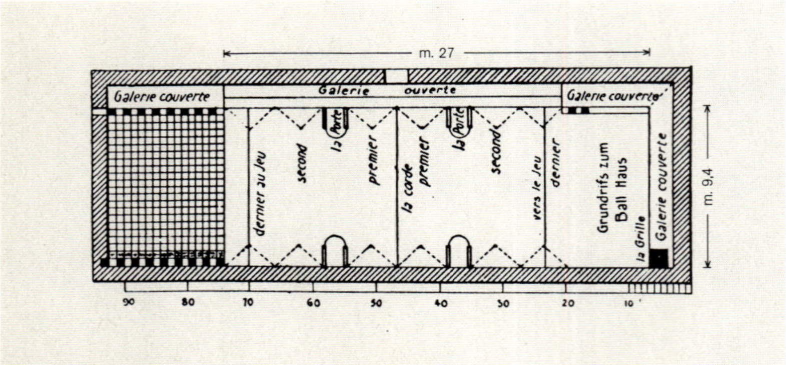

FLORINUS 1719

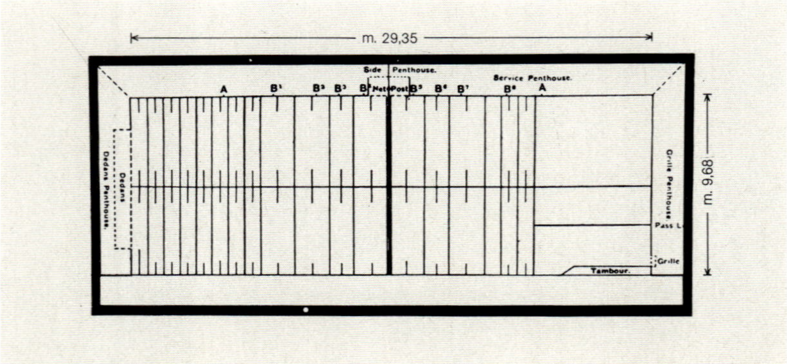

PRINCE CLUB 1889

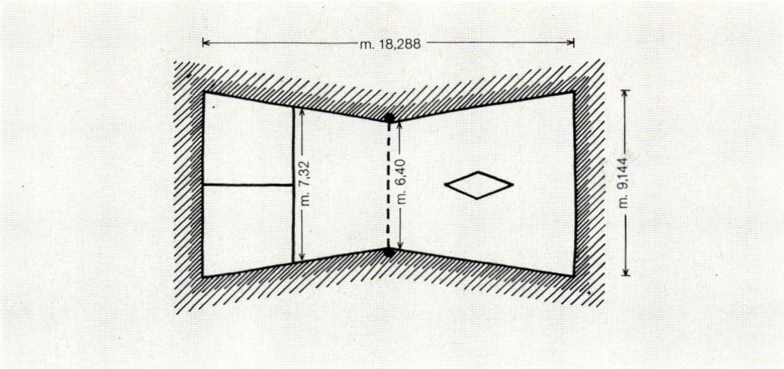

WINGFIELD 1874

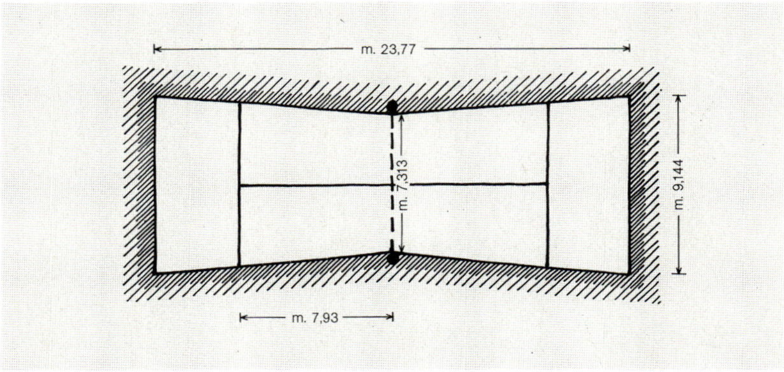

MARYLEBONE 1875

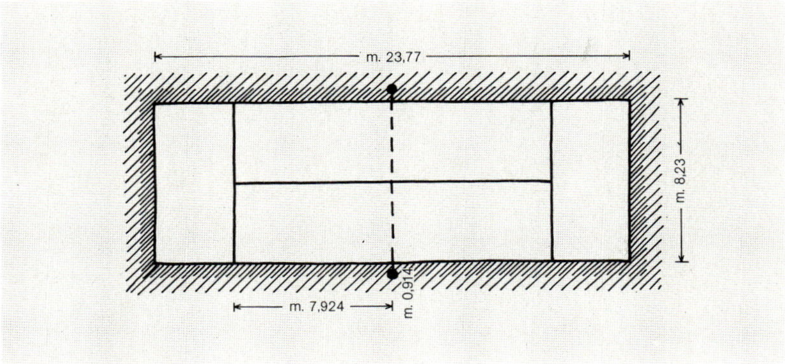

WIMBLEDON 1877

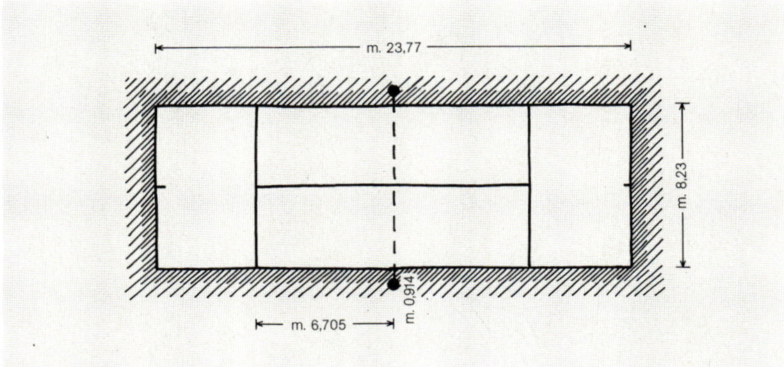

1878

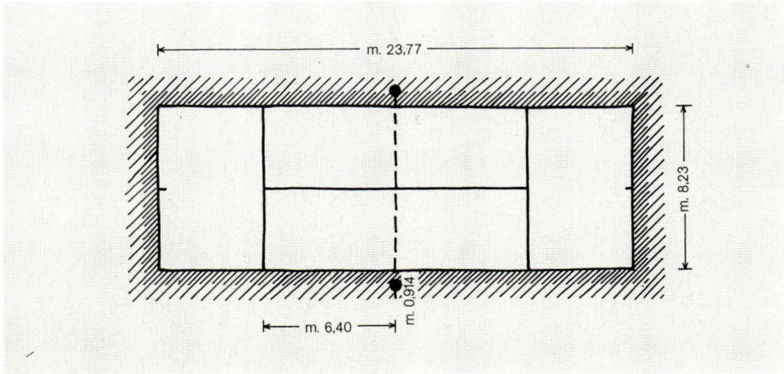

1880-1974

The history of the tennis court is reproduced here on a reasonable scale, from the days of Hampton Court in 1529 to the present moment. The measurements of the playing field of the English kings are conjectures from Noel and Clark (1), but the three designs from Scaino's work of 1555 are authentic. The one at the Louvre (2) is actually a large field, forty meters by twelve. 3. Here is Scaino's plan for the game of racket, according to the architect, to limit the rules by creating a reasonably-sized playing area, and (4) his blueprint for "the interior court for play with a cord using either paddle or hand." 5. Here is Florinus's 1719 design of a German court in which lines for keeping track of the chases occur for the first time. 6. The dimensions of the court at Fontainebleau as it appeared in 1732. 7. The high point of the jeu de paume *court, designed by Garsault in 1767. 8. The Bordeaux court as it appeared in 1788 in a rendition of it in 1822. 9. The Tuileries in 1862. 10. The English Prince Club as it appeared in 1889. 11. In the first court designed with a modified spider waist in 1874, the serve was made from the diamond and had to fall between the base line and the service line in either right or left service court. This was the new outdoor lawn tennis patented by Major Wingfield, which made a definite break with indoor royal tennis with its covered ceilings and openings for scoring purposes. 12. Under the modified rules of the commission of the Marylebone Cricket Club in 1875, the court was lengthened and the service area still remained very large. A faulty service went to the opponent with no point lost. 13. In 1877 the court at Wimbledon was constructed in a rectangular shape and the net posts moved outside the side lines. 14. The service court became smaller in 1878, and alleys were made mandatory for doubles play. 15. In 1880 the service area acquired its current size. The net posts were shortened to 1.06 meters (3 ft. 6 in.) in 1883, and the court acquired the dimensions upon which we play in the Year of Our Lord 1975.*

1

2

3

4

5

6

7

8

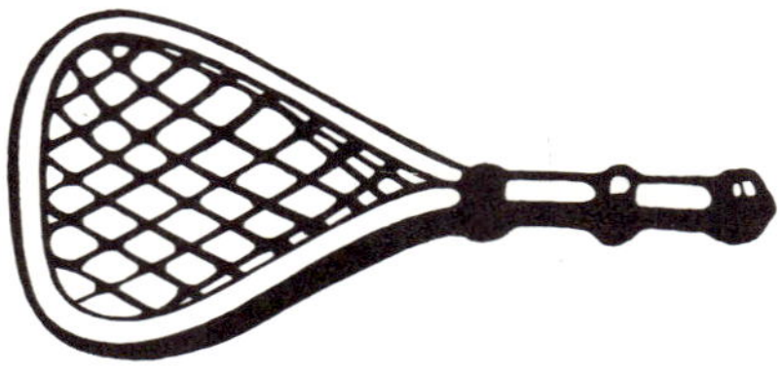
9

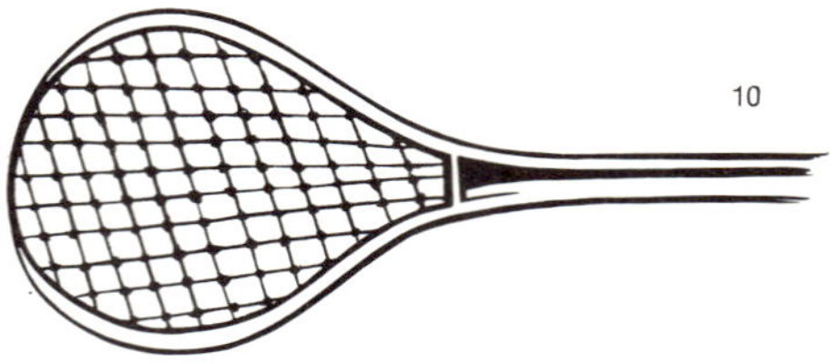
10

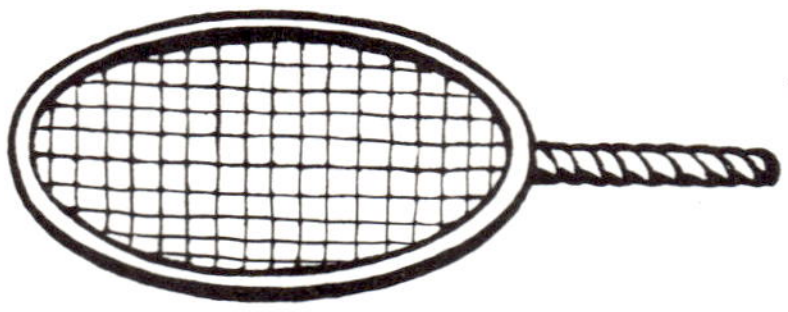
11

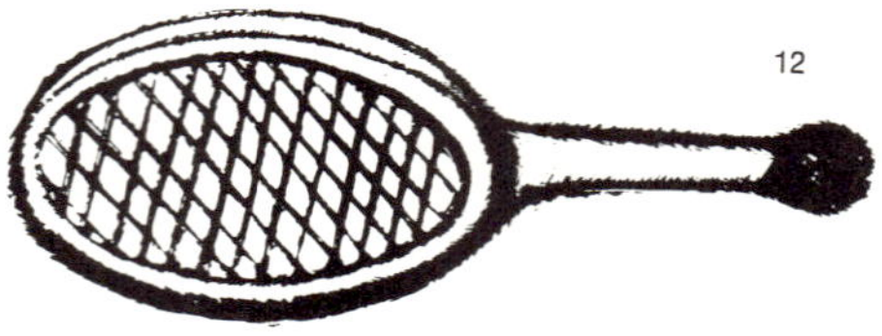
12

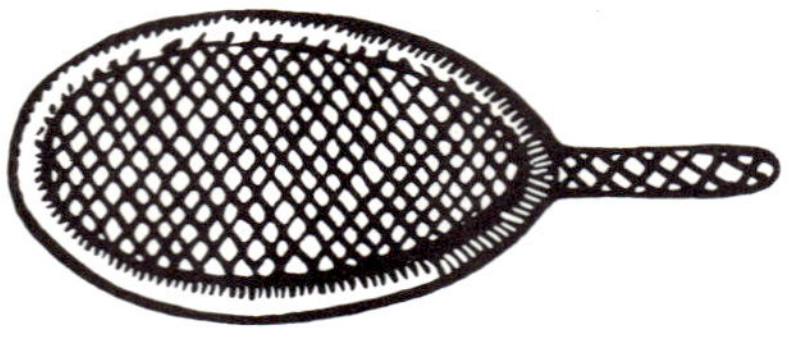
13

14

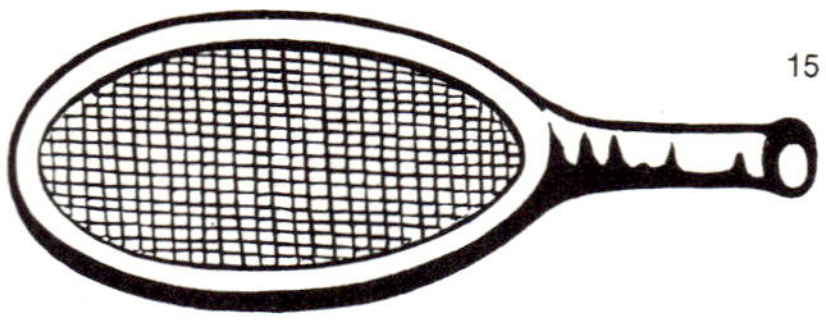
15

16

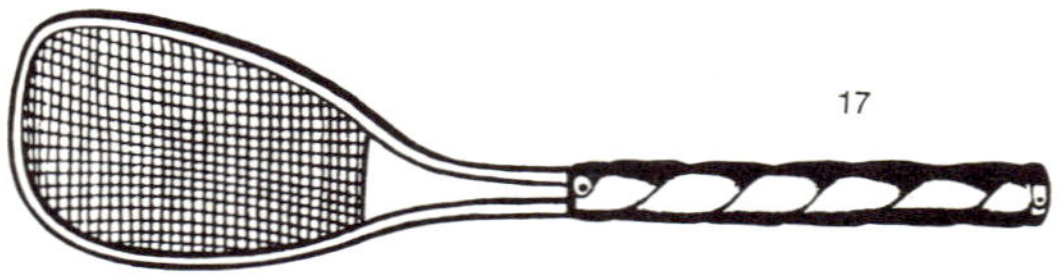
17

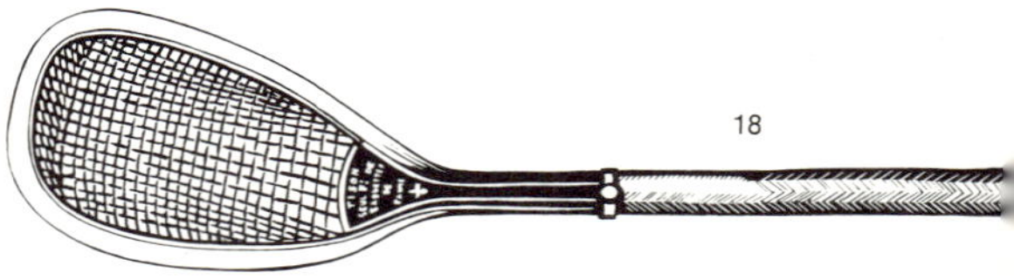
18

19

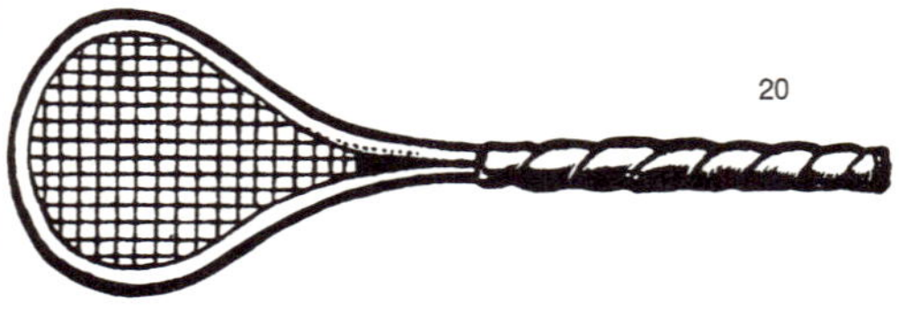
20

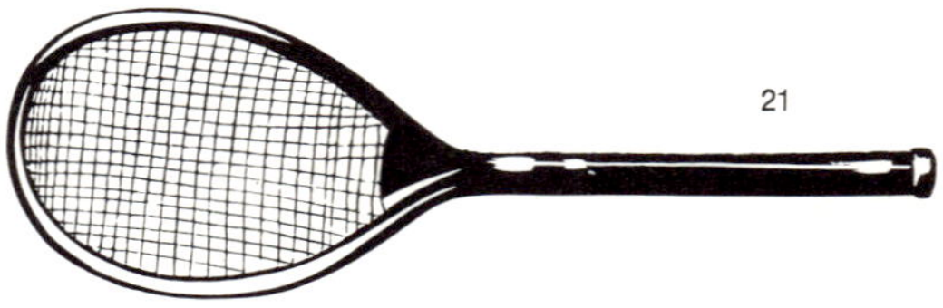
21

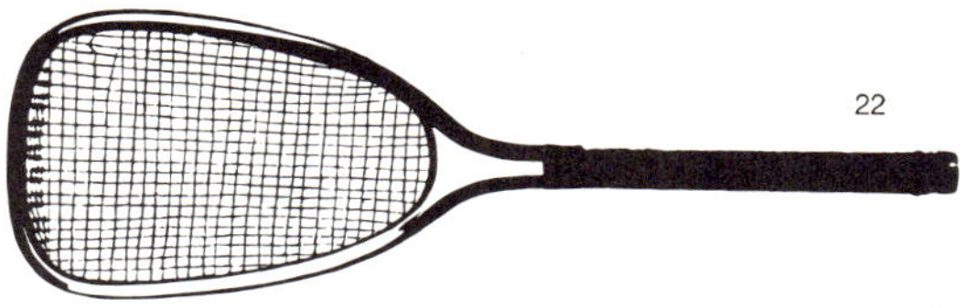
22

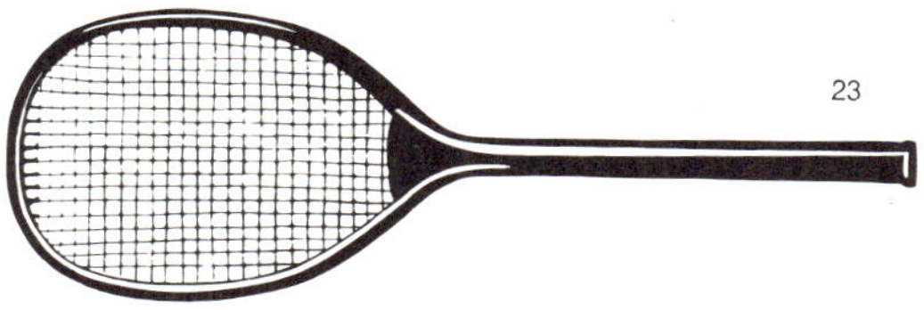
23

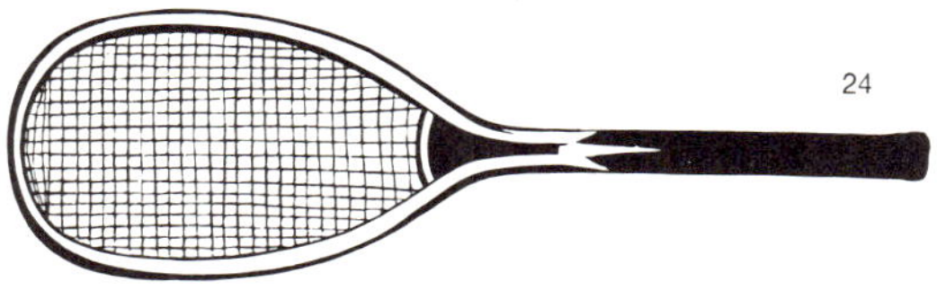
24

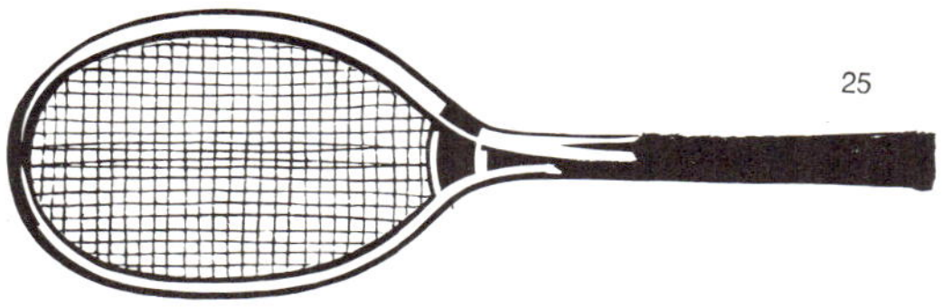
25

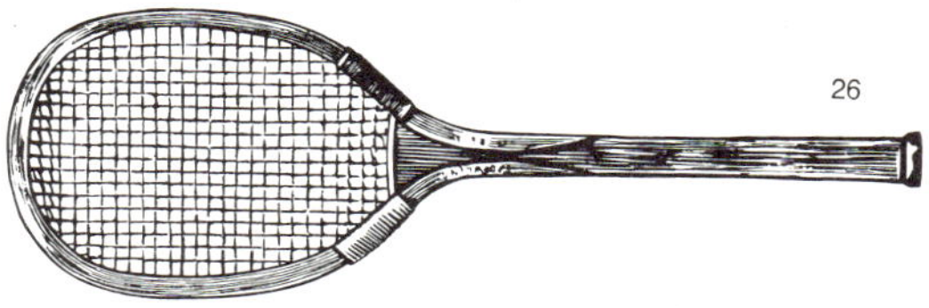
26

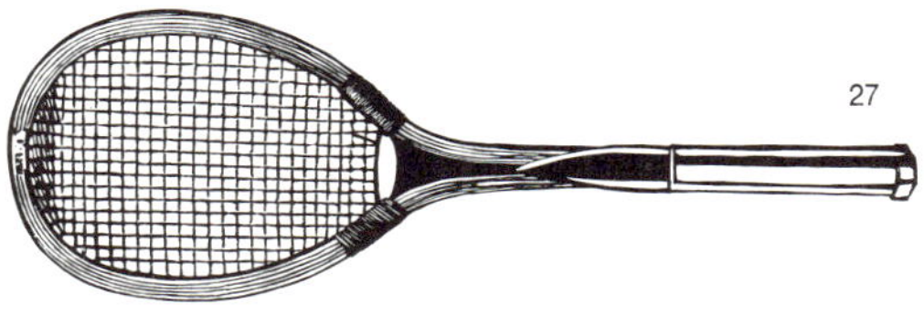
27

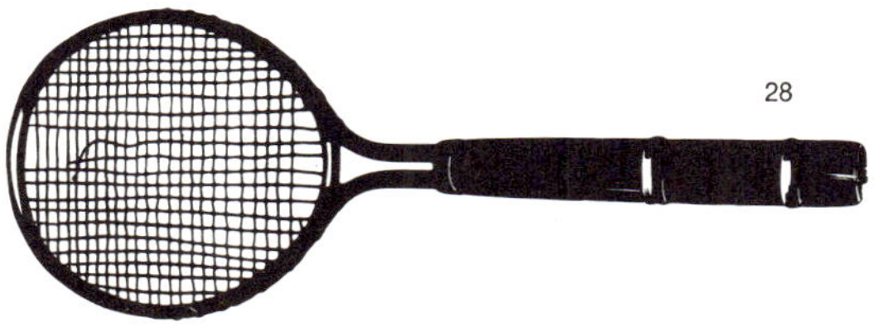
28

29

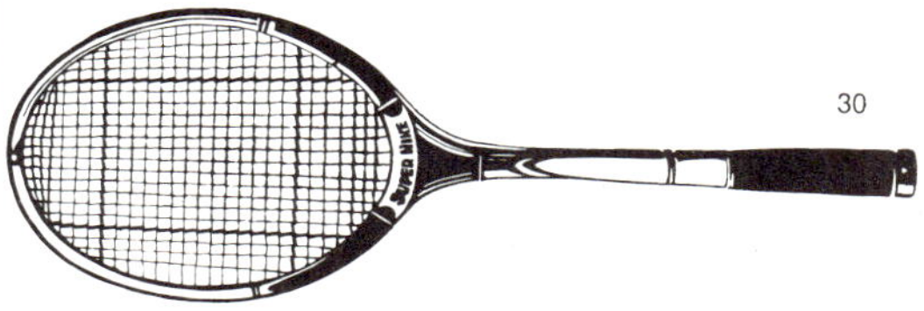
30

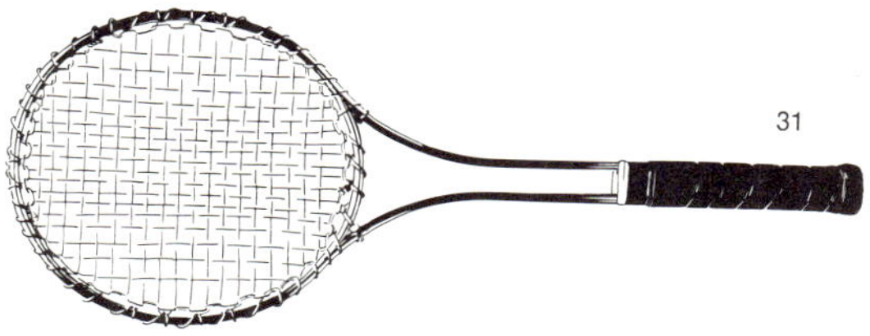
31

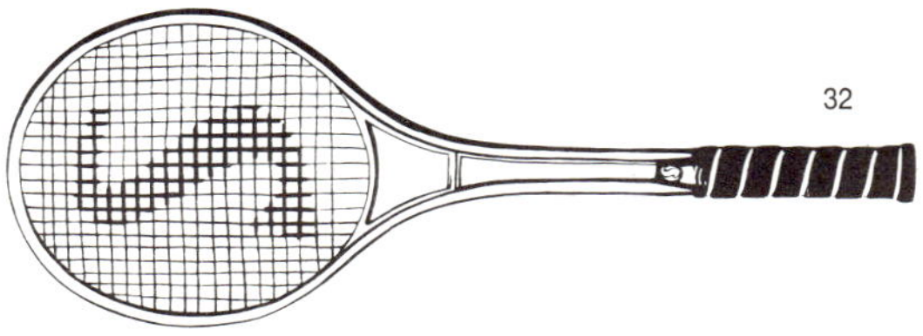
32

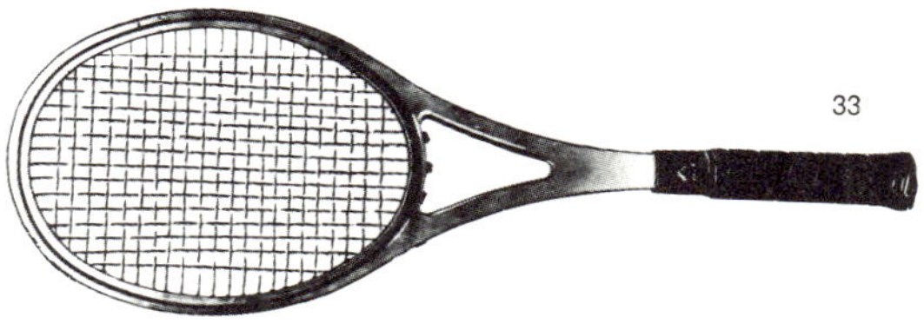
33

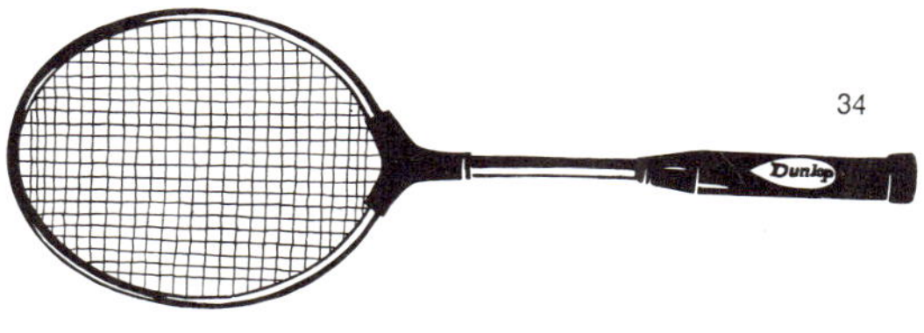
34

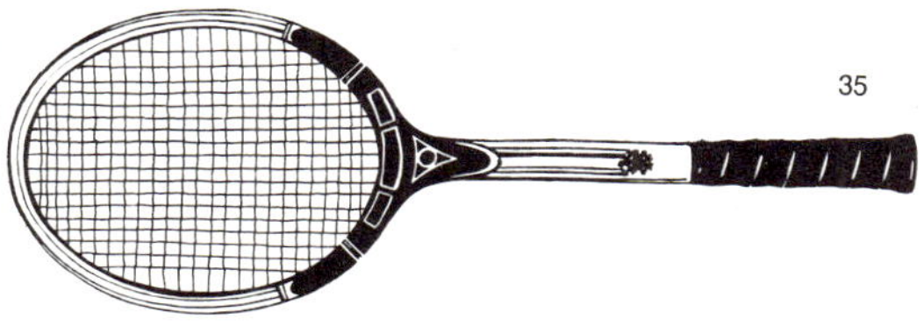
35

Racket is probably derived from the Arabic ràhat, *"palm of the hand," or from the Latin* reticulum. *The first reference to this equipment is in Ovid, the second in Cinnamus in the 12th century, and the most explicit one in Chaucer (1370-1380). The game was first played with the bare hand (1) (from the* Histoire de Lancelot), *which was later covered with leather thongs (2) (from Mercurialis), and then with a glove (3) (after the Harleian Manuscript 4375). The crude bat (4) (from the* Alexander Romance) *in 1344, became later a more complicated glove for the hand (5), and lastly a* battoir *(6), often covered with costly parchment and conserved for us in Bayonne. The two paddles from Scaino (7 and 8) are pleasantly formed, as is the splendid racket (9) with its net strung obliquely and double grip handle from 1555. 10. Patiently strung with a knot at each juncture of the strings, the princely little racket of Charles IX stems from the same period (1552). 11. The racket of the Unknown Gentleman dates from 1583 and is the first to have an oval frame and to be strung in the modern way, perpendicular and horizontal to the handle, which is about 20 cm (8 in.) long. 12. The racket designed by Crispin de Pass in 1608 hails from Strasbourg, with its oval frame and net again strung obliquely. 13. The 1641 racket of the Duke of York shows few changes. 14. In 1675 the Bologna designer Mitelli used tiny holes along the frame and a fabric-wrapped handle. 15. The implement of the German Ballmeister dates from 1723, and (16) the one designed by Barcellon, master of the king of France, dates from 1753. For the first time the handle is fashioned separately with a compact binding. The racket is still strung with a knot at each juncture. 17. The Garsault racket dates from 1767, and the knots are simplified with a twist at each horizontal crossing. The Tison of 1820 (18) and its descendant of 1861 (19) are slanted to pick up the lowest balls or those close to the wall. In 1874 Major Wingfield's racket is once again straight (20), and its contemporary (21) from 1876 is of more efficient design, as are the two following (22 and 23), dating from 1886 and 1891. The knots on the strings are gone and from then on, the frame begins to flatten out, both to reduce the tensions upon the wood and to limit the amount of dead space. Around 1900 the oval shape of the racket is the norm—note the two rackets that date from 1898 and 1902 (24 and 25)—and the different stages of assembly have both been refined and increased in number, as in the 1910 Dowling (26) and in the French Mass (27). Dayton's attempt to use steel for both handle and strings (28) dates from 1930. The Spalding from 1930 (29) resembles the Super Nike of the first postwar period (30). Lacoste perfected his metal racket in 1965 (31), improving the balance and moving the center of gravity. The 1968 Spalding Smasher (32) chose aluminum, the Head (33) rather gravitated toward a layer of resins like modern skis, while Dunlop narrowed the handle of the Titan (34), and Davis perfected the wooden assembly (35).*

Parte of the Litle Parke
The Garden plott graunted by Patent
of the Litle Parke

Tennys Courte
B

Color plates on the preceding pages
Across from page 32: Upper panel: "The Ball Game" by Goya from the second half of the eighteenth century. At this time the bat used by the young man dressed in red was rounded, but it had not yet taken on the oval form of a racket. In Spain the racket was much less widely known than in Italy, France, and England, and the poorer people fashioned for themselves equipment of wood. Lower panel: A miniature from the Cantigas *by Alfonso the Wise, which is treated extensively in the text.*
Across from page 33: Upper panel: On parchment, John Norden has sketched the outline of the castle at Windsor. Lower panel: Here we see a detail of the above sketch, showing the "tennys courte" set comfortably between the castle and the fortress. The racket was still strung diagonally, and many documents inform us that this court goes back to the beginning of the 1500s, although this particular sketch dates only from 1607. On that royal playing field, the first international handicap tournament took place between Philip the Fair and the Marquis of Dorset in 1506, a few months before the death of the unfortunate husband of Joanna the Mad. And then in 1522 an international doubles match was played here, pairing Henry VIII and Charles V.

which is to say *tenetz!* (Here it comes!) Erasmus wrote in 1527, but more than a century later an imaginary game between Louis XIII and Philip IV is described in the *Carmen de Ludo Pilae Reticulo* (Poem of the Racket Ball Game). Richelieu is acting as referee in this match. We read that the French king invites his opponent to ready himself for the serve with "Excipe!" The same word was already used by Seneca. The scholarly Marshall observes that James I was preparing an advice for his beloved son Henry around the time of the appearance of the poem. Among other sports, James suggested "caitche or tennise," making the English term synonymous with the word derived from Latin. Thus this simplified Rosetta stone of tennis brings our research on the development of the term to a satisfying conclusion.

Gower, in fact, wrote his three major works, one each, in Latin, French, and English: so that in the church in Southwark he rests on three stone cushions that symbolize his contribution to the three languages of England: the cultured, the courtly, and the vernacular. There would be nothing easier than for a highly learned man like him to think in Latin while he wrote in English, and thus "tennis" would have been born in Latin and slowly corrupted into English. All this is well and good, despite the thorny question of why no Frenchman might have felt the need to warn his opponent in French, and continued to do so only in Latin.

There is another complication that arises in a country where *paume* was never called by this name: in Italy itself, which is, according to many historians, the grandmother of tennis to those who prefer to call France its mother.

In his *Cronica di Firenze* (*Chronicle of Florence*), Donato Velluti speaks of 500 French knights, the most stylish people that he had ever seen, all noblemen and barons of great wealth. A certain Tommaso Lippaccio becomes their friend and begins to play ball everyday. "And from that time on," Velluti concludes, "they began to play *tenes*."

So, unless we wish to believe that all the French chroniclers conspired for several centuries to make no reference to that accursed *tenes*, it is hard to resolve the puzzle. For the document of Florence is very old and makes references to the year before the Battle of Altopascio, when on September 23, 1325, almost all these brave gentlemen lost their lives.

For the present it is better to drop the matter altogether, until a more conclusive document can be uncovered. Let us rather turn our attention to the first international match of some social pretensions, which took place at Windsor on January 31, 1505.

Philip, the archduke of Austria and newly crowned as the king of Castile, matched his wits with the Marquis of Dorset, while Henry VII observed the contest: "But the kyng of Casteele played w. the Rackete and gave the Lord Marques XV (that is, an advantage of fifteen points)."

It is clear that one could play both *paume* (with the palm) and *tenes* (tennis with a racket) at the same time.

But the racket was a great advantage. Henry VIII had seven of them, according to the inventory of the palace at Greenwich. Sebastian Giustianiani writes that the king was a great tennis devotee, and that it was a real pleasure to watch him play, his slick body hair matted against his fine linen shirts, damp and translucent from sweat.

After the game, Henry would dress again in his beautiful robes of black and blue velvet (also listed and their purpose described), and would man the gaming tables to all comers, be they Lombard merchants or French hostages. The king would lose eight hundred ducats in one afternoon. Punctual in his payments, he would recoup his losses with his usual violence by driving off the master of Hampton Court and taking over and refurbishing that famous compound.

In 1523 Henry hosted Charles V, and the two "playd at tennice at the Bayne against the princes of Orange and the Marques of Brandenborow." The doubles play ended with a tie score after eleven games. Thus, at least, speaks the report of Hall's Chronicle, but perhaps one of the bars was lost on the Roman "XII," which was thereby read "XI" in error!

Even though this was probably the most important doubles match of the century, it should not lead us to the conclusion that tennis was the exclusive domain of the court in England.

A French traveler, Maistre Estienne Perlin, writes in 1558: ". . . this land is very rich, and the businessmen earn more in a week than their German or Spanish counterparts do in a month. As a result, artisans like carpenters and hatters can be seen playing tennis for a crown, something that happens very seldom elsewhere, especially on a workday."

The sport was flourishing everywhere. What was needed was someone to define the rules and codify them. The first individual to compose such a volume was Antonio Scaino, a Lombard from the tiny hamlet of Salò on the blue shores of Lake Garda in northern Italy.

1

Changes take place in costumes and in equipment used by our twenty-one champions, well known and unsung, of the history of the evolution of rackets, that is paume *or royal tennis. The Roman gentleman (1) is the least cumbered with clothing, while his Spanish counterpart of the end of the thirteenth century (2) has hitched up his tunic around his waist, an idea that apparently has not occurred to Baroness Wentworth (21) six centuries later. The woman is, however, the only one of our stalwarts in short sleeves, though the player of the sixteenth-century rackets (4) and Barcellon (17), tennis master to Louis XIV, have rolled up theirs. In order to protect themselves from the cold of playing fields heated only by charcoal braziers, some of our players wear hats: young Charles IX in 1552 (5), the student of Sambucus in 1576 (6), the unknown gentleman in 1583 (7), the young woman in the painting* l'Enfant à la Raquette *from the sixteenth century (9), the* Ballmeister *(11) from 1650, the mime (12), the German player from 1723 (14), and his French contemporary (15).*
Some of our players are even wearing three-cornered hats, for example, a member of the corporation of the Raquettiers-

2

3

4

5

6

7

8

9

10

11

12

13

14

15

16

17

18

19

20

21

Brossetiers (13), an institute founded in 1457; and the elegant eighteenth-century gallant (16). The ballplayer of Harleian (3), the young player in 1633 who will become James II (8), and the possessor of a fine backhand in 1632 (10) have their locks bared to the wind, but they wear much more elegant dress than does the celebrated professional Masson in 1765 (18). With the great technician Barre (19) and Noel (20), the author of a fine book on the game of kings, tennis attire takes on the characteristics of lawn tennis.

The players of royal blood are so numerous that some sort of process of elimination is required. The ones remaining are:
1. Alfonso the Wise, portrayed in the midst of reading his Cantigas, *which contain some lovely verses pertaining to* pelota.
2. Francis I who dotted his realm with tennis courts and was even able to play on shipboard going up the Loire in 1539.
3. Charles of Orléans, a captive at Wingfield, who wrote some of the most beautiful poetry dedicated to paume *while in prison.*
4. Henry II, according to Brantôme, the best player of his day, even though his amateur status kept him from winning the most important trophy, the Eteuf d'Argent.
5. Louis X, who died of pneumonia after a game played in the Forest of Vincennes.
6. Philip, the archduke of Austria, appeared at Windsor in 1505 in one of the first international matches, offering a handicap of fifteen points to the Marquis of Dorset, who played with his bare

1

3

4

6

2

5

5 Antonio Scaino da Salò. The Treatise

Transported from his native Salò on the beautiful shores of Lake Garda to the learned Aristotelian lectures of the University of Padua and to the ball games of the arena there, Antonio Scaino found a friendly welcome at the court of the Este family and even became a member of the close circle of Duke Alfonso II. The times were bad. Spain was making preparations to take possession of the country. At court the games were played with a grim determination that revealed a compulsion for diversion and a nostalgia for the good old days of Cossa and Ariosto.

Almost every day the duke would go down to pit himself against his friends and the professional players, "Vincenzo Flisco, his valet, a young man of rare courage and unusual force, and Nardo Veneziano, a rare and equally famous talent in the game."

Alfonso would divest himself of his robes bordered in ermine and cheetah, his brocades shimmering with jewels, his silks interwoven with silver, to dress as did his courtiers and servants. He "stripped down to his doublet, with supple trunk hose reaching amply and safely to his thighs as in the common modern use, his feet lightly shod with buffalo skin."

The rules of the various ball games were well known only in oral form, and their interpretation often caused arguments. One day the duke himself and Scaino argued over the awarding of a point. The young abbot not only knew that he was right but also that he was one of the most knowledgeable experts in the game. Why, he probably thought to himself, should I not fix the rules for tennis as Achille Marozzo, Andrea Aliciato, and Camillo Agrippa did for fencing and Federico Grisone for the art of horseback riding?

Vacation time had just arrived. Scaino's master from Ferrara, the philosopher Maggio, had freed him from the daily task of commenting on Aristotle. From his desk Scaino lovingly removed the piles of commentaries on the *Metaphysics* and on the letters of Saint Augustine. Late in life, these writings would make Scaino famous as a learned commentator at the papal court. He began to pen, one after the other, elegant sentences to decorate the rigid Aristotelian pentagram: in his style, references to music and philosophy were the backdrop for the less imposing "art of the racket, the most appropriate sport for the man of letters."

Any awkward effort of mine to cover the 315 pages of this *Cortegiano* (*Courtier*) of the tennis world with its rules of style and manner, would do the kindly abbot an injustice.

hand.

7. Henry VIII, among his many matches and wagers with the Lombards and French hostages, played a doubles match teamed with Charles V on June 6, 1522. It is doubtful that Charles V (9) played against Francis I at Orléans in 1530.

8. Under Henry IV, paume *had its heyday, and a papal envoy counted 250 courts for 300,000 Parisians.*

10. Galeazzo Maria Sforza was the most enthusiastic patron of the Sala della Bala *in the Castle of Milan and much stronger a player than* Ludovico Moro *(12).*

11. Alfonso II of Este had two professional trainers for the sport.

7

8

10

11

12

9

It will be worthwhile to explain how the game was played at the time and how the various forms of the sport were similar to each other, for there was a great deal more of interchange, diversity of opinion on rules, and mutual tolerance than is the case with the ironclad sports of the present day.

For example, in the second part of the work where Scaino speaks to us of the difference between the various games, leaving soccer out of consideration, he makes the fundamental divisions in accordance with the shape and size of the ball used. His divisions were so sensible that Mercurialis soon adopted them to catalog the Roman games, as we have seen before.

The ball can be "hard, filled with wool" or "light, filled only with air, with a remarkable bounce and mobility." The difference between the two balls leads to a difference in hitting them: the ball may be put into play with the open hand (with the palm or *paume*) or with the clenched fist supported by an armguard. The covered fist can be replaced by a bat, the *scanno* (a carved wooden bat) or a racket.

Depending on the range of the ball, one can play open-air tennis (*longue paume*) or close tennis (*courte paume*) with a cord or net

1

2

5

7

1. Seneca: With a good player, no holds barred.
2. Martial: If you know how to return my shots with a speedy left hand, I am yours.
3. Ovid: Light balls bounce lightly upon a large racket.
4. Horace: If the Roman sports bore you, play ball as the Greeks do.
5. Avicenna: Playing ball sums up all other sports.
6. Petrarch: If this game is tolerated, play it in a quiet and gentlemanly manner.
7. Mercurialis: Playing ball is far and away the best sport.

3

6

4

in walled-in and covered courts. With these two types of balls, Scaino continues, six different games can be played. With the light ball, *pallone* can be played, which requires the use of the fist with an armguard or the *scanno*.

With the hardball, also called the small ball, open-air rackets or handball can be played. The hardball is also suited for playing handball with the cord or net, or rackets with the cord or net. Of the six, let us look closely at the last two games of close tennis, with or without the racket.

The ball, filled with wool shearings, can be placed either with the hand or the racket. Scaino speaks of an academic dispute between two students at the University of Padua, one French and the other Spanish, concerning the advantages of the two kinds of game. The Frenchman correctly notes, among other things, that "the rallies can be of much longer duration in the game played with the racket than in the other," and further that "the game played with the racket does not make the hand swell as does the other, causing the player often to leave the game due to the pain involved."

Scaino was decidedly in favor of the racket, and subsequent events proved him right, for the game played only with the hand was soon limited to a few areas in Italy.

After describing the ball and the equipment used to put the ball into play (palm, armguard, *scanno*, racket), the abbot shows the several outlines for playing areas in his text. First he takes up the

8

10

12

14

9

11

13

15

8. Castiglione: It is a noble and proper game, which requires manly strength.
9. Erasmus: Nothing exercises better all parts of the body than ball played with the bare hand.
10. Chaucer: But canstow playen racket to and fro.
11. Brantôme: Henry II was an excellent second and the best third in the realm.
12. Shakespeare: When we have match'd our rackets to these balls, We will in France, by God's grace, play a set.
13. Caravaggio: See how this feels, now! (As he killed Ranuccio Tommasoni with his knife.)
14. Cellini: I had in my castle a game of cord ball, which I found to be quite useful.
15. Rabelais: A ball in one's breeches, a racket in one's hand.

one at the Louvre, the labor of "that most Christian and most valorous King Henry."

Less able historians have quickly noted the oddity of a Lombard using a French court as a model, if the game was indeed known in northern Italy.

Had they read more carefully the original Italian text, which they frankly labeled "complex and involved," they would have discovered that, "since both the larger and the smaller enclosed courts are used for the game of rackets, I thought that the example of the Louvre in Paris would serve our purposes very well since it is built in the grand architectural style and is worthy of the purposes of a king." Scaino also feels it was guided by the best tenets of architecture available at that time.

Scaino observes that there are a large number of different enclosures available for the game from which he plans to select one of modest dimensions as a guide, based on the estimates of an expert and a competent architect so as to avoid the construction of odd-sized courts in the future. This is the first attempt to bring a standard measure to the construction of tennis courts, an idea that, up until the middle of the nineteenth century, will not again occur to a serious student of the sport.

Each type of game has a court adapted to its needs, and for royal or court tennis the one in the Louvre measures 36 meters (118 ft. 1 5/16 in.) by 12.38 meters (40 ft. 7 3/8 in.). The smaller one measures

AB HOSTIBVS

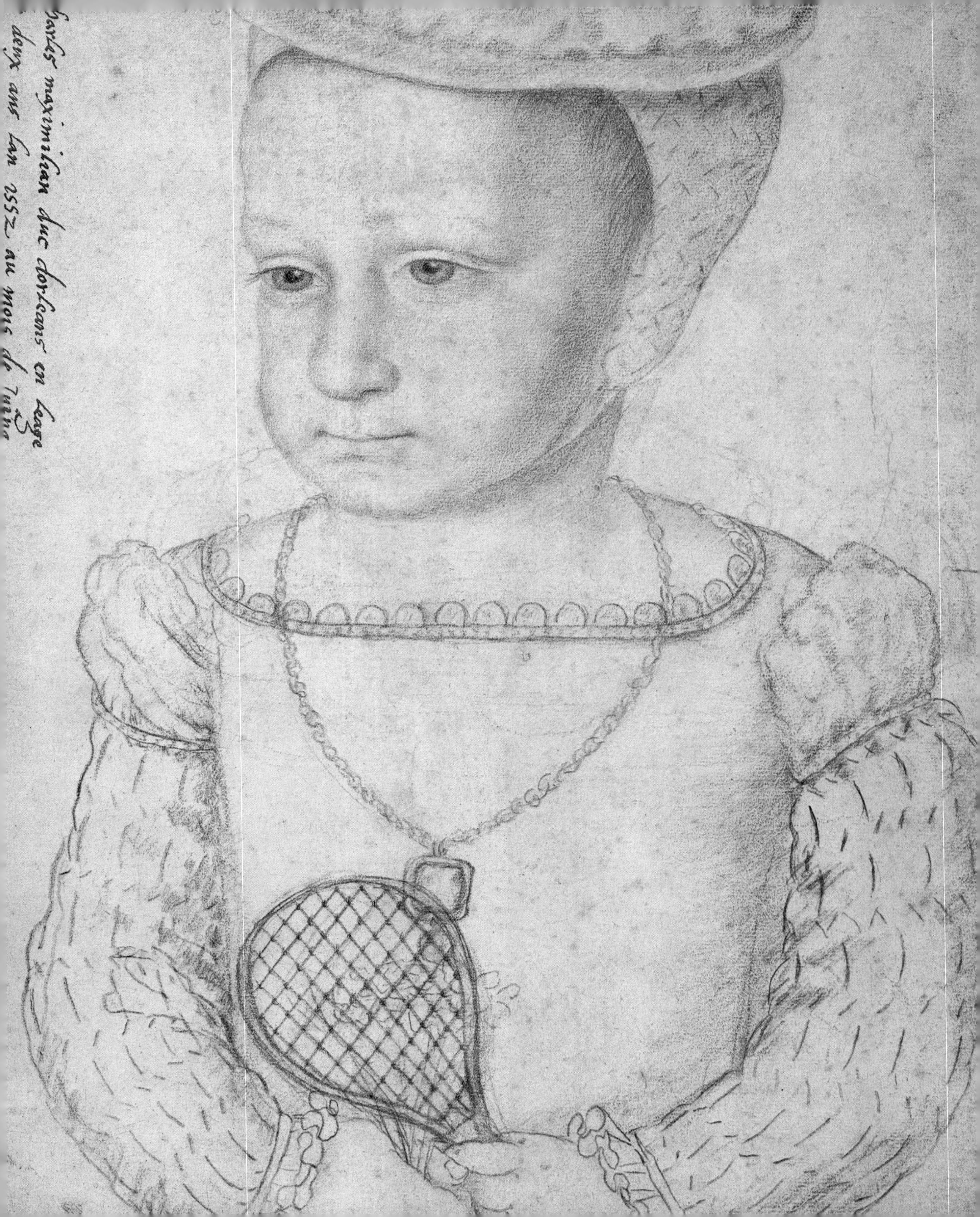
harles maximilian duc dorleans en leage
deux ans lan 1552 au mois de Juing

1. *A Flemish inscription from 1476 mentions "Kaetspeel," that is the game of chases, referring to the same game that in French bears the name* Jeu de Paume, *in Italian* Gioco della Corda, *in English* Royal Tennis, *that is the parent of modern tennis.*
2. *The signature of Pierre Gentil appears on a 1612 receipt for five hundred francs paid him for instructing little Louis XIII in tennis at the request of Marie de Médicis.*
3. *Diplomas of the tennis masters Henri Villiers from 1688 and Jean-Pierre Barcellon from 1767.*
4. *A document by the city of Piacenza awarding monopoly control to one Girolamo Quinzani, a promoter, in matters pertaining to all games of racket there.*

ghecstelike en waerliken ...

1

gentil

2

William e Mary

3

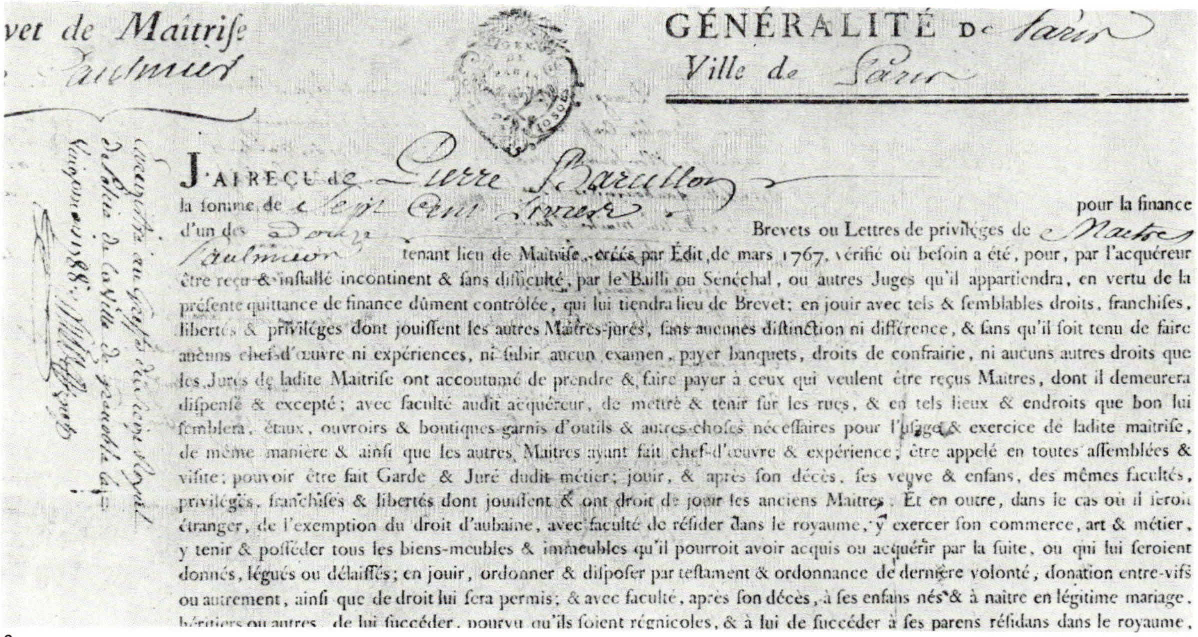
vet de Maitrise ... Paulmier

GÉNÉRALITÉ de Paris
Ville de Paris

J'AI REÇU de Pierre Barcellon la somme de Seize Cent livres pour la finance d'un des Douze Brevets ou Lettres de privilèges de Maîtres Paulmier tenant lieu de Maitrise, créés par Edit de mars 1767, vérifié où besoin a été, pour, par l'acquéreur être reçu & installé incontinent & sans difficulté, par le Bailli ou Senéchal, ou autres Juges qu'il appartiendra, en vertu de la présente quittance de finance dûment contrôlée, qui lui tiendra lieu de Brevet; en jouir avec tels & semblables droits, franchises, libertés & privilèges dont jouissent les autres Maîtres-jurés, sans aucunes distinction ni différence, & sans qu'il soit tenu de faire aucuns chef-d'œuvre ni expériences, ni subir aucun examen, payer banquets, droits de confrairie, ni aucuns autres droits que les Jurés de ladite Maitrise ont accoutumé de prendre & faire payer à ceux qui veulent être reçus Maîtres, dont il demeurera dispensé & excepté; avec faculté audit acquéreur, de mettre & tenir sur les rues, & en tels lieux & endroits que bon lui semblera, étaux, ouvroirs & boutiques garnis d'outils & autres choses nécessaires pour l'usage & exercice de ladite maitrise, de même manière & ainsi que les autres Maîtres ayant fait chef-d'œuvre & expérience; être appelé en toutes assemblées & visite; pouvoir être fait Garde & Juré dudit métier; jouir, & après son décès, ses veuve & enfans, des mêmes facultés, privilèges, franchises & libertés dont jouissent & ont droit de jouir les anciens Maîtres. Et en outre, dans le cas où il seroit étranger, de l'exemption du droit d'aubaine, avec faculté de résider dans le royaume, y exercer son commerce, art & métier, y tenir & posséder tous les biens-meubles & immeubles qu'il pourroit avoir acquis ou acquérir par la suite, ou qui lui seroient donnés, légués ou délaissés; en jouir, ordonner & disposer par testament & ordonnance de dernière volonté, donation entre-vifs ou autrement, ainsi que de droit lui sera permis; & avec faculté, après son décès, à ses enfans nés & à naitre en légitime mariage, héritiers ou autres, de lui succéder, pourvu qu'ils soient régnicoles, & à lui de succéder à ses parens résidans dans le royaume.

3

GRIDA
PER LI GIUOCHI DELLA RACCHETTA.

Per degnazione di S. Eccellenza il Sig. Marchese del Castellar Generale Comandante, e Governatore Interino dei Ducati di Piacenza, e Parma, essendo stati confermati al Sig. Girolamo Quinzani li Giuochi della Racchetta, che furono negl' anni addietro al medemo conceduti dal Sereniss. Sig. Duca Francesco di Gloriosissima Ricordanza, come da venerata Lettera in data de 7. del scaduto mese di Gennajo; ed avendo in seguito il predetto Sig. Quinzani fatta istanza per la pubblicazione, o sia rinovazione della presente Grida.

Quindi è, che per parte dell' Illustriss. Sig. Giacomo Maria Schiattini Dottore dell' una, e l' altra Legge Ducal Consigliere P. Governatore di questa Città, suo Territorio, e Maggior Magistrato; colla previa approvazione, e consenso della prefata E. S. si confermano li Privileggi, e facoltà di poter giuocare nel luogo di detta Racchetta alli Giuochi tutti ivi permessi, e soliti praticarsi: come pure si ordina, e comanda che Persona alcuna sia chi si voglia non possa aprire in questa Città pubblico Giuoco di Trucco, Bigliardo, o altro simile, nè a quelli far' giuocare senza espressa licenza del sodetto Sig. Girolamo, o di qualunque suo Affittuario in esso Giuoco sotto pena della perdita del Trucco, Bigliardo, o altro simil Giuoco come sopra, e suoi arnesi, o loro valore, ed altre pene maggiori ad arbitrio del prefato Illustriss. Sig. P. Gov. applicabili per una metà alla Regia Duc. Camera, e per l' altra metà al riferito Sig. Quinzani, o di lui Affittuario.

Procuri ogn' uno d' ubbidire, poiche contro li Trasgressori si procederà anche per denunzia, ed inquisizione ed in ogn' altro miglior modo.

Piacenza 7. Febbrajo. 1746.

G. M. Schiattini P. Gov., e Magg. Magist. &c.

Dicta die publicat. fuit in forma &c.

C. Sagliani de' Cancell.

PIACENZA, Nella Regia Stamperia del Bazacchi.

4

full tilt so high that the opponent cannot return it on the fly, and at the same time doing it slowly, so that the ball will rebound with delay when it reaches the back wall. This lag will give the player time to regroup his forces."

As a splendid example of a player on the defense, a strong figure of a man, Scaino cites "Gian Antonio Napoletano, held in high esteem by the distinguished and excellent gentlemen of Mantua." He also mentions a certain "Gian Fernando Spagnolo who, already advanced in age, played with the same measured grace (due to his rare discernment) as in his salad days."

Keeping score was not too different from current rules, albeit complicated by the chases or replayed points.

In fact, unless the player hit the ball either under the net, over a certain height on the walls, or into one of the openings on the upper back wall, the point was not awarded immediately. But "that spot in which the ball comes to rest after at least two bounces and while rolling on the floor, is taken as a mark. In popular parlance a mark is called a chase, that is to say, it is the token of the chased or pursued ball. Once the spot has been noted, the players change sides. The point goes to that team whose previous chase is closer to their corner than the one marked by the ball that has just come to rest."

In other words the chase is won if the ball comes to rest beyond the spot where the last chase was marked, within the boundaries of the game, of course. Each point has the value of fifteen, thus one arrives at thirty and then forty-five, which for reasons of euphony will soon become forty instead. When one of the players reaches forty-five, it is said that he has arrived at "one," needing one chase to win the game. Two chases are needed when the score is "two all" (in Italian "a due," from which the French *à deux* and the English *deuce* which means a tie in tennis).

The several ways of keeping score with fifteens lead to three kinds of victory—the "simple," the "double," and the "wild."

In the "simple victory," both contestants are awarded points, and at the end the winner is the one who has two more than his opponent.

In the "double victory," the winner scores four points to zero, thus he has a double victory. It is not a bad system, but totally unknown in today's play.

Finally, the player who is three chases ahead, that is 45 to 0, and then loses five in a row to his opponent, gives him the triple victory. This is a clever idea, full of humor and very just, punishing someone who, having gotten 45, cannot end the game and actually allows himself to be beaten: "seeing himself in the situation of losing five chases as well as the game, without being able to draw a breath or stand firmly, open-hearted and magnanimous, covered with suffering and shame, he becomes enraged or insensitive. And they are few and far between who do not go into some sort of strange and wrathful desperation in such a case."

Speaking of the various degrees of victory, Scaino also gives an explanation of that strange way of marking points: "In the wild game, the idea is to get five chases one after the other, which brings the winner a triple victory. Now, the number fifteen contains five three times, and three five times. We can thus say that as a result of the number of fives in fifteen, the five chases are meaningful, and of the three units comprised in fifteen, we glean the three prize awards (first, second, third) that go into the victory in the wild game: moreover, multiplying within the number fifteen, the three five times and the five three times, we can say that with that corresponding multiplication the proportion is declared that exists between the five chases and the three levels of award."

This argument is probably not the most convincing one of Don Antonio's. After citing others, even more disparate, the American Malcolm D. Whitman, author of the fascinating *Tennis Origins and Mysteries*, pays him homage, stating that his arguments, if not exact, cannot be denied at any rate. I hope that the description of the playing areas, the equipment, the balls, the different kinds of play and scorekeeping have given an idea of what "the game of cord and racket" was really like. Don Antonio never dreamed of calling the game lawn tennis, a term used later.

The need for recapitulation and the need to be clear, and I am hopeful that I have succeeded here, obliged me to leave out fascinating chapters and delightful argumentation (such as those on Aristotle and Plato, notes, music, mathematics, astronomy), reasons why the book was written, descriptions of rackets and balls, wise suggestions on how to hold the racket or the *scanno*, sorrowful criticisms concerning the confusion of rules and referees, further information about the ancients after asserting that there was a lack of documentation to discuss them, and evidence to prove that cord tennis is the best. Scaino's treatise also dealt with anatomical descriptions of the perfect player and of his moral and physical strength, philosophical accounts of the movement of the various parts of the body, medicine, the limitations of exercise, and the progressive possibilities of training, the crucial factor of starting out at a very young age in order to become a champion, the trajectories of the ball and its rebound potential with relation to the density of the air and the force of gravity. More than twenty pages of Scaino's work were devoted to analyze different strokes and shots, style, or, if you prefer, the biomechanics of the sport, as we would say today.

It is useless for me to try to tie together chauvinistic arguments to prove that Don Antonio was the most important writer of his day on the subject, even if I do not thereby imply that the copyright of the game is his.

It is a bit vexing to state that the book has been overlooked since it was written in our humble Italian, especially since in the nineteenth century it was considered convenient to divide the game between the English-speaking and French-speaking worlds exclusively.

It may be well to remind our readers here that Petrarch spoke of tennis before Chaucer, that the etymologies of racket, both *rahat*

Fatal accidents, due to the hardness of the leather ball, were not uncommon. To the left, in this seventeenth century print by Callot, we see St. Mansuy, *Bishop of Toul from 338 to 350, about to restore life to a young nobleman who has just been struck down. Above, in the absence of the saint to protect tennis players, we have the luckless nephew of Sir John Stanley, who touches his injured jaw struck by the tennis ball he holds in his left hand. The tomb inscription of the church at Elford records with marble gravity:* Ubi dolor, ibi digitus (It hurts where the fingers are.)

and *reticulum,* were traced to Italy, that the prohibitions to play on holy days are as old in Italy as in France, as can be evidenced by fourteenth-century documents in Pisa and Mondoví.

While the game was just happily being played more than two hundred years before Don Antonio, the second half of the fifteenth century witnessed a veritable explosion of interest in all the Italian courts. Among thousands of examples we choose the painting by Costantino da Vaprio on the vaulted ceiling, where the ball that is battered back and forth has given its name to the vast chamber: the *Sala della Bala* (Hall of the Ball) in the Sforza palace in Milan. Galeazzo Maria Sforza played his brother Ludovico Moro with great regularity and requested the treasurer, in a letter dated 13 January 1472, "that you take from his allowance, the thirty ducats of gold I won from him, and do this without fail."

Galeazzo Maria made it a habit of always playing with new balls, to the extent that, in 1470, he sent the following news to his preacher in Florence: "We wish for you to have one hundred of these made, but a little larger than the ones we received last time so that we can get a little better bounce out of them."

The beauteous favorite, Lucia Marliano, the Countess of Melzo, was never missing from the games, softly reclining upon "a cushion of crimson and green velvet, an arm and one-half in length and one arm's length wide." But her encouragement and the counsels given by the famous trainers were to no avail against the best player of the court, Count Galeotto Belgioioso.

"Be careful not to play with him," suggests Galeazzo Maria to his brother Ascanio, on September 10, 1475," because he has become such a fine playing master that he will win every game."

Important historical events are tied into the sport. The wounding, the subsequent assassination of Gaspard de Coligny, and the beginning of St. Bartholomew's Massacre were brought to the attention of Charles IX while the king was playing paume *at the Louvre in 1572. (He and his companion can be seen in the upper left of the picture.) "I can never get a moment's peace! Always these fresh annoyances!" the king is reported to have shouted out as he threw down his racket in disgust.*

6 Greatness and Decline

In order to write a book of this type in the space allowed, the author must learn the gentle and difficult art of what to leave unsaid. I am forced, therefore, to sketch in hurriedly the contributions of the other European nations to the game, before touching on the period of its rise to greatness and subsequent decline.

In 1476 there appeared in Flemish the *Kaetspele* (Game of Chases), a translation of the French *Jeu de Paume Moralisé* (A Moral View of *Paume*). It is a volume that seems just about as morally constructive as it is rare, for only two copies have survived to the present time. Rummaging around in a library, I came upon a reference to a certain *Jeu Spirituel de la Paume ou de l'Eteuf* (The Spiritual Game of *Paume* or Balls) written in 1435, and I have a suspicion that this confession of a penitent player, now unavailable, is the original from which the other French work and the Flemish translation are taken.

We ought to emphasize at this point that the first surviving French book on the sport was translated almost immediately for the Flemish, and that *kaetse* is the equivalent of Italian *caccia*, French *chasse*, and English "chase." It is all cut from the same cloth, even if the Flemish language prefers to call the sport "The Game of Chases" instead of "palm" or "cord" game (the equivalents of French *paume* and Italian *gioco della corda*).

The Flemish are also our source for the first painting that shows a game played with rackets. In point of fact though, from the viewpoint of the artist himself, the tennis players and playing field are not the center of attraction. Each of the nine different versions of the theme that I have been able to ferret out shows Uriah at the moment when King David delivers the letter that will ultimately bring about the former's death at the front lines. The group composed of David, Uriah, and the courtiers is in the foreground while the tennis game itself plays a distinctly minor role in a flight of perspective that encompasses an immense park and a bay. This painting indicates the same indifference to the plight of the individual that we see in the much more famous work by Brueghel the Elder, *The Fall of Icarus*.

The only one of the nine versions that has a clearly identifiable painter is the one signed by the firm hand of Lucas Gassel in 1540, the prototype of the others. The monogram "L. G. fecit" (Painted by L. G.) stands out clearly on the work, now the proud possession of Dr. Restelli of Lake Como.

Of the four versions reproduced in two color plates between pages 40 and 41, the one done by Gassel is most likely the best, with the softest hues and the most beautiful perspective. It has not been given the position of honor for the simple reason that the version hanging at Lord's, the London Marylebone Cricket Club, has the best draftsmanship and is the most appealing to the eye. The identity of the painter of this work is still in doubt, however, despite the questionable candidacy of the name of Joos Van Amstel, as is the work belonging to the other London resident, Lord Aberdare (upper left), which some contend was painted by Andreas Ruhl. The painting in the lower left is attributed with some justification to Herri met de Bles. It was brought from Italy to

Taken from the painting by David, this picture illustrates the Tennis Court Oath at the Jeu de Paume *in 1789, the official act of rebellion of the members of the Third Estate against Louis XVI. At Chénier's request, the court was first transformed into a national monument (Boilly's painting below) and then into a museum (bottom of the page).*

Boston by Elizabeth Stewart Gardner.

Though they are all outdoors, the playing areas in these works are not too different from those described by our friend Scaino. The surface is clearly paved in stone or brick, three times out of four in two different colors to set off the divisions of the court; the cord that divides them has not as yet developed into a real net.

The painting belonging to Lord Aberdare shows a doubles game in progress, witnessed from the gallery by a score of spectators. Gassel also depicts a doubles match, but one of the players is huddled low in a rather unusual stance. Perhaps his partner's shot has upset their opponent closest to the net, and the rally is almost over.

In the painting to the right, from the Stewart Gardner Museum, we observe a singles game. The positioning of the players is almost identical to those of the Marylebone piece, with the man on the left about to hit a hard forehand shot and his opponent readied for a high volley. The third man is, in all likelihood, in charge of retrieving the balls or of keeping score by tallying the chases. In all the paintings a small basket can be seen which is used for picking up the balls that are scattered about due either to wastefulness or carelessness, unless (and this is much more likely the case) they represent "chases," prior points to be awarded.

Another valuable picture of the sport, perhaps the first that shows a tennis lesson in progress, is found in a short satirical poem, the *Emblemata,* dating from 1576 and written by Dr. Zsamboki (Sambucus in the Latinate form), a Hungarian physician at the Court

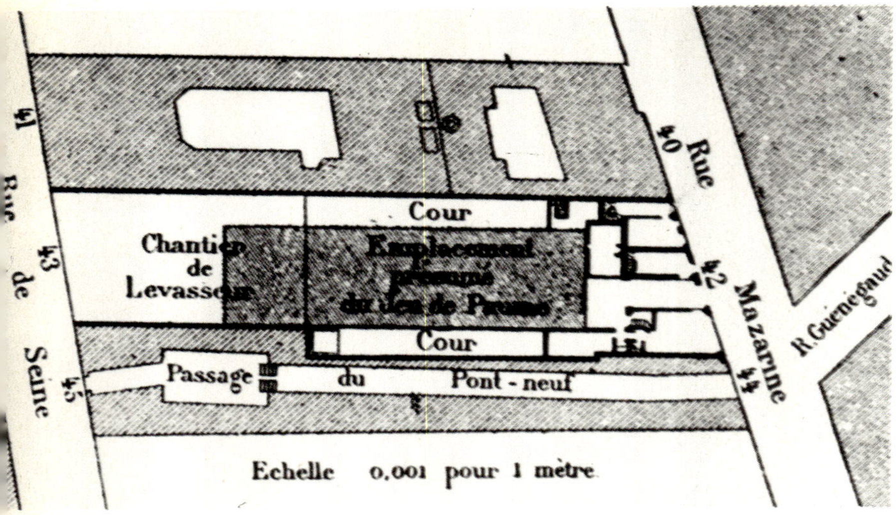

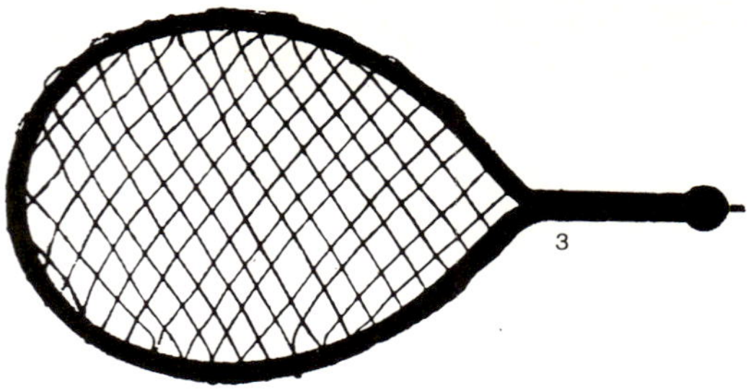

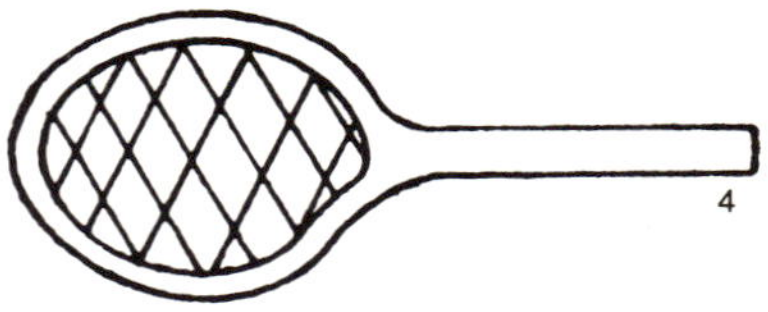

1. In the seventeenth and eighteenth centuries, paume *and the* comédie *often shared the same roof, as in the case of the* Jeu de Paume de la Bouteille (Jeu de Paume *of the Bottle) and the* Guéguenard *Theater, where Perrin's* Pomona *was performed on Tuesday, March 3, 1761.*
2. The peaceful coexistence of the two groups was often broken by altercations between robbers and their victims. This painting by J. B. Pater depicts such a rowdy affair.
3. The sign of a seventeenth-century building for jeu de paume *preserved at Rouen.*
4. An entry token shaped like a racket from a jeu où se donne la Comédie *("court theater") in 1784 at Angers.*
5. The emblem of the Corporation of the Broommakers, Brushmakers, and Racketmakers, dating from

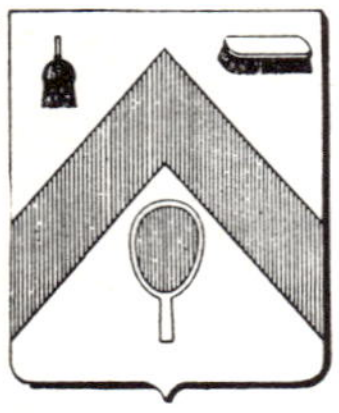

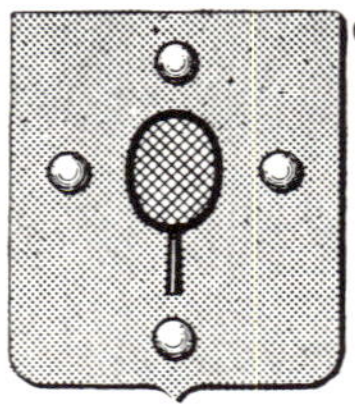

of Vienna. The instructor is actually gripping two rackets, perhaps in order to make his point more clear or perhaps to show his ambidexterity. Sambucus was a handsome and jovial sort, much opposed to indoor games, and it is hard to speculate as to the real reason behind the twin rackets.

We find reference to other important tennis lessons, dated July 9th, 1612, when Master Gentil affixes his signature to the bottom of a legal document in which he declares himself satisfied with the payment of 500 lire in exchange "for services rendered to Louis XIII in showing him the fine points of the game." This official method of payment must bear some relation to the documents of incorporation awarded on November 13, 1610 to the *Communauté des Paumiers Raquettiers, Faiseurs d'Eteufs, Pelotes et Balles* (Association of *Paume* Masters and Suppliers of Balls).

Such franchises, which date back to 1480 and which were favored by Francis I in 1537, had finally managed to raise *paume* to an art form. In order to enjoy these privileges of franchise, the aspiring player was required to demonstrate his ability by a special examination in which he not only had to beat two known masters, but also had to show himself capable of making both ball and racket.

In Spain the racket remained a very rare piece of sports equipment, as attested both in 1555 in the *Dialogues* of the Spanish philosopher Luis Vives and in 1618, when certain packing crates of poplar wood, sent by the viceroy of Naples, were needed to make paddles.

1475. The racketmakers took their leave from the builders of brooms and brushes around 1550 and adopted a new shield, a racket surrounded by four silver balls (6).

7. A family portrait of the Charriers, famous masters for three generations, from the eighteenth to the nineteenth century.

8. A group of players at the Tuileries during tournament play in 1891. Standing second from the end on the right is the well-known Ridgway.

9. Another group of players at Manchester at the beginning of the 1880's. Seated third from the right is John Moyer Heathcote, the inventor of the fabric-covered ball, and the person to the far left with the long beard is Edmond Tompkins, a great player of royal (real) tennis.

10. A nineteenth-century ex libris.

7

10

8

11

12

11. I Capricci *(Whimsy), a woodcut done by Bracelli in 1607, brings to mind the metaphysical players of Carrà, seen elsewhere in the book in a color version.*

12. The racket designed by the Bologna craftsman Mitelli in 1675 still has a very short handle, but it is covered with the fabric binding that has once again come into vogue at the present time. The diagonal strings of the first rackets have by this time disappeared.

9

Among the descendants of the Roman games, some retained the use of the bare hand, while others employed armguards and gloves, and still others provided equipment different from the racket for propulsion. Some of them are seen in the following panorama, offered without being in any sense complete.
1. These instruments are English copies of Scaino's descriptions, as we see them in order, a ball, two pumps, a scanno, an implement whose popularity was brief, and an armguard used to propel the ball.
2. Another armguard together with a paddle used in pelota.
3. More examples of armguards.
4. The tamburello is used in playing a game by the same name, which is still popular in some European regions and resembles pallone to some degree.

2

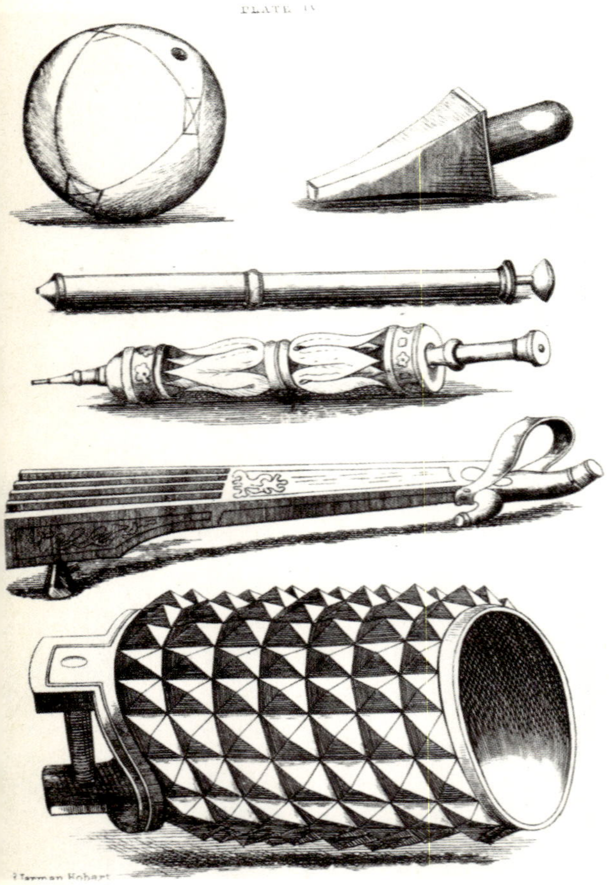

1

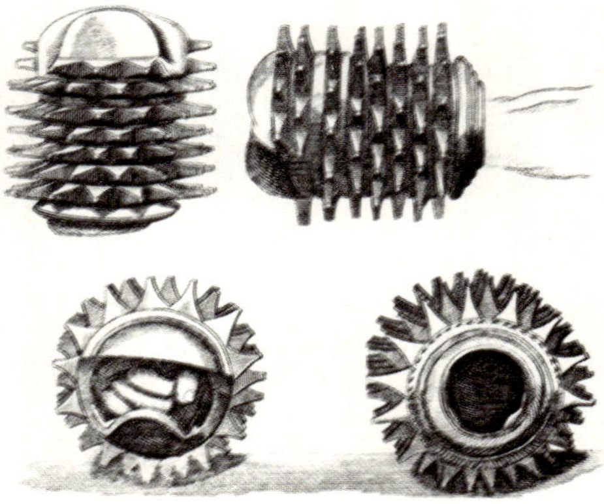

3

7

5. This nineteenth-century portrayal of an Italian player of pallone comes to us from Australia.
9. Here is another example of the same game from the Bertarelli Collection. 8. In this picture from England, the player, called mandarino, is about to serve the ball to the batter, illustrating the origin of the tennis term "serve" or "service."
6, 7, and 10. Illustrations of the game of pallone as played in the eighteenth and early and late nineteenth centuries.
13. Another game played by teams of three men each in France. The game that Burckhardt called "the classical game of the Italians" was also well known in France,

4

6

5

12

8

9

especially as played by teams of four, using the small armguard and following the same rules as those of chases. Pallone with the larger armguard is played by three without the use of chases, but this form of the sport is also dying out.

14. Pallone being played at the Quattro Fontane (Four Fountains) in 1814.

15. The same game at the Prison of Saint-Lazare in Paris, painted by Robert Huber.

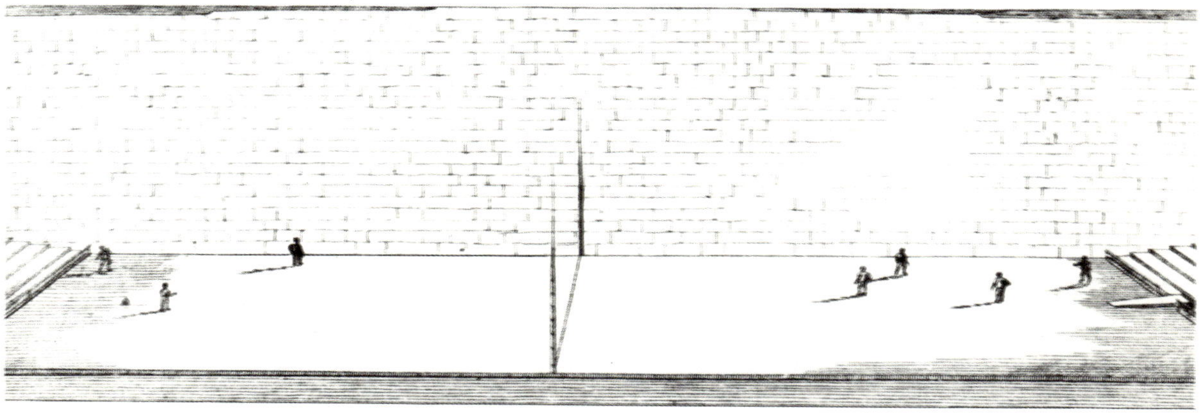

10

11

13

16. Another popular scene by Domenico Olivieri from the 1700s.

11. Another nineteenth-century descendant of the Flemish Kaetspel *as seen in an advertisement to a match taken from the important book,* Kaatsen in Friesland (Chases in Friesland) *by Dr. J. L. Kalma.*

12. A game contemporary with early lawn tennis, called the Belgian ball game by an unknown English artist. Notice the very interesting and unusual gloves for the whole palm similar to the ones that probably formed the link between hand and racket games.

14

15

16

1

8

A few descendants of the Roman and medieval games are still in existence, even if they are less popular than tennis. Photos 1 through 6 show stances that are remarkably similar to one another and to certain positions in tennis.

7

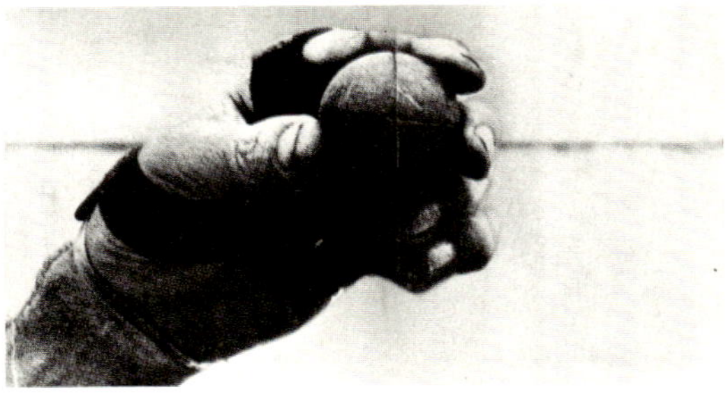

1. *Jose Letroye, Belgian champion of* balle au tamis *(ball and sieve), a game similar to Italian pallone, and like the latter played with a springy ball.*
2. *Spanish pelota, also played with the bare hand.*
3. Pallone elastico *(springy pallone), so called from the springy nature of the projectile, played in the Piedmont and Ligurian regions of Italy, with pockets of activity in the areas of Nice and Bergamo. The game is played with the bare hand, sometimes protected by a thin wrapping.*
4. *Already known in the seventeenth century, a game of* tamburello *is still considered great fun in Northern Italy and in France. It is played with a rubber ball weighing some 70 grams (about 2½ oz.), and, since 1954, with teams of five players each. Here a* tamburello *player reaches for a difficult shot.*
5. *We see Spanish pelota, played by young men in the tradition of King Alfonso the Wise and also as depicted in the country scene by Goya, appearing in color elsewhere in the book. The player,* pala *in hand, is about to strike the ball.*

2

4

5

3

6

9

10

6. *The player of Spanish cesta wears a helmet to protect his head from the leather ball, which is as heavy as its Renaissance ancestor and can produce devastating injuries. The helmet resembles the type used in American high school and intercollegiate wrestling.*
7. *In a player's hand, we see a ball used in Valencian pelota. The most vulnerable points of the hand are protected with strips of leather for a blow from a ball weighing about 3½ ounces.*
8. *The* pallone elastico *is the center of attraction at Piazza Galimberti in downtown Cuneo in Italy.*

9. *Place Morichar in Brussels is not less crowded during a match of* balle au tamis.
10. *The playing field of Macerata, a small town near Ancona, now used for open-air opera performances. The Italian poet Leopardi wrote eloquently of the* pallone *engagements that took place here.*
11. *Pelota, just like the bullfight, transplants well in South America. We can see a game being played in Buenos Aires with the* cesta, *a kind of wicker scoop.*
12. *A pelota game in progress in the Basque provinces, where the game is especially revered.*
13. *The playing field of Santo Stefano Belbo, highly favored by the contemporary Italian novelist Pavese.*
14. *A photographic witness to the historical five-day game played at Monforte d'Alba, a center both for the game of* pallone *and for fine wines.*

11

12

13

14

1

On these pages we see pictures of sports akin to lawn tennis. Major Wingfield referred to these sports to set up rules for lawn tennis played informally until then.

2

3

4

1, 2. Sketches of the game of rackets, from which the major took the point system and the rule of service, according to which a serve was lost when the server lost a rally. From royal or real tennis he took more the spirit than the letter of the law, dropping both the system of chases and the walled-in court, but later he used the point system.

3. A game of fives at Eton, the last

5

6

descendant of the hand games of the ancients.
4. *The squash-rackets court at Eton.*
5. *One of the last royal tennis courts in Paris, the* Passage Cendrier *(Cinder Path), torn down in 1861.*
6. *The famous tennis coach, Edmond Barre.*
7. *Children playing badminton at the turn of the century. Originally played in Malaysia and India under the name of* poona, *the game was renamed by the Duke of Beaufort. Wingfield adopted the net from this game, initially over 1.5 meters (4 ft. 11 in.) in height.*
8. *Court for the inmates of the Fleet Street Prison, described by Charles Dickens.*

7

8

Meanwhile in Paris, Lippomano, the Venetian ambassador, wrote that one thousand crowns were spent each day to purchase rackets, and Sir Robert Dallington was amazed to note that the French countryside was "alive with *paume* courts that seem more common than churches. The French are born with rackets in their hands, which are more numerous than beer pots in England."

In the midst of all this elegance, in 1579, Gosselin, the king's librarian, dedicated to Monsieur d'O, a court favorite, his *Déclaration des Deux Doutes qui se trouvent en comptant le Jeu de la Paume* (A statement of two difficulties which arise when scoring in *jeu de paume*). Gosselin's difficulties had to do with the mysteries of keeping score based on the number fifteen, and his two solutions were taken from astronomy and geometry, in accord with his own favorite topics of study. Only one copy of this book exists today, bound together with two other works, the royal ordinances on *paume* of 1592 in twenty-four articles, and the *L'Utilité qui provient du jeu de la paume au corp e a l'esprit* (Benefits derived from *paume* both to body and mind), translated from Galen's Greek original by Forbet the Elder, master of *paume*, and published in 1599. To make the researcher's task a little more complicated, both Gosselin's treatise on keeping score and Forbet's translation have often been attributed to a certain Hulpeau, who actually did nothing more than publish both of them again in 1632, together with a well-known engraving by Crébierre.

Unlike the more refined Gosselin, the *paume* master ranged in his twenty-four rules from his first maxim *bene vivere et laetari* (good living brings happiness) to his last *animus gaudens aetatem floridam facit* (a happy spirit makes for a happy life), ending his work with the motto *bon pied, bon oeil* (good footwork, and one's eye on the ball). The rules for keeping score were not too different from those of Scaino as far as winning an individual game was concerned. Sets, however, were awarded by the best of four or six games, and in case of a three-game tie, an advantage of two was needed.

Some of the royal articles referred to rules concerning the payment of drinks, settling gambling accounts, lawsuits, and there is a heavy emphasis on hard cash in general. Betting was so common that the word *tripot* (gaming house) took on the meaning of 'bawdy house,' and the frays were so numerous and so vociferous that they became the subject of the first novel written about the sport, the *Mémôires de Monsieur le Marquis de Montbrun* (Memoirs of the Marquis of Montbrun), penned by Sandrar de Courtils in 1701. The marquis departs for London in the company of the strongest professional player in the city of Paris, who has disguised himself as a gentleman's gentleman. He stirs up half the city of London and then reduces the dogged Count of Northhampton to rubble on the paved tennis court. The playing areas have become closely tied to the needs of the professional player, especially in France, and the increasing use of the closed court as a theater only confirms this fact. Voltaire will write on the subject: "What a shame that for the staging of *Mithridates* or *Tartuffe* there is nothing better than the *Jeu de Paume* at the Place de l'Étoile, with the audience forced to stand and a bevy of coxcombs wandering among the actors."

The few permanent theaters of that day were reserved for the

Here are some champions of royal tennis and lawn tennis, selected to illustrate differences and similarities between the two games. The upper tier of pictures illustrates royal tennis, while the lower tier demonstrates lawn tennis. The grips are less alike in the two games in the forehand (A, A^1) than in the backhand (B, B^1), whereas the angle between the forearm and the racket is much wider in lawn tennis (A^1, B^1). Actually, lawn tennis is a rough sport as compared to the refined astuteness needed for the game of kings.

1. The serve in the older game was executed from below, as demonstrated here by J. Pettitt.
2. A forehand shot demonstrated by the bearded J. M. Heathcote, struck much lower than is the case in 2^a.
3. In the preparation for the forehand, the swing is not so wide as in 3^a.
4. Old Biboche, one of the greats, gets ready for a backhand volley, with a style that is more up-to-date than the one of the lawn tennis player below!
5. While Renshaw is getting ready for a forehand stroke, the position of the racket permits him to

1

2

3

4

1^a

2^a

3^a

4^a

A
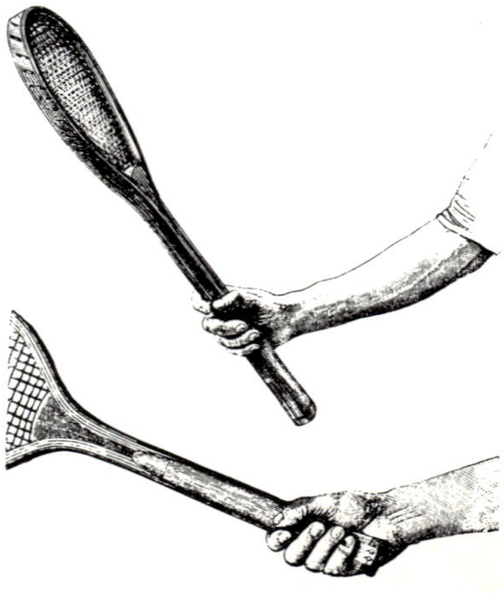
A^1

Court and for the aristocracy. During the great vogue of court tennis at the beginning of the seventeenth century, the actors had to make do with haphazard stage props, set up hurriedly when night came on and the players left the courts free. Once in a while, the ragged and tattered troupes would pilfer the clothing that the *maîtres paumiers* (tennis masters) had rented to the players. Quarrelsome arguments were occasionally the result, as can be seen in a painting by Pater. Nevertheless, as the game of *paume* began to decline, the stagings became more and more profitable for the owner of the *jeu de paume*, who did his best to obtain monopoly rights by transforming his *tripot* into a court theater, where plays were produced as well.

By the time of Voltaire's lament, many closed courts had already

assume a very easy stance that will not force him to hit the ball from beneath.
6. Biboche slices a forehand volley, while Renshaw begins his swing with the head of the racket too close to the ground.
7. The defensive position of this player of royal tennis suggests a volley very close to the net, much closer than in the case of Renshaw, below.
8. Two low backhand volleys. Once again, as in 6^a, Renshaw's stance is clumsy, but also defensive. A and A^1, B and B^1 offer the reader two examples of the grips for the old and the new tennis. The forehand grip of royal tennis is much wider in order to scoop up the ball and work on it. The angle of the forearm and the handle is reduced more than in lawn tennis. The positioning for the backhand (B and B^1) is similar. The angle between forearm and handle distinguishes them, as does the custom of gripping the racket further up along its length in royal tennis.

5

6

7

8

5^a

6^a

7^a

8^a

B

B^1

become permanent theater houses, with orchestra seats, loges, and a stage. In France this form of building (following the outline of the old *jeu de paume*) caught on quickly, and it was not until long after the semicircular floor plan had become common in other parts of Europe that the French finally abandoned the rectangular building. One cannot, however, blame the court theater for the decline of royal tennis, or rackets, in France: such an assumption would be a little too farfetched.

Jeu de paume, at least the *courte paume* variety played with rackets, ran into difficulty in the Renaissance, in the age that Neuendorff calls "the most unfortunate period of all times" for sports education. The first hint of this decline can best be appreciated in a lively scene from Thomas Corneille's *The Triumph of*

Giocco Della Racchetta
Gabriel Bella F.

Marino's long poem in which he contrasted racket and the discus throwing of Adonis to the lyrics of Chiabrera in honor of Cintio Venanzi da Cagli, pallone as played with the armguard slowly but steadily ousted *palla corda* (cord ball), a new name for the ancient game of *rachetta*, in the eighteenth and nineteenth centuries. The Renaissance authority Burkhardt called pallone "the classical game of the Italians," and the diaries of visitors to Italy, from Goethe to Fuseli, were crammed with references to this rougher sport together with thumbnail sketches of it in action. Our Italian poets, more devoted to rhetoric than to technique, went out of their way to praise pallone, as evidenced by Leopardi's ode to Carlo Didimi di Treia, composed one year after the start of the construction of a magnificent playing field at Macerata.

At this critical point the English began to play a major role. From the beginning of the seventeenth century, the tide began to turn in favor of this sport across the Channel. Partially withdrawn from the business world, feeling time hang heavy, the rich gentlemen farmers were too sprightly a lot to sit idly by with a pipe in their mouths or a pretty farm maid on their knees. Puritan laws stood in the way of further development, but the decrees of James I and Charles I helped court tennis survive, and the sport then continued its development unimpeded. Charles himself was up and about at six in the morning to practice with the celebrated master John Webb on one of the fourteen covered courts in London. And in 1663, even Charles II made an attempt at the new court built at his request at Whitehall, and apparently lost at least four pounds of excess weight, not taking into account all the powder sweated off his pomaded cheeks during such rough, male encounters.

Despite a de-emphasis of the sport under the Hanoverians, who were not tennis-minded, Walpole could recount the tragic death of the Prince of Wales, Frederick, who was struck down in 1751 by internal bleeding after a hard blow to the stomach with the ball. And while in Paris the covered courts at Versailles were turned into the headquarters of the National Assembly in 1789, the French *paume* masters found work across the Channel on courts recently financed by such patrons as the Duke of Wellington, Lord Plymouth, Lord Brougham, and many other less well-known but equally affluent and tennis-struck notables. In 1816 there actually was organized a "World Championship," won by Marchisio, an Italian from France, whose father had been a master at the Court of Turin in Italy. With a purse of three hundred sterling in the offing, Marchisio trounced the English champion Cox.

The returning popularity of the sport was accentuated by the publication of two sets of rules. One, by Randle Holm, was published by the Academy of Armory in 1688, and the other, which appeared in 1878, was a joint effort of the two most important French professionals, Barre and Biboche Delahaye, and the Englishman, Julian Marshall, a true scholar of the fine points of technique. But as Marshall was patiently annotating the valuable manuscript of *Annals of Tennis*, he was acutely aware that his effort would be a swan song to the sport as he knew it then. The new game that was developing under his watchful and curious eyes on the lawns of the English country houses during the summer would soon strike a death blow to the old sport of royal (or real) tennis, called court tennis in the United States.

Marshall's task had been to codify the old rules and enshrine them on the time-honored shelves of the British Museum, together with countless anecdotes of the sport as it had been played by celebrated monarchs and unknown champions alike.

By the time that the *Annals of Tennis* was completed in 1878, Major Walter Clopton Wingfield had already lodged his patent for a new game, called lawn tennis. Together with other former players of the sport of kings, Julian Marshall threw himself with gusto into the task of clarifying the rules of the new sport of commoners.

1

3

2

4

1. Julian Marshall, the author of the most famous account of the game of kings, Annals of Tennis, *published in 1878. 2. Albert de Luze, his French counterpart, whose* La Magnifique Histoire du Jeu de Paume (The Stirring History of Jeu de Paume), *appeared in 1933. 3. Marshall's* ex libris *carries the motto "The King of Games: The Game of Kings," together with a picture of Henry II and his favorite indoor court. 4. A gold plate commemorates Luze's winning of the "Golden Racket," the French court tennis championship in 1905.*

1

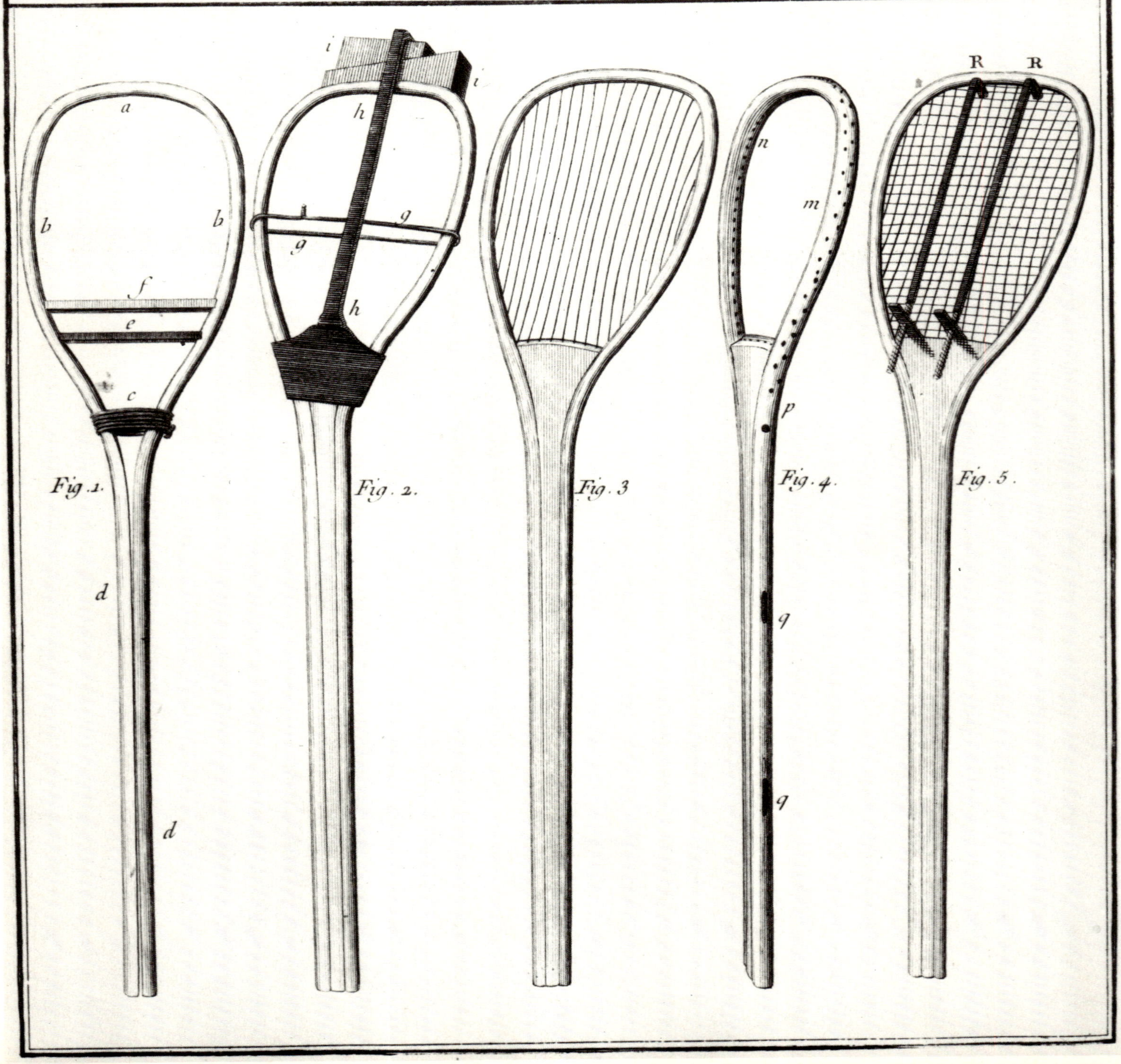

2

Three illustrations show the handcrafting of rackets in the eighteenth, nineteenth, and twentieth centuries.
1. An etching taken from Garsault. Three Tennis Masters at their workbenches: the man to the right is knotting a ball. Below we can see the way in which a racket was assembled and corded.
2. Similar work is being carried out in this French etching, which shows equipment being prepared for royal tennis.
3. A photograph snapped at the SIRT, the oldest Italian manufacturer of rackets, in 1922. The firm, located in Bordighera, is still very active.

3

THE PIONEERS OF LAWN TENNIS

Major Wingfield Patents a New Game. Miss Outerbridge Imports it Into the United States. Wimbledon is Born in 1877. Dwight Davis Invents the Cup Bearing His Name and the Doherty Brothers Win it. The Mythical Domination of Australasia, Wilding and Brookes. Continental Tennis. The Women. Wingfield's Box Arrives in Bordighera.

Here we see Major Walter Clopton Wingfield at the age of forty, posing with one of the rackets sold by his representatives for a pound sterling each. To his right can be seen the request for patent, dated 23 February 1874, for "a new and improved portable court for playing the ancient game of tennis."

A.D. 1874, 23rd February. N° 685.

A Portable Court for Playing Tennis.

LETTERS PATENT to Walter Clopton Wingfield, of Belgrave Road, Pimlico, in the County of Middlesex, for the Invention of "A New and Improved Portable Court for Playing the Ancient Game of Tennis."

Sealed the 24th July 1874, and dated the 23rd February 1874.

PROVISIONAL SPECIFICATION left by the said Walter Clopton Wingfield at the Office of the Commissioners of Patents, with his Petition, on the 23rd February 1874.

I, Walter Clopton Wingfield, of Belgrave Road, Pimlico, in the County of Middlesex, do hereby declare the nature of the said Invention for "A New and Improved Portable Court for Playing the Ancient Game of Tennis," to be as follows:—

The object and intention of this Invention consists in constructing a portable court by means of which the ancient game of tennis is much simplified, can be played in the open air, and dispenses with the necessity of having special courts erected for that purpose.

Price

On the opposite page is a reproduction of the title page of the first book of rules, which appeared in December 1873, and where we can read clearly "Sphairistikè or Lawn Tennis." The first name, which went back to the Greek origins of the sport, was quickly abandoned. It never caught on and gave cause for puns. As the text records, Wingfield was a flexible man who was more interested in economic success than in slavish attention to the details of the rules, and created a new synthesis of rackets, royal tennis, and badminton. On the following pages: 1. Wingfield outfitted himself with a new top hat, a new astrakhan overcoat, and did his best to increase the sales made by his agents, French & Company, who warehoused the box containing the equipment for the game, which for those days was anything but cheap in price. 6. The description of the rules of the game left by Wingfield, oddly enough, differs from the sketches made of the court and from his own commentary on the need for a wasp-waisted court. As matters went, the drawing attached to the first patent (2) and the first illustration of the court (3) are not at all rectangular, especially because of the difficulty involved in securing the net. 3, 4. We see how the game was played and how the serve was placed from the diamond in the center of one of the courts into the service courts of the opponent. 5. Here is a later edition of the court which, by 1877, had become rectangular.

7 Walter Clopton Wingfield Patents a Noteworthy Game

In 1873 at the age of forty, Walter Clopton Wingfield had no particular reason to consider himself successful. He had a fine name, inherited together with the remains of the family fortune, and had gone to the right schools. Wingfield had taken part in the only military adventure open to a young Englishman after the Crimean War, and now he faced the peaceful years of the Victorian Age. The time he spent in China as commander of a squadron of the Montgomery Yeomanry Cavalry had not, however, encouraged him to make the military a lifetime career.

He spent his time telling colorful tales about the Eastern opium dens, playing the quiet role of magistrate in Montgomeryshire, and organizing an order of gourmets.

He lost no chance to lead a worldly life and hence threw himself into every sport imaginable from the hunt to shuttlecock (given its new name "badminton" by the Duke of Beaufort in honor of his local country seat), and from sabers to croquet, an activity as important to women's liberation as all of the books of John Stuart Mill.

At a birthday party in Nantclwyd, the conversation chanced to turn to the games played by what Disraeli had called "one of the two English nations." The windows of the loveliest house in the village looked out over a meadow, bright green as set against the pearl grey of the winter day, and someone complained sadly about the harshness of the climate, so inhospitable to games played *en plein air*.

Another guest remarked that it was difficult to get up a match of court tennis, and a third recounted from hearsay that in Edgbaston at the home of a Spanish importer by the name of Pereira, a certain Major Harry Gem and his friends had been getting together for several years to bat back and forth a hollow rubber ball with their rackets. The ball rebounded well even on the lawn. Major Gem and his friend Pereira had gone so far as to organize a club for the new sport at Leamington.

The conversation around the fireplace grew more animated. A dedicated reader informed the group that nine years earlier in the garden at Ancrum, the guests of Sir Walter Scott had taken part in such a match as the one just described. Immediately thereafter a history buff went one better, going even further back in time to an almost identical occurrence, when, under the admiring eyes of Queen Elizabeth I, in the park of the Earl of Hertford at Elvetham, ten footmen had played "long fives," an English cousin of the French game of *longue paume*.

Major Wingfield kept his counsel while stroking his full growth of beard. All the enthusiasm and animated dialogue brought back to his mind an idea that had come to him often as he gathered the news clippings for a sportsman's guide he was preparing.

Soccer and rugby, thought the major, were fine for boys who liked to give themselves a mud bath. Track and rowing, more in keeping with university life, required a certain combative spirit. As for cricket, a large group of players was needed.

Up to that point, he reasoned, nothing better than that pale imitation of a sport, croquet, had been found for the yards surrounding the summer places of the well-kept grounds of the clubs. This game kept the charming young ladies in their hoop skirts amused, bemused, and out of mischief while they were being courted. And by mass-producing mallets and balls from wood with the aid of the new machines and by transporting them by train or steamship, someone had made himself a small fortune.

"A month ago in *The Field*," one of his most lovely guests was saying excitedly, "someone was talking about a sport that can be played on the lawn with a racket, and the writer went on to say that it wasn't proper to call it 'badminton' like the drink, but suggested that it be referred to as 'ladies' tennis!' "

Wingfield waited patiently for his old aunt to inveigh against such a revolutionary idea which must certainly have had its origin with that upstart Florence Nightingale. Then, in his customary nonchalant and commanding way, he got the attention of the whole group.

"Next spring," he asserted, "we'll have a new game to play right here in the garden, a game for all of us."

A few days later the guests assembled at Nantclwyd. All had received in the mail a brochure titled *The game of Sphairistikè or Lawn Tennis*, which was republished for a larger audience in February 1874, together with a claim to copyright set forth by the major, and the news that "a provisional patent protection had already been granted for the invention of a new and improved court for the old game of tennis." After a warm note to the group at Nantclwyd for their help, the major launched into a clear explanation of his plan.

"I set up two posts in the ground about twenty feet apart, between which I stretch a rectangular net. At each of the posts I place a triangular net, attached in such a way that the pole divides it into two right triangles, at the right angle of which a cord and rings connect the triangular nets to the rectangular one and the two points of which are held by pegs driven into the ground. The triangular net represents the side walls of the playing area."

Examination of the accompanying sketches from the patent request will help to clarify the above, and may also suggest to the reader that the wasp-waisted shape of the court might possibly have first been the result of miscalculation in the measurements taken from the major's written instructions.

It is clear that when Wingfield speaks of side walls, he still has in his mind the covered playing area of old court tennis, and the same sport certainly influenced him in his rules for the serve as well.

From the diamond area in the center of one of the half-courts, the ball was served into the other half-court, more specifically into either side of the divided area between the service line and the base line in modern parlance.

Taking after badminton, the net was about five feet in height, and the racket midway in size between a modern tennis racket and a rackets bat. Rackets itself was the model for Wingfield's system of winning points. Only the server, the individual who was "hand in" according to the slang of the sport, could earn points. If his opponent (who was "hand out") caused him to make a fault, the

1

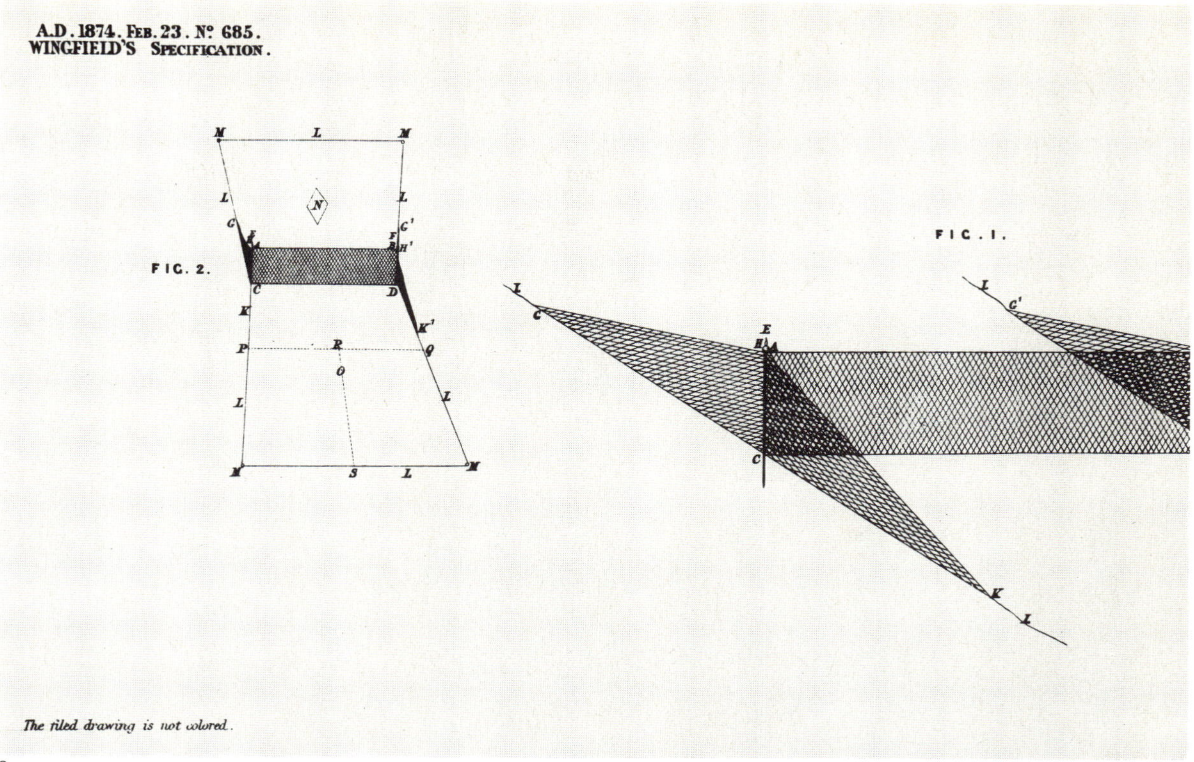

2

3

4

5

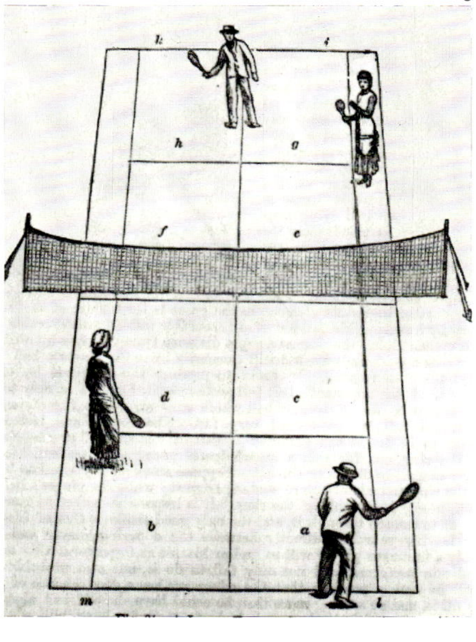

In 1880 the sides of the alleys had been defined, limiting the service area. In addition to tennis, Wingfield was also the author of a sportsman's guide and a bicycle handbook. Other than some financial comfort, the patent afforded him a gold watch, a billfold containing 200 pounds, and a marble bust, all gifts of a grateful committee of tennis enthusiasts. When he died, however, on April 18, 1912, there was no mention of the word "tennis" in his obituary.

6

BY HER MAJESTY'S ROYAL LETTERS PATENT

Price List

FOR CASH ONLY.

	£	s.	d.
Box of Sphairistike, the game complete as advertised	6	0	0
Extra-sized box, with Racquet Press, extra Bats, and a supply of Balls for several months	10	10	0
The Patent Court complete, in Box	2	7	6
Racket Press for six Bats	1	0	0
" for four Bats	0	15	0
Full-sized Sphairistike Bats	1	0	0
Ladies' Bats	0	15	0
Balls, per dozen	0	5	0
Sphairistike Tape Measures	0	2	6
Tennis Shoes, with India-rubber soles, which will not cut up the turf	0	18	6

BEWARE OF SPURIOUS IMITATIONS.

Every Box, Bat, and Ball is marked "Sphairistikè."

The Bats are expressly made for the game, of the original shape designed by the Inventor; the Balls are manufactured in Germany, and made specially of an extra thickness of Indian rubber, and not procurable anywhere else

SOLE AGENTS—

MESSRS. FRENCH & CO.,

46, CHURTON ST., PIMLICO,

LONDON, S.W.

1

1. *This sketch from the Todd Collection was drawn by Harry Gem, president and founder of the first Lawn Tennis Club in the world, the Leamington, in 1872. Gem is about to hit the ball, with his Spanish friend, G. B. Pereira, playing at his side. On the other side of the net stand Drs. Tomkins and Haynes.*
2. *Below is the first photo that has come down to us of the game, found through the good offices of Alan Little. It shows the same locale in 1874, and demonstrates the difficulties involved in stretching out a net.*

2

4

3

3. *A Christmas card which appeared in 1862, according to Jimmy Jones who lent it to us.*
4. *Perhaps the first cartoon dealing with tennis, from the* Punch *issue of 23 September 1876.*
5. *This drawing by Du Maurier depicts Wingfield's suggestion that the game be played on ice.*
6, 7, *and* 8. *Taken from* Punch *in 1874. The first of the three is probably the first picture of women's doubles.*

5

6

7

8

1

1. *An illustration of the first world tournament of the All-England Croquet and Lawn Tennis Club of Wimbledon, which is still the most important world tournament. The finals of 19 July, 1877, were witnessed by an audience of 200 who deposited with the box office one shilling each. Today the club can accommodate 300,000 spectators.* 2. *The second illustration by Harry Furniss gives us an idea of the tournament of 1879. At the top of the picture, the Reverend Hartley is beating Gould before 1,000 fans. The other subjects treated in the montage are a sudden rain, a spot of tea, and beautiful women: three ever-present elements of the competitions.* 3. *Here we have confirmation, in* Punch, *of the popularity of the game in 1880.* 4, 5. *Two different views of tennis. It is easy to end up chained to a racket!*

2

server lost only the right to continue to serve, which went to his opponent. To avoid charges of plagiarism, the major had had the idea of introducing deuce when the score was tied at thirteen all, as well as the vantage of old *paume*. Actually, in rackets the set ended at fifteen, but in the event there was a tie at thirteen, the player who first achieved that score could begin a new set of three or five points, and when the score was tied at fourteen, a three point advantage was needed to win.

Wingfield suggested to the readers of *The Field* magazine in the issue of March 21, 1874, that in order to better understand the rules of the new game, they should send in sixpence in stamps for further information. He told them that to play the game "a court, four rackets, and a supply of balls from French & Co. for the sum of five guineas" were indispensable. It almost seems too much of a coincidence that the same day and in the same paper Sir Gerald Fitzgerald wrote a feature on the new sport. Wingfield responded with his own article, confirming the issue of the patent, and stressing the fact that "his establishment would provide total satisfaction for any reader interested in the new game."

The readers of *The Field* who went to Wingfield's establishment found a wooden chest 36 x 12 x 6 inches containing, other than balls and rackets, a roll of tape, some large pins, and some wedges and a hammer. One of the readers was not altogether satisfied and complained to *The Field* that in order to obtain some balls, he had to outfit himself once again. "Can Mr. Wingfield's patent be valid," the reader inquired, "if many people have already been playing the game for some years in their gardens?"

The complaints soon turned into a chorus. It was suddenly remembered that Lord Henry, bishop of Bath, had proved himself in a similar game, and that James Lillywhite had published an advertisement a year earlier, describing that game as "The New Indian Outdoor Game, more pleasant, more healthful, and more fun than croquet."

Jokes were made about Wingfield's suggestion that the game be played in the winter on ice with skates. Julian Marshall, with his sharp

3

4

tongue, noted that a colonel who was a good friend of the major had confided to him (Marshall) that *sphairistikè* in Greek meant water clock (from the wasp-waisted shape of the court)!

Other critics were not less severe and quoted Charles Dickens, who had died four years prior to that time, claiming that his description of the rackets court in the Fleet Street debtors' prison was much easier to follow than all the major's instructions.

The most cruel of the lot chimed in and observed in addition that tennis could expect very little from a man who was a descendant of the jailer of Charles of Orléans.

Wingfield defended his position with a nonchalance matched only by his good business sense. He did away with the Greek name and had printed a small booklet of testimonials quoting, among other satisfied clients, seven royal highnesses, two princes, seven dukes, fourteen marquis, fifty counts, ten countesses, eight viscounts, twenty-nine baronets, and thirty-seven ladies, not to mention a rash of gentlemen and honorables. Moreover, Wingfield conceded to more flexibility in the matter of the court's measurements: the service, played from the base line and directed to the area between the net and the service line, would be acceptable.

The major also stated his willingness to go out on the courts himself in order to test Mr. Hale's suggestion of modifying *sphairistikè*. Mr. Hale considered himself the originator of a similar game, which he called Germains Lawn Tennis, named for his country house.

J. H. Hale contended that the second bounce ought to remain within the lines marking out the playing area, but this suggestion lost popularity after an exhibition match played by Wingfield teamed with Captain Thomson against Clement Scott and the famous cricket player Lubbock at Prince Ground (Hans Place).

The major was then happy to accept the proposal of R. H. Fitzgerald, secretary of the powerful Marylebone Cricket Club, that both Hale's and his games be tested simultaneously on March 3, 1875.

The wise old men of Marylebone then asked for the right to establish rules for the new game, and the major accepted graciously, pleased to have the approval of such an august group. The panel selected was the same one that in 1872 had drawn up the complicated rules for *paume*: together with the Honorables Ponsonby Fane, Hart Dyke, Chandos Leigh, it comprised two champions of the game, C. G. Lyttleton and J. M. Heathcote.

The major's "lawn tennis" passed the examination of these experts with flying colors. The playing area retained its hourglass shape, called *papillon* as well, the French word for "butterfly" also suggestive of its outline, and at the same time the net was made three feet longer and eight inches lower at its center. No changes were made in the scoring.

The custom of alternating the serve into the two service areas became mandatory. It was also made absolutely mandatory that the server stand with one foot outside the base line. Hitting the ball into the net gave his opponent the serve, whereas hitting the ball outside the service area meant the loss of a point.

Wingfield was totally satisfied with these rules and got ready to print a new updated version of his book, but in June 1875, after only one official exhibition match at Cambridge, events took an unexpected turn. Control of the game, which had been won with so much effort and some small measure of fame, was suddenly wrested from the hands of the major.

5

8 The Real Birth of Tennis at Wimbledon

In a letter to *The Field* dated 5 December 1874, John Moyer Heathcote stated his pleasure in having found a new ball covered with white flannel. The old champion of court tennis thought this to be a great advantage, for the ball had more elasticity than the ones in use at that time and it was much easier to control.

The letter came to the attention of the editor-in-chief of the journal, Mr. J. W. Walsh, and his right-hand man, Henry Jones, who was himself an authority on whist and used the stylish pen name of Cavendish. Jones was considerably younger than Walsh, but their friendship was a close one, the common bond being their passionate interest in sports.

They had met at one of Mr. Walsh's weekend lawn parties where the best of London's young people were wont to gather. Jones had taken it upon himself, and quite rightly so, to point out to Walsh that his guests, in their sport, were making a shambles of his flowerbeds and behaving rather badly, and he further convinced the older man to send one of his men to London in search of a proper piece of land upon which to set up a croquet club.

Turned away at the Crystal Palace and at the Prince Club and amazed at the outlandish request of 500 sterling in rent for six acres in Holland Park, the agent had finally run across something interesting, though not centrally located: four acres of delightful meadowland at a rent of 120 sterling per year in Wimbledon on Worple Road.

For an additional 425 sterling, the land was surveyed and newly seeded. In June 1870, the All-England Croquet Club was already in a position to organize its first croquet tournament.

Satisfied with his initial success, Henry Jones and his cousin Whitmore proposed in 1871 to elect Mr. Walsh as honorary secretary. The proposal was immediately approved in an atmosphere of gay cordiality. And a good idea it was. For if there was need, for example, of a steamroller, it was only necessary to elect Mr. Walsh's daughter as an honorary member and the piece of equipment appeared in a thrice. When the request came for washing facilities, it was Jones's turn to get in the act: he borrowed a small building from the owners of *The Field* and then pocketed the coins that the patrons paid to use it.

We must not be led to believe that all this familiarity would bring about a relaxation of the rules regarding attire. On the door of this tiny clubhouse could be read the following admonition: "Gentlemen are kindly requested not to play in shirt-sleeves when ladies are present."

The initial success of the operation made the membership think seriously of buying the property. It was not possible to raise the 2,500 sterling needed, and the result of the attempt was counterproductive. Some of the members, frightened by the large-scale plans of the indefatigable Jones, resigned, and in 1873 the club was forced to ask for a lowering of the rent to 100 sterling a year.

Jones was not the sort of man to give up hope. Every Saturday, "dressed in his white flannels, a white beret on his head, brandishing a white parasol bordered in green, he would set forth in detail the niceties of his ingenious theories for an admiring audience."

One of these conversations must have referred to Heathcote's letter on the new type of tennis ball and especially its fine properties on the surface of a lawn. The result was twofold: in the first place, a new game was born at Wimbledon, and in the second, the coffers of the establishment began to grow. In 1875 the management set aside twenty-five sterling for an "area reserved for lawn tennis and badminton." As soon as a subcommittee was set up to study the rules, complications arose.

The game, according to Wingfield, was still the same one described in the instruction booklets he had sold in his establishment. There were those at the Prince Club who had lowered the net to three feet in order to make the rallies more exciting. Others, on the other hand, claimed that, in the handicap competitions, the stronger players ought to use a supplementary cord set at seven feet from the ground. Amidst these ongoing arguments, resolved with Jones's customary aplomb, the name of the club was changed to the All-England Croquet and Lawn Tennis Club in 1877, and Mr. Walsh prevailed on the owners of *The Field* to offer a Challenge Cup, with a prize of twenty-five guineas, the tournament to augur well for the new name.

The problems with the rules had to be ironed out, of course, before such an undertaking could be begun, and Henry Jones convinced Walsh that no one was better equipped for such teamwork than C. G. Heathcote and Julian Marshall. Heathcote, the brother of the inventor of the covered ball, was setting himself up as an authority on lawn tennis, and Marshall, the author of *Annals of Tennis*, openly accused Wingfield of having plagiarized the old sport of kings.

The results of these investigations totally discredited the claims of poor Wingfield, and they were accepted with such acclaim that in a few days more than 7,000 copies of the new rules were sold. Thinking highly of Marshall, the Marylebone Cricket Club did not wait long to add their seal of approval.

As can be seen from the illustrations, the playing area became rectangular, the posts were moved outside the court, and the net was lowered. The scoring system of rackets was altogether abandoned, and the system of the older court tennis (also known as real or royal tennis) was adopted in its entirety, with points of 15, 30, and 45 in both games and sets. The players would change sides at the end of each set, and one game would decide ties of five games each. One error in serving was admissible.

The sage reflections of the trinity of Marshall, Heathcote, and Jones had given birth to a new game, which would attain its present form after minor modifications in 1883. The height of the net was reduced once again. The service line was brought closer to the net. The position of the server, which in 1877 was astride the base line, was moved outside the playing area. A ball that touched the net when served and then continued into the opponent's court had to be replayed, as had not been the case before. The balls were now lighter in construction.

Henry Jones, proud at the result of all these labors, decided to become the first referee in history, and he personally was responsible, in his role as secretary of the committee, for the following announcement that appeared in the June 9th issue of *The Field:* "The All-England Croquet and Tennis Club at Wimbledon proposes the organization of a tennis tournament open to all amateur players on Monday, 9 July and on successive days. The entrance fee will be one sterling and one shilling. Two prizes will be awarded, a first place in gold and a second prize in silver." A footnote indicated that the players would have to provide their own rackets and shoes without heels. Balls for their training sessions would be provided by the gardener.

Together with new nets, fifteen dozen new balls were ordered from Jefferies and Company in Woolwich, with the specific request that the flannel covers be sewn by hand with unbleached heavy thread and with uncrossed stitches. The weight of the balls could vary only from one and one-fourth ounces to one and one-half ounces. A neighbor provided seats for the spectators in exchange for the loan of a roller, a lawn mower, and four guineas. The contenders were numerous, twenty-two in all. The tournament, originally set for Monday the 9th through Thursday the 12th of July, was postponed in order to let everyone attend a cricket match between Harrow and Eton, and finally began the following Thursday on the 19th before a crowd of some 200 spectators, each of whom had eagerly paid one shilling for the privilege.

To the surprise and disappointment of C. G. Heathcote and Julian Marshall, who were both experts on the rules they themselves had invented, and of the champion of court tennis, W. C. Marshall, the Challenge Cup was won by Spencer W. Gore, a rackets player.

Why don't we interview the winner, using his *A Reminiscence of Fifteen Years* which appeared in 1904:

Reporter: Glad to have won the Wimbledon, Mr. Gore?

Gore: Of course, I am.

Reporter: Had you played tennis a great deal before this tournament?

Gore: Well, . . . yes, but certainly a lot less than rackets, which I played while at Harrow.

Reporter: And how did things go with the new rules?

Gore: Don't even talk to me about it. All of us racket players disliked the system of scoring in tennis. It was often terribly confusing. And even the umpires were confusing from time to time. They misjudged at least a third of my serves.

Reporter: Which reminds me, you have a very strong serve. How did you develop it?

Gore: I roll up my sleeves, and with the ball at shoulder height, I slice hard at it from below. The flannel-covered balls take the slice a great deal better. And then, the rectangle into which the serve can be placed is very large: it would be a good idea to make it smaller. Did you know that Mr. Jones has figured out that 376 games have been won on serves and only 225 games on returns. Does that seem fair to you?

Reporter: I read that in *The Field.* The journal maintained that the players of court tennis were favored by the height of the net.

Gore: That's right. Since the net in the middle is less than 53 centimeters (1 ft. 8⅞ in.) in height, the player who places cross-court shots has an advantage . . .

Reporter: On the other hand, you have used just perfect counter tactics.

Gore: Oh, don't exaggerate. I have taken advantage of the fact that most of my opponents played a middle-of-the-court game, and I decided to return my shots on the fly.

Reporter: Do you think that your offensive game has any future?

Gore: Not really. I think that the perfection of the drive, the forehand and backhand from the baseline will rather favor the defensive game.

Reporter: Mr. Heathcote, whom you beat 6–2, 6–5, 6–2 in the fourth round, maintains the opposite. He says that it was your wrist action in the volleys and your offensive play that destroyed all your opponents, him included.

Gore: Let's hope that Heathcote is right: We'll see how things go next year . . .

In 1878 Spencer Gore was beaten by a player who trampled down all the grass around the baseline without even grazing the net once. Like Gore, Frank Hadow had batted balls off the walls at Harrow, but the spirit of adventure had carried him to a coffee plantation in Ceylon. He had returned to visit London after three years in isolation, and his introduction to the new game at the covered courts of Maida Vale had completely captivated him and caused him to extend his vacation until the tournament was over.

At the outset, Spencer Gore paid Hadow no special attention whatsoever. He had rather watched young Lawford for trouble, as well as Erskine, who were doing a fine job in the fray of the All Comers, vying with each other for the title of challengers of the current champion. What bothered him most was a badly pulled muscle in his hand that kept him from putting away the ball before it crossed the net: a shot whose legality had provoked discussion.

The tournament was suspended once again for the cricket matches between Eton and Harrow, and both Gore and Hadow attended to cheer on their former schools. Hadow, used as he was to the outdoor life, did not think about head covering, and sunstroke confined him to bed for three whole days.

Gore attacked him with boldness mixed with occasional pity since he noticed that Hadow sometimes raised his hands to his temples, still not being fully recovered. After a few awkward at-

1. *The scoreboard of 1877 has no scores recorded, and no record of the Challenge Round, which does not as yet exist.* 2. *We have not been able to track down a picture of the first winner, Spencer W. Gore. We dedicate this drawing to Gore.* 3. *The championship cup was provided by the magazine* The Field. 4. *The Challenge Round final between Gould and the Reverend Hartley, winner of the third and fourth championships, whom we find in (7).* 5. *Lawford (winner in 1887), famous for his fierce forehand, as shown in (6). In 1881 he takes on W. Renshaw, who beats him 6–3 in the fifth set.* 8. *Hadow, winner of the second championship of 1878, photographed during the jubilee of the champions in 1926.* 9. *The Renshaw brothers, Ernest (seated, winner in 1888), and Willie (last on the right, winner in 1881–86 and 1889).*

1

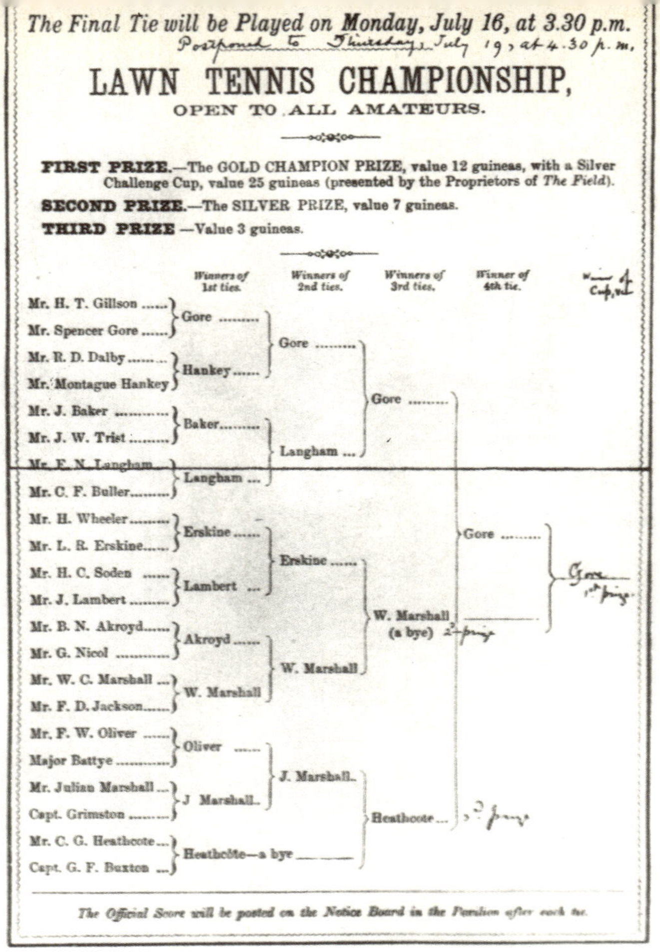

The Final Tie will be Played on **Monday, July 16, at 3.30 p.m.**
Postponed to Thursday, July 19, at 4.30 p.m.

LAWN TENNIS CHAMPIONSHIP,

OPEN TO ALL AMATEURS.

FIRST PRIZE.—The GOLD CHAMPION PRIZE, value 12 guineas, with a Silver Challenge Cup, value 25 guineas (presented by the Proprietors of *The Field*).

SECOND PRIZE.—The SILVER PRIZE, value 7 guineas.

THIRD PRIZE —Value 3 guineas.

	Winners of 1st ties.	Winners of 2nd ties.	Winners of 3rd ties.	Winner of 4th tie.	Winner of Cup
Mr. H. T. Gillson	Gore	Gore	Gore	Gore	Gore 1st prize
Mr. Spencer Gore					
Mr. R. D. Dalby	Hankey				
Mr. Montague Hankey					
Mr. J. Baker	Baker.........	Langham ...			
Mr. J. W. Trist					
Mr. E. N. Langham ...	Langham ...				
Mr. C. F. Buller.........					
Mr. H. Wheeler.........	Erskine	Erskine	W. Marshall (a bye) 2d prize		
Mr. L. R. Erskine......					
Mr. H. C. Soden	Lambert ...				
Mr. J. Lambert					
Mr. B. N. Akroyd......	Akroyd	W. Marshall			
Mr. G. Nicol					
Mr. W. C. Marshall ...	W. Marshall				
Mr. F. D. Jackson......					
Mr. F. W. Oliver	Oliver	J. Marshall..	Heathcote... 3d prize		
Major Battye					
Mr. Julian Marshall ...	J Marshall..				
Capt. Grimston					
Mr. C. G. Heathcote...	Heathcote—a bye				
Capt. G. F. Buxton ...					

The Official Score will be posted on the Notice Board in the Pavilion after each tie.

2

3

4

5

6

7

8

9

10

11

From the left, the others pictured are: Browne; the Reverend Hartley (winner, 1878–79); Grinstead; Maud Watson, winner of the first women's championships in 1884 and 1885; Lawford (winner in 1887). Seated is Lillian Watson. 10. Challenge Round of 1880. Hartley beats Lawford, the challenger, before a packed stand. 11. 1892. The Irishman Pim defeats Lewis in the finals of the All Comers (selection to decide the Winner's Challenge). 12. 1907. First victory of a foreigner. The Australian Brookes at the net in the All Comers, victor against Baby Gore. 13. 1910. First finals of the All Comers played between two foreigners. Wilding, from New Zealand, defeats Wright from the United States of America (seen volleying). Wilding is on the way to winning the first of his four titles (1910–1913). 14. 1913. First Challenge Round between two foreigners. Wilding will defeat McLoughlin, the U.S. Comet, seen running back to salvage a high lob. 15. Joseph Clark of Philadelphia, protagonist in the first international matches, along with his brother Clarence, in 1883. 16. The Americans, in knickers, were trounced twice by the Renshaw twins, one of them wearing a striped sweater. 17. The first Americans to do well in doubles play were Holcombe Ward and Dwight Davis. 18. Davis is serving his formidable American twist during the victory in 1901 against Eaves (at mid-court) and Hillyard. The Yanks lost in hard-fought finals play against the Doherty brothers.

15

17

12

16

13

14

18

1
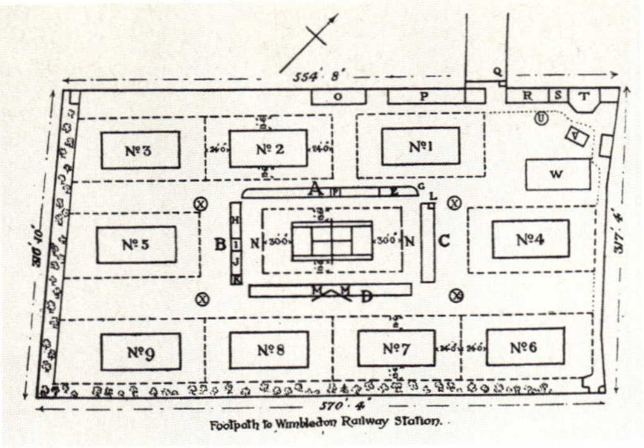

3

5

2

4

6

tempts at passing the champion down the middle of the net, Hadow risked a high overhead shot that Gore could not return.

This surprised Hadow and he tried the same shot again with results that encouraged him to apply a heavy dose of the same medicine on his opponent. Gore was more and more often driven to the back of the court, and, disheartened, he ended up losing two long sets 7–5 and 7–5. Only the final required a two-game lead. Upon being awarded the Cup, Hadow showed his better side; the lob was his only means of defense against such strong play, he stated bravely. He departed soon after for the plantation and was not seen at Wimbledon until the tournament jubilee, 1926.

He had influenced the course of the game in a less than brilliant way, even if the registrations, including some Irish players, reached the record number of forty-five entrants in the following year. In *The Field* and in the salons of Mayfair a great to-do was made of the favorites, of Erskine and of Gould, the Irishman with the pseudonym of St. Leger. No one thought of the young Reverend Hartley, who had just been convinced by a member of the Tabor family, an old tennis clan, to take up the old sport of royal tennis

7

8

1. The ground plan of the old club at Wimbledon on Worple Road.
2. The courts are new, the grandstands small, but the referee, Mr. Evelegh, who held the position from 1890 to 1904, is seen here ready for his role.
4. The spectators of the 1905 matches mill around among the tents where strawberries and cream are served with tea.
5. In 1907 the future King George, accompanied by Commander Hillyard, makes his first visit and accepts the honorary presidency. It is the official blessing.
3. The Queen has her own club, which will attain importance as a training ground for Wimbledon.
6. Foreigners become more and more numerous, and the Belgian De Borman, proud possessor of a powerful forehand, is the first individual from the Continent to reach the semifinals in 1904.
7. Ending the domination of the Englishwomen, May Sutton arrives from Pasadena in 1905.

9

10

11

12

8. She beats Miss Douglass (later to become Mrs. Lambert Chambers), and is seen here from behind as she places a forehand shot to her.
9. Meanwhile the scoreboard was perfected in 1907 for the finals (10) between the Americans Wright and Behr against Wilding and Brookes, the winners. Behr is seen rushing the net.
11. 1911 brings the first victory from the Continent by the Frenchmen Gobert and Décugis.
12. Here the Frenchmen are in action, with a forehand shot by Décugis, against Ritchie and Wilding.
13. The line keeps growing longer as crowds gather to purchase the precious few tickets in 1913.
14. The German Froitzheim loses the finals of the All Comers matches of 1914 to Brookes.
15. The Frenchwoman, Miss Broquedis, winner of the Stockholm Olympics, who partnered Wilding in the Wimbledon finals of the mixed doubles in 1914. War will soon cast its shroud over the sport.

which he had given up when he graduated from Oxford.

The young minister never really gave a thought to winning, for he wrote: "I had made no provision for someone to cover me in the pulpit in Yorkshire. As a result, I had to return home from London on Saturday evening, have a quick breakfast Monday morning at the crack of dawn, guide my horse the ten miles to the station to arrive in London at two and at Wimbledon barely in time to play my first match, famished and dog-tired as well.

"I came close to losing the semifinals against Parr: but luckily for me it began to rain. We were forced to stop, and after a nourishing tea I felt much better, and the match went well for me.

"The following day in the finals of the All Comers, I ran across St. Leger, now known as 'Gould of Montecarlo' [accused of chopping up a woman and sending her back to England in a trunk]. At that time he was a happy, impetuous Irishman, the champion of his own country, and, all in all, a fine player. He was given to volley more than any of the rest of us, but there must have been something amiss with his game, for after a good night's sleep, I beat him easily in three sets."

Hadow was forgotten among his coffee plants in Ceylon, and the good reverend won the challenge round by default.

13

14

15

9 The Renshaws. Mary Outerbridge Imports the Game into the United States

It was certainly one of the Reverend Hartley's good habits to raise his eyes heavenward. During the finals in 1881, he was forced to repeat that act of resignation not fewer than one hundred times in the space of thirty-seven minutes. On the other side of the net stood a young man with neat blond hair and manicured moustache, wearing elegant flannels and a military belt, the sleeves of his shirt carefully rolled up. He smashed all Hartley's lobs with a violence that really proved the staying power of the new Ayres balls.

Hartley sighed, closed his eyes, and then opened them to try to find solace among the 1,300 spectators that jammed the new stands. He could not hold back a low moan when he thought he made out the stiff collar and top hat of his smiling rival among the fans. With his customary calm, slight amusement and distant demeanor, Ernest Renshaw was watching the first Wimbledon final of his brother William, inventor of the smash. For ten years, their only competition being the clumsy, violent, and dogged Lawford, the twins won all there was to win. At Wimbledon Willie won seven singles and Ernest won one, the latter still able to get into the finals four times. And from 1884 on, they won all the doubles matches with the exception of one due to Willie's withdrawal with the first recorded case of tennis elbow.

The Renshaws won three singles at the very beginning of the prestigious and gala Irish championships at Dublin and numerous cups and medals at the tournaments on the Côte d'Azur, where they had their winter training camp among the sea pines of the Hôtel Beau Site at Cannes.

Willie and Ernest were the first in the history of the sport to be called by their first names by their fans, the first to sign autographs, and to see in the newspapers the choice bits of gossip that up to that time had been the province of opera stars only. They were actually not only excellent tennis players, but set off from the common crowd, and also quite different one from the other.

In continual movement, a spirit on fire, "Willie was aggressive as a fox terrier, and you would have taken him for a Spaniard, the Manuel Alonso of his time. He hardly gave the ball boy the chance to feed him his ammunition or his opponent to position himself before he let fly his service. Extroverted, chatty, Willie felt so much at his ease as the center of attention that his favorite pastime, other than tennis, was acting. He had a natural ability for the game, and "a couple of weeks of training was enough for him to get in shape." He had perfected the overhead serve, a then recent invention of A. T. Meyers, improving on it by increasing its speed, and "Renshaw's smash" was the most famous shot of its time.

After Willie had played for a couple of years very close to the net, the changes of the rules in 1880 and the final rules of 1882 caused him to improve his volley from the service line, and actually made him understand that an aggressive player could volley even from the backcourt against the players of pat ball in the old mollycoddle style.

The new shots, the new tactics, were naturally tempered with a bit of genius: Willie never felt himself defeated, even on those occasions when no one would have bet a red cent on him.

In 1889, the year of his last victory, Willie was down one set to two, and two to five, against Barlow. Playing "like a cat," he canceled out three match points, but, as he was dashing for the net in the fourth, he slipped and fell headlong, losing his racket. Barlow "felt that a lob was enough to win the point and executed one." "Willie picked up his racket, dashed back in pursuit of the ball, caught up with it, and won the exchange," and then the set 10–8.

He wasn't finished yet. Willie seemed terribly worn out, though. Barlow surged ahead 5–0. In the stands, W. C. Taylor, who was a betting fiend, offered to take Willie at a hundred to one odds. Commander Hillyard, the best-known expert of that time, told him plainly that he was a stupid ass. "Are you trying to take my money?" he chided. A few minutes later, Willie had indeed won, 8–6.

In the finals Willie was to beat Ernest, who had wrested his only singles title the year before from Lawford, the number one enemy of the Renshaw family. The twins grudgingly played against each other. Willie was able to muster some spirit in those matches of brotherly love, but Ernest seemed to be put out by the whole idea. "He just was not trying," he muttered.

He didn't even like to practice with Willie in private, and it was his brother's indifference to handicap tournaments that spurred him to give his very best in these competitions. Handicap tournaments were much in vogue at that time. The awarding of the handicaps themselves provoked arguments as involved as the mathematical computations needed to define them. In handicap play Ernest felt freed from the anxiety that the increasing importance of the competitions made him feel.

A mere fifteen given or taken transformed the match into a fun game, grim duty into derring-do. With one *bisque* in his favor (that is a point he could ask for at any moment of the game), Ernest easily beat both his brother and Lawford at an exhibition match at the Prince Club.

On another occasion, after listening with amusement to Mrs. Hillyard's complaints about the way the voluminous hoopskirts and the hat she was forced to wear ruined her game, Ernest proposed a handicap of ½–40. He then appeared on her court at Thorpe

1

The magic twins, Willie and Ernest Renshaw, dominated the game in the 1880s. Willie won seven times at Wimbledon, Ernest only once. Nevertheless, the latter made the finals four times. Ernest also did not enjoy playing against his brother, and he preferred to avoid such matches by pushing himself into handicap tournaments. 1. The brothers before the finals of 1883, Willie decked out in a striped sweater, if we can trust those who knew them better. 2. The magic twins in finals play in 1882. Willie won both matches in the fifth set. 3. Willie in a close-up and in the drawing (5), executing a backhand with the same face of his racket used for his forehand. 4. Ernest in a serious moment.

3

2

4

5

1. Wingfield's first box arrived in New York in the spring of 1874 in the company of Miss Mary Outerbridge on the steamship Canima. 10. A *year later, another box was delivered to the house of James Dwight's (10) uncle in Nahant, Massachusetts. The beginnings of the sport in the United States are marked by numerous innovative changes, even more so than in Great Britain, and for a time the Americans played four persons to a side. 2. The first printed sketch of the sport in the United States*

1

2

3

4

goes back to 1876, but instead of a ball, a shuttlecock is being batted back and forth. 3. This page from the rotogravure section of the New York Daily Graphic *dates from the following year. The gentleman surrounded by the group of women on the right is the president of the Staten Island Cricket Club, where the Outerbridges' net was first set in place. 4. A detail shows a tennis player exclaiming to his friend, "Violent exercise this, by George!"*

5

6

7

5. The court is rectangular by this time as can be seen in this 1880 view of the Staten Island tournament, the first American event of this sort to achieve historic importance. 6. In May of 1888, the Americans got ahead of the English by forming the National Association. The club at Newport, Rhode Island was chosen for the first championships, pictured here on August 31 in the same year, and again in 1885 (9) and in 1888 (7). The Casino at Newport is now the seat of the Tennis Hall of Fame, the only museum of tennis in the world. It is directed by Jim Van Alen who has helped us in our work. 8. Women continue to stand out in American tennis, represented by the four best women players from Philadelphia between 1884 and 1887. Pictured here are (from left to right) Bertha Townsend, Margaret Ballard, Louise Allerdice, and Ellen Hansell, who later married Louise's brother. The dress of the beautiful Ellen, she remembers, was red and blue, and she had the same shade of red hair as the Venus of Cranach. *10, 14. A low forehand shot placed by Dr. James Dwight, who was at the same time the pioneer, champion, and driving force of tennis USA. He was the first to have the bright idea of developing closer relations with the more experienced English players. 11, 12, 13. Dick Sears, Dwight's student and partner, was also from New England and won the championships from 1881 to 1887. In doubles competition, the two put together five victories. In Europe, however, Sears could not manage to give the Renshaw twins any trouble in 1883, and Dwight was able to reach number eight only with great difficulty in the English seeding. Having given up active participation in the sport, the doctor became president of the association and until his death in 1917 was a powerful force in the history of American tennis.*

9

8

10

11

12

13

14

1

2

4

5

3

6

7

8

1. In the United States, Henry Slocum followed Sears and proved to be a reliable player of modest talent who could not be worn down. He won the championship in 1888 and 1889. 2. Oliver Campbell defeated him and then took his place. Champion from 1890 to 1892, Campbell was a fine volleyer, and in his only experiment with center-court attacks. His career was marred by rheumatic fever he contracted in Cuba, serving as a volunteer during the Spanish-American War. 5. Malcolm Whitman was the most reliable of the American pioneers. He perfected the all-over court attack and in the years of his greatest activity (1898–1900) was

European try he was putty in the hands of the English. 3. In the finals of 1889 we see him glued to the net, his racket held up almost as if to protect his face from the cannonball passes dished up by Slocum. 4. Bob Wrenn was an excellent athlete and represented Harvard in football, hockey, and baseball.

He won four titles within the span of five years (1893–94 and 1896–1897), and he was the first to practically unbeatable. He then made a serious study of the sport and authored one of the most important works in the annals of its history, Tennis Origins and Mysteries. *6. In this cartoon the Englishman Eaves laments over Wrenn's conduct during the finals of the U.S. Championship of 1897. Willie Renshaw should never have tried those spiked shoes in his repertory is the gist of his sage comment. 7. Larned, who was by no means inferior to Whitman when in top form, lasted a good deal longer and won*

9

10

both in 1901–1902 and from 1907 to 1911. Then he retired, offended by the elimination of the challenge round. He is portrayed here in the process of executing an almost perfect forehand shot. 8. Born in Geneva, Switzerland, one of the fortunate survivors of the Titanic disaster, Dick Williams was a good-natured player who always shied away from lukewarm victories. He won from 1914 to 1916. 9. Dwight Davis, the donor of the Davis Cup, and Holcombe Ward, singles champion in 1904, won the doubles from 1899 to 1901. 10. Beals Wright was a pusher and developed a devastating chop. A champion in 1905, he was the first American to make it big on the foreign circuit. 11. Maurice McLoughlin was called the Comet due to his sparkling play and the short span of his career. He won both in 1912 and 1913. Here he is wickedly engaged in one of his devastating backhand serves. 12. The proud possessor of the strongest serve, Lindley Murray in action, on the way to winning the 1917–1918 Patriots' Tournament. 13. Another noteworthy server, Fred Alexander, in finals of doubles play for seven years in a row and winner in 1907–10. 14. The Royal Pinciana Hotel of Palm Beach, center of tennis and of earthly delights.

11

12

13

14

Spy

white stalk of asparagus, 1.87 or 1.88 meters (6 ft. 2 in.) in height, with an enormous court control."

In the interviews that followed the match, Woodhouse confessed that he had barely been able to beat the Renshaw twins at Wimbledon, two players with a highly promising future. That tournament had been won by Lawford, who had not let Woodhouse have even one set in the finals matches and was almost unbeatable. He had a devastating forehand that people were calling "the Lawford shot."

Woodhouse also told them with all candor, amid murmurs of surprise, that the overhead serve was by now very popular in England and that the rackets score had become as obsolete as the dodo.

Both Dwight and Outerbridge were on pins and needles while the Englishman was being interviewed. Outerbridge quickly told a group of his friends that the time seemed ripe to begin serious plans by drawing up a book of rules and forming a tennis association.

In the meanwhile, Dwight was frenziedly consulting the timetables for the steamship departures; he wanted to see Lawford, play against the Renshaws, and try to wheedle out of them their most up-to-date secrets. Then, he reasoned, Dick Sears could put them into practice!

Outerbridge was the first to see his dreams realized. In May of the following year, in parlor F of the Fifth Avenue Hotel in New York, thirty-four charter members organized the United States National Lawn Tennis Association.

In order to resolve the antagonism between Outerbridge and Dwight, General R. S. Oliver of Albany was selected president, and the two antagonists formed an executive committee, together with Clarence Clark from Philadelphia, who had the backing of at least twelve Pennsylvania clubs.

The organization of the first National Championship was planned for the Newport Casino, R.I., and in August of 1881, twenty-one players, equipped with English rackets, with the latest rules and a good supply of Ayres balls, prepared to do battle on the splendid courts, shielded from the sea by a heavy stand of trees. With Dwight to guide him from the sidelines, Dick Sears won the championship without the loss of a single set. In 1882 the champion won again so easily that Dwight requested and was granted the chance to select and send to England the best American doubles combination the following year.

But Dwight's plans were upset and he and Dick were both defeated by the sudden appearance of two brothers, Joseph and Clarence Clark. The trip to Wimbledon by the Clark brothers was, as we have seen, a total disaster. James Dwight declared that he knew that this would be so, and he and Sears both threw themselves passionately into the business of training for the next year. When Dwight was defeated by his own pupil in the finals of the National Championship of 1883, he decided on his own to make the big trip. In the early months of 1884 he was busy signing up for all the tournaments to be played on the Côte d'Azur, where the Renshaw twins had the habit of spending the winter in Beau Site.

Refined and soft-spoken, the twins must have found that strange tourist a bit hard to take. They treated him courteously, but with a certain reserve. Dwight was totally out of his element. His theories of attack, based on his strange serve executed from the left of his head, did not work well on those soft reddish courts.

After he had been beaten several times, he sent an urgent appeal to Dick to join him, in hopes of being able to regain credibility in doubles play. In view of the urgency of the situation, Dick acquiesced, rejoining his friend at Cannes where he began a period of intense training, devouring handfuls of oats, which were, according to Dwight (on the basis of his knowledge of medicine), of great benefit to a tennis player.

At the height of his powers, Dick finally met Lawford in the Irish championships: the drive of the Englishman reduced him to a cipher. In their first doubles match against the Renshaws, the Americans were able to scrape together three games.

A less stubborn individual would have retired to the sidelines. Not James Dwight. The following year he was back there right on time, and the English began to realize that Dwight was a force to be reckoned with: after observing him in the semifinals at Wimbledon, they seeded him number eight.

Dwight was exultant. For between America's number two player and England's number eight, there was not a shred of difference! All he would have to do was to find another Sears to perfect in the Lawford drive and the Renshaw smash, to nourish him with whole oats, to train in the winter the way those two accursed twins did . . . and all Wimbledon would be on its feet, cheering the triumphant Americans with amazement in their voices!

Livingston Beekman seemed to be the chosen one of the Lord. He was a youngster of seventeen that even Sears had had a difficult time in beating in the finals of his sixth successful National Championship. With his authority as president of the association, Dwight convinced the lad's parents to entrust their son to him, and they left once more for the south of France in quest of the unbeatable twins.

Day after day, in some mysterious way, despite the generous rations of oats supplied him, the young man seemed to suffer more and more from some sort of drowsiness. Dwight was about to refer to a specialist when the hotel manager let slip the awful truth: Beekman had been returning to his room at dawn! The young *bon vivant* was sent directly home right away, and Dwight girded up his loins alone to face the final battle at Wimbledon.

The opening matches were only one day away and the courts lay green and inviting when Dr. James Dwight suddenly realized he was thirty-five years of age.

He left on the first sailing vessel.

But he did not return home a dejected man. The years spent going back and forth between London and the Côte d'Azur had both taught him a good deal and made him more aware of his adversaries' feelings. And in the United States he had still one more doubles title to win, not to mention his dear friend Dick's last victory.

In 1894 Dr. Dwight once again took on the presidency of the American Association, and his first thought upon doing so was to begin a one-man crusade against the descendants of the Renshaw twins.

10 The Doherty Brothers. The Beginnings of Davis Cup Competition

Majestic in height, the waxen whiteness of his cheeks in strong contrast to his dark wavy hair, Reginald Hugh Doherty was in the habit of playing with his cuffs unbuttoned, and the flutter of his sleeves accented the long and graceful strokes of his racket. His profile, standing out against the golden background of the cover of *Lawn Tennis*, which he wrote with his younger brother Laurie, brings to mind the studied elegance of the illustrations in *The Yellow Book*, a magazine that Reggie used to hide under the pillow in his garret room at Cambridge. On the title page of *Lawn Tennis*, across from a photo of the two brothers stretched out on the grass in a court, the dedication pays homage to the Grand Duchess Anastasia, who delighted in the game. Her imperial highness was a companion of both men, but she seemed to be especially happy at Reggie's side at the tournaments of the Côte d'Azur and of Homburg, the watering place where German tennis was born.

For many Englishmen of that period, 1897 was not only the year of the diamond jubilee of Queen Victoria, but it also marked the beginning of the Doherty Era; and 1906 was not only the date of a great swing to liberalism, but also the end of that same sporting era.

Reggie won four titles at Wimbledon from 1897 to 1900, and when his weakening health no longer permitted it, Laurie took his place for five years in singles competition. In doubles play, the two carried the day eight times at Wimbledon, and in those ten years of almost complete monopoly, they lost a total of four matches. Their firm support served to revive the ailing fortunes of tournament play which had sharply declined after the retirement of the twins.

The Baddeley brothers, whose number one enemy was the Irishman Joshua Pim, had replaced the Renshaws and their stubborn rival Lawford. The Baddeleys "did nothing spectacular, but they did it well." Like a Neapolitan fisherman, Pim wore a multicolor silk scarf around his waist, and he was powerful enough to outclass the stronger of the Baddeley brothers, only to be badly beaten in the next match.

The London audiences did not seem to enjoy the Baddeley brother's successes, nor did they feel any joy over the victories of the three Irishmen: Hamilton, Pim (called the Ghost because of his slight build), and Mahony, "a champion without a forehand." The 3,500 spectators that had induced the Southern Railways to make a special stop near the entrance of the club in 1885, had dwindled so much ten years later that the secretary was forced to announce a deficit of thirty-three pounds. The tournament of 1896 was possible because of the readmission of the croquet players, who once again saw their sport included in the official emblem of the club after being unceremoniously ejected in 1883.

In 1906, enthusiasm for the Doherty brothers had brought 30,000 people to trample the grass of the surrounding paths and 2,000 pound sterling into the astonished secretary's hands. That year little Laurie Doherty, nicknamed Little Do by the fans, won his last singles match, while in doubles play the brothers were trounced by Riseley and Smith, due to Reggie's obvious inability to keep his form for more than three sets. He had confided to a friend that he did not know what real good health felt like. On another occasion when his younger brother was teasing him, he retorted, "If I could run like you, Laurie, I'd spot you an advantage of fifteen!" Little Do's face grew sad at the admission, but only for a moment, since he knew that his brother was right. Reggie won more often when his training routine was such that he could select the best time of the day, get enough rest, and stop his practicing when the strain became too great.

Unlike the Renshaw brothers, the Dohertys played very intensely and willingly together, with a spirit of fair play that seemed as ingrained as their masterful strokes. Reggie's 1.83 meters (6 ft.) in height permitted him to play his drives from above, as he kept varying his grip slightly on the racket and hitting the ball hard without sacrificing any accuracy. Big Do served deep into the court and compensated his comparative lack of speed by a half-volley of exceptional sensitivity when he rushed the net. Small, solidly built, ten kilograms (22 lbs.) lighter, Little Do, on the contrary, moved quickly and with perfect balance. He could jump and kill lobs from almost any part of the court. He played less violently than Reggie, but his shots were equally well placed; while his brother's shots were often inspired and touched with genius, Laurie had an almost classical form, "the best for a rank beginner to imitate."

The Doherty brothers met only once in Challenge Round: that of 1898. Very few of the spectators sensed that their smiles and the few words exchanged when they switched courts hid a deep-seated desire to prove themselves. Reggie took the first two sets and then won 6–1 in the fifth.

Three years later, both Reggie's family and the doctor prevailed on him to retire, at least from singles play, and Big Do finally began to wean himself away from that exhilarating sport that was slowly ruining his lungs. He thought, as did everyone else, that Laurie would be the one to receive the Cup from him, in a simple ceremony without frills. Laurie, however, who was shaken by the prospect of such an honor, played badly in the All Comers finals. He was beaten by Baby Gore, a hardheaded businessman who divided his time between office routine and stubborn and unrelenting attempts at winning the title.

Hardly had the last of Little Do's balls gone crashing into the net, that Reggie was heard to remark: "I cannot refuse to defend my title against Gore: if he is to win, let it be fair and square." Reggie brought one set to zero and 5 to 2, and then weakened, but without any visible signs. Gore's last handshake was followed by an almost imperceptible bow. The following year, 1902, signaled the beginning of Little Do's own career when he devastated Gore to take the first of his five titles.

Together with the rise to fame of the Dohertys in the last year of the nineteenth century, the history of the sport was to be changed by an idea set forth by the young American Dwight Davis and nourished by the highly commendable zeal of James Dwight. Up to that time, from North America to South America as far as Brazil and from Sweden to India, tennis had made its way by emphasizing rugged individualism and by being a sport of the ruling class. Once the Championship at the end of June drew to a close, the gates of the All-England Club were closed to all except the few members. The same was true of the gates of Dinard, of Monte Carlo, of Homburg, and of Bordighera. Sleepy coachmen and a few chauffeurs, their hands covered with grease, waited for the boss to take his exercise and then change clothes in a dressing room separate from the one used by the coach.

In the United States the spectators would arrive at the Championships at Newport by crossing their neighbors' gardens on foot. The Americans were probably more noisy and less chic than the inventors of lawn tennis. They certainly were not less rich or important. The heavy sweaters worn by the players carried the initials of the Eastern universities in large letters: Yale had its Slocum; Harvard its Sears, Hovey, and Wrenn; and Columbia its Campbell.

Dwight Davis came from St. Louis, but the prestige of the Eastern schools had attracted him to Harvard where he met a delightful partner in Holcombe Ward. The latter was small, slim, timid, and not attractive physically, while color blindness made the green grass seem brownish to his eyes. He was clever enough to realize that he could never hope to ward off cannonballs and play an offensive game himself for the whole span of a singles match. He looked around, took old Dr. Dwight's serve as a model, perfected it, and then taught the serve to Davis.

Behind those balls flattened out by their spin until they almost resembled whirling tops, Davis and Ward stormed the net, digging into the turf with the iron cleats of their dark leather shoes. It was impossible to defend oneself against those serves and that push: the two partners won the university championships and then, in the summer of 1899, the nationals as well.

Davis's and Ward's joy was somewhat dimmed by the realization that they were champions only of the Atlantic coastline and by the fact that the public was showing less and less interest in the game. The competition of golf and the departure of many young men for the Spanish-American War, including the two champions Larned and Wrenn, had reduced the club membership from 107 to forty-four in 1898! It was necessary to get on the move, to invent something new to regain the public's enthusiasm, and, at the suggestion of Dr. Dwight, Davis and Ward asked two good friends to accompany them to the West Coast.

The two friends came from Boston: Beals Wright, also a left-hander, was the son of the well-known baseball player George Wright, and Malcolm Whitman, the national champion, was the most important tennis talent to be developed in the United States. When the mission had returned from California, the young Davis was beside himself with enthusiasm. "The West," he said, "has an enormous potential for the development of tennis, and I have learned from this trip that a large international competition would help the development of the sport not only here but in other countries as well." Dr. Dwight could not hold back his joy when Davis requested that 217 ounces of silver from Shreve, Crump and Low, Boston silversmiths, be melted down and that the resulting cup, with the name of the International Lawn Tennis Challenge Trophy, be awarded annually. As is the case with most names that are too long, it was soon shortened to the Davis Cup.

Back from the foundry and the engraver's, the massive bowl shone and waited for the inscription of the first nation to win it. Dwight began a heated flurry of letters, but the English were busy with the disasters of the Boer War and seemed less than enthused over the new project. As a result, the Dohertys could see no purpose in spending August on the other side of the Atlantic.

For many years prior to that time, several individual tourists had discovered the technical superiority developed by the inventors of tennis. In 1896, Larned had amazed Wimbledon by winning the first two sets from Herbert Baddeley, but his luck turned against him afterwards when the strings broke on his only racket. In 1898, Clarence Hobart had made the finals of the All Comers Doubles, but in the singles he was devastated by Little Do.

The Irishman Goodbody, on the other hand, got as far as the challenge round of the 1894 American Championships by beating young Larned. Three years later it was actually two Englishmen who fought it out in the finals of the All Comers. Eaves won out over Nisbet and held off the winner, Bob Wrenn, for five sets before succumbing.

In light of these results, the Lawn Tennis Association (LTA) in Britain (which had been organized in 1888 in a successful attempt to break the monopoly of Wimbledon) thought that a second team, without the Dohertys and the doubles experts Risely and Smith, would be enough to teach those bloody Yanks a lesson. Baby Gore had reached the All Comers finals at Wimbledon where he lost to Sidney Smith, and in the doubles challenge round, Herbert Roper Barrett and Nisbet had kept the Dohertys at bay for five sets. Gore and Barrett's team achieved a more representative status with the selection of the number one Scotsman, Ernest Black, and departed on the steamship *Campania*.

"The fearless trio," as the monthly publication of the LTA had described them, disembarked in New York on the morning of August 4, 1900. There was no fanfare, no welcoming committee, not even an official representative—they were tied up in Boston: Mr. Stevens could not get away from the office and sent one of his men. The employee offered to give the fearless trio a hand with their grips, but he could suggest nothing better than Boston for their practice. He explained that New England was only six hours away by train. Once they had arrived, the friends of Mr. Stevens would

1

2

3

Reggie and Laurie Doherty were champions more often than anyone else between 1897 and 1906. They perfected their game to become a model for all tennis greats until the outbreak of the First World War. Laurie, called Little Do (3), won five Wimbledons from 1902 to 1906 and was the first foreigner to win the title of U.S. champion in 1903. In five challenge rounds for the Davis Cup, he was never defeated and won seven singles and five doubles. Reggie, called Big Do (reclining with his brother Laurie in picture 5), managed to win four times at Centre Court from 1897 to 1900 and was then struck down by a serious disease. The brothers dominated doubles play in the international championships of Great Britain from 1897 to 1901 and from 1903 to 1905, and were beaten altogether only four times. They were the first to win the U.S. championships in 1902 and 1903.

4

5

6

7

8

1. Reggie Doherty, against the backdrop of the famous court constructed for the Renshaw twins at the Hotel Beau Site in Cannes, where the Doherty brothers also spent their winter practice sessions.
2. The Hillyards' home at Thorpe Satchville. Laurie and Reggie (with a beret) are the last two on the right. The other men are Commander Hillyard and Cazalet. The women are, from the left, the American May Sutton, Miss Wilson, and Blanche Hillyard.
4. Laurie is the second from the left; Reggie is seated in the armchair, representing the university team of Cambridge against their opponents from Oxford, in blue jackets.
7, 8. The covers of the highly popular American and English editions of the Doherty brothers' technical book on lawn tennis, dedicated to Her Imperial Highness the Grand Duchess Anastasia of Mecklenburg-Schwerin (6), a patron of the sport and a dear friend.

certainly see to providing them with a place to train. Despite this delightful logic, Baby Gore and company decided to train in Niagara Falls.

Without having touched a ball for more than twenty days, the Britishers showed up in Boston on the eve of the contest, the organizers beside themselves with worry, while Whitman, Davis, and Ward were putting the finishing touches on their practice sessions.

"The playing surface was terrible," Barrett was to write a few years later. "Just imagine an English court where the grass is as high as possible, multiply by two, and you have a good picture of the situation at Longwood. The net was absolutely frightful, held in place by double cords that continually went slack to five or six centimeters (2 in.) every few games, making constant readjustment necessary. As concerns the balls, it gives me a royal pain even to mention them. They were in terrible shape, overly soft and lifeless and, served with that American spin of theirs, they were the deuce to return. I am not exaggerating when I say that neither Beals Wright, nor Holcombe Ward, nor Karl Behr could get such results from the balls we use at Wimbledon. Not only did they wobble in the air, but they also rebounded at least four or five feet. The disadvantage for our team was devastating. We had no experience with that kind of serve, and we were totally ill-equipped to return them. The spectators were very gracious, and the women spectators not unpleasant to feast one's eyes upon."

The difficulty in controlling those serves was heightened, according to Black, by the misguided benevolence of the umpires who failed to notice the foot faults. "Our opponents were astonishingly fast in getting to the net," and moreover, "they had the fine advantage of taking a seven minute break after each set, a custom we were not at all used to."

These justifications for the team's poor showing, which can be interpreted as desired, only serve to confirm the fact that the first British team to visit the United States was too presumptuous and unprepared.

The matches began on August 7, Wednesday, a day late due to rain. Davis began the hostilities, his nerves on edge after losing the first set to Black. Gore had come on a nearby court, overly confident of outclassing Whitman.

While Davis regained his composure and got ready for further play, Gore, who had believed that only the Dohertys knew how to stop him from using his formidable forehand, found that Whitman also could exploit the weakness of his backhand, and he won only six games from the American.

In the doubles, Barrett and Black were confronted with new unexpected customs of these American natives. The reporter for the

1

Sportsman noted with amazement that "the Americans play altogether differently from us. Davis, who is left-handed, stands far outside the service line, returning his balls with his backhand." Ward's position was classified as unorthodox, but his serve could nonetheless only be returned with a lob. The reporter's surprise was complete when he noted that "there was practically no volley play unless initiated and sustained by the English. When the Americans were not serving, they took great pleasure in raising lobs to a height of forty or sixty feet, which then fell precisely on the base line.

"The Americans felt at the time that retaining the serve was extremely important, and they not only did their utmost to keep it, but also were glad to go on the defense when the Britishers were winning."

It seemed likely that by the time the finals rolled around on Friday, the underdogs, by now used to the courts and the balls, would be able to make some sort of decent showing.

Gore had more luck against Davis with his forehand, but he still lost the first set 9 to 7, and tied at 9 all in the second, when one of the numerous summer thunderstorms that the Atlantic Coast is famous for burst over the Longwood Cricket Club.

The English took part in a dinner given in their honor and declared their inability to continue: they were rushed to take part in some exhibition matches at Southampton and then to set sail for home.

2

8

3

The Davis Cup, annual world team championship based on four singles encounters and one doubles, was born out of an idea that occurred to Dwight Davis. It was contested for the first time in 1900 between the U.S. and Great Britain. Before the matches, there were numerous interchanges of players.

2. In 1897 at Longwood there were numerous Americans and Britons together for the championships. From the left, G. Wrenn, Sears, Bob Wrenn, Whitman, and seated with Larned (second from left), are their guests Eaves, Nisbet, and Mahony, respectively

4

ranking as three, sixteen, and two in the British classification.
1. Gore, Roper Barrett, and the Scotsman Black.
3. The Longwood Cricket Club at Boston, the site of the matches. The poor condition of the grass provoked loud complaints of the visitors from abroad.
4. Around the cup, Whitman, the donor Davis, and Ward.
5. The finishing touch to a very lifted forehand shot by Ward, ranked as number two.
6. The English number one Baby Gore busy with a forehand volley. In order to play 58 games, Gore put up with five weeks of round-trip travel. After the defeat of Great Britain in 1900 and the brilliant success of Davis and Ward at Wimbledon in 1901, the Doherty brothers consented to cross the Atlantic to take on the possessors of the Davis Cup.
7. A violent left-handed smash by Davis, Ward's partner in the doubles.
8. Whitman, the number one American player, executing a drive with excellent follow-through.

6

5

7

1

1. The 1902 encounter was played at the Crescent Athletic Club, in Bay Ridge, New York, and for the first time large numbers of Americans flocked to watch.
2. In the group we see some of the key figures at the matches. Seated, from the left: Ward, Laurie, Collins, Reggie, and Davis. The Cup matches were the scene of the first obvious error made by a team captain, when W. H. Collins (4) chose Pim, out of condition and the champion of 1893 and 1894, over the Wimbledon title-holder, Laurie Doherty, for his lineup. The English lost three to two, but the following year the two brothers (3) had their chance to take advantage of the Americans, who supported a has-been player, Bob Wrenn (7) out of a feeling of loyalty, instead of going for Larned (6), who had

2

8

9

3

5

performed well in both matches.
5. The participants in the second match that took place at Longwood; from the left, G. Wrenn, Collins, the English backup man Mahony, Bob Wrenn; and seated, Laurie, Larned, and Reggie. In the four very rare photos at the bottom of the pages in numbers 8 and 9, we see two candid photos from the doubles victory of the Dohertys over the Wrenns. In both cases it is George's (the younger Wrenn's) ball, against whom the Englishmen concentrate their attack.
10, 11. The two decisive matches are depicted here, both won by the brothers in the fifth set. In number 10 Reggie (to the left) is at the net, taken unaware by a lob. In number 11 we see Larned's backhand volley, with Laurie streaking like a bat out of hell to position himself. This was the first time in the history of the Davis Cup that an ambiguity of play had to be decided by the referees in favor of the English guests. Times were indeed different from the rule-plagued present.

4

6

7

10

11

2a

2b

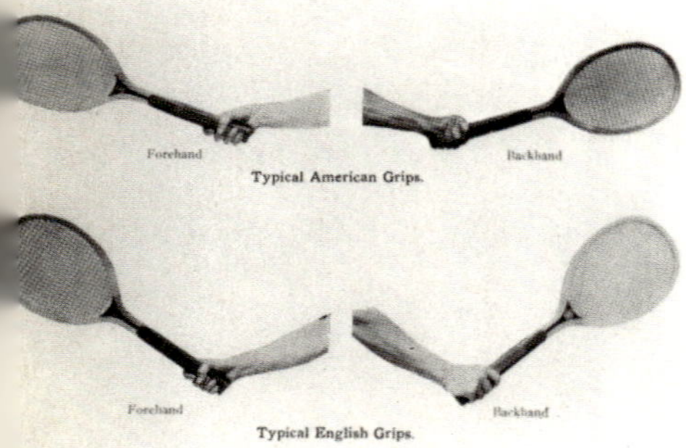

x

y

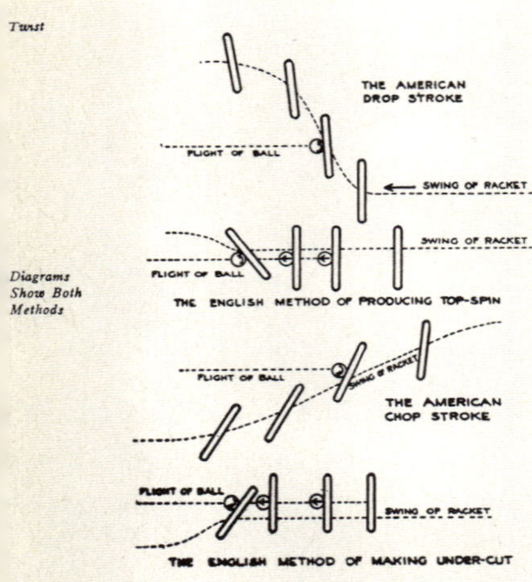

The technical aspects of the English and American schools of tennis at the end of the century are considered here. To the upper right, Larned, the most titled American player, and the best exponent of fundamentals. To the left, Mahony, an Englishman known for his purity of style, is held by Doherty to one slim victory at Wimbledon. In tiers 3, 4, and 5 Laurie and Reggie. The basic difference between the two schools is shown by the grip on the racket and by the angle between the forearm and the racket handle (see x below). The English grips for backhand and forehand are similar and the angle more acute: they resemble what even today is called a Continental grip. The American grips differ considerably between forehand and backhand and resemble the present-day Eastern grip, very popular in the Atlantic seaboard states of America. The diagrams (see y below) show the two approaches to the ball that result from this difference in style of gripping the racket. The photographs of Larned show the sequence of the forehand (1, a, b, c), followed by that of a backhand (1d, e, and f), and demonstrate an exaggerated forward thrust of the spine. This is due to the self-consciousness of the model, for other photos of Larned snapped in play show him in a much more natural and nearly upright position, even if he fails to follow the hidebound dogma of 1974 which insists that the spine be poker-stiff and perpendicular to the ground. Mahony finishes his strokes perfectly (2 a, b), and seems to lean even more than Larned at the moment of impact: doubtless due to some distortion caused by the lenses used at that time to take these extraordinary pictures. Mahony's two strokes are slightly undercut, whereas the American's shots are flatter and hit further in front. The tier-4 series of the Dohertys is taken from their famous book of 1903, the covers of which for both American and English editions are shown elsewhere. 3a. Laurie's forehand grip shown here is a little less open than Mahony's. 3b. Modeling a slightly more inclined stance than would be the case in actual play. 3c. The weight is on the left foot for proper form. 3d, e, f. Reggie is demonstrating the corresponding position for the execution of the backhand. Here,

1a

1b

1c

3a

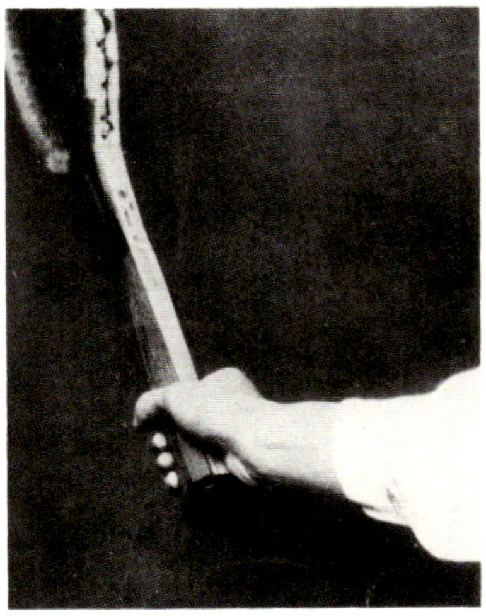

3b

4a

4b

5a

5b

1d

1e

1f

too, the grip differs from the classical models seen in diagram (x). 4 a, b. Two strokes taken from actual play, showing control by Laurie that would make any current champion green with envy. 4b. The lifted follow through is also very up-to-date.
4 c, d. A demonstration of two excellent backhand drives that would also fit well into today's play, given the time needed to set them up. 4e. An undercut training volley by Laurie. 4f. A long volley executed by Reggie, who, though reaching for the shot, exhibits excellent control. 5 a, b. Two stages of an American service by Laurie. 5 c, d. Two slightly sliced serves by Reggie, easier for him on account of his greater height. 5e. A letter-perfect smash executed by Laurie. 5f. A less violent smash by Reggie on a lower ball.

3c

3d
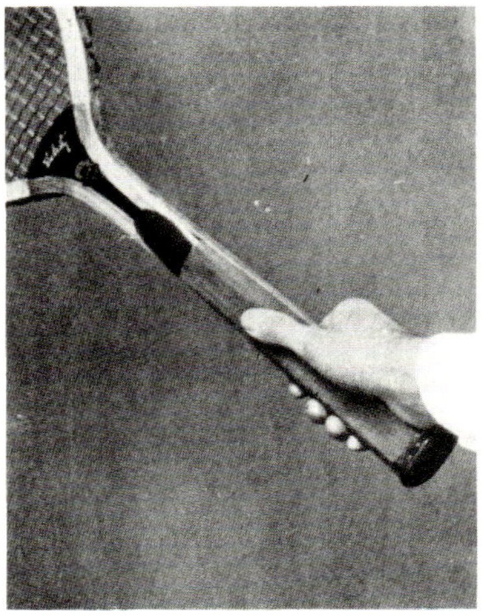

3e

3f

4c

4d

4e

4f

5c

5d

5e

5f

11 The British Win the Cup

Reggie

Laurie

The Americans renewed their challenge the following year, in 1901, but the English response was that their best team was not in shape to make the crossing. They might take the Americans up on their kind invitation at some future time.

Dwight Davis took things with his customary calm, an attribute that equaled his good sportsmanship. He registered for Wimbledon together with his faithful friend Ward, and he fended off all of the strongest English teams as far as the challenge round.

For the first time, the mossy citadel of the sport was in serious trouble. Would the Doherty brothers be able to withstand the terrible American onslaught of serves?

The superiority complex of the English public seemed a bit shaken, but the brothers seemed to be up to the challenge. In the first place, they began to send back all the American twists, even first service faults, in order to become used to the bounce. Laurie, who had a great smash, told Reggie to play closer to the net. At one set each, a storm interrupted the contest, and the brothers had all the time they needed to realize that the rotations of a left-hander like Davis were controlled differently from those of a player like Ward. The following day, although hard pressed to do it, the brothers turned out an impressive 9–7 victory in the fourth set of the match, replayed from the beginning.

The applause that greeted Doherty had a quality of gratitude about it, and at the same time there was a feeling of respect for those proper adversaries of the United States, well turned out in their black shoes and behaving like the fine gentlemen they were.

The English responded enthusiastically to the challenge letter sent them the following year. This time the brothers did not have to be asked twice: Reggie, who had been limited to doubles play at Wimbledon and had watched his younger brother's first victories as a spectator, thought that a real crusade ought to be armed. Mr. W. H. Collins, the president of the LTA, who himself served as captain, had chosen old Joshua Pim in addition to the Doherty brothers. Pim had won at Wimbledon in 1883 and 1884, but had since stepped out of serious competition and played now only for the pleasure of a good clean shower.

Collins offered to go along with Doherty as a sparring partner, under the condition that he would go out on the courts only in the event that an accident to one of the brothers made his appearance necessary. Pim accepted.

In the meantime, the Americans were getting things ready in a big way. Together with the doubles experts, Davis and Ward, they had selected the national champion, Larned, for singles competition, and asked Whitman, who had retired undefeated in 1901, to come back.

William Powers, who was responsible for the organization of the event, had had the idea of snatching the match away from the refined citizens of Boston or even of Newport to bring it into an association that was interested in more than one sport, the Crescent Athletic Club of Bay Ridge. Powers was also responsible for a fine promotion campaign stressing the fact that admission was free: a written request was all it would take to get the best seats.

On Thursday, August 6, slowly moving trams began to transport more than 5,000 jammed and enthusiastic spectators from New York City. Some of the fans had even come by boat down the Hudson and across the Bay. The few among the spectators who knew tennis well were astounded to see Dr. Joshua Pim warming up with Reggie Doherty.

Although Dr. Pim had arrived in the States after the brothers and had lost more than 12.5 kilograms (27½ lbs.) in six weeks of practice, he had been selected by Captain Collins over Laurie, who had won at Wimbledon and was by this time by far the steadier of the two brothers.

"The Americans' greatest advantage is in a fresh doubles pair," Collins had told the astonished journalists, "and with the possibility of hot weather, I cannot risk the chance of coming up on Friday, the hour of decision in doubles play, with two fatigued athletes. Pim is playing extremely well, and there is no reason why he should not have the chance to show the Americans some of his old fire-eating qualities."

Collins's forecast turned out to be absolutely correct. Pim went out on the courts against Whitman when the singles play between Reggie and Larned had hardly begun: after less than an hour, a storm unleashed a deluge over the club, just in time to keep disaster from striking. The old doctor had lost 6–1, 6–1 in the first two sets, but Reggie was not much better off, down two sets, 2–6 and 3–6.

Dr. Dwight, the referee, decided that the first two singles must be finished the next morning and the reverse singles played in the afternoon. Pim won the third set but lost the fourth 6–0. Reggie, however, put the British back on level ground by beating Larned in five sets.

After 29 games in the morning Big Do hardly had time for a light lunch before he was faced by Whitman who had had 13 games of match practice against Pim. The American had a style which would always present problems for Reggie, and he countered all his maneuvers with a splendid variety of strokes. Reggie reached 5–4 in the first set and then faltered. Collins was nervously stroking his moustache on the sidelines. Laurie, biting his nails, would have loved to rip off that moustache.

Pim won only eight games against Larned, who embraced Whitman wildly. They had won 3–1! Aroused by this victory over the inventors of the sport, the fans increased twofold in number for a doubles match that could not turn the tide. The brothers defeated Davis and Ward and announced that they would stay in the United States for the National Championship.

In the quarterfinals, Whitman should have played the winner of the match between the two brothers. Laurie retired in favor of Reggie, who was well rested and defeated the American in four sets. Once more his delicate constitution was not able to recover. Larned repulsed his attacks in the challenge round, winning three hard sets after having lost the first.

The Doherty brothers, who were not less graceful in social engagements than on the courts, were quick to congratulate their opponent, the audience, the condition of the courts, and they had kind words for poor Pim and also for Collins's misfortune.

A few days before the selection of the 1903 team, the Dohertys invited Captain Collins to one of their parties, at which Reggie gave an impromptu demonstration of his excellent voice. Over a cup of tea and a roll, they let him know their conditions for the proposed trip to the United States: they would need a reserve player like Mahony, stronger than Pim, to use in an emergency. Collins was so highly impressed with their logic that he ran the risk of making yet another mistake. During the practice tournament at Nahant, Reggie had felt twinges of pain in one arm. He didn't pay any attention to it, but suddenly found that he could not even grip his racket.

Collins asked Larned, the captain of the American team, if he thought it would be proper for him to play Mahony in the first singles match and Reggie in the last one. Larned checked the matter out with the referee, Dr. Dwight, the author of the rules, as well as with the learned jurist Richard Olny. Dwight objected, noting that it seemed impossible to him to substitute a healthy player like Mahony, and Larned told the Englishman that he was "awfully sorry." Collins thought the matter over. The Americans were a little weaker than they had been the previous year. Still led by Larned, they had replaced Davis and Ward with the new doubles champions, the Wrenn brothers. As second in the singles play, they had preferred Bob Wrenn, not only to Whitman, who had definitely retired, but also to Wright and Ward as well, who were above him in the ranking list.

By 1897 Bob Wrenn had won the national title four times, and in 1898 he had voluntarily left for Cuba with the Roosevelt Rough Riders. He received an honorable mention and caught rheumatic fever for his trouble. When they realized that he would love to be selected, the joy of the patriotic officials knew no bounds. The draw brought him against Laurie. Collins was convinced that Wrenn was out of form. "Laurie can wear Wrenn out for me so that Reggie can recuperate," he reasoned, and he decided to take the risk. Fools rush in where angels fear to tread. Collins informed Reggie of his thinking and withdrew him from the first singles against Larned, giving the astonished Americans a point. Laurie made mincemeat out of poor Wrenn. With the rain that began to fall during the match and that did not let up for three days, Wrenn began to suffer from rheumatism; by which time Reggie's arm had almost healed. The doubles match, which was disputed for the first time on the second day, was a real struggle, but the Doherty brothers climbed back from 5–6 in the first, 6–7 in the second, and closed the match in the fourth.

Six thousand fans in their straw hats, with starched collars going limp in the sun, crowded round the two central courts of the Longwood Cricket Club to witness the decisive singles matches. The matches betweeen Reggie and Bob Wrenn and between Laurie and Larned began at the same time under conditions that Collins defined as "a refinement in cruelty." Only the umpire's chair separated the two courts, and during the alternating of the sides and even during the rallies, Laurie could not help but hear all that was happening to Reggie, while Larned squinted anxiously over at Wrenn.

These fateful matches had an unusually parallel outcome, in that both were tied in the fifth set. Reggie and Wrenn were three games, Laurie and Larned four all. Larned, exultant over Wrenn's good showing, climbed to 40–15 on Laurie's serve. Laurie served and rushed to the net, only to have a return pass him and hear the umpire, Mr. Mansfield, declare solemnly: "Game to Larned, leading 5 to 4."

On the other court, Reggie, suddenly downhearted, looked at his brother. Laurie was near the net talking to the umpire, and trying to clarify where the service linesman ought to be positioned. Surprisingly, the man's seat was empty, although no one had noticed the fact.

Reggie and Wrenn stopped their match and came over to the other court at the same time as the referee, Dr. Dwight, ran up. Laurie repeated his question: Was the service long or not? The umpire could not make up his mind, and Dr. Dwight ordered that the point be replayed. Laurie served, rushed the net, and took the point, and then three more in rapid succession. Now he held the advantage, 5–4.

Reggie recommenced play. He no longer felt any pain, but rather a deep sense of well-being. After a few minutes of play, the English had taken the two singles matches and won the Davis Cup.

During the American Championship a week later, the conversations dealing with the events at Longwood were still going strong. The linesman, it was determined, had said before the matches began that he would leave for personal matters at a prearranged time: what had happened was that his substitute had failed to show up to replace him.

Larned felt that Dr. Dwight's action was a noble one, but not justified by the circumstances. The decision ought to have come from the umpire. Mansfield meanwhile confided to his friends that he thought the serve out, but had no way of being sure about it, because the linesman should have decided. As a result, he had been both pleased and relieved to take Dr. Dwight's suggestion on the matter. Laurie refused to comment. He knew the best way for him to prove himself was on the court. In the quarterfinals, the draw once again pitted the two brothers, as it had the year before, and

1

2

3

4

The Davis Cup opens its doors to the world. In 1904 the Americans are unable to make the trip, and Great Britain trounces the Belgians in finals play, losing only one set. 1. Seated with the Doherty brothers we see Lemaire and De Borman. 2. In 1905 the Americans invade Wimbledon with (from left to right) Ward, Wright, Captain Dashire, Larned, and Clothier, but the English (3), strengthened by Reggie, Captain Collins, S. H. Smith, Gore, Laurie, beat them five love. 4. In 1907 the Cup embarks on the long voyage down under to Australia. In our photo, Brookes, the southpaw, is beating Behr in the semifinals against the U.S. played at Wimbledon. 5. In 1908 the Australians admire their own team for the first time, hard pressed by the Americans. Wright, who is rejoining Alexander at the net, will win both of his singles matches. 12. Some shots of the Melbourne courts taken the same year. 14. Wright seated, with Alexander. 13. The two young stalwarts sent by the United States to Australia in 1909: Long, seated, with McLoughlin standing by his side. 7. Wilding pushing McLoughlin in the last singles match of the tie. 8. The semifinals of the same year, won in Philadelphia by the United States over Great Britain, five love. Little and Hacket play against the Englishmen Parke and Crawley. 9. The semifinals at the New York West Side Club between the United States and Great Britain. McLoughlin fires a lob at Dixon. The Americans take the match four to one. 10. The English bring the Cup home from Australia in 1912. Seven countries entered in 1913. The Australians make their first trip to the United States, but the only point scored is the one made by

5

7

8

9

12

13

14

6

Doust and Jones against McLoughlin and Hacket, to the left of the net. The same doubles players take the decisive match in the Challenge Round at London. 6. Hacket is volleying against the English doubles team. 15. The contenders are always the same: Roper Barrett, Dixon Hacket, and McLoughlin. 11. Another shot of the 1913 English team: Parke, Captain McNair, Dixon, and, seated, Gore and Barrett, the same team that saw the English defeated for the first time in the United States in 1900!

15

10

11

Color illustration opposite page 96: From the left, (1) Tony Wilding in a service and a smash, and Norman Brookes executing two very typical volleys. Below, the pair seen sitting in the park at Brookwood after a practice session. Opposite page: (2) Max Décugis, as seen in a painting by François Flameng, hung in the headquarters of the Racing Club of France in Paris.

Though his work was better carried out on foot, the umpire would seek a chair to rest in when fatigued. A platform was placed beneath the chair to aid him to see the court better, and then another was added for even greater visibility. At this point, a ladder was also required to climb to the vantage point above. From this arrangement, the bright thinking of one of the umpires invented the umpire's stand (seen to the upper left). Another invented the line marker (seen below), a real time saver to the harried grounds attendants. To the lower right can be seen the brave woman player, ready to serve, used in the advertising program of Elliman and Sons to market their all-purpose liniment.

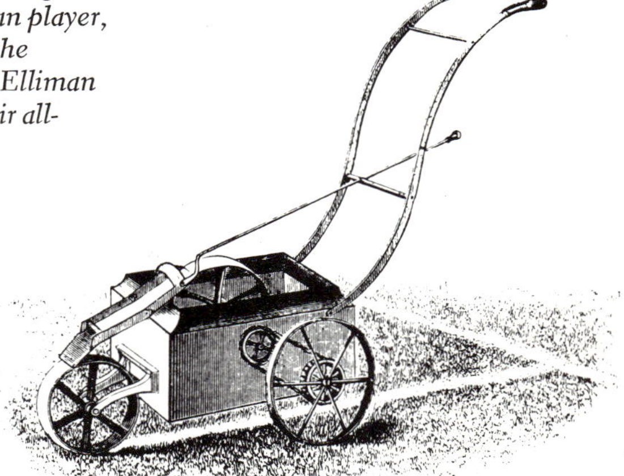

1

2

3

August 13, 1914. Before 12,000 fans packed into the West Side Tennis Club at Forest Hills, New York (1), the American titleholders confront the Australian contenders Brookes and Wilding. The Dominions are already at war, heightening the Aussies' combative spirit. In the first match, Wilding (wearing a cap) contains the brilliant beginning logged by Williams, and goes on to win 7–5, 6–2, and 6–3.

The second match is the occasion for one of Davis's longest sets, as well as the crowning of a new champion in young McLoughlin pitted against that old warlock Brookes.
The American Comet (3) serves twelve aces, one of them depicted perhaps in photo (2). Brookes is crushed 17–15, 6–3, and 6–3.
On the fourteenth of August, the Americans hesitate until the last minute on how to face

4

5

Wilding and Brookes (5).
Prompted by McLoughlin, they select Bundy over Behr. Wilding does not make one mistake, often playing behind Brookes (4).
McLoughlin tries to force the issue, causing the American team to go down to defeat 6–3, 8–6, 9–7.
August 15. The older and wiser Brookes is anticipating Williams (8) and is just about to put the game away when he runs out of steam. Williams mistakenly asks for a time out, allowing Brookes to regain his composure, who then counterattacks (6) and puts Williams away 6–1, 6–2, 8–10, and 6–3.
Australasia has regained the Cup. Wilding, in the last match, sees no reason to wear himself out against the superior McLoughlin (7), who takes him 6–2, 6–3, 2–6, and 6–2.

6

7

8

12 Australasia: Wilding and Brookes

At Trinity College his friends called him the Australasian, and had been doing so for the past few days. They would show him world maps and maps of the various countries of the South Pacific, asking him with feigned perplexity where that new realm, Australasia, was located.

Tony Wilding would laugh that gentle laugh of his, the good and patient man that he was. Even he thought it a little strange that his native New Zealand had gone in with Australia, in order to get a Davis Cup team together, even though they had both Dunlop and him. As far as he could see during the six days of sailing through placid seas, those Aussie shipmates of his were not much better at the game than his fellow New Zealander and he. In 1904 their representative, Norman Brookes, had founded the Australian Association, and until the next year had never shown his face at Wimbledon, although he was already twenty-seven years old.

That very Saturday Brookes was to have met Baby Gore, the stubborn old rival of the Doherty brothers, in the finals of the Kent championships at Beckenham. Wilding put on a leather vest over his striped team captain's sweater. In a little more than an hour, his powerful two-speed 7/8 Bat Jap had taken him to Beckenham, just in time to run into a slender young man with a pensive look, long dangling arms, and one slim powerful hand tightly clutching an old triangular racket. Could it be possible, Wilding thought to himself, that this quiet man could be one of the most well-known individuals in Melbourne?

"Brookes?" he asked hesitantly. The Australian turned his piercing look toward him, staring at him with his two bright blue eyes.

"That's me, mate."

Wilding made mention of their approaching common goal at the Davis matches. "Do you think you can take Gore?"

"Take him?" Brookes huffed. "I'd be ruddy surprised if I didn't."

When Tony knew Norman better, he had no problem in finishing off the story. He wrote that Norman's thoughts before any match were always the same: "Could it be that my opponent would have the cheek to dare take me, Norman Brookes, on? Would I beat him? Of course, I would beat him!" It was hard to picture two such different champions together.

Wilding, blond and ruddy-faced with a heavy frame, was capable of waiting thoughtful hours on end for his opponents to tire. Brookes, with a Mediterranean darkness of complexion, was unpredictable, aggressive, and always ready to attack, though he often used poorly timed strokes. Wilding's progression was mathematical in its perfection. After launching his career in 1904, he won the title at Wimbledon in 1910 for the first time.

Brookes, bested by the younger Doherty in 1905, made a comeback in 1907 and won both Wimbledon and the Davis Cup, only to disappear from the tennis scene in Europe altogether. He would return home loaded down with work from which he freed himself once each year to defend the Cup. In 1914 Brookes landed for the third time in England, and, in answer to the reporters who asked him what had prompted him to try again, he stated: "Everybody says that Wilding is unbeatable. I want to see it for myself."

Wilding was at the height of his powers at that time. He had won four Wimbledons in a row, from 1910 to 1913, and had also taken the World Clay Courts Championships in Paris, a tournament that had been organized to celebrate the founding of the International Lawn Tennis Federation (ILTF). Tony asked to have the challenge round eliminated to show his good sportsmanship and to get ready for the competition. But it was too early for such a change: 68 of the competitors agreed with Wilding, 46 were opposed, and 24 abstained.

Tony had to wait for Brookes, helped by a linesman, to get out of the clutches of the German Froitzheim, and almost as if he had been hypnotized, he was beaten in three solid sets.

Brookes had been nicknamed the Wizard because of the unbelievable ease with which he could sense his opponents' every move, even the most carefully concealed and violent shots.

In 1961, the year in which this reporter had the honor of meeting Brookes in Melbourne, the Wizard had already been knighted, and though his back was somewhat hunched over, his eyes still retained the sparkle of younger days. I rashly asked, at the risk of being impolite, if Wilding had not been a bit too fair in considering him even better than Little Do.

The old gentleman gave me an imperious glance and said generously that Wilding himself had been an excellent player. Then he returned to a quiet conversation already begun with the man who had lost a match by a few points a few days earlier and had gone on to become prime minister.

1

2

3

4

E. Smith Travers (1) introduced the game into Australia, but the first match goes back to 1885, when it was played between South Wales and Victoria at Sydney. The Englishman Eaves (2) became the first foreigner to make a name for himself, in 1902, while H. A. Parker (3, 4), who was learning the American reverse twist service, took the New Zealand title. 5. Rose Payten became the Australian star at the turn of the century, but she never faced the rigors of the voyage to Europe. 6. Mrs. Cater-Howitt was the champion of two Australian tennis-playing states, and Constance Lean (7) was the first woman New Zealander to attract attention in Great Britain.

5

6

7

1

2

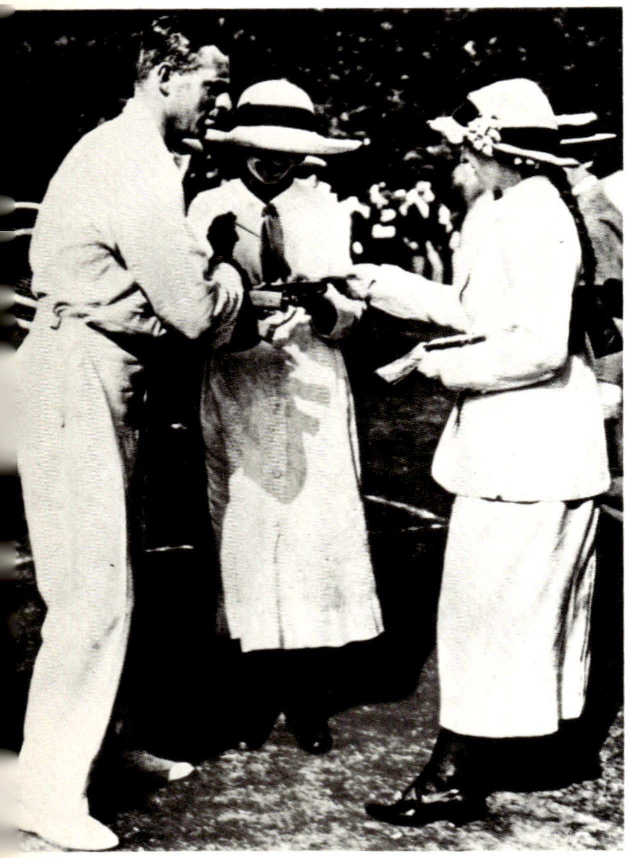

3

4

5

6

7

Tony Wilding was the most reliable, if not the most talented, of the tennis greats who followed the Doherty brothers. He was a New Zealander and, together with Brookes, he represented the mythical realm of Australasia in Davis Cup competition. Tony's short life, which ended on the battlefront in Belgium, had the excitement of a novel of chivalry. He won Wimbledon from 1910 to 1913, and his outstanding devotion to physical fitness made him almost invulnerable in the clay-court tournaments of Europe, his adopted homeland. Student at Cambridge (1), friend and doubles partner of Lord Balfour (2), idol of the female college population in England (3), he would zip from one tournament to another on his powerful Bat-Jap motorcycle(8). In 1907 he was awarded the cup presented by the most prestigious German tournament, Bad Homburg (5). He tries in vain to salvage (4) one of McLoughlin's volleys, at Wimbledon in 1913, but still will go on to beat the Comet 8–6, 6–3, 10–8 (4). A very worthy serve (6), struck slightly low for modern tastes. 7. A backhand shot in accord with the English grip, very much in vogue at that time.

8

1

2

3

Norman Brookes was the first of the great Australian champions and the first foreigner to win the title at Wimbledon in 1907. Thanks to him and to Wilding, the Davis Cup arrived in the homeland of the kangaroos the same year and stayed there until 1912, to return Down Under once again in 1914. Until he was twenty-nine years old (4), the physical isolation of his homeland robbed the Wizard of the international acclaim due him. But even at the age of forty-seven, the Wimbledon tennis-goers would applaud his incredible victorious match against the number two American, Hunter. 1. For his backhand, Brookes still used the pioneer style à la Renshaw, striking the ball with the same face of the racket used for the forehand. His sensitivity and legendary wrist permitted him to overcome this handicap with ease. His friend Wilding once remarked that he changed grips ten times in a sustained rally. 2. Brookes, seen returning a serve with almost effortless ease, his racket held at midhandle with wrist well blocked. 3. Here the backhand grip has changed, and the stroke played is more modern in form. 5. About to strike a lifted drive with such coordination as to suggest a warm-up. 6. We see him returning a low forehand volley on the famous French court at Dinard, one of the first constructed on the Continent.

If Wilding was extraordinary, less artistic, and stronger than the magical brothers, the Wizard influenced the whole course of Australian tennis with his authority while he was president of the association for twenty-nine years, from 1926 to 1955.

In 1901, at the time of the visit of that world traveler, Dr. Eaves, Norman Brookes was the unknown son of a man who had crossed the sea from Northampton with nine pounds sterling in his pocket, and who had later become one of the most important Australian magnates of the timber industry.

When he returned to Great Britain, Eaves told his friends of this young left-hander from Melbourne who had learned the American twist as well as the reverse twist in only two days. If he ever got to Wimbledon, chances were good that the Doherty brothers would go down in defeat. As matters turned out, in 1905 the sorcerer's apprentice missed his target by a very narrow margin, but by 1907 his assortment of serves had increased to four.

The English fans, who had adopted young Wilding, accepted the victory of the newcomers. At least Brookes came from the Empire, and his success keynoted the enormous international popularity of lawn tennis.

Had not an American girl won the women's singles, a pretty miss by the name of May Sutton? Had not the doubles gone to Brookes and Wilding? Had not even the Prince of Wales been seen on the courts in the company of the beautiful woman who would become Queen Mary? And moreover, had not the prince "graciously accepted" the title of president of the club?

All of this was more than cold comfort and could have been reason for general rejoicing, had not Brookes had the good fortune to carry home the Davis Cup as well, losing only one set in four singles matches against the Americans and the English.

But what could be done after all? After the retirement of the brothers and of Sidney Smith, where could new champions be found? Grudgingly, the English had been forced to turn back the clock and make use of the team formed at the baptism of the Cup seven years earlier: old Baby Gore and Roper Barrett. And, after

4

5

6

1a

1b

1c

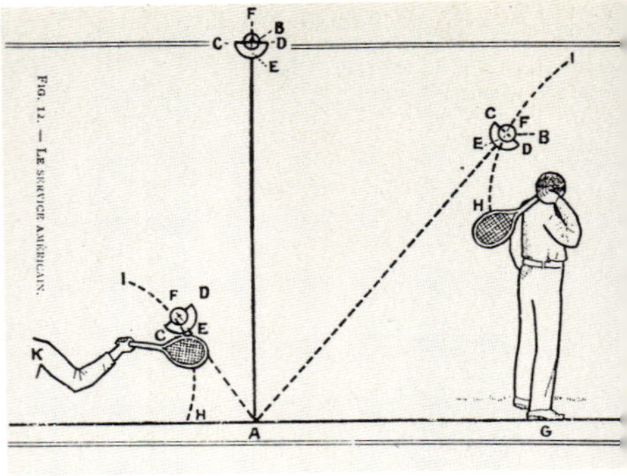

x1 x2

2a

2b

2c

Both Brookes and Wilding began self-taught, and they later refined their tennis to become consummate stylists. Brookes shows us the difference between a normal American serve (2) and the reverse American serve (1), which was used by almost all of the best players of the day. The diagram (x) helps us understand where the ball had to be hit.

In (x1) the racket describes a semicircle from right to left (for Brookes, who is left-handed, the situation is reversed), imparting top spin to the ball. In (x2) the racket produces both sidespin and top spin (for the left-hander, again the situation is reversed). The alternate use of these serves produced varying results and confused the opponents.

3. A serve by Wilding, much less laborious than those of Brookes. 4, 5. A forehand and a backhand. Wilding stands between the English school, from which he has adopted the backhand grip (z), and the American, which favors a more closed grip for the forehand (y).

y

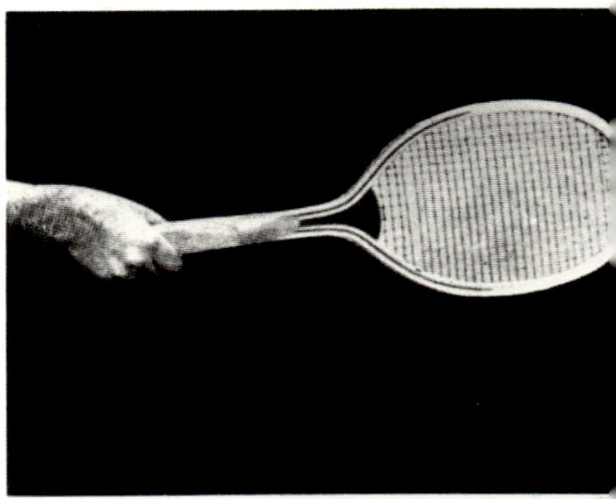

3

4

5

z

all, it was a good deal better to count on Brookes and Wilding than on the American team of Beals Wright and Karl Behr, beaten by a burst of power, three to two.

When Australasia won the Davis Cup, the competition became more difficult. They had to be challenged on their own ground, but they wanted Wilding to make the journey to Australia.

He repeated several times that he would like to spend his vacation at home, and the trip, when it finally came, ended up by making him wonder if the tours were worth it: for the three glorious days of the challenge round cost him two inactive and almost totally sedentary months on board ship.

Astride his motorcycle, Tony went across Europe from one tennis club to the next. At Wiesbaden, Frau von Meister invited him to a ball in honor of the emperor, while in Vienna the members of the tennis club welcomed him with open arms to show him "that the beautiful Austrian women were no less elegant than their Parisian counterparts." At Kormend, in the summer home of Prince Batthyany-Strattman, he was able to exercise his natural penchant for agrarian life, enriched with Central-European refinements. "There is no one who loves horses the way the Hungarians do when they truly care for their animals," he wrote, thinking of the pony that he had ridden as a child at Fownhope, "where none of us wore shoes before the age of ten."

The important figures in European tennis were charmed by this delightful young New Zealander who had won both Wimbledon and the Monte Carlo handicap with equal ease, the latter in doubles play with Lord Balfour, who knew how to ride a colt and could quote Horace's poetry at a *soiree*. From time to time, Tony sent Norman Brookes a card from the most out-of-the-way places. Aloof in faraway Melbourne, Norman had used his own funds to construct new grandstands, enlarge the factory, and beat his brother, his only trainer, giving him a thirty-love advantage. Displeased at the poor performance of his adversaries, he spent many hours in the billiards room, going over and over the various ball combinations for a carom. "It was as if," his wife Mabel wrote in *Crowded Galleries*, "he had been divided into two different people. As a young man he had been introverted, obstinate, hard even on himself, and grimly determined to succeed. He himself saved the money for his first trip overseas. When later on he had developed a different view of things, he still retained a sort of defensiveness, and the natural desire to give of oneself was a quality that he always had difficulty in acquiring."

This man, who had the misfortune to suffer from an ulcer during the years of the important tournaments, once a year went down in one of his two Fiats to pick up Wilding at the ship.

"He was deeply loyal to his friends," Mabel assured us, "and other people did not have very much importance for him."

In his huge sea chest, Tony had brought with him a few changes of clothes as well as a large number of new rackets and many Slazengers, the name that had replaced Ayres in the tennis ball market.

Raising clouds of reddish dust from the roadbed, the Fiat carried the two great champions to Brookwood, and here Norman, with no advance practice, submitted himself to the rigorous athletic training laid out for him by his friend under the bright sun of the dry southern winter. During one of his first jaunts on a train that was taking him to Cannes, Tony had run into a medical officer of the British armed forces in the East Indies, who was now receiving pension. Their acquaintance quickly ripened into a friendship, and the tennis player began to follow religiously the methods prescribed by the sportsman doctor:

7 A.M. A very weak cup of tea followed by a brisk walk and some jogging.

8:30 A.M. Breakfast.

11 A.M. Practice volleys followed by three, four, or preferably five sets in rapid succession and played as hard as possible.

1:30 P.M. Lunch.

3:30 P.M. Three doubles sets, followed by more practice. If the player's smash is not fully up to par, special training must follow. And, to finish off, a little rope jumping, a few practice strokes against the wall, and a short jog. After each practice session, bath and massage.

10:15 P.M. Lights out!

P.S.: Don't forget the breathing exercises.

The training program grew so difficult that Brookes found himself at the point of being burned out. Warm as toast in his fur-lined sleeping bag, Wilding slept out-of-doors, as he always did in Paris on a balcony not far from the St. Cloud Tennis Club, and at the Park House in Wimbledon. Ever since he had gone out on the family courts as a ball boy and had been promoted to player by the unexpected departure of a friend, Tony Wilding had ached to be a champion.

Even though at first he hit both forehand and backhand with the same face of the racket, long hours of study had taught him to prefer the English grip for the backhand, with the thumb held pointing along the handle of the racket. Wilding had, however, retained his powerful "colonial" drive and was the first to declare that it was stupid to speak of cut-and-dried grips. In his autobiography, *On the Court and Off*, he writes that "dynamic studies and diagrams demonstrate that in this area all dogmatic statements are futile." He goes on to say that one had only to see the number of times that Brookes changed grips in an exchange to understand the validity of this statement.

Wilding also maintained that the American style à la Karl Behr, frenziedly set on controlling the net with a winning volley, was a method suited to winning quick victories but ill-adapted to marathons of five sets each. For, all things considered, those terribly laborious serves of theirs "that make the ball sing," could easily be contained with two solid drives, and finally ended up by tiring out the server.

Brookes finally was convinced as well, and he began to worry more about the length and the speed of his left-handed serve than the force of the spin.

Among those who shared Wilding's viewpoints was a large,

1

2

4

3

5

solidly built, excellent American player by the name of Beals Wright. His active participation in putting these views into practice was set back by a silly accident that could have cost him a lot more trouble. Before leaving for Wimbledon, Beals had tried to pry open a bottle of Vichy water, using a toothbrush as a lever. The neck of the bottle shattered, and a sliver of glass lodged in his hand. During the trip, the wound became badly infected, and he lost a finger during surgery. Beals set about overcoming the handicap with the same tenacity that Wilding put into his practice sessions. The American assured his friend that he would prove the validity of his theories by trouncing him badly!

The Davis Cup matches in Melbourne in 1908 were a splendid exhibition not only of excellent play but also of good sportsmanship. Before seven thousand wonder-struck fans, who found in tennis a game no less exciting than cricket, Beals Wright beat both Wilding and Brookes. The doubles match, which decided the encounter, saw the four players divide their bar bill in friendly camaraderie and intervene in helping the linesmen make difficult decisions. The combined Australian-New Zealand team was down three love in the fifth set, when Brookes, the old Wizard, who had seemed at the end of his powers, suddenly regained them and turned the tables.

Having been so close to victory, the best Americans refused to make such a long trip again, and the Association sent McLoughlin and Long, two twenty-year-old players from the West, to represent it.

Maurice McLoughlin was the first tennis player from the United States who had come from the middle class, and he had made his name by playing on cement courts in public tournaments. His forehand had the force of a pile driver, his serves were meteoric, and he was noted for rushing the net. His play let it be known in no uncertain terms that the long reign of Larned was about to draw to a close, and that Wilding and Brookes had come across a grim adversary.

Despite McLoughlin's brilliant play, the two Australian players closed the match five love, and the American Association was discouraged at the outcome.

The following year, after a dogged interchange of telegrams with the English, the U.S. team retired, and the Australians took advantage of a curious clause that allowed the holders of the cham-

6

7

8

9

Maurice McLoughlin, the Comet, was the first American champion to arrive from the cement courts of California (1, 2). Unlike the stars that had preceded him and who had their beginnings in the fashionable society of the Atlantic Coast, he hit his first balls on the unyielding cement of public precincts. His entry into the exclusive white house of tennis USA produced a kind of revolution. Others had already applied a fight-to-the-death technique to the sport, but tennis players like the Dohertys or Larned had overcome them with their overall court game. The new style of play was imposed by McLoughlin's untiring drive, his vitality, and his courage. The Comet grew red in the face, turned combative and aggressive, and attacked the ball with a very close grip, especially in the forehand, as can be seen in photos (4) and (5), producing a very accentuated lift spin. Nor were his serve and his forehand a laughing matter. Brookes and Wilding always found it difficult to return his cannonballs and to check the rebound of his elaborate second service (7, 8, 9). In view of the work involved in changing his grip, his backhand was not very effective (6), but the low volley (10) was played with admirable ability. His career in the United States was blocked by Williams, and even more by Little Bill Johnston, who beat him 10–8 in the fifth during the finals of the 1915 championships (3), the same year that he scored such remarkable victories against the Australians.

10

pionship to judge the challengers of insufficient ability and thereby stand off the challenge.

It was the English team that was thus treated by the lads from Down Under. Two years later the English vindicated themselves by sending a team to Melbourne strong enough to defeat the Aussies, who had to get along without Wilding. Encouraged by the return of the Cup to Europe, seven squads registered for tournament play in 1913.

Australasia (Australia-New Zealand) descended into the lists without either of their champions. Wilding was in the Swiss Alps climbing mountains and making plans to become a pilot. Brookes had married a lovely seventeen-year-old girl, whose family had graciously given Napoleon's house on Saint Helena to the French government. While the newlyweds were cutting an enormous wedding cake sent from England, decorated appropriately enough with net, balls, and silver rackets, ten bridesmaids carried Mabel's long train, which had been embroidered in Venice. A columnist quipped that it seemed odd to him that a wizard should have chosen a fairy princess as his bride.

13 The Others: The French and the Germans–Décugis and Froitzheim

"Paris," Wilding wrote in 1912, "has become one of the most important tennis centers in the world, and a team from this city could easily beat a team from London. The enormous talent of Max Décugis has greatly favored the advance of the sport, and Gobert and Laurentz are first-class players. It is a fact that there are at present more promising young players on the continent than in England and the dominions combined."

Toward the end of the forties, this journalist met the aging Décugis, who had retired to the Côte d'Azur and never missed a match if he could make it. At that time, Coco Gentien, the secretary of the International Federation, was finishing his latest book, *Aventures d'un joueur de tennis* (Adventures of a Tennis Player), one of the most interesting and perhaps the best written of the myriad accounts of tennis.

Décugis and Gentien endlessly discussed the anecdotes and tennis personalities in the book, while this young reporter often sat entranced as he listened to them.

Gentien: When I was young, my governess took me to the Bois de Boulogne, to the meadow at Croix Catelan. I would press my nose against the chain fence of the Racing Club, where tennis was being played. And that is where my passion for the sport was born, even though my genes may have sent me in that direction.

Toward the end of the century, my maternal grandmother had fallen in love with the new game at first sight and had an English architect build a court for her in her garden at Auteuil. It must have been one of the first ones in France . . . .

Décugis: I don't doubt that. The first tennis club was organized in 1877 at Décimal in Paris, but the groundwork of the one at Dinard, where the English used to come in the summer, could not have been laid after 1878. A truly beautiful court was erected for the Renshaw brothers at Beau Site in Cannes in 1875. Those were the times!

Coco, do you remember that poem by Heredia, "Les Champions" (The Champions)? *D'une gloire indomptée* . . .

Gentien: That's not quite the way it begins. (He recites the whole poem).

1

4.The young Marcel Proust, French author later famous for his magnificent cyclic novel Remembrance of Things Past, *kneels at the feet of the diminutive and oh so young Jeanne Pouquet to pay her court with an imaginary racquet serenade. 5. The court at Beau Site in Cannes, erected to provide the Renshaw twins with their practice sessions far from the fogs of Old London Town.*

2

3

1. The legend at the bottom of this unusual photograph from the Wollerner Collection reads "1774." The year is incorrect, and the right one, 1874, indicates that tennis arrived early on the other side of the Manche ("the Sleeve," as the French call the English Channel). To the left, together with Wingfield's carton can be seen a parasol. To the right, the little girl with her Florentine straw hat is holding a fish net, and the fourth woman in the doubles game has taken the crying child into her arms.
2. The Island of Puteau on the Seine, the site of one of the first French clubs, and the very first to be reached by boat.
3. The legendary court at Dinard where the first international tournaments were disputed, as well as some delightfully animated doubles matches played by three men and one woman.

4

5

D'un courage indompté que leur orgueil banda
La chemise percée et la face tomate
Ils luttent, Yankee glabre et moderne Sarmate
Sous un soleil cuisant d'Alger ou de Blidah.

Courage undaunted, by their pride increased,
Their shirts torn and their faces red from strain,
They struggle on the court, the beardless Yankee and the modern Sarmatian,
Under the broiling sun of Algiers or Blida.

A coups de lemon-squash et de whiskey-soda
Ils chassent de leurs nerfs la torpeur qui les mate.
La balle va, revient, suit le geste automate:
Lutte épique, égalant les hauts faits de l'Edda.

Bolstered by gulps of lemon squash and whiskey soda,
They drive from their bodies the tropic heat:
Their movements machinelike, the ball goes back and forth,
An epic match this, taken from the pages of an Icelandic Edda.

Mais la Fortune enfin fait son choix et bascule.
Quinze, trente, quarante . . . A Roncevaux, Roland
Lui-même succomba. Dans un ultime élan
Ix bondit sur le lob trop court qui s'émascule,
Et d'un smash foudroyant, tel un assassinat,
Gagne le jeu, le set et le championnat.

But then Lady Luck makes her choice and tips the scale,
Fifteen, thirty, forty. At Roncesvalles, even
Roland went to defeat. In a burst of speed
Ix pounces upon a short lob that misses the mark,
And like an assassin, with a devastating smash,
Takes game, set, and championship.

Décugis: Very good. And that one by Marcel Schwob, how did it go?

Gentien:

Si vous la baisé comptés quinze;
Si vous touchés le tetin, trente
Si vous avez la motte prinse
Quarante-cinq lors se présente.
Mais si vous metés en la fente
Ce de quoy la dame a mestier,
—Notés bien ce que je vous chante—
Vous gagnez le jeu tout entier.

Reporter (Clerici): Mr. Gentien, please: how do you translate *fente?*

Gentien: All of it has already been translated from a fifteenth-century text. I hope that Max will not want me to translate that, too.

Décugis: What a memory you have! I'll bet you even remember the first tournaments at Auteuil.

Gentien: Only what I have been told. The heroes of my childhood were the Englishman Briggs, winner of the first championship in 1891, and Schoepfer, who won the following year and who became the Nabokov of his day under the pen name of Claude Anet.

1

2

1. *Both player and manager, Canet was one of the French pioneers. In the sequence of photos (2) he shows us, above, the simple serve with no spin, and, below, the American reverse serve, a typical weapon of the period. 3. Of the two Vacherot brothers, the second, Marcel, on the right, achieved good international rating, despite his poor health. In 1895, the year of the inauguration of the French indoor championships, he defeated the Englishmen Hough and Hetley and the German Voss. 4. A picture of the same championships from 1900, shows, from the left, the English Caridia, Ritchie, Simond, and Norris getting ready to play. 5. The turnout was very encouraging, and the tournament ended with a banquet provided by Monsieur Lecaron: we see here the 1902 menu. 7. Décugis, the first French champion of international fame, studied in Great Britain and won the Renshaw Cup for juniors in 1898. At the age of twenty he already stood out in indoor play, launching a career that would carry him to twenty-eight titles as French champion in various categories and to the Wimbledon doubles victory in 1911. Décugis was the translator of Vaile's* Modern Lawn Tennis, *the highest technical authority available at the turn of the century, from which photos 8, 9, and 10 are taken. Evidently they are candid photographs that were taken during practice warm-ups, showing a low volley with good follow-through, a well-prepared backhand, and a forehand lifted with great impetus. 11. Décugis in the company of Germot.*

3

5
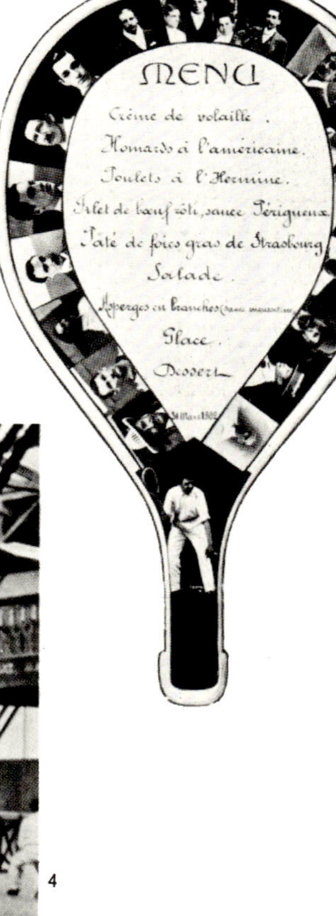

4

6

7

11 12

12. A forehand volley, well braced by the arm, despite the unexpected passing shot. 13. With the aid of Décugis, smiling Gobert won Wimbledon in 1911, but he preferred to play doubles with Laurentz (14), who, as a result of one of Gobert's shots, lost the use of an eye. 6. The beautiful Art Deco sitting room of the Tennis Club, Nice, and the main court of that club (15), seen while play is in progress among Décugis, Wilding, Ritchie, and Doherty in 1907. 16. Dating from the same year, here is a view of the club at Monte Carlo, another winter training ground for the tennis world.

8

9

14

13

10

15

16

1

1. The four young French women from the early years of this century are Madame Gallay, and Mademoiselles De Kermel, Cécile and Jeanne Matthey. The first was known as the "Queen Bee" since she was the most imposing of the four. We may also assume that she was slowed down by her large hat. 2, 3. The delightful Broquedis, the strongest French female tennis player before the advent of Lenglen. The strokes seen are both forehand volleys, the first slightly improvised, the second anticipated with excellent balance and accuracy.

6

2

7

3

4. The beautiful lady's greatest success, the Stockholm Olympics in 1912. The King of Tennis, Gustav V of Sweden, presents her with her prize. 6, 7, 8. These lovely models are from 1909; the attire of the first is reminiscent of Broquedis; the second is like the clothing worn by the Matthey sisters. 5. Jeanne Matthey, the strongest of the sisters and champion from 1909 to 1912, is seen at the end of an excellent overhand serve.

8

4

5

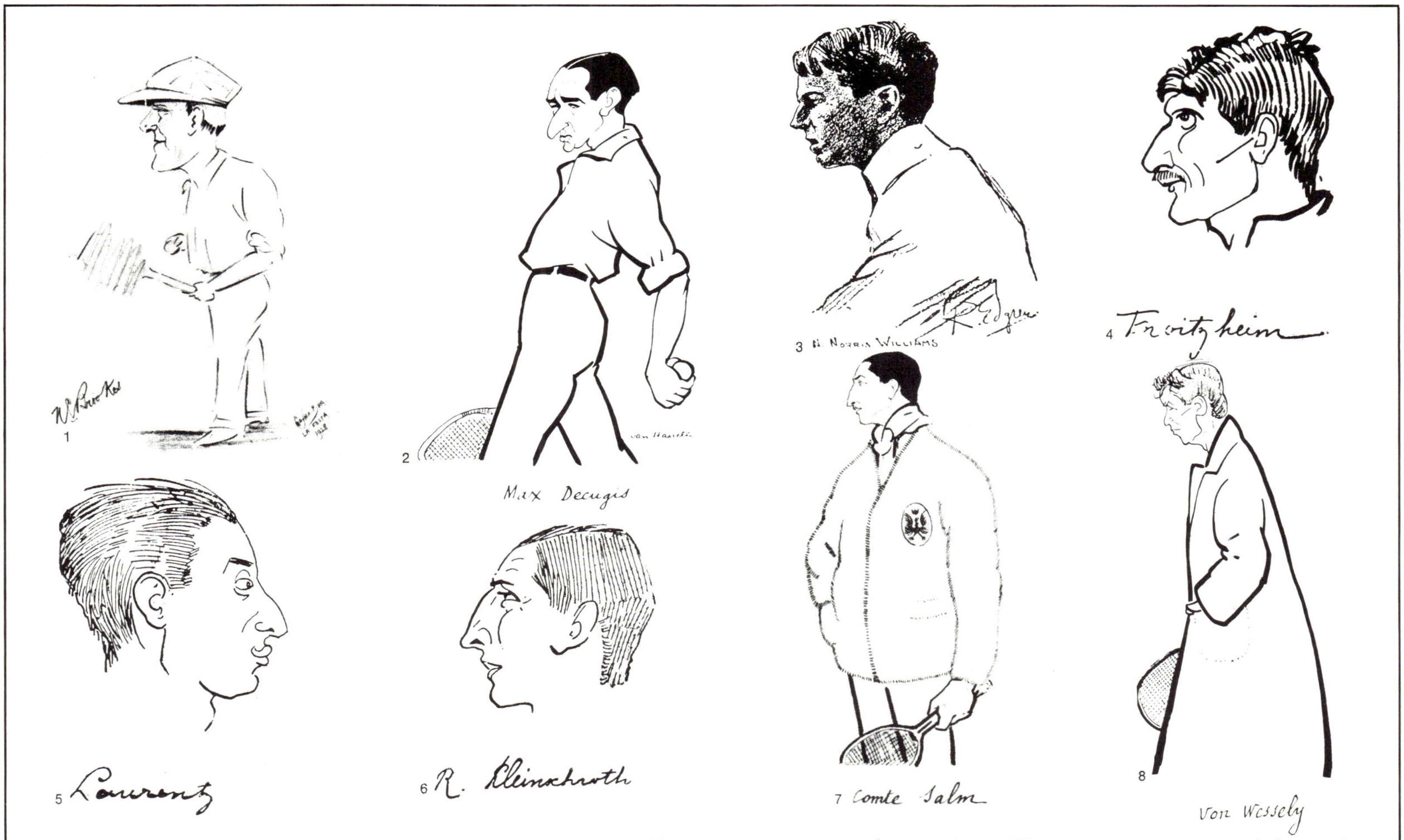

Caricatures of some of the greats of that time: 1. Brookes. 2. Décugis. 3. Williams. 4. Froitzheim. 5. Laurentz. 6. R. Kleinschroth. 7. Salm. 8. Von Wessely. 9. Sutton. 10. Hillyard. 11. Lambert Chambers. 12. Reggie Doherty. 13. Collins. 14. Laurie Doherty. 15. Wilding.

1

2

3

4

1. Just like France, Germany was at first an English colony as far as tennis was concerned, and Bad Homburg, seen here in a photo from 1876, competed for patrons with Dinard and the Côte d'Azur. In 1897 four Englishmen played in the final here. 2. They are, from the left, Reggie and Laurie Doherty, amazingly enough, defeated for the fourth and last time in their careers by Ball-Green and Hillyard. Tea is taken under the oak trees (3), and the heir apparent, seen third from the left in photo (4),

Décugis: Don't forget the Massons. Nadine won all the handicap tournaments, and her husband, Willie, organized the first French open championships for indoor play at the Tennis Club de Paris. When one of the two English players, Hough, told him that the playing surface was not good enough, Willie had it all torn up and burned, replacing it with a brand-new oak parquet. He had earned a good deal in Canada, but he certainly could be generous with his money.

Gentien: From 1898 on, games were also played at the Racing Club and at the Bois de Boulogne. And even more on Puteaux Island, where the players went in canoes. My grandmother, Kate Fenwick, who was French champion seven different times, told me about a women's doubles final. They began at two in the afternoon, and by seven o'clock the score was tied at five in the third set. Then one of the young women playing against Kate broke up the proceedings by calmly coming over to the net and stating that she had a dinner engagement in the city and would have to leave.

Décugis: What about Count Voss, the German champion? As soon as the score went against him, he took it as a personal affront and excused himself. "I can only accept defeat at the hands of the Kaiser," he would say.

Gentein: And the Kaiser would only play in the privacy of his castle. At that time you were already becoming our idol, Max. Back and forth you would go to England, then you got engaged to Bobette, the daughter of François Flameng. My uncle, Pierre Gillou, kept a diary bound in black leather for us, in which tennis events were recorded. He called it "The Elegant Drive," and I am sure it was the first daily account of the sport written entirely by hand. . . . Every one of your victories is recorded there.

Reporter: Mr. Décugis . . . Sir . . . Which one of your many victories do you remember best?

Gentien: My Lord! Are you still underfoot? Couldn't you leave us in peace and go and work on your forehand? You'll never become a champion player at this rate.

Gentien was right about my game. But Décugis, older and more patient, answered my question. And this young reporter took his first notes which he would later send to the *Gazzetta dello Sport* (Sports Gazette), published by Gianni Brera, a newspaperman who was thirty years old.

Max Décugis, the little Frenchman who was never still a moment, his hair plastered down, his India-ink eyes snapping, spent eight years studying tennis and English at Woodford and at Twickenham. By the age of fifteen he had already won a doubles handicap with the great Mahony as his partner, and at the age of sixteen, the Renshaw Cup for the Junior Championships of England. By the age of twenty-one he was stronger than the Vacherot brothers, as well as Aymé and Germot, and made a good showing in his first national championships. He would win the men's singles eight times and the men's doubles, with different partners, a total of thirteen times from 1902 to 1914.

The match that gave him international prominence was the finals of the European Championship against Doherty in 1900. That same day Santos Dumont was the first to fly over the Eiffel Tower in his tiny dirigible, and, from the court below, Décugis suddenly saw him lean out, madly waving his straw hat. As they found out later, he was not signaling to the matches on Earth below but was rather trying to put out a small fire!

Among his many memories, Décugis loved to dwell on his victory against Wilding at Brussels, one of the most unbelievable comebacks in the history of the sport. From a score of zero sets to two, love five and love forty, instead of shaking his opponent's hand, he had attacked him and won in the fifth set, à la Rocambole!

The center attack, which has been attributed in error to Cochet, was in reality Max's invention.

In October 1904, upset at the prospect of having to face Gore, he turned to Vaile for advice:

"Play long shots along the center line and then rush the net," the technique-conscious New Zealander had recommended. And

5 

6 

7 

8

9

while Max looked at him in amazement, he added wryly, "If you draw two imaginary lines from your farthest reach on the volley, making their point of intersection the spot where Gore strikes *your* ball, you will make it impossible for him to slip you a passing shot."

Max tried the technique, won handsomely, and, to show his gratitude toward his mentor, translated into French *The Modern Lawn Tennis*, a real masterpiece of technique.

Décugis was the first player to be embroiled in an investigation of charges of professionalism.

The tennis champions of that era were, as has already been noted, men of means who were able to travel at their own expense, build their own private courts, and register with ease for Olympic competitions. Tennis had been one of the ten sports included in the pantheon of the modern Olympic Games, though no one had taken it very seriously.

If the tournament winners were lucky enough to get this recognition three years in a row, they also obtained the additional recognition of the Challenge Cup along with other keepsake awards.

Tired of piling up silver cigar cases and crystal vases, Max proposed that these prizes be replaced with coupons that could be redeemed for prizes. Although he always denied it, in this way he was able to purchase a car. He was a man very hard to get along with, and yet at the same time very much envied. Soon there were complaints about him taking money for transporting early spring vegetables, grapefruits, and strawberries while en route by car from the Côte d'Azur to Paris. Among the witnesses who testified on his behalf was André Gobert, who, side by side with Max, was to win the doubles competition at Wimbledon in 1911.

Gobert is certainly the first good example of a champion *manqué*, despite the fact that he won the Olympic title in 1912 in Stockholm, Sweden, and made the finals of the All Comers at Wimbledon. Gobert was absolutely unbeatable when he was in top-flight form. He was 1.92 meters (6 ft. 3 in.) in height, with a well-developed physique and a second serve as herculean as the first. All that it took, however, was the arrival of the English monarchs, or an unexpected gust of wind to unnerve him and make him lose his pace, just like a trotter in harness racing.

During a Davis Cup match that Gobert had almost won, his team captain, Allan Muhr, saw him suddenly walk over to the umpire's chair and put on one of the sweaters that he always took along with him. It was summer, and the heat was like a furnace. Muhr kept his mouth shut, but one game later, Gobert was back again to put on another sweater. "I've got a chill, and I'm really freezing," Muhr heard him say through chattering teeth. Not long afterward, Gobert managed to worm into the third sweater and to lose the match.

10 

goes out on the courts with Lieutenant Otto von Müller, Frau von Maesler and Miss Duddel. 5. Simond shakes hands with Kreuzer and Wilding with Froitzheim. 6. A very modern backhand shot by Kreuzer, the second-ranking German player after Froitzheim (7), who vied for a long time with Décugis to be the best European. 8. The Berlin Rot Weiss tennis court. 9. Grand Duke Michael of Russia and his wife, with the Doherty brothers sitting directly in front of them, at Heligendamm. 10. Heinrich Kleinschroth, doubles finalist with Rahe at Wimbledon in 1913.

1

2

3

4

5

6

Tennis became very popular with the high society in Europe and the Dominions toward 1880, but successful organization did not begin until the turn of the century. 1. The king of Belgium was an avid fan. 2. De Borman was on the team that defeated France, and he got as far as the Davis Cup Challenge Round in 1904. 3. The star of the Ostende tournament in 1901 was a newcomer, Louise Gevers, who became national champion in 1902. 6. From

Having played tandem with Décugis, Gobert went on to form a solid doubles team with Laurentz, the third member of the great French triumvirate of that period. Laurentz was of Belgian descent and had been trained by the old coach Burke, the Irish professional of the Paris Tennis Club. Laurentz saw his career interrupted almost permanently when one of Gobert's serves that had ricocheted off the wood of his racket hit his eye, detaching the retina. Laurentz was only eighteen years old at the time. When he returned to the courts, he noticed that Gobert avoided him, and he himself went over to suggest that they play together.

Laurentz's life was destined to be tragically associated with tennis. During the world championships, played at St. Moritz on covered courts, he contracted pneumonia, and for six long weeks he was the only guest in a large hotel, whose employees awaited his departure to close for the winter. When the doctors finally decided to take him to Paris, it was already too late to save his life.

The Germans were the traditional enemies of the French in the early years of this century. Wilding, that unbeatable paragon of play, thought that Décugis was stronger than Froitzheim, the number one Prussian. His judgment betrayed an obvious love for France, and perhaps a vague premonition of things to come.

The 1913 Davis Cup Match, the first one played on clay courts and won by Germany 4–1, contradicted Wilding's views.

In Germany the sport had also been born in a resort area called Bad Homburg where many Englishmen went for the cure. Kaiser Wilhelm readily patronized tennis, too. Wilhelm himself never ventured forth from the walls of Monbijou, near Berlin, or from his castle at Homburg, but the heir apparent took part in the tournaments together with Lieutenant Otto von Müller.

The courts at Homburg were seven in number, divided by a green parkway that was shaded by huge oaks into whose dark shadows the ball often disappeared. Even the King of England, Edward VII, praised the beauty of the site, but was rather surprised to find out that the boundary lines were made of wood. Had he ever visited the Lawn Tennis Turnier Club in Berlin, his astonishment would have been even greater, for there the six hundred members trod upon dividing lines of iron painted white.

The patron of the club was the sister of the Kaiserin, who presided in much the same fashion as the Grand Duchess of Mecklenburg-Schwerin at Heligendamm and the Grand Duke Michael of Russia at Baden-Baden. The champions of these noble clubs were Count Voss, noted for his forfeits, and the Countess Schulenberg, who pushed herself into the Wimbledon competition in

7

the left are the Danes Larsen, Hillerup (champion in 1902), Hansen (champion in 1901), and Gudmann. 7. The Hotel Kulm tournament of 1899 in Saint Moritz. 8. A photo souvenir of the participants in the tournament. 9. In Holland the game began on asphalt courts at the Hague: the champions of the 1902 doubles are Van Groenou and Mundt. 10. The Van Aken sisters, blissfully unconcerned at the net. 11. King Charles plays nonchalantly in his suspenders at Cascais in 1901.

8

9

10

11

The heir apparent to the Swedish throne, Gustav, began the sport as a small child and continued in tourney play his whole life long under the pseudonym of Mister G. In photo (4) he is seen with Princess Ingeborg of Denmark and in photo (5) with some of the loveliest young women in the kingdom.

12

1908 and whom the critic Flavelle ranked eleventh among British women players. It is no surprise that, with the worsening of international relations, the title of representative of the country should pass from Count Voss to Otto Froitzheim, chief of police at Wiesbaden.

On the court, Froitzheim exhibited all the qualifications of the profession: his game was remarkably error-free, he showed no mercy, and his reason was never clouded by fantasy. Old Heinrich Kleinschroth, still very much alive in 1973, told this reporter that when Froitzheim was on the court, his friends would bet whether he would pass his opponent on the first or the second shot. Usually it took only one.

"Froitzheim was a sort of Lacoste, and, only errors by the linesmen kept him from beating Brookes in 1914, and probably also the Wimbledon title the same year. For almost twenty years he was the strongest player in the country."

Heinrich Kleinschroth himself, a very rapid doubles partner, light and Machiavellian, arrived at the challenge round of 1913 together with Rahe. Rahe was the owner of a large supermarket, and both he and the Kleinschroth brothers could afford expensive winter vacations on the Côte d'Azur.

The number two man on the first team, Kreuzer, was the exception that proved the rule: he never came to the winter practice quarters at all, for he was from a poor family, had a large number of brothers and sisters, and earned a few extra pfennigs playing a fine game of soccer.

Having beaten the French in 1913, the Germans tried their luck in the United States the following year, where the Americans had regained the Cup from the English. The American team seemed stronger than ever, with the terrible "Comet" McLoughlin backed up by Williams, a character worthy of *The Ambassadors* and its live-all-you-can theme.

Brought up in Lausanne, a junior Swiss champion at the age of twelve, Williams was miraculously saved during the shipwreck of the *Titanic*, while his father, Douane, who had donated the World Cup, perished. Williams brought to the game a kind of exaggerated perfectionism which was even more pronounced than the rugged play of his partner McLoughlin.

Germans and Australians clashed in the first elimination round at the Allegheny Country Club in Pittsburgh. It was August 30, and the fuse lighted at Sarajevo two months earlier was sputtering, now very close to bursting into flame.

Froitzheim and Kreuzer both stated later that if the news of the declaration of war had reached them on the court, they would

13

12. Tennis under the Hapsburgs at Marienbad at the turn of the century. 13. In 1903 at Moffat, the finals of the Scottish championships went to Anthony Wilding, who wrote a book about his one thousand motorcycle journeys. 14. The English champion of Bengal, P. G. Pearson, describes Ilahi, the ball boy from Allahabad, as the best Indian player of that time.

14

1

1. Wingfield's service, with the feet within the diamond directed between the service line and the base line, lasted as long as did the major's influence.

2

2. According to the rules of the Marylebone Cricket Club of May 24, 1875, it became mandatory to place one foot behind the base line and place the ball into alternate service courts.

3

3. In 1880 it became mandatory to have one foot directly on the base line, and the other foot had to remain in contact with the ground. The new rule is here demonstrated by none other than Willie Renshaw.

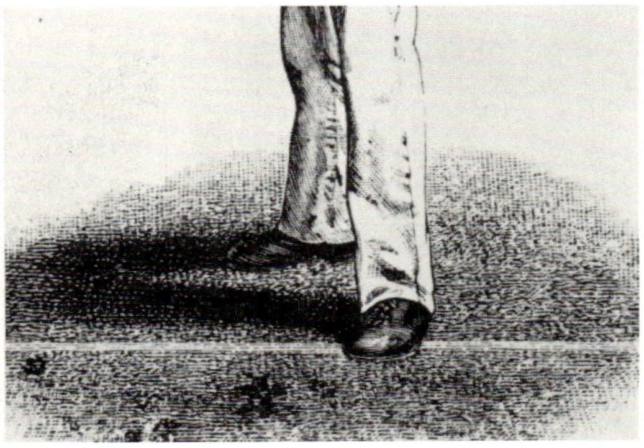

4

4. In 1884 it became legal to lift the foot further from the base line. Our moustached player demonstrates this rule, and at the point of impact with the ball, he will lift his foot even more.

5

5. On December 17, 1902, it was decided that both feet must remain behind the base line. This provision became official on January 7, 1903. Laurie Doherty demonstrates in this picture.

6

6. At the beginning of 1960, it became legal to jump into the air with both feet, and hit the ball with greater freedom, where the scissors leap permitted the player to project himself more quickly toward the net. The maneuver is illustrated by Fred Stolle.

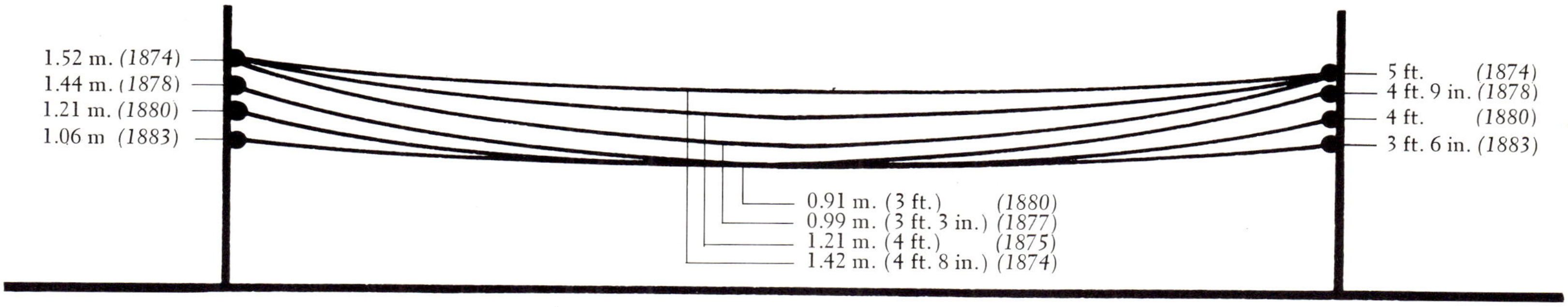

The service, given that name because it originally was served to the batter, was slowly transformed from a courteous way of initiating play to the most aggressive stroke in the entire game. The rules changed as well to keep up with this evolution. At the very beginning, the player could miss the serve as many times as required, but then the rules of rackets took over, and the error entailed the loss of the service (no point awarded to the opponent). A short time before the birth of Wimbledon, with the updating due to Jones-Marshall-Heathcote, the definitive two-ball service was finally arrived at.
Meanwhile, as has been shown in another table, the height of the net was reduced, and the service line slid toward the net, restricting the service area. This writer himself feels, that in order to limit the exaggerated importance of the serve, this area should be reduced even more.
The development of the net in lawn tennis was a painful process. To make things even more difficult, it was very hard to keep the net taut at the beginning, and this made it impossible for rules and reality to jibe fully, as can be seen in photographs of that period. Even in 1900, twenty-six years after Wingfield lodged his patent, the English players lamented the fact that the American net would sag some ten centimeters (about 4 in.) every few games during the first Davis Cup match.
For the reader who has the patience to study the above table, the following data will be helpful in dramatizing the lowering of the net: In the center of the chart, 1.42 meters (4 ft. 8 in.) in 1874. 1.21 meters (4 ft.) in 1875 at Marylebone Cricket Club. 0.99 meters (3 ft. 3 in.) in 1877 at Wimbledon. 0.91 meters (3 ft.) in 1880 at Wimbledon. At the posts, the net descends from 1.52 meters (5 ft.) in 1874, to 1.44 meters (4 ft. 9 in.) in 1878, 1.21 meters (4 ft.) in 1880, and 1.06 meters (3 ft. 6 in.) in 1883, at which point it has remained fixed to the present day. In 1877 the posts themselves were moved apart an additional 0.91 meters (3 ft.).

have thrown down their rackets. The match began in an atmosphere of terrible tension, which Froitzheim was successful in controlling, while Brookes took it out on the ball boys, the linesmen, and the fans, who favored the Germans. In a rain of lively winning shots, the Wizard made a comeback and Wilding defeated Kreuzer.

The declaration of war was announced two days later, at the very moment in which the last tennis ball flew out of bounds. The Australians and the Germans shook hands stiffly, and the defeated team jumped aboard the first outbound steamship only to be stopped at Gibraltar and detained in the United Kingdom.

Froitzheim sent a letter to Commander Hillyard, who was secretary to the All-England Club and very close to the King, asking permission to fight for his country. With equal gallantry Hillyard responded that he did not have the power to authorize such a request. Otherwise, he certainly would also have kept his champions from combat in order to save them, so to speak, for tennis.

Meanwhile Brookes and Wilding, against their will, were finishing the final obligations of Davis Cup play. They defeated the English and then the Americans, despite the fact that McLoughlin qualified as the player who had made the most progress, winning both his points. His first set against Brookes, a violent drawn-out 17–15 which was played entirely on serves, shattered the magic defenses of the old Wizard.

On May 8, 1915 in a trench at Neuve Chapelle, Belgium, Tony Wilding had the chance to relive the match lost against the Comet, and the final at Wimbledon, with his fellow tennis player Barnes.

"We can't always be at our best," he concluded with a tired smile before dropping off to sleep.

The following morning Tony's remains were pulled out of the trench in a mixture of shrapnel, earth, and sandbags. His face was intact. A golden cigarette case, a remembrance of his success presented to him by his partner Craig Briddle, had slipped out of his pocket.

1

2

14 Women Star in Their Long Skirts

The grandstands at Wimbledon were constructed of well-seasoned timber. Commander Hillyard, afraid that the suffragettes might destroy his establishment, contracted with a night watchman, whose name was inscribed in the personnel files simply as Joe.

Excited about the important task entrusted to him, Joe was carrying out his first tour of duty when a suspicious noise reached his ears from B stands. He rushed to the scene and managed to lay hands on the clumsiest of the women assailants who had been trying to set the place on fire.

The following morning, Hillyard accompanied the prisoner to the police station and gave Joe the special reward of a sovereign.

Joe blushed, pocketed the coin, and then disappeared. That evening he returned with an enormous rope, running into Hillyard as the latter was leaving the office. The commander could not hide his surprise, and Joe, with a crafty look on his face, explained:

"It's this way, your honor. If those terrible firebugs are worth a sovereign each, it's a good idea for me to have a rope to tie them up with as I catch them."

It is not unlikely that among these discontented suffragettes were to be found some of the women players rejected by the Wimbledon committee and prevented from competing for a cup awarded by a member who favored women's liberation in 1879.

The Irish proved not to be such misogynists. As early as 1879, in Dublin, they had opened their championship competition to members of both sexes, allowing Miss May Langrishe to make her mark as the first female tennis titlist in history.

Five years later, even the conservatives of the AEC decided to take the plunge, and Maud Watson won the first of her two titles by beating her sister Lillian. With understandable overstatement, Maud complained that the medieval mentality of the organizers had kept her from succeeding for years: from the day of her début at Edgbaston in 1881 until 1886, at Bath, Miss Watson lost none of the fifty-five matches she played, and her opponents totaled only eleven sets wrested from her!

Maud and her sister Lillian were the first players to dress exclusively in white. "In my day," she reminisced, "women played in skirts that reached to the grass, with bright-colored dresses, veils on their hats that were wrapped round their necks, and high heels. We switched over to white, and our blouses had long sleeves, but we avoided starched collars."

At Bath, the city where the Romans had played *pila trigonalis*, Maud saw her excellent record spoiled by a fourteen-year-old girl, Lottie Dod. Lottie had the enviable advantage of skirts that were a good deal shorter, and in view of her tender years, she could play without a hat, wearing a simple coif that often fluttered off into the stands after a violent smash. Even serving underarm as had Maud, Lottie Dod rushed the net in pursuit of a strong forehand, and volleyed high balls with little effort. In 1887 the smiling girl won her first Wimbledon with extraordinary ease at the age of fifteen, and she continued to dominate English tennis until 1894. At the height of her powers, she decided that she was bored by it all and chose to throw herself wholeheartedly into golf. She quickly became the champion of England.

3

4

1. The year 1879 is written at the bottom of this print, which many have taken for a sketch of Wimbledon. The first ladies' championship was organized by the gentlemanly Irish in Dublin in 1879. It is possible that this picture from The Graphic Dramatic Journal *was taken from that source.*
2. Maud Watson was the first woman to win at Wimbledon, where women were admitted on the courts only in 1884. She remained unbeaten for five years, and with her sister Lillian, they were the first to wear white for play.
3, 4. Pictures of the first U.S. competitions, both from 1884. The first is from the Staten Island Ladies Club, the site where Mary Outerbridge set up the first net in the United States. The second is from the Orange Lawn Tennis Club at Mountain Station. In contrast to the English, the American women played dressed in bright colors, as is evident from the picture.

The year before Lottie's reign began, the title had gone to Miss Blanche Bingley, a young woman of whom it was said "that she would never touch her fish with her knife nor a ball with her bare hand." Indeed, Miss Blanche played with her fingers covered in immaculate gloves of calico, which attracted the attention of Commander Hillyard. His curiosity quickly extended to Blanche's other attributes as well, and they were soon married and became the most celebrated family in English tennis.

At their home in Thorpe Satchville in Leicestershire, the most famous greats of the sport could be found on weekends: from the Renshaw brothers to the Doherty duet, and from Dr. Dwight to his pupils Davis and Ward. The court, perfectly tailored due to the happy presence of gentle flocks of sheep and rolled with the collaboration of a horse that was specially shod for the task, was one of the most beautiful in the whole world.

In that Athenian school of tennis were played not only secret return matches but also handicap games between champions, both men and women, and elated mixed doubles. It was there that Dr. Dwight induced Mrs. Hillyard to experiment with a highly controversial technique, the man at the net and the woman in the back court, and when it was Blanche's serve, Dwight would look at her with anxiety, hopeful that she could see the service court. "I can see it very well, right over your head, Dwight," she assured him thoughtlessly, forgetting that the Achilles' heel of that tireless scrapper was his lack of physical stature.

Thanks to her ability to get along with the world's tennis greats, Blanche Hillyard improved her own individual drive until she was finally able to cover up her weak backhand and volley. Capable of beating any young man foolish enough to give her a ten-yard start over 100 yards, Blanche would station herself in the left corner of the court and fire her terrible shots from that quarter.

Mrs. Hillyard never succeeded in defeating little Lottie, but she beat the latter's record, winning six Wimbledon crowns against five for the fickle tennis champion turned golf enthusiast.

Fourteen years passed between Blanche's first and last title, years that were full of garden parties, romances, and journeys; years that brought her in mixed doubles on the same court with four sovereigns, and finally led to her winning the championship of Germany. Her most important rival was Chattie Cooper Sterry, who beat her five times between 1895 and 1913.

Chattie Sterry's nephew Terence recounts "that Chattie was a confirmed health faddist." She would ride with Mahony on his velocipede, the same champion who later died instantly after a bad fall in a curve. After an especially grueling match, Chattie even had the audacity to ask her disappointed rival what the symptoms of a headache were. Her superb physical condition allowed her to play a game of constant attack, and the only hope that her opponents had was the infrequent occasions when she would entangle herself in her voluminous petticoats.

Those terrible long dresses, topped off at the neckline by a harsh and primly starched collar, with its lace festoons, veils, and ribbons, could not help but slow down the imprisoned players. May Sutton was the first woman with the courage to show up at Wimbledon in a dress that could almost be considered short, and her

1

2

3

4

5

1. This picture from 1885 shows the strongest English women players of that period. 2, 3, 4. Miss Blanche Bingley, six times the champion at Wimbledon. In the first picture, she plays wearing gloves. The caption for the third reads: "She has a naturally fine and penetrating serve." 5. Dublin, site of the first women's open tournament in 1879. 6. The Challenge Round at Wimbledon in 1901 between Mrs. Hillyard and Mrs. Cooper Sterry. 7. The challenger, Mrs. Sterry, will win 6–2, 6–2. Her backhand was much better than that of the titleholder. 8. The legendary Miss Dodd won the title at the age of fifteen and later became a golf champion.

6

7

8

1

2

3

4

5

6

Here are views of turn-of-the-century English women tennis champions, as seen in the ovals of their family albums: 1. Ethel Thomson (Larcombe), Wimbledon, 1912. 2. Gladys Lamplough, Indoor Championships, 1907. 3. A. M. Morton, finals of the All Comers, 1902, 1904, 1908, 1909. 4. A. N. G. Greene, Eastern England, 1903, 1905. 5. Blanche Bingley (Hillyard), Wimbledon, 1886, 1889, 1894, 1897, 1899, 1900. 6. Violet Pinckney, London, 1907, 1908. 7. Dora Boothby, Wimbledon, 1909. 8. Chattie Cooper Sterry, Wimbledon, 1895, 1896, 1898, 1901, 1908.

7

8

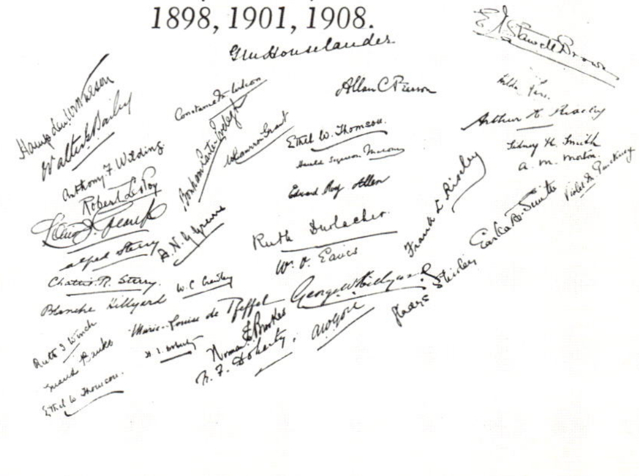

1

2

3

eccentricity in so doing was grudgingly tolerated since she came directly from so barbarous a country as the United States.

Following the tennis rituals of the day, May arrived at the Hillyards' home at Thorpe Satchville, bearing a letter of introduction from Marion Jones, the American champion whose own visit to the United Kingdom was considerably more successful in a personal sense than on the professional level. Marion owed her fame primarily to a match she had *lost* to Elizabeth Moore in the finals of the All Comers Round of the U.S. Championships in 1901. The scores (4–6, 1–6, 9–7, 9–7, 6–3) made the management think things over, and the tournament, which began officially in 1889, was reduced to a more reasonable two of three sets.

Accustomed to hunting, the Hillyards were not easily impressed by the athletic prowess of the American girls: their technique was much more roughhewn than Blanche's. The hosts assigned a pleasant room to the big girl, studied her game, and decided that she was just another outsider. Their judgment was certainly a little premature. At Wimbledon, May really took off, using her overhead serve and attacking the ball with even more enthusiasm than she did her enormous meals.

Once she had won the title in 1905, the first won by a foreigner, May Sutton comforted her desolate opponents with the revelation that she too was part English. She had, in fact, been born at Southampton before her father, a naval officer, received his pension and tried his luck in the New World.

"Dad's passion for tennis was so great," May explained, "that after he had bought ten acres of land in Pasadena, he made my sisters Ethel, Florence, Violet, and me, together with our horse, all pitch in to help him build a court. A short while later the earth embankment collapsed on one side, making it necessary to run slightly uphill in forehand play."

The Suttons quickly got so good that the saying began to go around in California that to beat a Sutton it took a Sutton, and the South California Championship was humorously rebaptized the Sutton California Championship. The four sisters had won a total of eighteen times. Attending one of the first finals matches in 1902 was a girl, only a few months younger than May, named Hazel Hotchkiss.

Though she came from Massachusetts, the cradle of American tennis, Hazel had never attended a match, and she fell in love with the sport immediately. She threw herself wholeheartedly into making up for lost time, getting up at dawn to use the court at the Berkeley campus of the University of California, off limits to women after 8:00 A.M.

At last, when her game seemed good enough to her, she set out in hot pursuit of the four sisters. In 1906 she succeeded in beating the first one, Ethel, at the Pacific Coast Championships.

In the meantime, May had won the American Championships in 1904, where she found the going too easy. She next tackled Wimbledon, where she triumphed in 1905, lost in the finals of 1906, and then proved herself in 1907, the year that Brookes shone as well.

Hazel's winning streak did not catch up with May until the spring of 1910 at the finals of the Ojai Valley tournament. The chubby little queen of Wimbledon easily won the first set 6–2, but in the second she was not able to do the same. At the end of the third set, which she lost six love, she left the court in a huff, refusing even to shake Hazel's hand.

Six months later, the two met again at the Pacific Coast championships, and the whole California tennis world crowded around the central court at the Hotel Del Monte. By dint of tremendous forehand strokes, May won the first set, but as soon as she began to tire, Hazel appeared at the net, ready to destroy her with smashes that were worthy of any man.

The best women English tennis players of the day seen posed in photos (2) and (6), together with the best known men players (except for the Dohertys). Current opinions to the contrary, the game at that time was not so different from the contemporary one.
1. An attack by Chattie Cooper Sterry, on Miss Morton's forehand, during the 1908 Wimbledon finals, won by the former 6–4 and 6–4.
5. Miss Thomson, backed by E. R. Allen, plays the net, while Miss Lambert Chambers places an aggressive drive, and will probably meet Wilding at half court.
3. The Misses Meyer, Pinckney, and Thomson on tour.
4. Miss Martin, women's champion of Ireland in 1902, seen with her basset hound.
7. Miss Stawell-Brown's over-the-shoulder smash and her bow tie, as worn by men, are both far ahead of her day.

4

7

5

6

At the beginning of the third set, Hazel was about ready to serve, when she noticed that her opponent was still seated comfortably next to the umpire. The poor man, covered with embarrassment, informed her that May wanted some tea and a pastry and would not budge from her seat next to his until she had them. Hazel waited, pacing back and forth like a caged lion. Twenty minutes later, nourished and rested, May finally returned to the court and easily took the set from her rival 6–4.

Two years later Hazel married George W. Wightman, who would later become president of the Association, and she left California in the hands of her enemy. Their rivalry continued, however, on a long-distance basis. In 1923 Hazel was successful in instituting a sort of Davis Cup for women, the Wightman Cup, a challenge invitational between the United States and Great Britain. May answered her in 1938 by sending her daughter Dodo to win the Australian championships, the first American woman to do so.

It was from Australia, while May and Hazel were going at it tooth and nail, that exciting news had been received concerning an extremely strong player, Miss Payten, a girl capable of following the serve to the net and of carrying on strong volleying. That world traveler, Dr. Evans, had admired her greatly, and Stanley Doust would assert that she was even stronger than May Sutton, and perhaps even more gifted than the new English star who had replaced Blanche Hillyard.

Dorothea Douglass Lambert Chambers, daughter of an Anglican vicar, had begun by playing against a wall of her parents' home, as many other children did. The little girl must already have had a premonition of greatness, for she lined up all her dolls, bears, and other patchwork animals along the edge of her imaginary center court. Faced with a live turnout at the Centre Court at Wimbledon in the three finals matches hotly contested against May Sutton between 1905 and 1907, Dorothea realized that even she could stand room for improvement.

Between 1910 and 1914 Dorothea was able to perfect a game that Hillyard, the husband of one of her opponents, defined as "extremely talented." "The surprising thing about her was her ability at angle shots. It seemed that she had a mental image of the pattern of strokes at the same time. No other champion, not even Roper Barrett, had been given the kind of talent that the Good Lord saw fit to bestow upon her."

While Dorothea was winning her seventh title in 1914, setting a woman's record that seemed unbeatable at that time, in France a fourteen-year-old girl, Suzanne Lenglen, was awakening the enthusiasm of the residents of Paris with phenomenal exploits in the domain of clay courts. It would take five long and tragic years for Dorothea and Suzanne to meet on the Centre Court at Wimbledon one bright, sunny afternoon.

1

2

3

4

8

5

Dorothea Lambert Chambers (2), the English female tennis star with the greatest popular appeal and winner of seven Wimbledon crowns, is seen in vigorous attack strokes. 1. A high forehand volley. 4. A static serve. 6. A backhand volley. The clips of Marion Jones (5) are much more graceful. She was the U.S. champion in 1899. 7, 3. Two more serves, overhead and underhand, by Mrs. Larcombe, the Wimbledon champion of 1912, and by Miss Robb, the victor of the same tournament in 1902. Surprisingly enough, the earlier pose demonstrates the more modern style. The server keeps her foot on the base line, legal until 1903. 8. A montage of photographs of the strongest French women tennis players of that era. From the left, Suzanne Amblard, the Belgian Mme De Borman, the oh-so-young Lenglen, Berthe Amblard, Mme Golding, Mlle De Poujade, once again Mme Golding, and Miss Broquedis executing an American serve.

6

7

1

3

2

Daughter of an English Navy captain who had moved to Pasadena, California, May Sutton was the first to encroach upon the British domain at Wimbledon. She won in 1905 at the age of seventeen, lost in the 1906 Challenge Round, won it back in 1907, the year of the foreign occupation when Brookes took the singles and Brookes-Wilding the doubles. May was the first to come on the court in half-length sleeves, and her youthful ways, by turns, fascinated and upset the stands, used to the health faddists in their antiseptic white. Her game, which was based on a forehand attack with a good deal of lift (2, 4), often took her to the net. Her serve veered between an over-the-shoulder format (seen in slow motion in 3) and a reverse American serve (6).

8. Waiting for the return in a very awkward pose, during the winning finals match against Lambert Chambers in 1905.

The Sutton sisters, photographed with their father (1), played their doubles game at the net, if this snapshot is to be used as evidence. The picture was taken at the summer court that they themselves built.

7. A strong forehand by Hazel Hotchkiss-Wightman, the great enemy of May Sutton. Hazel won three years in a row from 1909 to 1911.

9. The winner of the U.S. Championships of 1908, Barger-Wallach.

10. Elizabeth Holmes Moore, who won in 1886, 1901, 1903, and 1905.

11. Mary K. Browne, winner in 1912, 1913, and 1914.

12. Molla Bjurstedt Mallory, champion in 1915.

7

8

4

5

6

9

10

11

12

15 Wingfield's Magic Box Arrives in Bordighera

The early history of tennis in Italy is indebted to the activities of British colonialism rather than to native enterprise. In back of the well-attended Anglican Church in 1878, the Bordighera Lawn Tennis Club was engaged in friendly rivalry with the English Committee presided over by the Bishop of London and Gibraltar. Before World War I began in 1914, the two clubs combined had a total of nine courts. When the conflict was over, the British community had swelled to some three thousand souls, and the Colonial English Cooperative for Sports rushed to ready six more courts.

Tiny Bordighera, on the Riviera di Ponente, the Italian section of the Riviera, west of Genoa, had not seen the like before. Where titled Englishmen, or even mere civil servants, used to the warmth of the colonies and enjoying financial advantage based on the strength of the pound sterling over the lira, failed to spread the gospel, a traveling uncle, a friend in the diplomatic corps, or a guest of refined upbringing disclosed the wonders of Major Wingfield's magic box to the eager young Italian gentlemen.

"The unforgettable Senator Pecile . . . presented his son Attilio and his friend Carlo Braida and others of their set with that carton which cost no more than fifty lire and contained four rackets, the net, two end poles, and twelve balls. . . ."

Udine, northeast of Venice, was the site of the beginning of tennis in 1890 due to the good senator's generosity. The procedure was the same as elsewhere in Italy. The sport first took root among the affluent with their country homes and family circles, while the development of tennis clubs came later because it was a new feature in Italian life. The cordial welcome extended to the sport sometimes knew no bounds, and perplexed family members would lament afterwards the destruction of prize firs or plantain trees that later were found to be out of the right of way of the courts and had thus been needlessly sacrificed.

These fragments of old letters, of columns from newspapers, and of specialized journals, must have been known to the anonymous translator of *Wilfred Baddeley's Lawn Tennis*. With his usual foresight, Ulrico Hoepli, the publisher and bookseller to the Italian king, brought out the Italian version of this book in 1898.

In his introduction he estimated that there were between five hundred and seven hundred courts of varying quality in the country: "Those of fair dimension (the few) and those (too many) where the rules are not respected, some of clay, cement or asphalt, and a very few of grass.

"That in itself is something, or at least a beginning. May I note, as well, that of the above figure more than half are scattered in the large cities and in the country residences in Northern Italy, especially in the lakes region. The remainder is to be found divided about equally in the area between Florence to Rome and in the South of Italy. In the past few years the sport has made considerable progress due in large measure to the Italian Association, which has its headquarters in Rome. . . ."

The Association was founded in Rome on April 16, 1894, "with the purpose of promoting and developing the game with all the methods that may be considered most appropriate, especially by awarding prizes and organizing the National Championships." Among the founding fathers were Rome, Milan, Genoa, Turin, Venice, and Vicenza. Many of the individual clubs were organized throughout the last decade of the century: the Lawn Tennis Roma in 1890; the Tennis Club Milano in 1893; and Genoa in the same year. Viareggio and Florence respectively in 1896 and 1898. Arezzo and Premeno both in 1899. By far the oldest of the clubs was the one at Turin, not too far from Bordighera and the Riviera di Ponente: "It was the fourth of April 1880: at the Café Fiorio in Turin several of Count Enrico Cigala's friends had gathered to celebrate his return from London, where he would go every year to spend some time with his English mother's close relatives. Former cavalry officer, a well-known wit, accomplished in every sport, he would make his palatial homes the scene of riding to the hounds, jousts with the foils, and tennis matches. Especially pleased by this new game, at that time still unknown in Italy, he expounded his sporting plans for his friends on the evening of his return from England and invited them to join him in organizing a small tennis club in Turin. Without any trouble he was able to enlist the aid of ten of his friends, among them Count Casimiro Faà di Bruno, Count Emanuele di Rorà, the Squire of Fernex, the Count of Cervignasco, the Marquis Carlo Compans of Brichateau, Count Alfredo Malabaila of Canale, and the Marquis Emanuele of Bagnasco. Not having access to the well-manicured lawns that England was famous for, and hoping to begin practice sessions as soon as possible, Count Cigala turned to the local pallone society, which was located in the moat of the ancient citadel."

Since it was the count who had made the request, after

1

2

3

It was in Bordighera, not far from Turin, that the first tennis game was played officially in Italy in 1878. The English set up there Major Wingfield's net, and the few documents that have come down to us from that period do not show the name of one Italian as having played either on the first court (1) or on the second (3), which was constructed soon afterwards near the Anglican church.
2. The same is true for the presidents of the club, none of whom was Italian up until the Ethiopian war broke a beautiful tradition in 1935. The list of presidents, beginning with 1896, makes this quite clear.
4. The only Italian to be seen is the ball boy, here shown holding a metallic line tracer.

4

much deliberation, the pallone managers conceded to him the use of the court for three hours each week. "There was, however, a striking difference between the rough-and-tumble game of pallone and the more reserved game of tennis, and the guffaws and catcalls of the spectators would have quickly driven off the ten players with their lightly-stroked rallies if Count Cigala's stubborn will to win had not prevailed, keeping his members from breaking rank and giving solid support to the infant sport."

The history of each of the first wave of Italian clubs is similar to the one above. Despite the fact that all the pioneers came from the nobility and were wealthy, the clubs had rough going and were often forced to move, beset by numerous difficulties. The jeering of the pallone players forced the pioneers of the game in Turin to move from the city to a single court in Valentino's park, in 1890. By 1912 they possessed three courts there with 132 members, but the fair of that year evicted them. . . .

In 1883 the municipality of Milan provided the land for five courts on Via Mario Pagano, across from the Church of Corpus Domini. The first cup, which was offered by the president, Count Felix Scheibler, attracted only five registrants: Gabriele d'Annunzio, the famous poet and dramatist who later did much to persuade Italy to join the cause of the Allies in World War I, was one of them, but he had no burning desire to go out on the courts. "He preferred," said Rosetta Gagliardi, "to watch the well-turned heels of the women tennis players."

But it was later necessary to move even from Via Mario Pagano to Via Alberto da Giussano when a radical power block forced

1

Gino de Martino was the first Italian player of international fame. 1. At Wimbledon in 1911, the year of his retirement. 2. A picture taken at the time of his greatest youthful vigor, already symbolically (and in point of fact) crowned with rackets in a photo taken at the Porta Pia Tennis

2

4

3

Club in 1892. A marvel of determination, de Martino won the championship in 1895 and then once again in 1911. 3. One of his attack forehands, showing great vigor. 4. In a white car coat at Territet, with Kleinschroth and Décugis. In that tournament de Martino defeated Wilding. 5. The sumptuous summerhouse of the tennis club at the Cascine, the lovely rambling gardens in Florence, in a photo taken in 1898. In 1910, after an earlier attempt had failed in Rome in 1894, the Italian Federation of Lawn Tennis was founded, presided over by the Marquis Antinori (6), who passed the baton to Beppe Croce from Genoa in 1913, the real father of Italian tennis (7).

5

them out, and then again in 1908 to the Cagnola. In 1914 they transferred operations to Via Domodossola, still operating five courts as they had done twenty years ago. Not a great deal of progress was made, even if there was "a small shelter with a stove made from tin sheets," at the *Circolo di Lawn Tennis* (Lawn Tennis Club) in Rome by 1910, as Augusto Serventi tells us.

6

7

The tennis played in the nineteenth and early twentieth centuries, up to the time of World War I, was not too important in Italy: Wallis Myers, author of the well-known *Tennis at Home and Abroad*, covered the activities in nine European countries, as well as Brazil, India, and what were then the Dominions, but not one line of reference to Italian play was made in the work. Enrico Cigala, the pioneers' champion was, nonetheless, a fine player, more than able to hold his own against the foreigners. After an almost unbelievable victory against the great Wilding at Territet, he retired, satisfied with teaching the game to his sons James and Gingi.

Gino de Martino, obviously a count from his very name, was successful in becoming the first president of the Italian Association of Lawn Tennis in 1894, and, at the same time, the first Italian champion in singles and doubles in combination with his brother Uberto. Among so many gentlemen with classical beauty, Gino was a real athlete with a strong, rugged face, gifted with a powerful Western drive and the ability to follow it closely to the net. His courage as a tennis player was sometimes translated into absolute rashness in everyday life. On New Year's Eve, the astonished passersby saw him set up a large plank extending out over the

1

1. *The first tennis club founded by Italians was the one in Turin in 1880, through the good offices of Enrico Cigala, whose mother was English.* 2. *The first photo of the Turin establishment that we have been able to track down dates from 1906, and the conditions of the court do not offer much encouragement.* 3. *The court at*

2

retaining wall along the Tiber River. Seated calmly astride his bicycle, he hurtled along the length of the board and then flew off in an elegant arc that ended gracefully in the muddy waters, with Gino still calmly in the seat and the maneuver accomplished flawlessly. He won his bet. De Martino's career was unique: he won two titles sixteen years apart.

The founding of the Association had run into a large number of difficulties, not the least of which was the fact that the tennis enthusiasts themselves, instead of taking care of their problems, preferred to play and then to quarrel among themselves, individual against individual, and club against club. After Lionel Hirschel de Minerbi had won the title in 1896, 1897, and 1898, the championships, which had managed to scrape together a dozen registrants, were suspended by the disbanding of the Association.

In 1910 the Florentines were successful in carrying out a brilliant marriage between political and sporting interests, and the

3

devoted players all their lives, and one of the pair, Amadeo, will become an excellent doubles player. 4. A photograph of the spectators at Florence in 1890. 5, 6, 7. Toward the end of the century, Premeno was jokingly called the little Lombardy Wimbledon. 5. The principals of a doubles match in 1901: Lionel de Minerbi, champion of Italy from 1896 to 1898, Tom Antongini, who was better known as a writer and Gabriele d'Annunzio's secretary than as a tennis player, Cornetti, and Wilkinson. 6. The father of Placido Gaslini, one of the most important doubles players of 1930. 7. This young woman, according to the caption on the photograph, is the somewhat mysterious "ladies' champion of Premeno."

4

5

Perugia seems better cared for in this 1901 photo. 1. In this shot from Venice in 1905, the charming woman with her veil and her racket takes a back seat to other matters. The boys on the table top are the two young dukes of Aosta brought by their father to see the matches. They will be

Association was founded once again, on May 18, 1910, with the name of Federazione Italiana di Lawn Tennis (Italian Federation of Lawn Tennis), under the presidency of the Marquis Piero Antinori. The following year, de Martino regained the title, defeated Wilding, lost to Williams in the finals at Territet after five sets, and then retired due to a weak heart. His enemies (and some of them are still living) were rather of the opinion that his illness was feigned and that he was afraid of the younger players, such as the Milanese Suzzi, who was clever and especially able at net play as well as doubles, or Mino Balbi de Robecco, a student of the Marquis Negrotto Cambiaso, a man of classical features who was noted for never playing without his monocle. The natives began to improve with the reading of the English tennis manuals and after a few brave forays on the courts of the Côte d'Azur and Saint Moritz.

Towards the end of this early phase, an English player of average

6

7

After Gino de Martino, Italy had no further champions of international quality but rather amiable gentlemen, dedicated to vacation tourneys and garden tennis. The national championships, interrupted in 1898, began again in 1911, and in 1912–1913 they were taken by Alberto Suzzi from Milan, whom we see here (1), casually smoking his cigarette before descending to the lists.

1

3

ability, like Neville, could come to Milan and defeat the local champions, Toni Antongini and Leonino, leaving him sadly complaining, "He has beaten me, and he is going to stay here for two years!"

Alberto Bonacossa and Gilberto Porro Lambertenghi compiled the first Italian tennis manual with great zeal. At the same time the two Macquay sisters were facing the Bellegarde sisters at Florence, while George Prouse was often losing at the hands of Cesare Colombo. Rosetta Gagliardi and Giulia Perelli thought of themselves as still in their salad days, as did the even younger Riccardo Sabbadini, "the most graceful backhand in the world," according to himself.

2

4

5

6

2. *The Marquis Gilberto Porro Lambertenghi was another moderately good player, but better known as a serious student of the game's strategies, shown here in the cockpit of his plane. He was later shot down in World War I. In 1914 he and his colleague, Alberto Bonacossa, published the first Italian guide to tennis, a superior booklet tiny only in its size. When the war ended, Bonacossa finished the construction of the Milan Tennis Club on Via Arimondi,*

7

"We played without teachers, each of us inventing his own brand of tennis. With the exception of de Martino, none of us knew how to put two strokes together at the beginning. Learning the backhand was everyone's greatest problem. Then we began to improve, and Balbi learned the American serve at once," Serventi tells us.

A serious student and given to endless experimentation, the Marquis Mino Balbi worked doggedly on the construction of airplanes that even managed to lift slightly off the ground, and he also concentrated on new techniques of tennis. Watching him from the edge of the court with his benevolent, gentle, and paternal air, was Beppe Croce, the man who was finally able to organize the Italian federation in the years prior to the war.

8

where he gave the central court his friend Lambertenghi's name to honor the dead hero. 4, 5. Two pictures taken from the manual, posed by Mino Balbi di Robecco, from Genoa, who won the last prewar championships in 1914. Here Balbi demonstrates the American kick serve, the most advanced offensive maneuver of that time. 3. The principals of the 1914 championships seen on the courts at the Cascine in Florence. From the left we see George Prouse, a New Zealander relocated to Italy as a sporting goods representative, who won the mixed doubles together with Giulia Perelli, the charming young woman dressed in a sailor outfit in the center of the group. The second from the left is Riccardo Sabbadini, a terrible tease who won the doubles with Count Balbi, who is in the very proper striped jacket on the right. To his left is Rhoda de Bellegarde, the young Florentine winner in 1913 and 1914, who died in the war and was awarded the silver medal. 7. Another view of Rhoda as seen by the photographers, also in the center of photo (6) with her sister and Margery and Maud Maquay, good doubles players both and Florentines of English descent. 8. A very elegant view of Ms. Perelli. Her low-cut blouse is a little ahead of those Edwardian days, and seems to presage her brilliant career later on.

THE GOLDEN AGE OF MODERN TENNIS

The Divine Suzanne. The Immortal Big Bill Tilden Beaten by the French Musketeers. Fred Perry and the English Revenge. Queen Helen Wills. Don Budge Wins the Grand Slam. The Nobility and Subsequent Condemnation of Hitler's Enemy von Cramm. Tennis in Black Shirts. The War Years.

16 The Goddess of Tennis

Suzanne rubbed her eyes nervously, noticing that her mother had raised the shades in her room halfway, the customary sign in the family that her father was at home for a change. As the heavyset figure in its gray wool suit came in and cast its shadow across the spring light flooding the room, Suzanne suddenly remembered that it was her thirteenth birthday, May 24, 1912!

Her father's face was radiant, and he carried a brand new Driva Champion tennis racket in his hands. His words had a hopeful ring: "Dear Suzanne, here's hoping that this will be the year when you learn that high volley for which Mr. Caudery is so famous!" Suzanne barely had time to reply before her father continued: "If you don't, your father will be very unhappy. Promise me, swear to me, that you will heed my advice and learn it!"

Her mother, seated near the window, nodded in friendly encouragement. Suzanne shook her head in happy assent, and her father hugged her with glee.

The birthday racket was not her first one. Two years earlier, at their summer home at Compiègne, her father had given her a little racket, so light that it looked like a toy. To her usual recreation with the bow and arrow in the Picardy countryside, Suzanne could now add the new pastime of tennis.

At Compiègne, Suzanne would train in the granary of the mill, and when the heat became unbearable, she would go down by the old waterwheel and cool herself in the river. Watching her from the pasture was the only one of her grandfather's 800 horses that her father had refused to sell along with the bus lines that had made the Lenglen family fortune in Paris.

That winter Mr. Charles Lenglen took his two ladies and their inseparable companion, the Pekingese Gyp, to the Villa Ariem at Nice, where the terrace looked out over the clay courts of Parc Impérial. Suzanne had been the terror of the Promenade des Anglais since her early childhood, beating within an inch of his life any boy who dared to challenge her. She began to consider the courts as her own property, as a sort of extension of the garden surrounding the villa.

The secretary, Mr. Caudery, would follow Mr. Lenglen's teaching techniques with amusement as he spread the courts with handkerchiefs, so that Suzanne might try to hit them with her strokes and thus earn a prize of candy. Little Suzanne would play between noon and 1:00 P.M. when her customarily long school day allowed her this luxury. And in the evening, when her homework was complete, it was her father's duty to take her to dancing school, a proper gymnasium for the physical preparation of a future world champion, as far as he could see.

After mass on Sundays, the whole family, including Gyp, of course, would go in a body to the central court of one of the clubs in Menton, Monte Carlo, or Cannes to enjoy the finals of the spring tournaments. Always staying near his daughter, his index finger pointing out a masterful stroke or an error, Mr. Lenglen would advise her to follow the champions' play and would sharply criticize the underhand serve and the lobs of the participants.

Suzanne was determined to play a man's game of tennis and be a real champion, or nothing at all. Her father's admonition was that a star was neither male nor female, but something beyond that crass human distinction, and she set out to reach that happy Valhalla, faced by opponents who were amazed at her virtuosity.

At the Picardy championships in 1912, her first adversary, Madame Butloc, almost refused to go out on the court against that child, who was busily engaged, while waiting for the match to begin, in attracting swarms of black birds by imitating their call! And at the time that her mother accompanied her to Bordighera for the first interclub match, the secretary thought that Mrs. Lenglen was competing and tried to send her into the locker room instead of her daughter. But the little girl could easily handle things on her own. Amused at the incident, the child star went on to leave her adversary, Miss Dale, only one game in two sets.

Suzanne improved with each match she played: capable of returning three hundred balls in a row in her workouts, she certainly was no slave to routine. She served overhead, and the curve described by her strokes, which passed a good half meter above the net, always came within a few centimeters of the boundary lines. As light as a ballerina on the points of her hemp sandals, she quickly dashed to the net to the total consternation of her foes, who had thought that a slow lob would be enough to get by her modest height. Suzanne, who could jump the net with her feet together, would leap quickly into the air, never missing the chance for a smash. Whereas most of her opponents found her quarrelsome, headstrong, and even downright monstrous, the most intelligent of the tennis stars adopted her. Count Salm never missed one of Suzanne's matches and let forth with some unprintable salvos that scorched her opponents.

Dressed in formal attire as a joke, Wilding came out to Villa Ariem to ask Suzanne to play with him in mixed doubles. During their victorious partnership, Wilding never failed to voice his approval, and Suzanne would rise up on tiptoe and let him kiss her nut-brown cheek at the end of each match. Only a few days before the beginning of World War I, Suzanne won the worldwide championship at the age of fifteen, beating Madame Golding in finals play in the shadow of the ancient trees at Saint-Cloud.

The very day of the finals, July 5, 1919, Commander Hillyard, then secretary at Wimbledon, convinced President Wilson Fox that it was time to move to Worple Road to build a new stadium capable of accommodating all the fans who had begun to throng to the box office. In the royal box, a full span above the top hats of her entourage, the gray bonnet of Queen Mary could be seen alongside the derby of George V. The queen was a totally committed fan, and she feverishly recounted for her husband the steps that had carried the tiny French lass to the challenge round:

Suzanne had beaten, in turn, Mrs. Larcombe, the absolute master of the slice, Miss McKane, the best of the young English women players, and finally, 6–4, 7–5, the American Elizabeth Ryan, who rushed the net like a charging young heifer. Mary explained further that in that match Suzanne saw herself tied at five each, but then a rainstorm had given her the chance to catch her breath and to finish off her opponent in two games by following her serves to the net.

The conversation was interrupted by the arrival of the two op-

ponents. At the venerable age of forty years, Mrs. Dorothea Lambert Chambers did not seem any less vigorous than she had been in 1904 while winning the first of her seven titles. Her long and capacious cotton skirt and her blouse tightly closed at the collar gave her gait a certain mechanical air. Suzanne seemed even more diminutive at her side and even more supple, totally at ease under her wide-brimmed beach hat, her arms chestnut brown and exposed by the very short sleeves of her light dress. After the curtseys, which Mrs. Chambers made with the grace of a changing of the guard, the two adversaries squared off to warm up.

Suzanne often came to the net, as unconcerned as if it were a simple training game, to drive back Mrs. Chambers's powerful forehand shots with her tiny forearm held valiantly in front of her body. Her jaws grim to the point of pursing her lips beyond recognition, Mrs. Chambers put a couple of bad shots out of court, and then moved toward the base line to await the little one's first service. Having shut her opponent out in the first game, the champion changed courts with regal bearing, but she had scarcely had time to serve when the ball was returned, out of her reach.

For four straight games, stroking with ease her cross-court forehand, her base-line backhand, her devastating volleys and smashes, Suzanne never let her opponent get control of the ball and made Dorothea feel for the first time uneasy, out of style, and powerless: in a word, old.

It was at that moment, while her whole world was crumbling around her, that Dorothea showed what she was made of. She began to avoid the backhand shots and to muster long forehands from the left-hand corner of the court. Having driven her rival out of bounds, she hit terrifying drop shots which died in the grass ten meters from the young Frenchwoman. Building from 1–4 to 3–5 and lastly to 5 all, with her tiny opponent's set point dramatically reversed by a drop shot, Dorothea played as she never had before. The score 6–5, on her first set point, she thought she had carried the day, but Suzanne, with her typically light touch, cancelled out her opponent's advantage with a high volley, exchanging at the same time a meaningful glance with her father, who was nervously grasping his wife's arm in the section reserved for the special guests.

The game continued, the score tipping crazily back and forth, Suzanne trying to avoid her older opponent's two lethal shots, until it stood at eight all. Here the youngster staked her all on a couple of *en plein*, was successful, and took the first set 10–8.

But she still had work cut out for her. Despite her severe training routine, her endless rope jumping, the hundred-meter sprints, and the strict curfew imposed by her father, Suzanne was not used to concentrating for long periods. Her game, though it was still beautiful to witness, lost its vigor, and at 1–3, a long unsuccessful sustained rally made her raise her bleary eyes toward her father. Mr. Lenglen got to his feet and tossed a shiny object to his daughter. It was a tiny silver flask, and while the umpire, Mr. Hillyard, threw an incredulous glance at Max Décugis, one of the linesmen, Suzanne took two deep draughts and immediately returned to the attack. The good vintage cognac was quickly burned off in a series of flaming volleys.

The photo of Suzanne on the preceding page was snapped by Henri Lartigue when the diva was only fifteen. In our photo album (1, 2, 3, 5), the three most important matches of the tennis goddess. Moments from the first Wimbledon victory in 1919 against Dorothea Chambers, the holder of seven titles. The twenty-year-old Suzanne won 10–8, 4–6, 9–7, saving two match points. 1. Suzanne is serving. 2. Mrs. Lambert Chambers swings into position for one of her terrible forehand shots. 3. The Englishwoman at the net while Suzanne is passing her with a drive. 5. The goddess once again, serving, under the admiring eyes of Queen Mary. 4, 6, 11, 12. Testimony of the only match she lost during her triumphant career, when she withdrew in 1921. 4. Suzanne in her fur coat seen with her rival Molla Bjurstedt Mallory. 6. Under attack on the Central Court of the West Side Tennis Club in New York, with Mrs. Mallory at the net. 12. Comforted by the French representative de Joannis, Suzanne leaves play, the victim of a bout of coughing and weeping. 11. A wicked caricature showing the dominator in turn being dominated. 7, 8, 10. Photos of what was later defined as the match of the century at the Carlton Tennis Club in Cannes. 8. The goddess seen with Helen Wills, then twenty-eight years old. 10.

1

2

3

4

Wills congratulating the victor. To the right of the photo a hand can be seen with palm upraised, a gesture intended to stop the proceedings and continue the game. The voice that had called the fateful match point was that of an overexcited fan, not one of the linesmen as had been supposed. 7. The match continues, and although attacked by violent drives from her opponent, Suzanne will avoid disaster as always, going on to win 6–3, 8–6. 9. The goddess together with her favorite doubles companion, Bunny Ryan. No other doubles partners ever bested their performance.

5

6

7

8

9

10

11

12

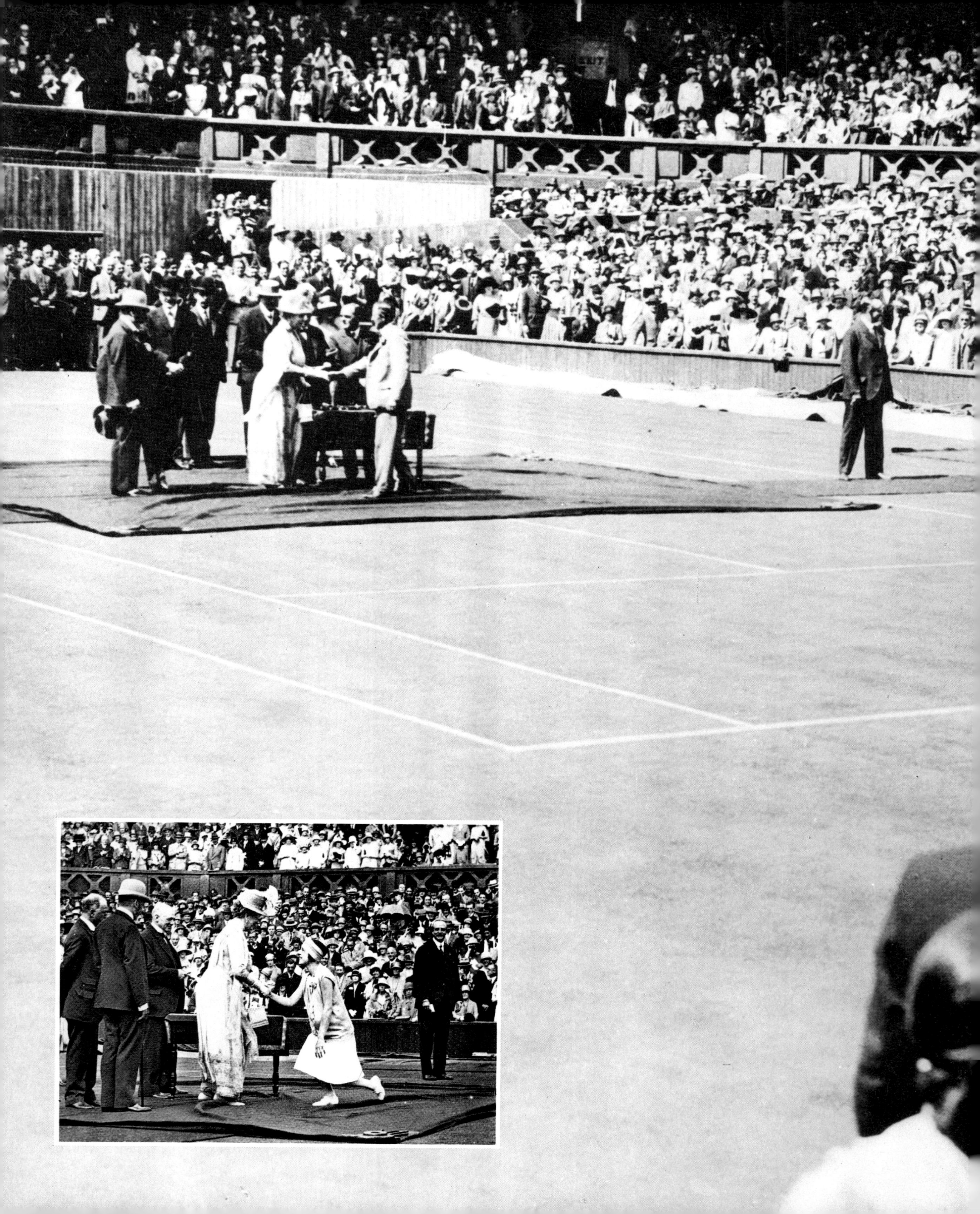
EXIT

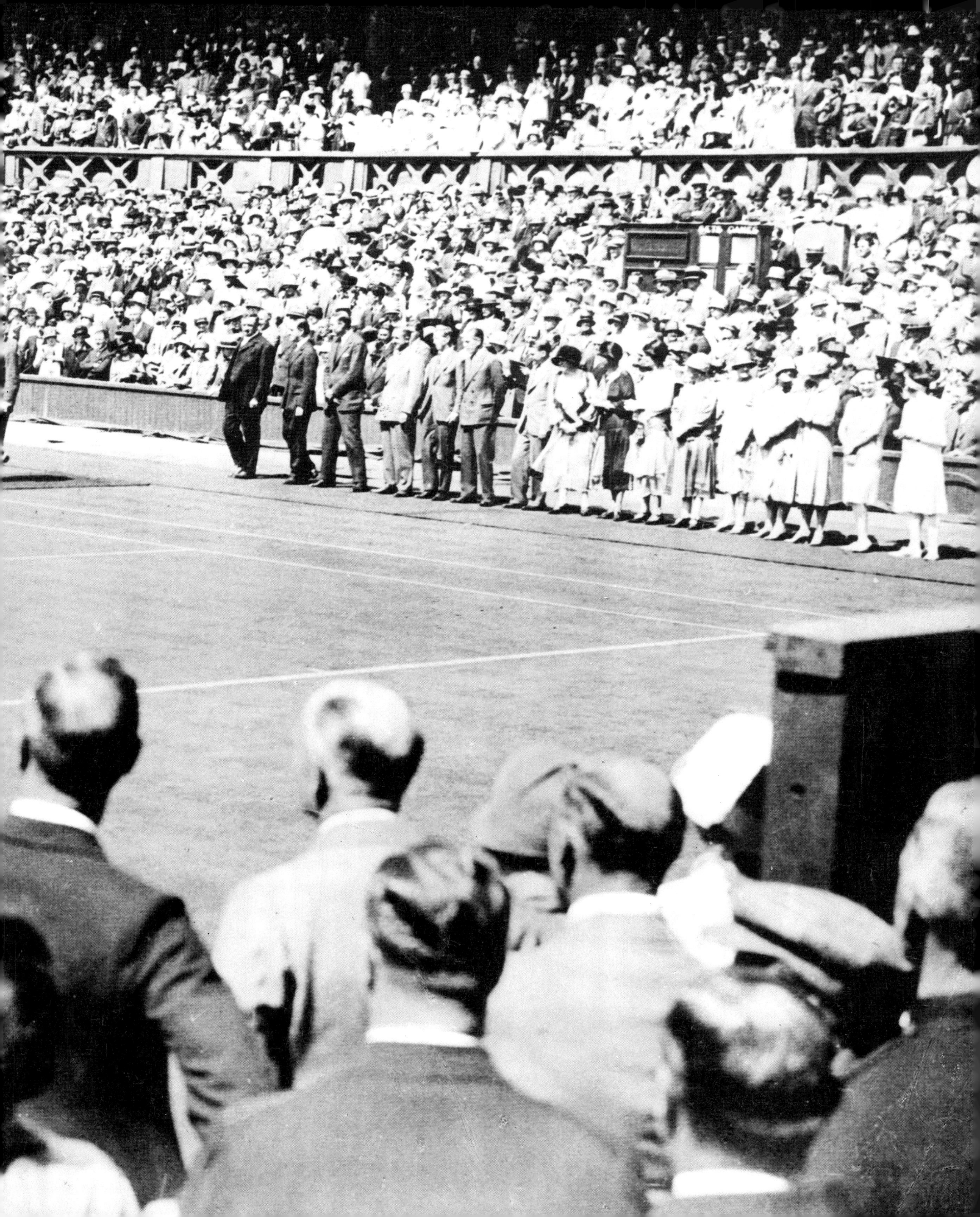

On the preceding pages: Awarding the prize to the winners at the 1926 jubilee of the Wimbledon matches. In the large photograph Suzanne is the second in line from the right and in the small insert she is seen curtseying before Queen Mary and King George (in the homburg). A few days later, due to having missed a scheduled game, Suzanne had lost favor with the monarch and retired both from the tournament and from the game itself. A few samples of Suzanne's style follow on these pages: a brand of tennis of incredible athletic tone and yet with a light touch that actually seemed to defy the law of gravity. 1. A volley slightly behind the service line. 2. The follow-through of a lifted backhand. 3. A violent attack drive from the left.

1

3

2

4

4. A scissors leap to get the smash, observed by the goddess's favorite mixed doubles partner, Toto Brugnon. 5. Another extraordinary leap into the air, during the execution of a backhand volley, admired by Patterson. 6. This attack flight inspired the choreography of Debussy's Jeux, *a ballet which was staged in Berlin in 1931.*

5

6

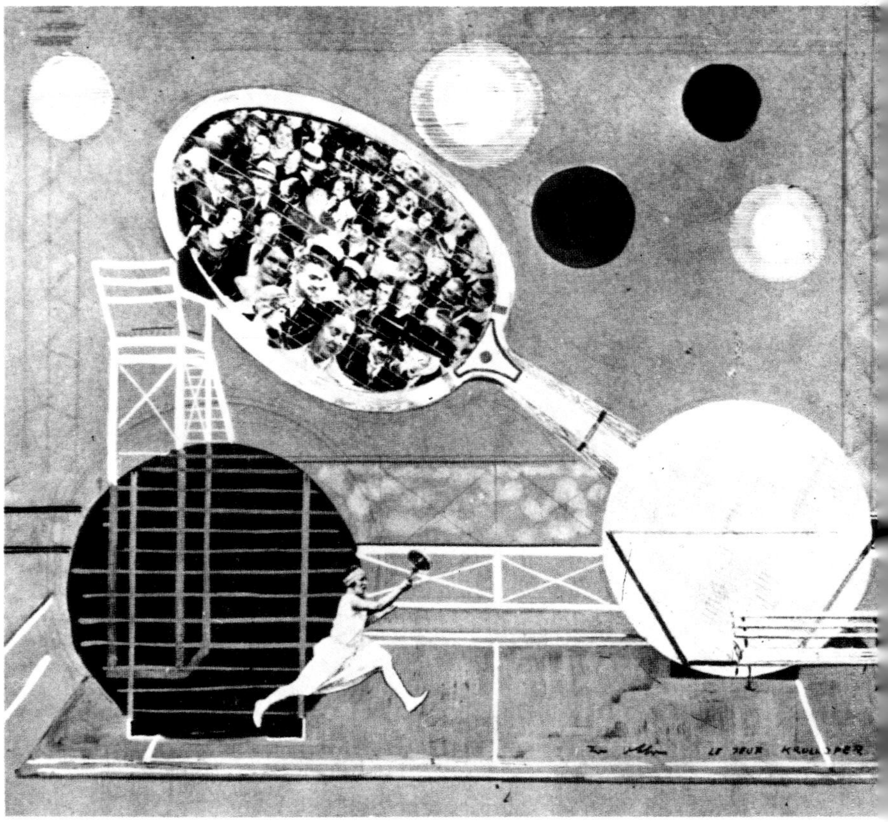

Back to four games each, Suzanne found herself unable to end the set, and Dorothea tied the match at one set all. After twenty-eight games, the elderly queen and the heir apparent to the throne were still tied. Suzanne began to push, but her lack of energy rendered her ineffectual at 4–1. With methodical ferocity, Dorothea caught up with her and then took the lead and garnered the vantage of two match points (6–5, 40–15). She waited, at the base line, for her opponent to rush the net. Suzanne, who was by this time completely exhausted, was acting from raw courage.

She moved to the attack instinctively and stretched desperately for Dorothea's passing shot, playing the ball off the frame without seeing where it landed. To her amazement, she heard from the gasp in the stands and then the applause that the ball was good. Dorothea did not have time to recover her composure. Suzanne's deep backhand caught her off balance. Her cheeks aflame and her eyes glistening with happiness, Suzanne once more took control, and the older woman again felt the helplessness of age. The tiny marauder finished her work 9–7 and rushed to embrace her victim, while Max Décugis himself rocketed toward the two of them to congratulate her with a kiss. Queen Mary smiled as she saw the youngster break away, cross the court like an arrow, and bury herself, wild with joy, in her father's arms.

Suzanne was probably better described as unreachable than unbeatable. The finals match against Dorothea signaled a series of victories against all the opponents who tried their strength against her. She was so much better than all of them that they soon counted their blessings if they were able to wrest at least a few games from her, not to mention a set. The following year at Wimbledon, the bruised and beaten Dorothea was able to take only three games from the Frenchwoman in the finals. The same year, when asked to participate in the Olympic games at Antwerp, Suzanne lost only four out of sixty-four games.

Her fame quickly spread far and wide, and soon the term Suzanne the goddess, was born, though it is unknown who coined it. She was without a doubt the first real prima donna that the game of tennis had ever seen. Patou became her modiste, and she became the pattern for fashion-conscious tennis players everywhere. Suzanne held her dark hair in place with a headband of tulle, which she constantly changed, along with her gay sweaters. She was one of the first to bring colors out on the court and was careful to coordinate her color scheme with the green of the grass and the red of the clay.

At the Côte d'Azur handicaps, Gustav V of Sweden argued with Manuel of Portugal to decide which of them would have her as partner in the mixed doubles, and after the game, the Swedish monarch joined Suzanne's intimate circle of friends at Villa Ariem. Among the chosen few were Henry Gerbault, who was leaving tennis for the sea, Coco Gentien, Claude Anet, and Pierre Albarran (her biographers), the Romanian Mishu, who cheered everyone up by sitting at the piano and improvising crazy ditties, Toto Brugnon and Elizabeth Ryan, who had been chosen as her partners in doubles play. In that bourgeois parlor, where the heavy

1

2

Suzanne Lenglen was the first woman to turn professional in 1926. 1. She shakes hands with her opponent, the American Mary Browne, during a night match at Philadelphia. 2. Seen here with William Tilden. The two stars detested one another and this is the only photo of the two smiling. 3. Suzanne with her mother and with one of the great loves of her life, the American tycoon Baldwin. 4. Back in Paris, she follows the ballet mistress Pavlova and teaches tennis according to the canons of dance.

mauve cretonne draperies kept out the sun and the thousand or so trophies that the divine one had won in the dark, many notables met and chatted, such as Rudyard Kipling, Arnold Bennett, Douglas Fairbanks, Mary Pickford, the Maharajah of Kapurtala, and Lord Rocksavage.

Suzanne's lack of physical beauty was totally overcome by her gay, vivacious nature, and she was no plaster saint, being the first to suggest dinners, balls, and entertainment. Every season she thought anew that she had found the man in her life, and every season she returned to her mother's arms, tearful and disillusioned, asking her father's pardon for having forsaken her training routine for a romance. Monsieur Charles would patiently hold her tiny hand with its long, brightly lacquered finger nails, then lead her like a child to the tennis court where the handkerchief targets had already been scattered. It suddenly seemed to Suzanne, as she got back in stride, that all the weeping that she had gone through was nothing more than a bad dream. After a half hour of practice she had found her magic touch again. And after jumping rope a hundred times, she felt once again unbeatable and happy with her lot.

If Monsieur Charles had not loved her more than life itself, and if he had not, for once, let himself be influenced by his wife, Suzanne would still be the only women's tennis player with an unbeaten record. He could not resist the entreaties of his two ladies, however, who joined forces to insist that he accept the invitation of Miss Ann Morgan to a series of benefit matches to raise funds for the regions devastated by World War I.

Down with a hacking cough, Suzanne was forced to promise that she would not play in the United States Championships, but when she arrived in New York she let the French representative, Monsieur Albert de Joannis, enroll her against her better judgment.

She was coughing badly, she probably suffered badly from asthma, and seasickness had all but wiped her out. Deprived of the support of her father, besieged on all sides by myriad requests, she just did not have the strength to say no. The draw assigned her a very easy first round, but then her opponent, Miss Goss, decided to withdraw, and this left her faced with Molla Mallory. Molla had come to the United States from Oslo, Norway, in October 1914, saddled with the difficult family name of Bjurstedt, a nurse who was also licensed as a masseuse and endowed with an irrepressible *joie de vivre*. As the Norwegian champion, classed third in the 1912 Olympics, Molla sensed at once that tennis was an excellent shortcut to society. Enrolled in the tournament sponsored by the Seventh Regiment Armory, the most "in" of the indoor clubs, she won and soon became the darling of society.

She was a fascinating woman, with high cheekbones and dark almond eyes, a reminder of her Lapp heritage, endowed with the bright sparkle of a courageous and indefatigable player. Her terrible Western forehand, her ability to play a game of attack from the base line, and her indomitable fortitude carried her quickly to victory over the strongest American competition. She won the U.S. championships in both 1915 and 1916.

In June of 1921 Miss Bjurstedt became both champion and the wife of a wealthy man, and finally transported her baggage to Paris and Wimbledon for the two most important world tournaments. At Saint-Cloud she lost in the finals, winning five games from Suzanne; at Wimbledon she was defeated by Bunny Ryan's terrible slices, and then saw her, in turn, go down to defeat at the hand of the divine Suzanne, with only two meager games to her credit. Molla had, however, one advantage over all of Suzanne's other rivals: she was not under the spell of the divine player, she harbored no special hatred for her, and, above all, she did not believe her gifted with any mystical invulnerability.

This serene attitude, coupled with Suzanne's hacking cough, was enough to make Molla the only one to beat her. The victory was no ordinary one, for Suzanne, having lost the first set six to two, could only muster two sustained rallies in the second, finally fell to the grass coughing badly, and had to retire from the lists amid the jeers and catcalls of the spectators. In the midst of the confusion, while Julian Myrick, the president of the American Association, was requesting the disqualification of the Frenchwoman, Mr. de Joannis was doing all he could to avoid coming to her defense. The physician finally diagnosed that she was suffering from whooping cough. Molla came through it all with flying colors and even offered Suzanne the chance to rest before continuing the competition.

The newspaper accounts that followed were often somewhat lacking in objectivity, and though the Norwegian clearly analyzed the reasons for her victory, at the same time she failed to bring to the public's attention the fact that Suzanne was not in good health. It is also true that many people were tired of Suzanne's reign, and even more of the excesses that marked it. The next encounter of the two women, at Wimbledon in 1922, was therefore able to awaken greater enthusiasm on the part of the fans than had the Lenglen-Lambert Chambers affair.

In a burst of husbandly enthusiasm, Mr. Mallory had bet more than $10,000 on his helpmate. At the same time Suzanne's father and family doctor had implored her not to compete since she was nervous and in low spirits. Suzanne and Molla got to the finals with little effort, and had to wait almost two hours, from five to seven, for the rain to stop its endless staccato on the canvas tent that covered the stands at Centre Court with its crowd of the faithful.

In her dressing room Suzanne argued with her mother, then asked her friend Bunny Ryan to leave her alone. A few minutes

3

4

later she sent someone in frantic haste to look for Bunny, then tore off her tulle headband, and redid her lips at least ten times with the lipstick that she carried constantly in her hand. Those nerve-racking minutes spent in front of her magic mirror had made her taut and brittle. On the court her Driva Champion strings failed to respond somehow to her touch, and her every stroke went foul. At the end of the first two games, which she quickly lost, it seemed that her end was near. Her splendid limbs offering her solid support and a picture of health, Molla could not refrain from a smile as she began to punish her opponent with her straight and true forehand shots. But suddenly, as if by magic, Suzanne's balls acquired speed and precision, and she began to place them further and further away and closer to the sidelines in a progression not unlike musical notes. Suddenly gone stale and covered with shame, Molla found herself unable to face the curious glances of the eight thousand onlookers and their pitying and encouraging applause. Suzanne quickly won twelve games in a row in twenty-two minutes. Then she shook her rival's hand while hacking softly, and quickly turning her back, went toward the central pavilion to receive the congratulations of that other and older queen.

Suzanne's reign had begun again. She was becoming more famous and more exact in her refinements. She was more and more lionized, and above all, more and more worn down. Molla stubbornly insisted on taking her on once again at Nice, and for her trouble was severely trounced in duplicate six love sets.

The public no longer asked who Suzanne's rivals were and began to balk at attending tourney play at which the tennis goddess did not appear. The organizers would go to any lengths to insure her presence. They would offer Monsieur Lenglen one thousand francs as a wager that his daughter would not participate, and he, smiling craftily, would take them up on the bet.

Placido Gaslini, one of the diva's best friends, recounts that they went from Venice to Saint Moritz in a private railway coach, and that as soon as they arrived Hans Badrutt greeted Suzanne with a carriage and eight horses.

John Tunis reminisces how a little elderly English woman showed up in the office of the secretary of the tennis club in Monte Carlo to purchase a ticket to Lenglen's first match. The secretary, Mr. Henley, responded that Suzanne was unfortunately suffering from jaundice and could not participate in the tournament. The elderly woman walked off shaking her head. In a few minutes she reappeared to ask if at least Suzanne was planning on *attending* the competition. When told that Miss Lenglen was indeed going to attend, she happily purchased a reserved seat as near as possible to where the tennis goddess was supposed to sit.

Suzanne's health had become very weak. Her biographers speak of two types of jaundice, of insomnia, of frequent uncontrollable crying spells. Only one of them makes any mention of the time when she pleaded with her father to allow her to leave the court. Suzanne only met with the grim response that she could do so only when she had won. In 1924 the goddess had to bypass the Olympics, and at Wimbledon the physician insisted that she withdraw after her exhausting match against Bunny Ryan.

When in 1925 she returned to play and win, it seemed that her illness had taken its toll, if not of her style, at least of her strategy. She no longer took risks and preferred to handle her opponents with long cross-court shots, bring them to the net and then devastate them with backhand passing shots, as they stood speechless and totally off balance.

This new edition of the old Lenglen, less brilliant but more dependable, once again took the Wimbledon crown with a total of five games lost in as many matches. The reporters in desperation decided that the only one who could beat her was Helen Wills, the same girl who had won the gold medal at the Olympics during Suzanne's illness, had reached the finals at Wimbledon, and was now the dominant force in the United States.

Helen had a straight nose, a well-rounded mouth, a lovely oval face that framed large, coldly intelligent eyes. Her expression reflected great intensity. The reporters, according to a ditty current at the time, "a ribald race, had called her little poker face." She never spoke to her rivals on the court and had learned to accept the most poorly founded judgments of the umpires with a fatalism that stood in marked contrast to the vitality of her game. The pesky attacks of small-minded reporters, vainly in search of tidbits of gossip, caused her no concern once she decided not to buy the newspapers; for she decided, she could get a better idea of herself without such reading.

Helen was born in the country, and as soon as the family was established in Berkeley, her father, who was a doctor, enrolled her in the club there, noted for its illustrious traditions. Under the guidance of Pop Fulmer, she quickly began to play only the boys. She was looking for something to substitute for the games of cowboys and Indians, the duck hunting expeditions with dog and gun, and tennis permitted her painless entry into the adult world, because she had long believed in Santa Claus.

Her impressive forehand, unequaled among women players, was developed during the visit of Little Bill Johnston to Berkeley. Clutching with difficulty the enormous handle of that fifteen-ounce weapon, identical to the one used by Little Bill himself, she would repeat softly, "I am Johnston, I am Johnston," and she soon began to resemble him, at least in the forehand. When she was only fifteen years of age, she won the American championship

1. Suzanne Lenglen died of leukemia at the age of thirty-nine. Brugnon and Borotra sorrowfully follow her funeral cortege.
2. At Nice a street was named in her honor.

1

2

Helen received a kiss and a marriage proposal from a handsome young man, Freddie Moody.

A sudden attack of appendicitis, which had the whole American colony in Paris talking, prevented Helen from her rematch with Suzanne. The goddess of tennis sent her rival a huge bouquet of red and yellow peonies and then left for London. Suzanne was looking forward to a seventh triumph, which would have equaled the record of Dorothea Lambert Chambers the same year as the jubilee of the championships.

With Helen out of the way, the competitors were her old and overly affectionate friend Bunny Ryan, the heavier Miss Mallory, and the Englishwoman Miss McKane, who was now Mrs. Godfree. Despite the fact that the stubborn omission of the seeding procedure had assigned Suzanne an opponent like Mary Brown in the first round, the only one who could give her trouble and had the talent and personality to replace her one day, was Lilí de Alvarez.

A Spaniard born in Rome, with the modern outlook to the point of wearing tulle trousers under her skirts that captivated King Alfonso's attention at Wimbledon, Lilí played a game that was all her own, sparkling with continual attacks, hazardous shots, and half-volleys. The heedless luxury of such improvisation would have required the sacrifice of the sort of rigorous athletic training that Lilí had no intention of undertaking. Her most interesting matches were often those where she missed victory only because of her poor condition. Because Suzanne was a victim of insomnia and poor nerves, Lilí was the only opponent that the Divine did not feel confident of beating easily.

The wife of the French ambassador, Madame de Fleuriau, had plans to present Suzanne at Buckingham Palace immediately after the tournament. During the presentation of the champions at Wimbledon, which brought together about fifty celebrities on the Centre Court, it was Queen Mary herself who introduced the star athletes. Amidst smiles, applause, and testimonials, Suzanne gave a tired imitation of herself. Lady Wavertree put her huge black touring car at Suzanne's disposal, her mother calmly put up with her tantrums, Coco Gentien amused her with adventures of the writer Marcel Proust as a tennis buff, and Commander Hillyard followed her like an obedient slave.

Queen Mary herself, fascinated behind her dark glasses, did not miss a single point, and, after the first singles victory of Suzanne over Mary Brown, she let the organizers know that she would attend the matches the following day. Up until that time either the secretary Hillyard or one of the French players had been in the habit of letting Suzanne know when she was scheduled to play. With Hillyard absent, no one thought of informing Suzanne, and she left the club with the idea that she was to compete only in the doubles. To please the queen and bring that insufferable star into line, the referee Burrow decided to set another time for her to play singles competition, two and a half hours before the doubles.

At this point the sources contradict each other. Some confirm that Suzanne, who was not in the habit of reading the newspapers, was never informed of the singles encounter. Others are just as sure that Didi Vlasto, the new partner assigned her by the French Federation, told her toward eleven o'clock in the morning, and that Suzanne at once sent word to Burrow that she could not break a previous doctor's appointment. The referee and the most loyal monarchists assert that Suzanne Lenglen, in a burst of foolish pride, tried to impose her authority over that of the association and Queen Mary herself. However that may be, Suzanne finally arrived at the club around three-thirty in the afternoon. Her dark glasses staring at the empty Centre Court, Queen Mary had been waiting in silence for more than a half hour. The bureaucrats called an emergency meeting with their rebellious starlet. She brazenly stated that she had no intention of tiring herself out before a decisive doubles match, and they in turn upbraided her and threatened her with disqualification. Her English was not equal to the occasion, and Suzanne stalked out of the office, shouting invectives in French, and closeted herself in the dressing room reserved for the lady champion. Shaken with sobs, she stubbornly refused to come out, deaf to all appeals. Not even the entry of Borotra, blindfolded with a towel and guided by Didi Vlasto succeeded in moving her.

This was the last attempt of the terrified officials. Borotra went to the royal box and apologized profusely to the queen in his name, in that of the team, and in the name of the French Republic. Stating wisely that the most gifted tennis player was less important than the Wimbledon matches, Burrow recommended that Suzanne be disqualified. Her singles and doubles opponents disagreed and insisted that the games be played the following day. After numerous discussions, the conservatives were defeated and Suzanne's two matches were put off, as she herself had requested, with the doubles competition to be played first the next afternoon.

Suzanne and Didi Vlasto were twice within a point of victory and then lost, but eventually the rain allied itself with the tennis goddess and her inevitable victory against a certain Mrs. Dewhurst was put off for a day. On Saturday Suzanne returned to Centre Court, having been deserted by the queen, and was greeted by a stony silence charged with bitterness. Borotra, her partner, dispelled the tension with a few witty antics, but the tennis goddess felt herself crushed down by the accusing silence of those thirteen thousand fans who had idolized her up until two days before.

Suzanne spent a nightmarish Sunday, and on Monday announced her retirement from the tournament. Once back in Paris, she accepted $100,000 from the American entrepreneur, Charles Pyle, for taking part in a tour of the United States, accompanied by Mary K. Browne, Vincent Richards, the Olympic champion in 1924, Howard O. Kinsey, and Paul Peret. If the tour was an almost total disaster, Suzanne at least met Shaky Baldwin, whom she loved desperately for four years, until boredom set in about the same time that his divorce was finalized. Miss Lenglen returned to Paris, and, more and more like Pavlova, organized and directed a school where tennis was taught in accordance with ballet methods. She died of leukemia on July 4, 1938, when Helen Wills was taking her eighth victory at Wimbledon, smashing all previous records.

17 The Immortal Big Bill

Once while William Tilden, known as Big Bill, was signing autographs, a rather forward young man asked him why he only signed his last name. Big Bill stared at the questioner with his knowing, slightly wicked look, and then burst out laughing, "Do you think that Garbo signs her autographs any differently?" The son of a fine pianist and a businessman with an interest in politics, Bill had taken after his mother, and his whole life was a continuous and rather pathetic effort to become what he called in vague general terms "a creative person." Despite the fact that he managed to collect two thousand opera records, his froglike voice never let him do more than sing in the bathtub, and he had to wait for the push that came from his tennis popularity to become even moderately well known on the stage. Even then he did not overly impress the Broadway critics and was successful only in getting the part of Dracula in a sixteen-week road show. His friendship with many movie stars like Katherine Hepburn, Charlie Chaplin, Mary Pickford, and Douglas Fairbanks, did not keep his film career from being limited to two tiny parts in two silent pictures. His plays have been lost, and the two books of short stories that he was successful in publishing are not great literature, tied to the trite theme of the friendship between the veteran champion at the sunset of his career and his radiant young disciple.

Unfortunately a failure both as a theatrical and literary talent, Tilden made his weight felt in the minor art of tennis as had no other. With hard work that began to show results when he was twenty-seven, he devised a very modern all-court game, a synthesis of Larned and Whitman's ground game and McLoughlin's net attacks. He was without doubt the first real intellectual of the game, and the first to introduce elements of psychology, tactics, and even ballistics in his splendid technical writings: the best of his books is titled *The Art of Tennis and the Spin of the Ball.*

Bill's perfectionism, his capriciousness, and his unbridled egocentrism set him in opposition to the establishment. Authentic snob that he was, he spent a good deal of his life scandalizing, ridiculing, and even insulting the directors of the Association. They responded by directing against him their unstinting dislike and even disqualifying him the night before a Davis Cup finals on one occasion, only to eat their own words when the State Department intervened on his behalf! His frustrated theatrical ambitions, paired with his deep strain of narcissism, combined to make him a much more interesting personality and certainly just as well known as a Bobby Jones, a Babe Ruth, or a Jack Dempsey, the other sports heroes of his day.

Whenever Bill was out on the court, one could expect a fine job of acting, but according to someone who knew him well, it was impossible to know what role he would play at any given time. He was indeed acting like a second Maecenas when in Davis competition he gave a whole set to the Australian Anderson in order to correct the judgment by a linesman who awarded him a set point in error at the end of the second set. On another occasion he was rather an irate Achilles, who, after sulking for a time in his dressing room, returned to the court to play dead against his friend Johnston after erroneous judgments by the linesmen and an unnecessary change of court. Finally, at Wimbledon, against a Cochet who thought himself beaten, two sets down and 1–5 in the third, Bill suddenly had the characteristics of a Hamlet, incapable of any action or any decision making until all of seventeen points had been lost!

These extravagances did not negate his fair play toward his opponents, and there was no one among his victims who did not think highly of him both as a person and a player. Big Bill was certainly no ingrate where his opponents were concerned, and returned in kind *their* kind words, praising Johnston more than anyone else, "the man who forces me to bring out the best that is in me," and Cochet, "a revolutionary who has brought tennis one step higher in the area of technique; the only one to beat me more times than I did him in our days as amateurs." The only two that he thought very little of, to be frank, that he detested cordially, were Suzanne Lenglen and Jean Borotra.

Of the first-named he indulged in poor taste when he wrote that she seemed to combine the characteristics of a streetwalker and a prima donna. "With a white fur wrap over her tennis outfit, and a turban of a brilliant red color on her head, I was deeply grateful that no bull showed up in the area." Once he was able to lure her out on the court in Paris, he devastated her with a violent six-love set, and then fed her lack of self-confidence before her match with Miss Mallory by blurting out in her presence that the Norwegian would destroy her.

Of Borotra Tilden said that he attained "first-class results with second-class technique, and that he had the enchantment, the color, the charm, and, most important of all, the insincerity of Paris." In brief, he was at the same time "artist and charlatan, the greatest showman and the greatest huckster in the history of tennis." It boggles the mind to try to understand how a man like Borotra, who never beat him in outdoor competition, could have given Tilden such trouble. Borotra had the Parisians whipped up to fever pitch, had stirred up the English, including the queen, and even in the United States his brand of theater tennis went over well, where his style of histrionics provoked less criticism than did Bill's.

The American public, not to mention the establishment, always took the side of Johnston, Tilden's best friend and at the same time his fiercest rival, whom they renamed "Little Bill." Johnston, who came from the cement courts out in California, made a name for himself ahead of Big Bill Tilden despite being a year younger. He ranked number one in the U.S. classification of 1915, and reappeared on top in 1919 until he was beaten by Big Bill by a very small margin.

The physical contrast made their duels even more memorable. "With his sandy hair, thin and with an anemic wanness, dressed in a jacket and tie, no one would have taken him for a great champion;

2

1

1. Tilden and Johnston at the entrance to the Center Court at Forest Hills. The occasion is one of the seven finals matches of the U.S. Championships that the two hotly contested. Johnston took only the first in 1915. 2, 3. Johnston's legendary forehand drive. 4, 5. Tilden's forehand. Johnston has a Western grip, his arc is very pronounced, the movement a synthesis of many other similar strokes that were typical between 1910 and 1920. Tilden's play is much more modern, with an Eastern grip and perfect dynamics of movement. Backswing and follow-through are both ample, the stance is regal and unfortunately totally unattainable. Jet tennis is too rapid to permit such full movements.

3

4

5

1

4

The U.S. team at Wimbledon in 1920 (2): on the far left, Tilden; on the far right, Johnston. 1. Challenge round at Wimbledon. Brian Norton, passed by Tilden, will lose 7–5 in the final set, after two match points. 3. Norton's aggressive backhand. 4. 1920: at Auckland, New Zealand, play in honor of Wilding. Johnston (serving) and Tilden will defeat Patterson (returning the serve) and the aging Brookes. The Cup departs for the United States.

2

3

for Johnston was tiny, only 1.68 meters (5 ft. 6 in.) in height, and weighed fifty-five kilograms (121 lbs.). His irrepressible forehand, his magnificent volley play, combined with his goodheartedness and his unquenchable will to win, made of him an all-time great, a tennis immortal," Tilden writes of his opponent.

It was precisely that marvellous forehand, with its Western grip and incredibly wide backswing which ended well to the left of his body with a sudden closing jolt, that made Big Bill aware that his own defensive game and especially his backhand were both deficient. Big Bill decided to go away for a whole winter to study his own weaknesses, just as he had done at the beginning of his career, when the Academy of Germantown had entrusted him with the task of advising their aspiring tennis players. For four months he remained with Arnold Jones in the pleasant cloisters of a home in Rhode Island. Jones was one of the first charming disciples in Bill's long career as an ill-fated teacher. When Bill reappeared to the world, his backhand, now braced by the thumb placed against the handle, was almost as strong, varied, and fearful as his legendary forehand. Thus prepared, with a serve that had been clocked at 124 miles per hour, Bill was ready to become the number one player in his country and then in the whole world.

The English and the Australians had suffered so badly in World War I that the United States abstained from participation in the first postwar Davis Cup in 1919. In 1920 both Bills easily took the Cup home from New Zealand, where the competition was held to honor Wilding. Tilden remained a fervent admirer of the aging Brookes, who managed, at the age of forty-three, to wrest a set from him, but he found that Patterson, the new Australian star, was far less refined than the old Wizard. Solidly built, with the

5

5. *The American team that beat the Japanese in the 1921 Challenge Round: Tilden, Williams, Washburn, and Johnston. 8. Tilden, seen here with Zenzo Shimizu examining two rackets, will beat the latter with difficulty. 6. Shimizu in the near court, giving a sample of his very personalized style, seen more clearly in (9), a style that carried him to within two points of victory. 7. The Australian Patterson, winner at Wimbledon in 1919 and 1922, but always in the shadow of Big Bill.*

7

6

shoulders and arms of a lumberjack, Patterson had adopted assault tennis technique à la McLoughlin, but, despite his two successes at Wimbledon in 1919 and 1922, Tilden did not see fit to mention him in his personal classification of the tennis immortals nor in his listing of the possessors of classic shots.

In his engagements with Little Bill, Big Bill's new backhand lengthened the duration of the rallies, and after a couple of hours of play the smaller man began to weaken. Beaten on the court but still a scrapper, Little Bill stubbornly tried to regain his 1919 title on six different occasions, and six different times Big Bill fought him off.

Those finals games were a potpourri of excitement. In the first, vintage 1920, a pilot that was taking pictures of the event, much to Tilden's displeasure, lost altitude and crashed next to the stands, missing the structure by no more than one hundred meters (110 yards). The players were totally absorbed in their game, and the match continued uninterrupted, very few of the 10,000 spectators evacuating the Forest Hills stands.

In 1921 Tilden rushed to retrieve a ball that would mean both game and set, and in the process he almost hit the service linesman in the back of the neck as well as a spectator in the nose. But he did get the ball, which cannonballed at ground level behind the umpire's stand to drop in the corner of Johnston's court.

Little Bill was badly shaken by such skill, but he had regained his composure the following year to the extent that he managed a lead of two sets to one with a three-love advantage in the fourth. Interest in the match was increased by the U.S. Champion Trophy that both Bills had won twice. A third victory would lead to the permanent award of the Cup, and Little Bill could retire to

8

9

2

1

3

Wimbledon moved from Worple to Church Road in 1922, and in the new Centre Court, capable of seating 16,000 spectators, Little Bill Johnston dominated the scene in 1923 during the absence of Big Bill. 1. One of his drives, shorter than usual. 2. On Centre Court, playing against Vinnie Richards, the child prodigy who was a student of Tilden and who won (3) the U.S. Championships together with his mentor at the age of fifteen in 1918. In 1924 Richards won the last Olympic tennis matches against Cochet (7) in Paris and turned pro at the age of twenty-three. 4. A view of the new courts at Wimbledon with Richards and Jacob in action.

4

5

6

8

7

9

10

5. Tilden with the only woman student during his long career as a teacher: Cilly Aussem, the enchanting German winner of Wimbledon in 1931(8). 6. A caricature of Tilden the actor, "the Edwin Booth of tennis." 9. Tilden in one of his unfortunate appearances on stage. 10. At Cannes with Van den Berck, one of his many students.

1

2

3

4

contemplate his laurels. A little shaken, Tilden was changing courts, when the president of the Association, Julian Myrick, said condescendingly, "It has been a great match, Bill." "Keep watching," Big Bill snarled through his teeth. In a whirlwind of winning strokes he pinned down six games in a row to win in the fifth. Between championships in the States, Tilden had found time to make two trips to Europe and to win Wimbledon twice, in 1920 and 1921.

Bill's excellent English, spoken by the high society of Philadelphia, which had heaped so much ridicule upon him at home, helped him feel more at ease than in his homeland. His tall profile, like a long stretch of bent wire, his pleasant and yet critical look, his enormous heavy wool sweater, fraying around the edges, suggested to Nellie Melba the nickname of the Blue Grizzly, a name that stuck with him.

In 1920 Bill whipped a diminutive Japanese by the name of Shimizu in the finals of the All Comers. Shimizu's precise game was all slices and feints and letter perfect. Down 1–4 in the first, 2–4 in the second, and 2–5 in the third, each time Bill found the speed necessary to come out on top over his strong Nipponese rival.

In the Challenge Round at Wimbledon in 1920, Bill controlled Patterson's serves with superhuman ease and then destroyed him, attacking his weak backhand with drop shots. In a little over an hour he became the first American victor of the important tournament. The following year Tilden was saved by the postponement of the elimination of the Challenge Round until 1922 and by a mistake. A victim of poisoning, he was nevertheless determined to carry on and win the Paris tournament. He arrived in London after the Paris matches and went straight back to bed. Bill left the clinic the Monday of the opening of the tournament to appear in the audience at Wimbledon, still shaky and muffled up in shawls. Only five days before the Challenge Round he was strong enough to start practice sessions with his good friend Arnold Jones, while his probable opponents sized each other up.

Beating Lycett, who brought bucket and champagne to Centre Court, Shimizu became the favorite as a result, but the Spaniard Alonso in turn took him before a record crowd, to the great delight of Suzanne Lenglen. In the finals of All Comers, Alonso, who played an inspired and aggressive brand of tennis, managed to take two sets and stood 5–2 in the third before going down to defeat, one hand almost inoperative from blisters, to Babe Norton.

Paler than usual and weighed down under his blue sweater, Bill rapidly lost the first two sets of the Challenge Round. At the begin-

5

6

9

7e année Nº 116 1er OCTOBRE 1925

TENNIS ET GOLF

Organe officiel de l'Union des Golfs de France et de la Fédération Belge du Golf

Paraît une fois par mois le 16 de Novembre à Février inclus

Paraît deux fois par mois le 1er et le 16 de Mars à Octobre inclus

RÉDACTION ADMINISTRATION PUBLICITÉ

30 rue WASHINGTON PARIS (8e)

ABONNEMENTS: FRANCE ET COLONIES 50f ÉTRANGER 70f

LE NUMERO 3 fr. 50

JANE RÉGNY COUTURE SPORT

7

8

The United States dominated Davis competitions from 1920 to 1926. The competition having increased, two zones are established in 1923, the European and the American, and in 1925 twenty-five teams enroll (4). 1. The French team of 1922 is made up of Borotra, Gobert, and Cochet, with their captain Allan Muhr. 2. The Spaniard Manuel Alonso, who was classified number two in the United States in 1926. 3. The Belgian Jean Washer, one of the strongest European players of the twenties. 5. The Chinese players, Wei, Kong, and Huang, enroll in 1924 and win fifteen games in all against the Australians, Gerald Patterson and O'Hara Wood, beaten in turn 5–0 by two American Bills, Big and Little (6). The Spanish team in 1921, Flaquer, José Alonso, Manuel Alonso, and De Gomar (7). The Japanese team of 1926, Fukuda, Shimizu, Harada, and Isawaki (8). Harada defeated both Lacoste and Cochet in Cup play. Another Frenchman, Borotra, lies injured by one of Patterson's shots, seen on the cover of Tennis et Golf *(9). The victim will soon get to his feet, and the attack against the United States will begin.*

ning of the third, he tried a few drop shots in a desperate attempt to shorten the rallies, and one section of the stands, apparently unaware of the game's rules, jeered badly. Such vulgarity offended Bill, but it upset Norton even more and he threw away two sets to spite the spectators.

Then a Bill who was almost recovered and a Babe brought back to his senses began their fifth set, which, after an advantage of four to two, saw the South African twice at match point, 5–4. Bill wiped out the first with an ace, and while trying to undo the second after an exchange of cautious drives, he hit hard, and certain of having made a mistake, ran toward the net to congratulate the victor. The ball suddenly seemed almost to drop from its trajectory, fell within bounds, and Norton, seeing Bill at the net, tried a passing shot which failed. "If he had gotten it across the net, I couldn't have done other than watch it sail by," Bill commented, still in disbelief twenty-seven years later. Champion now of Wimbledon and of the United States, once again victor in the Davis Cup, against Shimizu and Ito Kumagae, Bill was at the height of his power and could forgive the incessant arguments of the American officials.

Little Bill represented the United States at Paris and London the following year, and his victories confirmed the fact that Tilden was by this time unbeatable. The American Association made Big Bill keep track of his expenses and refused his princely expense statements. The Association also did not approve his requests to travel in a private cabin and to be lodged in the luxury hotels together with doubles partners of his own choosing: greats like Vinnie Richards, who, like he, won the American championships at the age of fifteen, or hopeless cases like Jones or Sandy Wiener who could not even defend one third of the court, much less one half.

Big Bill, in turn, refused to be a knight for that round table of hypocrites. He no longer crossed the ocean, and limited his activities to defending the Cup, winning against all comers from 1920 to 1925. Is there anyone stronger than I anywhere in the world? he seemed to be thinking. If so, let him come over here and prove it if he can.

18 The Musketeers: Cochet, Lacoste, Borotra, and Brugnon

The challenge was not long in arriving. Not one individual, but a team of four young men, as different one from the other as an Alpine from a Parisian or a Basque. Toto Brugnon was born in the French capital on May 11, 1885; Jean Borotra in Biarritz, near the Spanish border, on August 13, 1898; Henri Cochet in Lyon on December 14, 1901; and René Lacoste in Paris on July 2, 1905. All four of them arrived in the tennis world in roundabout ways, which were often in sharp contrast to the high-flown rules of a society that lived apart on the Island of Puteau, at the Bois de Saint-Cloud, and at the English colonies along the French Riviera.

The first breach of the facade of this Arcadia had come from Suzanne Lenglen's Driva Champion. As the tennis goddess's partner, chosen personally by her father from about a hundred aspirants, Toto Brugnon was promised a bright future in doubles competition. By the age of seven, Henri Cochet, the son of the custodian of the Lyon Tennis Club, already knew the fundamentals of the game; whereas Lieutenant Borotra hit his first ball during an Army tournament at Wiesbaden.

The only one to arrive according to the proper rules of the English-speaking world, holding his enormous club halfway up the handle, was René Lacoste. His first descent into battle, however, against Coco Gentien, was such a disaster that the senior Lacoste had no compunctions about suggesting that he change sports. Several months later the stubborn youngster had already staged a comeback, and to reward him his delighted papa had a small Hispano-Suiza specially built at his car factory. Two years later René Lacoste was outdoor champion of France: it was a meteoric ascent second only to that of Jean Borotra. In 1924, in his fifth year of play, Jean was successful in winning the French championships and Wimbledon!

He was certainly favored by background for this extraordinary success, for he had played Basque pelota from a very early age and had the additional training of covering twelve kilometers (about 7.5 miles) each day to and from school either on foot or by bike. His education would have pleased more the French novelist Montherlant, with his emphasis on the active life, than the more contemplative Rousseau: Jean played sports, had a job, supported an entire family, and at the same time got a degree as a polytechnical engineer and doctorate in law. People were used to seeing him get out of a taxi in his white flannels, his businessman's grey suit rolled up under his arm. He changed clothes on the run, he lived on the run, and above all, he played on the run.

When Jean was twenty-two, his brother Fred, also a good player, enrolled him in his second tournament, and there he discovered the volley quite by chance. Down 0–6, 0–4, he was attracted to the net by a sudden drop shot from his opponent, Le Besnerais: he instinctively dove upon the passing shot, returned it, and won the point. Wonderstruck, he raised his eyes to the heavens: so it was permitted to hit the ball on the fly! To play like football and rugby! Delighted with the revelation, he began to play, diving like a goalkeeper, dusty with red clay and happy. Le Besnerais did not win another game. "If the lob did not exist," Lacoste observed dryly on more than one occasion, "Jean would be totally invincible."

While Borotra, unconcerned about his weak serve, drove his bayonettelike attack to the desperation of his oppoents, René Lacoste began a program of research that was supposed to help him eliminate the errors in his game. "In order to win, I need two things that are easy to come by: a complete collection of books on tennis and a cement wall that I can wear out by playing against it and have it plastered each year." René had too logical a mind to be content with just that. He got himself a pile of notebooks and began to fill them painstakingly with notes. Precise and detached as an entymologist, he ran through the whole tennis world with his pen, dissecting his opponent's play until he knew its functions better than they did.

After finishing with his rivals, René began to consider the scoring system, attributing different values to the diverse combinations and thereby awarding each an unlike margin of risk. Unhappy with the forehand stroke and even more displeased with volley play, he had a special movie camera set up that photographed his movements in slow motion. When his coach Darsonval, totally worn out, began to complain about the length of the practice sessions, René designed and constructed the first ball-throwing machine.

Once he had arranged the classification of his adversaries and the technical matters, René took time out for meditation. On the days when his most important matches took place, he began to eat alone, actually attaining a sort of self-hypnosis. "I do not play well," he tells us, "unless I concentrate deeply on my matches." All his scientific reasoning and the rigor of his program did not keep René free from sudden and unexpected crisis of self-doubt. When he had broken a lamp or a mirror while practicing his serve, he would come out of the room completely unnerved and tell his friends simply that he had missed the mark somehow. Cochet quipped in retort one day that if he had missed the mark and wished to find it again, he had better consult with Saint Antony of Padua, who was famous for tracking down missing items.

Everyone, even his closest friends, thought Henri Cochet to be the exact opposite of the delightful Borotra and Lacoste, who had in common, at the very least, an absolute passion for practice sessions. Cochet trained very little and spoke even less. On the court his soulful dark eyes stood out from his ivory skin and often seemed to be elsewhere in a kind of dream world or simply concentrated on the ravishing beauty of one of the female spectators. While Borotra logged kilometers in his endless trips to the net and

Lacoste burst his lungs in shuttling back and forth along the base line, Cochet reached the ball with two quick and elegant steps, and returned it with great economy of movement before it had reached the high point of its trajectory.

His service did not appear any more violent than Borotra's, and his backhand was certainly technically no better and only a little more orthodox. When he felt in top form, his strokes moved like forked lightning: smashes that angled smoking away, magical half-volleys, homicidal volleys, with an irresistible quality.

If Henri Cochet did not take the trouble to organize a tennis game that seemed almost spitefully easy, he must at any rate have suffered at having to put up with a world more complicated than his own. At the beginning it was his lot to spend his free time on the courts that his father smoothed and watered from dawn to dusk. Nor did his life improve a great deal after he had beaten his friend and boss Couzon, thereby rising to number one player of the region. The tennis trips were always brief and secondary to his job in the silk factory. The military offered him for the first time the opportunity to prepare his tennis career in comfort. In two years he went from second division to become champion of France and then world champion on clay. However, his family laid a trap for him and his presence and name were used in furthering a sporting goods business. Hours spent behind a counter certainly did him no good at keeping in shape and at renewing his earlier triumphs.

Vinnie Richards's volleys, or perhaps Captain Décugis's ice packs, were lethal to Henri in the finals of the 1924 Olympics. For three months he dragged himself around, the victim of a mysterious debilitating case of influenza. He fell at the same time to third position in the rankings, behind Lacoste and Borotra, who were making a clean sweep at Wimbledon, and to some of the more impetuous journalists he seemed to be through. He was actually about to begin the second phase of his career that was to be directed by one of the few truly great officials: Pierre Gillou.

The product of a home where tennis was daily fare, already a good player himself by the turn of the century, Gillou had become the father figure of French tennis. At the beginning, his friendship with Borotra, a fellow member of the Racing Club, did not ingratiate him with Cochet, who had defeated the Basque on many occasions.

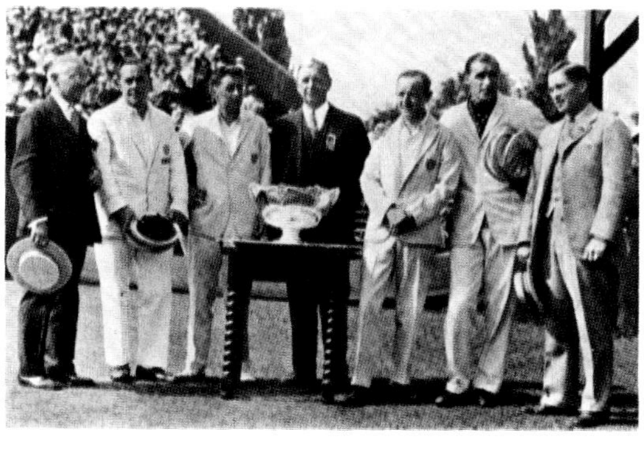

Opposite page: The four Musketeers brought together for the first time by the matches with Ireland in Dublin in 1923. From the left: Cochet, Brugnon, Captain Muhr, Lacoste, and Borotra. In the large photograph above: Four years later, they have just won the Cup from the U.S., 10 September 1927, on the courts at Germantown in Philadelphia. In their midst stands Pierre Gillou. Bottom left: The U.S. team with Garland, Big Bill, Little Bill, the donor Davis, Williams, Hunter, and Myrick.

2

Three moments of the Challenge Round of 1927 between the United States and France in Philadelphia. 3. Lacoste is at mid-court in a backhand volley against Little Bill who will win 6–3, 6–2, 6–2. 1. Big Bill is successful in defeating Cochet (whose forehand has hit the net): 6–3, 2–6, 6–2, 8–6. After the American

1

victory in the doubles, the old champion will no longer be able to sustain Lacoste's rhythm (2), who will cruelly lure him from the base line with a longline forehand shot and go on to win 6–3, 4–6, 6–3, 6–2. Cochet will finish the job beating Johnston 6–4, 4–6, 6–2, and 6–2. 4. The Davis Cup leaves for France.

4

3

1

2

The first attempts on the Davis Cup, poorly prepared and even worse directed by Allan Muhr, convinced Gillou to replace the American, to remove Captain Décugis, and, above all, to recall Cochet. Finally admitted to the luxury of a Mediterranean winter, Henri was able to practice with trainers like Albert Burke, Kozeluh, and Najuch. His future was now secure, and after an absence of three years from both America and Wimbledon, he returned to the team.

"If tennis had good years like wine," the sommelier smiled as he poured the Bourgogne for the French players, "1927 would be a good year to put some of our talent away." The players, Pierre Gillou and Madame Cochet, both smiled and nodded in agreement. It was July 27, and the Davis team, with the exception of Borotra, had set sail two weeks earlier than the year before.

Gillou had realized that excessive errors had prevented the team from doing its best during the five previous attempts in America, all of which ended in failure. In his account of the trip in 1926, published in *Tennis et Golf* by Daninos, Gillou had had the good taste to overlook many of the mistakes made by his predecessors, but he had hammered away incessantly at one idea. A new stadium ought to be built, and as soon as possible, large enough to contain more than 10,000 persons, for the next challenge round of the Davis Cup. It was the captain's considered advice that the Musketeers were now ready for the grand adventure.

In the fall of 1926, Tilden, who had not been beaten in the Davis Cup competition for six years, was defeated by Lacoste. Upset by defeat and nursing an injured knee, Big Bill once again fell in the quarterfinals at Forest Hills against Cochet. That tournament, which had been fatal to foreigners ever since Doherty's victory there in 1903, suddenly became the home of the French tricolor. Johnston was beaten for the first time by one of the Musketeers, Borotra; three Frenchmen made the semifinals, Lacoste won his victory against Big Bill, and there was a champagne supper and the Marseillaise played by a jazz quartet.

Big Bill had disembarked in Europe, having made peace with the American Association, and finally received from them the right to select his travel companion and doubles partner. He had been in Germany with Hunter, the first representative of an officially allied team, and had admired the indefatigable tenacity of old Froitzheim. He then went to Belgium where he defeated Jean Washer and visited Holland and Denmark. At the Paris finals he once again met Lacoste. The city itself was frenzied with joy over Lindbergh's transatlantic flight. In the fifth set, after four hours of struggle, despite many foot faults called by Allan Muhr, Big Bill was still leading. At match point, 13–12, 40–30, he found the energy to unleash one of his cannonballs which seemed to have gone fair, but to his shock, the linesman called it out. Cochet sat tensely edging forward in his seat, and Bill had the good taste to remark that,

3

4
5

6

7

8

1. Lacoste attacks with his forehand during one of his famous duels with Tilden, this one at Saint-Cloud in 1927. The Frenchman will win 6–4, 4–6, 5–7, 6–3, 11–9. 2. The photo memento of the victory. 6. Lacoste winning the U.S. championship in 1926, the first foreigner to do so after Laurie Doherty in 1903. This shot is a lifted forehand. 7. One of his fantastic backhand shots, a sideline attack. 5. Borotra, seen here shaking hands with Big Bill after a Davis Cup match in 1930, was never able to defeat the American on an outdoor court. 3, 4. The Bounding Basque seen in two volleys: a stretching forehand and then a backhand drive. 8. A scissors leap on a smash, during the second of the two victorious Wimbledons for the French in 1924 and 1926.

whether long or not, Henri was the person best qualified to judge the ball. The physical exhaustion that plagued Lacoste after the match prevented him from doing his best in the Wimbledon semifinals against the titleholder, Borotra.

Big Bill met Cochet again, the latter having climbed painlessly back from two sets down against Hunter in the quarterfinals. With his detached air, the Frenchman began very slowly, whereas Big Bill unleashed a forcing game of aces and winning returns. His success that day was such that he soon found himself two sets in the lead, and standing 5–1 and 30–0 in the third set. Perhaps Bill was trying to force more; perhaps he let his mind wander, thinking of the victory ahead, and the deep depression that would cast its pall over his usual victim, Borotra. At any rate, he put out one, then two drives. Cochet, when he changed courts, minted four points, then another four. While the silence that accompanies great moments descended upon Centre Court, Cochet racked up seventeen points in rapid succession and won the set 7–5. From then on he led all the way against an adversary who was more struck by disbelief than shock.

In finals play Cochet found himself face to face with Wimble-

The least flamboyant and the weakest in singles of the four Musketeers was Toto Brugnon, still able to make the Wimbledon finals by a hair. He played in the doubles with all three of his companions, a real man of the team, and never failed to come through when the chips were down.
1. With Borotra, the last of his three partners.
2. His famous lifted drive.
3. A highly authoritative volley.

1

don's darling, the man whom the English had baptized the "Bounding Basque" due to his habit of flying through the air, his blond hair held down by a blue beret. More at home on the grass than any of the Frenchmen, Borotra had won the title in 1924 and 1926, leaving it to Lacoste in 1925, with his nickname "Crocodile." Cochet, diffident, solitary, incapable of putting his laconic comments into English, had no nickname, but his personality was certainly no less intense than that of his companions.

Even against Borotra, who opened like a meteor, Cochet started down two sets to none, was able to equalize, but ended up faced with a match point. With his customary aplomb, he managed to cancel it, then did the same for two more, but later, during a very lucky volley, Borotra complained to the umpire that the ball had been struck twice and that the point was his. Cochet waited calmly for play to recommence, cancelled the seventh and last match point, scraped together ten points of his own, then bowed to the queen, and ran to the dressing room where a bottle of champagne awaited him, uncorked by the referee Hillyard. Borotra refused to toast. "I'm a teetotaler," he said simply. Without the Bounding Basque around to contribute (he, as usual, had been detained by his employment as a happy constructor of gasoline pumps), these were the anecdotes that the Musketeers recalled on the boat in intervals between gymnastics and paddle tennis.

Listening to Lacoste and Cochet analyze Tilden's game and their battle plans made Gillou see Big Bill in his mind's eye, sitting with his head between his hands in the old dressing room at Saint-Cloud, muttering disappointedly, "You have found the way to beat me, René." Or later, at Wimbledon, Gillou remembered Bill say to the astonished reporter Wallis Myers, "I can't explain how it happened. Cochet played a brand of tennis that I was not acquainted with." The idea was germinating in Gillou's mind of using in the singles the two men that had shaken Bill's strong self-confidence and of saving Borotra for the doubles along with Brugnon, who had won both the Butler Trophy and Wimbledon in tandem with Cochet that year.

"When Borotra is in shape," Lacoste repeated to Gillou with irresistible monotony, "he is the greatest doubles man in the whole world. Toto Brugnon, even when not in top form, is the strongest." At that time, Brugnon had won only one Wimbledon, and had recently lost there in finals play against none other than Tilden-Hunter. Confirming Lacoste's enormous faith in him, he would win three more titles and two second-place awards. To Gillou's anxious entreaties Toto responded calmly: "Let's see how the matches go once the first day is over. All I have to do is serve and return the best I can, no matter which of my friends on the team I play with: after all, they'll be making the points."

When the Musketeers began their practice sessions with the aid of Washer, at the rigorous pace established by Lacoste, they noticed that there were arguments on the other court. Just back from France and freshly arrived on the scene from the groaning boards of a banquet, Tilden had just had it out with the fourteen gentlemen of the board of directors. He had underlined the danger of losing the Cup if there was no adequate preparation, only to meet the response in fourteen different ways that such a danger was even more remote than an oncoming inflation. Not content with that, the orthodox directors had attempted to force him to desert Hunter for the more brilliant if disjointed Williams, and only Bill's threats of forfeit had forced them to abandon that plan.

While Tilden was wearing himself out arguing and winning one tournament after another, the Musketeers trounced the Japanese in Boston. Their strongest player, Harada, was a man small only in stature: he had beaten both Lacoste and Borotra the year before in the Davis Cup play.

Still in Boston, in the American doubles championships, Cochet-Brugnon and Borotra-Lacoste were beaten by Lott-Doeg and Hennessey-Williams. The rain was a concern to all, in that it did not allow them to practice properly.

Little Bill Johnston seemed to be in even worse shape than that famous procrastinator Borotra, and Bill's cavalier attitude in starting to train only a week before the event itself sent Tilden into a rage. In his vivid imagination, Big Bill pictured Johnston as the bugbear of the French: they had met him seldom and beaten him only once.

Tilden was also tormented by the thought that he had to win all three of his matches and gnawed by the fear that he might not do so. Not even the fact that he was in familiar territory on the courts at Germantown helped too much. The evening before the matches Lacoste confided to the English reporter Wallis Myers that he thought the draw a decisive factor. A well-rested Tilden, in as good spirits as at Paris, was virtually unbeatable, despite the age differential of twelve years. "We can win," René concluded,"only if I play Johnston in the first match."

In charge of the drawing, Myers lifted out of the cup the tickets with the names of Johnston and Lacoste. He could not hold back a smile, while René looked at him in amazement as if he were some sort of sleight-of-hand expert. Thursday, by three-thirty in the afternoon, after an hour of play, Johnston, out of breath and lacking accuracy even in his forehand, jogged over to compliment Lacoste

2

3

on his dazzling victory.

As he had thought would happen, Bill had to save the reputation of the United States. Cochet's big mistake was in not taking the advantage at the very beginning, unless his natural slowness kept him from doing so. According to Lacoste, Bill played so well that afternoon that not a man alive could have taken him. Cochet, only twenty-six, stood under the shower totally worn out, while the aging Tilden went over to complain about the doubles formation with his team captain Chuck Garland. The loudspeaker had just announced the pairing Borotra-Brugnon and Tilden-Johnston. Big Bill was furious and termed the choice an international blunder. Garland was able to replace Johnston with Hunter, but after the banquet at which the American managers showed their optimism, the situation was reversed again. Bill spent the night tossing and turning, only to hear the following morning that Johnston seemed to be worn out and that perhaps, all things considered, Hunter *would* have been a better choice!

The doubles were a hard-fought contest, with the French continually on the attack and the Americans superior in serves and returns. In the fifth set Big Bill vented all his wrath with an impressive series of aces and winning drives and succeeded in closing the match with a six to zero. His captain later found him worn out under the soothing hands of the masseur.

In the first encounter on Saturday, Bill started badly and was trapped by Lacoste's juggernaut. Crocodile played down the middle of the court to prevent him from using his long, powerful shots, pushed him back and forth by varying the length of his own strokes, and lastly, in reponse to his most aggressive drives, placed half lobs to his backhand, a deceptively easy ball.

When Bill, somewhat discouraged after the loss of the first set, had managed to take the second and had gone on the offense, Lacoste, with almost superhuman skill, began to fire jabbing crosscourts followed by dizzying lobs. "I thought I was playing against a machine, his strokes were so exact and impenetrable. It made me want to crack him across the mouth with my racket," said Tilden. Nevertheless, he hurried to congratulate his opponent and sat next to René to witness the decisive match.

"I was so nervous," writes Lacoste, "that, despite the bright sunshine, I put on three sweaters, one after the other, and even a hat." Cochet was aware of the importance of that match, which could make his name go down in the annals of tennis and resolve once and for all his financial difficulties. He suddenly anticipated Johnston, and then began to work him over with his forehand shots and his crisscross volleys. After one set, Little Bill, thinner than usual, hunched together his frail shoulders: suddenly he was having difficulty in breathing. Cochet arrived at the interval with a worry-free advantage of two sets to one, and he returned to the court with Lacoste, who had replaced Gillou, too nervous to stay seated in the captain's chair. At five to two in favor of Cochet, Johnston must have felt totally lost. "The audience was aware of it," said Cochet. "Little Bill began to attack every ball with a violence that surprised me, and the crowd, forgetting the rules of fair play, shouted so loudly that I lost control.

"My nerves were frayed from the very beginning, and I suddenly felt empty and uncoordinated, incapable of connecting with the ball.

"Lacoste asked me what was wrong, and his calmness helped me regain my composure and take the last game."

"It was the end of an endeavor begun in 1922," Lacoste wrote later, "of seven Atlantic crossings, of month after month spent dreaming of that moment." Then, suddenly returning to his plain style, he admitted, "Tilden, who could not be beaten by one player, was taken by a team."

The Musketeers held on to the Cup for six years, while Tilden tried desperately to find the talent necessary to bring it across the ocean to reside in the basement of the association he hated so much. Having seen how vulnerable Tilden was on the court, the officials accused him of professional journalism and disqualified him on the eve of the 1928 semifinals against the Italians.

Pierre Gillou, who had sold the 36,000 tickets to raise funds for the new stadium dedicated to Roland Garros, the athlete who fell in the war, ran to the American embassy, and Myron Herrick immediately cabled Washington. Big Bill was requalified in time for the final matches, beat Lacoste in five sets, sustained Hunter until the last set of the doubles, and finally collapsed completely exhausted in the duel with Cochet.

With the insidious rapidity of the Inquisition, the officials nailed down an airtight case against Bill and dismissed him from the courts for six months. A less determined man, with less love and respect for the sport, would have given up the ghost. The announcement of the retirement of Lacoste, who was soon to marry Simone de la Chaume, the golf star, and who fell ill the very evening before the Challenge Round, pushed Bill to decide to reenter competition.

"Your poker is less certain: you no longer have four aces in your hand," whispered Tristan Bernard to Gillou, while the latter was preparing to receive the President of the Republic in the tightly packed stadium. "It'll be up to Jean to prove you wrong,"

Henri Cochet carried in triumph after the victorious defense of the Davis Cup in 1929. He whipped Tilden 6–3, 6–1, and 6–2. In the six finals matches disputed in the Roland Garros stadium, from 1928 to 1933, the genius of anticipation was bested only twice, in 1932 by Vines and in 1933 by Perry. In the small photo, unconcernedly he has just placed a backhand volley.

Gillou retorted angrily. The American captain, Dixon, was kind enough to select George Lott to play opposite Borotra (the latter was afraid of Hennessey), and in a rain of well-played volleys the Basque carried the day.

To back him up in his quiet and discreet way, almost ironically uninvolved, was Henri Cochet, who was by this time world champion. From 1928 to 1933 Cochet lost only one match of the ten he played at Roland Garros. All it took was for Borotra or Brugnon to carry the day in one of the other matches, and a rain of poppy-colored cushions covered the court while the audience sang the *Marseillaise* and the Musketeers were carried in triumph by enthusiastic dervishes, first among them the gargantuan umpire Redelsperger. It was difficult for the young Americans, under the tutelage of the aging Tilden, to defend themselves against the verbal assaults of 12,000 shouting spectators, totally heedless of anything other than love of their country.

The 1930 trip also brought failure. Big Bill chalked up his last personal victory at Wimbledon by winning it ten years after his first visit, and he left the ranks of the amateur by accepting a contract from Metro-Goldwyn-Mayer. Without his magical support, the young Americans were easily eliminated by Great Britain, where successors to the Doherty brothers finally materialized in Fred Perry and Bunny Austin. But with the English defeated in the finals, the Americans returned to the fray in 1932.

The French were totally worn out. Borotra, immersed in business dealings to the extent that he let his faithful chauffeur Albert sign autographs on his behalf, refused to risk his reputation in view of the defeats already suffered against the British. When Lacoste, the captain who was not himself playing, begged Borotra to start conditioning, Jean replied testily: "You feel well, you're rested, why don't you go in for me?" Lacoste dusted off his notebooks, oiled up his automatic ball deliverer, and plastered the wall. Then he made his reentry in the French internationals, beating the holder

1

2

1. *Cochet, approached by Gillou from behind, has just beaten Tilden in 1928. The world classifications will retain him in first place for four years, until 1931. 2. A fluid volley to be followed by net play. 3. A forehand shot played on the run, with the ease of walking on air. 4. The photographic evidence of the most adventuresome of his matches against Big Bill. At Wimbledon in 1927, down 2–6, 4–6, 1–5, Cochet managed to win in the fifth. In finals play against Borotra (6), Cochet made an incredible comeback with six match points and went on to beat the Basque 4–6, 4–6, 6–3, 6–4, 7–5. 5. Still at Wimbledon, the handshake between the winner Lacoste and Cochet in 1928. Between 1924 and 1929, with one exception, two Frenchmen contested the first place at this London tournament. In the French championships from 1925 to 1933, not one foreigner won, and from 1926 to 1928 the Musketeers also prevailed in the United States. Borotra even won in Australia in 1928. 7. In 1930 the indomitable Tilden, at the age of thirty-seven, kept Borotra from a third victory, and renewed his victories from ten years before. It was the end of an era of great duels on the court.*

3

4

5

7

6

2

1

of the Wimbledon title, the American Sidney Wood, with a score that spoke for itself: 6–1, 6–0, 3–6, 6–8, 7–5. His delicate constitution could not stand the strain, and on the eve of the Davis Cup, he himself had to beg Borotra to take over for him.

Indignant over the spiteful criticisms leveled at him the year before, the Basque had made a public sworn statement that he had retired from Davis competition. But he could not refuse his sick friend's request, the flattery of the crowds and of the newspapers, and the sweet smell of success. The annals of the 1932 Challenge Round register two of his victories, the first obtained directly from the world champion, Ellie Vines, and the second against the number two American, Wilmer Allison. The word "heroism" often occurs in the French accounts of the event. The Americans were quick to claim theft: "The United States has won the Cup," wrote Al Laney in the *Chicago Tribune*, "but the trophy remains in France. A linesman kept Allison from his just victory. Borotra committed a double fault in favor of the American while at match point, but the umpire apparently suddenly suffered from blindness."

With both singles matches won on the first day and the doubles lost, the French were two to one. Borotra was the first out on the court against Allison, while Cochet and Vines waited in the stands. In order to slow down Vines's cannonballs, the French had drenched the court until it was a deep purple, but Borotra was the first to be hurt, down two sets, although he had tried to slow the game by changing his hemp sandals right in the middle of the second set.

The Bounding Basque recovered in the third and then won the fourth set, allowing himself another interval to change shoes once again, to the general hilarity of the audience. Those sandals must have been very fragile, because during the ninth game of the fifth set, after canceling out five match points, Jean, with his big toe protruding through the light fabric, gestured wildly toward the stands, showing the audience the hole in his sandal. Once again the sandals had to be changed and with good reason!

Against all the rules, which required that the game be continuous, Borotra staggered over to the captain, the ball boys, and a nearby fan, who quickly helped him off with the pair of sandals and shod him for the third time that day, while Allison, fuming with anger, sat cooling his heels on his racket.

Restored by sucking on an orange that a thoughtful person stuck in his mouth, Borotra returned to the court. He served at 40 all, lost the rally, and Allison reached a new match point. The linesman, Gérard de Ferrier, called the first service out. The second went as follows, according to the witness of one of the ball boys, Simon Giordano: "He hit it out a palm's length. My brother Angelo, who was next to the linesman, stood up and murmured 'What good fortune!' De Ferrier said nothing."

Allison, who was on his way to the net to shake his opponent's hand, was invited by the umpire, Mr. Redelsperger, to continue play. Behind Captain Bernon Prentice an American fan by the name of Baker was shouting furiously, "Thieves! Thieves!" Allison could no longer manage to connect with the ball.

I would be a very bad reporter if I failed to point out the error as well as establish how it came about. De Ferrier, still an active reporter in the year of Our Lord 1973, has told me that "the ball dropped very slowly, for Borotra was at the end of his strength. It somehow slowed down in the air and shortened its curve as it came to rest. There was really no contest at that point, at least until the Americans had won the last match, the one that Vines played against Cochet. Only then did they take it into their heads that it might be possible to take the Cup home with them.

"I have been a line judge in at least twenty-five Davis matches," De Ferrier concludes sadly, "and I have never seen anything like that before or since. . . . As for the other accusation, that I managed to be unavailable after the match. . . . It is totally unfounded, and I never really thought that anyone would want to talk to me then."

The theft was not malicious. It is difficult to prove otherwise, even if Simon Giordano were to maintain that his brother lied, and that Borotra had done his best to weaken the structure of his sandals so as to create an incident and stop the match. As a confirmation of the natural mischievousness of the three ball boys,

3

7

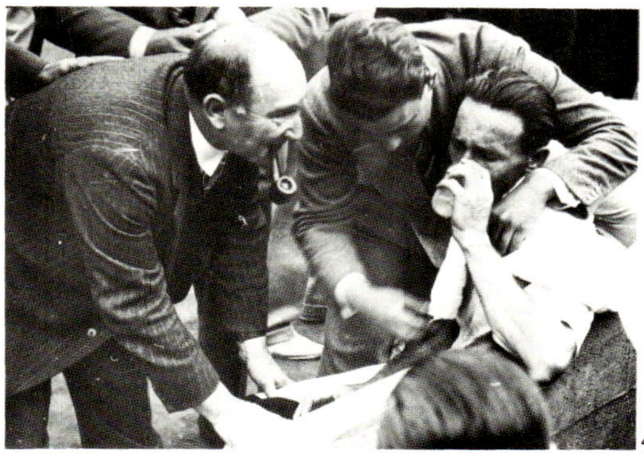

4

5

1. Lacoste, ill, is confined to the role of captain: here he discusses with Lenglen and Brugnon how to defeat the Americans in 1932. 2. Borotra is successful in impressing the new world champion Vines, seen here placing a forehand. 3. Borotra leaves the court visibly upset. 4. Even more distraught, during the singles against Allison (6), he violates the rules three times to change sandals, caricatured here (5) by the artist. 7. The Cup is safe for one year more.

6

the two Giordano brothers and Canavese, all native Italians, Cochet had to admit with his total frankness that the loafers always had a new ball in their pockets ready to hand over to him for the serve, if the point was a decisive one.

In response to the American accusations, Borotra himself declared during the farewell banquet that even at the Germantown Club in 1927 the judgments of the umpires had not been faultless. He was brilliant both on and off the court. In his memory, good devil's advocate that I am, I offer the following excerpt from the *New York Herald Tribune*, of September 11, 1927:

"Aware that the Davis Cup was for all practical purposes lost after the defeat of Big Bill, the fans lost some of their control, applauding noisily all of Cochet's errors, and raising a great hue and cry whenever Johnston made a mistake. . . . The umpire, Paul Gibbons, had to raise his hand several times to ask them not to applaud errors and to keep silent while the ball was in play. But he had no luck, and many of Cochet's errors, when he was ready to smash, were the result of savage yells at the very moment of impact of the racket with the ball."

With his laurels slightly singed, after challenging the critic Didier Poulain to a duel, Jean retired from Cup play, but certainly not from tennis itself. At the age of fifty-one he was champion of England on indoor courts for the eleventh time! Lacoste went out on the courts only to give advice to a disheartened Cochet or an aging Brugnon.

The English returned, and the French backed a young player by the improbable name of Merlin. He was filled with good will and miraculously managed to lead by a set and set point against a grudging Perry in the decisive encounter. While returning a very easy lob, the boy suddenly stiffened from a painful cramp and drove the ball into the ground. That was a better performance than Lacoste had expected of him, a poor child who entered our tennis annals with no other glory than this attempt.

Cochet saluted the astonished Roland Garros. Tilden was waiting for him in the Valhalla of the professionals, where they would continue their duel.

1

2

3

1. Son of the owner of the Hispano-Suiza Company, René Lacoste had the technical background to invent a training device. Here we see him with his automatic ball returner, which he would follow with the first metal racket many years later.
2. This photograph records his marriage to the world golf champion, Simone Thion de la Chaume, shown in a drive (3). Their daughter, Catherine, also becomes a golf great.
4. One of the grand tours made by the Musketeers: Brugnon, seen here in a beret, will describe it in his book Around the World with Tennis. *Cochet sits astride the dromedary to the left.*
5. Ready to climb aboard a plane for a daring flight from Paris to Vienna.
6. In 1967, forty years after their début, the ever-popular Musketeers are present at the dedication ceremonies for a court named in their honor at the Lys Tennis Club. From the left, Cochet, Lacoste, Borotra, and Brugnon are applauded by an array of champions from the sixties: Pellizza, Deniau, Kermadec, Ulrich, Morea, Darmon, and Pietrangeli.

4

5

6

19 Vines, Champion for a Year. Gentleman Jack

No one else had ever won both Wimbledon and Forest Hills at the age of twenty, to become world champion and enter the professional ranks at twenty-one, all after having had a disastrous season. No one hit the ball so energetically until World War II, with the sole aim of making the point always uppermost in his mind.

Tilden had invented all-court tennis and theorized on the spins. Lacoste had raised the sport to an exact science, and Cochet had thrown it into disorder. In the midsummer of 1931, while the French were bravely defending the Davis Cup against the new English and American champions, a tall, thin young man with a rolling gait and a pale, bony face hidden under a white, visored cap, scored heavily among the old tennis clubs on the West Coast. Ellsworth Vines, called Ellie by his close friends, had been born nineteen years before in Pasadena and was introduced to the game at the age of thirteen or so on that city's public cement courts.

During Vines's first match at Seabright, many spectators were amazed at his performance: in the flight between his racket and the lines of the adversary's court, the ball whistled with a trajectory closer to a straight line than to a curve, and some of the sharp-sighted fans attested that as it passed, the brand name was clearly visible on its bright surface. To the utter amazement of the officials, who had sent four other boys to serve as practice for the English at the Davis competition, Vines grew accustomed to the grass court as if he had always played on it. In rapid succession he took Seabright, the Longwood Bowl, and Newport, to make a clean sweep at Forest Hills, putting Perry out in the semifinals and Lott out in the finals. The hue and cry that resulted from those victories troubled Ellie not at all, for, stroking ever more vigorously, he continued quietly to win, even on the cement courts of Los Angeles and San Francisco. He finished the season classified third in the world by Wallis Myers.

Vines's easy assault seemed endless, as witnessed by events of the following year after his landing in Great Britain. In a thoughtful and depressed manner, the highly refined critics observed those serves of his that smacked against the low walls at the end of the court a few instants after being struck, resembling the firing of a double-barreled shotgun. His drives, always played with the smallest possible margin of safety, kicked up clouds of dust, and one smash that rebounded from mid-court ended up in the royal box amid gasps of concern mixed with admiration.

Ellie seemed content to let only seven games go to the Spaniard Maier in the quarterfinals, but even the great Crawford took only six games from him, and the darling of Wimbledon, Bunny Austin, was similarly devastated by him, finishing the final with a love set. Vines *did* win too often, but how could you fault him for that, how could you not appreciate his kind and generous nature, especially when, at the moment of his success, you saw him forget his own joy to comfort the loser Austin? The critics began to compose songs of triumph for the overdue return of the Davis Cup, and comparisons, always invidious, ran riot. One of the most fanciful likened Vines to Nijinski compelled to dance a solo to only three notes, symbolizing his three great shots, the service and the two drives.

In Paris, it seemed as if Vines opened his eyes to life for the first time, like the prince in the fairy tale by Oscar Wilde. Confused by Borotra's attacks, by the praise that the old huckster heaped upon him each time they changed sides, distracted by the shouts of the fans, dusty from the court, he lost the first singles, which turned out to be decisive, even though he beat Cochet in the last match.

His return to the United States, even without the Cup, gave Vines a certain sense of security. At Forest Hills he salvaged a semifinal match against Sutter, made it clear to Cochet that he was indeed world champion in only fifty-nine minutes, and immediately received an offer from Tilden to begin a long series of profitable professional encounters. Vines was almost twenty-one, deeply in love, and did not want to postpone the wedding. He felt hedged in by both admirers and advice givers. He decided to put off a decision on Tilden's offer, and made use of his honeymoon to think the matter over. At the same time he lost the Australian championship to McGrath, a youngster of sixteen who played a strange sort of backhand, holding the racket with both hands.

In March, before leaving for Europe, Big Bill approached him again. "If you win Wimbledon and the Davis Cup, the Association will do all it can to get you under contract," he told Ellie. "Will you keep your engagement with us?" "And what if I lose both places?" Ellie asked. Big Bill offered his hand on that as well. During his whole time in Europe, Tilden later wrote, the directors of the Association made Vines's life impossible. The inquisition reached fantastic proportions when Ellie had to turn over a letter signed by Bill that contained best wishes for success at Wimbledon. The poor guy had had it up to here—*ad nauseam*, Tilden said.

In the finals at Wimbledon in 1933, Crawford's serenity prevailed over Ellie's lack of balance. It was one of the most brilliant and dramatic men's title matches. The critics were finally able to find something wrong, and happily claimed that Ellie's touch was ineffective, his positioning too far from the net, and his strokes monotonous. Ellie was even more unlucky in Davis play. He twisted his ankle during the fourth set played against Perry, but stayed out on the court since his captain did not insist that he leave. At 6–7

1

2

3

4

5

6

7

In 1931, at the age of twenty-one, Vines overturns the tennis world by winning both at Wimbledon and Forest Hills. 1. His terrible cannonball. 5. A backhand volley. 4. The finals at Wimbledon in 1931, with his victim, Austin, who will win only six games in all and finish down 6–0. 6. The award of the cup for the U.S. championship being made by Carruthers. At Forest Hills, Vines defeated Lott (8) in 1931 and a weary Cochet (2) in 1932. George Lott, seen executing a difficult low volley, was one of the great doubles players, as were Van Ryn and Allison (7). Lott won only two Wimbledons as opposed to Brugnon's four and Van Ryn's and Borotra's three, but he took five U.S. championships with three different partners. 3. Evidence of the participation of the sixteen-year-old Sidney

8

in the fifth set, match point for the Englishman, Vines served and suddenly fell, his pallor a strange contrast to the clay court of Roland Garros. They carried him off the playing area while he was still unconscious.

At Forest Hills, Ellie lost at the hands of Bitsy Grant, a tireless retriever 1.60 meters (5 ft. 3 in.) in height. While the critics were roasting Ellie with their comments, Big Bill slipped into the dressing room and put last year's contract before his eyes.This time there was no hesitation. Ellie signed it without saying a word.

Resembling a joint performance of two greats of the arena, their tour was highly successful. At Madison Square Garden, 14,637 spectators produced $30,125 in revenues and applauded the comeback of the old pro Tilden. Big Bill and Ellie fought it out, according to best reports, in seventy-two cities. Ellie won forty-seven times and took home $52,000. He retained his primacy among the professionals until the arrival of Don Budge on the scene in 1939. At that time, freed from the agony of tennis, Ellie threw himself wholeheartedly into his beloved golf, reaching the semifinals in the Championship of the PGA in 1961. Now faced with the smallest of the white balls, on a much larger green than before, Ellie was finally able to strike the ball to his heart's content with no opponent to share it with. And most important of all, he could finally play alone.

GENTLEMAN JACK

The man who in all likelihood forced the issue of whether or not Vines would sign a professional contract was a lazy and peaceful sort of person. He played an old-fashioned brand of tennis with a pear-shaped racket, wearing long trousers and long-sleeved shirts. Only once in his life, at the end of the Wimbledon final of 1933, was Gentleman Jack Crawford ever seen to jump the net, in a moment of unaccustomed vitality. He suddenly pursed his lips and looked back quizzically at the obstacle that he had just dared to hurdle. A favorite of Queen Mary, who esteemed him as much as she loved Borotra, Jack brought back to Wimbledon the aura of wholesome Victorian days that still survived in Sydney as nowhere else in the world.

Since the year when the name of poor Tony Wilding had stirred the older spectators, never was a victory greeted with greater enthusiasm. Someone wrote that the racket with the flattened oval had belonged to a pioneer grandfather, and that Jack had found it at home, where he and his six brothers, under their father's direction, had built their own court. The new racket was a fine instrument, produced to play low volleys better, skimming over tennis shoes. Its serviceability in this regard never convinced

1

2

Wood at Wimbledon in 1925, seen here with Lacoste. Wood quickly matured and won the tournament in 1931.
Ranked among the first ten from 1932 to 1937, Gentleman Jack Crawford replaced Vines in 1933 as world champion. He beat the American in an unforgettable match at Wimbledon (6), and got to within one set of the Grand Slam, losing the fourth and fifth at the hands of Perry at Forest Hills. His game, made up of elegant and wide strokes, reminded many of Reggie Doherty. 1. A backhand with lateral displacement, very similar to one (3) photographed only moments before. 2. A very accurate forehand. 4. A half volley promptly returned toward the center of the court. 5. A low volley of elusive difficulty, aptly masked by an engaging smile.

6

3

4

5

the real experts, though thousands of rackets were sold. With this weapon, which also allowed him to strike the ball in areas where the cords were less taut, Jack won his first Australian championship in 1931, and then amiably triumphed on courts all over the world, remaining among the finest until 1937.

His slowness was compensated by intuition only inferior to his acumen. His 85 kilograms (187 lbs.), well placed at the base line, returned the balls with a deceptively light touch that had real muscle behind it. Although he played an excellent net game, he was rarely called upon to venture there. His service was not as explosive as Vines's; it was long and struck slightly to the right of the shoulder to fall within the lines. Then Jack himself would begin his placement game, which, after a few cross-court shots, made his opponents lose their balance, then make mistakes, finally collapse. For Australia, a country with a tennis community that looked to roughhewn and astounding models like Patterson and Anderson for inspiration, Jack was a major step toward civility.

Jack's international acclaim permitted the Australian Association to invite foreign representatives. Americans, Frenchmen, Englishmen, and Japanese streamed in, all seeking to capture the Australian title, which was only contested at home until the arrival of Borotra in 1928. It was, in fact, Vines's first visit which made Jack realize that the fearful cannonball could be returned using its own violence, much as a mirror reflects a ray of light cast upon it. Jack would have taken all comers at arm wrestling had he wished to excel at that typical, port-of-call activity among the sailors. He learned to oppose the American's projectiles with a fused unit of handle-wrist-forearm, held tense for a moment. Vines, to his dismay, found the balls dancing at his feet, like boomerangs.

In the legendary finals matches of 1933, "played on a bluish-grey day, perfect for tennis, refreshed by a light breeze that was contained by the high walls of the stadium," Gentleman Jack was able to stave off Ellie's cannonballs for three hours, with the exception of three aces per set, until Vines weakened in the fifth set. Jack's last four points raised four neat clouds of chalk dust. Crawford thus had arrived, with the utmost discretion, at his third important success of that happy year. By winning the Australian championships, he discouraged Cochet at Roland Garros, and now was taking Brookes's place at Wimbledon. The American championship was all that he needed to make his success complete by claiming the oft-sought Grand Slam, the title of which, by a lucky choice, owed its origin to the bridge parlance of the tennis players on their off hours.

Despite the fact that Jack was tired and suffering from chronic asthma and a nervous condition that brought into his dreams visions of tennis balls being played, he felt he had the world in his pocket until that fateful day when evil Bitsy Grant sprang Vines upon him. The evening before the finals match against Perry, Jack confided his painful dreams to Vinnie Richards and his friend offered him a mysterious remedy. There would be no bad reaction to the brandy that Jack took for his asthma, Vinnie added. Jack drank the concoction, slept well, and went out on the court to lead a brilliant battle of forehand shots, interrupted only by further sips from Vinnie's magic mixture while courts were being changed.

During the intermission, Jack sat conversing merrily with his wife while Perry took a quick shower. When Jack resumed play, his confidence had been replaced with sudden chills that ran up and down his arms, suddenly enormously heavy. Crawford never made his Grand Slam, and posterity has often wondered if the reason was Perry's forehand, a sudden attack of chills, or perhaps the bourbon whiskey that Vinnie had provided. The drink was certainly useful as a remedy against insomnia, but harmful to a tennis player who used alcohol only to fend off allergies.

20 Fred Perry, the Son of a Labour M.P.

"He is more American than any other American I have ever met," John Olliff wrote of Fred Perry, the Englishman, who, according to Tingay, "did as much for tennis in Britain as Lord Nelson did for the Navy." Combining the qualities of a fine international player with those of a man of letters with good study habits, John Olliff was certainly the best British critic of the sport. The man who beat Perry at his first Wimbledon, Olliff seemed qualified to make such a sweeping statement about him, but there is probably a strong hint of personal prejudice as well.

Another tennis writer, the same George Lott who was probably the best doubles player in the world, said that Perry not only looked like an Englishman, but also did his level best to heighten that effect by wandering about with an unlighted pipe clenched firmly in his teeth, from which no smoke had ever come forth. At the beginning of his career, Perry had tried to acquire the habits of the Doherty brothers, or even better, those of Austin, his teammate, who as a young man had often put on the blue jacket of Cambridge.

The legendary champions of the past, just like the heroes who had won at Waterloo by training for cricket, were beginning to lose their charm. Austin himself, who had dared enter the sacred grounds with pants cut off above the knees, assumed an even more nonconformist role in the movement called Moral Rearmament, and ended up, if not actually thrown out, at least *persona non grata* at the All-England Croquet and Tennis Club. At the height of his career, Perry saw his removal to professional ranks greeted by such a wave of resentment, that he, like Auden, would, hastened to apply for American citizenship. Even in Great Britain, the establishment did not want to admit that the times had changed, that there were thousands of spectators, and that balls and rackets were being manufactured in ever increasing numbers. Twenty years behind the mentality of the players themselves, the aging officials stubbornly dug themselves in, like bewhiskered old monarchs whose divine right to rule had been questioned. While Perry was winning his first Wimbledon, the professional troupe was on tour with Tilden, Vines, Cochet, Lott, and Stoefen, and the Central Europeans Kozeluh and Najuch, formidable retrievers who had always been too poor for tourney play as amateurs.

Fred Perry was the first great European champion who did not come from a family of means. His father was an intelligent craftsman, a union member, who came originally from Stockport, near Manchester, and moved to Ealing to represent the Labour Party in Parliament. Fred learned cricket and soccer in the public schools, and before he ever touched a tennis ball, he had already played a good deal of table tennis within the crumbling walls of the Brentham Garden Suburb Club.

It was table tennis that improved in him two qualities highly needed by the serious player of the lawn variety: in the first place, a highly unusual grip, an accentuated version of the Continental; and in the second place, the unforgettable thrill of victory after his success in the world Ping-Pong competitions of 1929. He won this title at twenty, was beaten with regularity by his contemporaries at tennis, and then undertook an experiment that exasperated his father's Labour colleagues as well as the more liberal directors of the company. Convinced by an amateur trainer by the name of Pops Summer that Fred ought to forsake Ping-Pong for tennis, then strike the ball on the rise and hit hard, Mr. Perry had taken his son out of school and given him a time limit of a year in which to prove himself or give up the sport altogether.

At first, those balls that were struck violently in full flight and smashed down with a snap of the wrist and forearm went far beyond the base line and sometimes even over the roof of the clubhouse, as Perry himself recounted. Slowly he began to develop a correct forehand, and, incredibly quick and solidly built, Fred succeeded in making up for his weak backhand "which was like the movement of a person trying to use a flyswatter for the first time. Not only did Perry manage to overcome the barrier of the qualifications at Roehampton, but he also did well on two occasions at Wimbledon. The following year he even entered the semiquarter finals, defeating a rather unpleasant individual by the name of Morpurgo who was classified among the ten best players in the world, and not easygoing at all.

Fred's first trip to the United States gave him the chance to send his father a trophy. Although it was won in doubles play as a second place award, that silver cup was a visible sign of success. When the American newspaper reporters asked him how he got into tennis, Fred replied that one day, at the age of fourteen, he had asked his father about the owners of shiny new cars lined up along the hedges at Devonshire Park in Eastburne. When the answer came that they belonged to tennis players, that game suddenly seemed to pave the way for him to have a new car as well.

Continuing his travels, Fred won his first important tournament, the Argentine championship, and due to the retirement of Lee, Gregory, and Collins, he found himself suddenly a member of a new and very young Davis Cup team. Other than him, the team sported Wilfred Austin in 1931, a frail and refined young man "who always had his nose buried in Shakespeare." Austin's friends at Cambridge had nicknamed him "Bunny" because he had teeth similar to those of a famous comic-strip rabbit and because of his ravenous appetite for greens. The best doubles man was Pat Hughes, who worked for Dunlop, and was the first player coura-

1

2

4

A dynamic, extroverted powerhouse, Fred Perry (3) dominates tennis for three years, from 1934 to 1936. Thanks to him and to Bunny Austin, the Davis Cup makes a triumphal return to Great Britain from Paris and remains there until Perry joins the professional ranks. 1, 2. Photo memories of the victorious Paris matches in 1933: Austin and Cochet, Perry and Merlin, the young substitute in Musketeer play. 4. The English team on Centre Court: Perry, Austin, Roper Barrett, Hughes, and Tuckey.

3

1

5

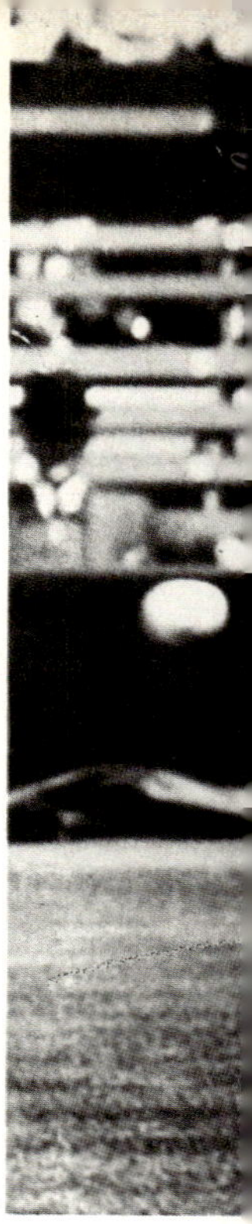

6

8

2

3

Perry won at Wimbledon in 1934, 1935, and 1936, the first player since Wilding to hold the title for three years. He won the U.S. championships in 1933, 1934, and 1936, Paris in 1935, and the Australian championship in 1934. In Davis he took 34 singles out of a total of 38. 1. A backhand passing shot against von Cramm in Paris in 1935. Result: 6–3, 3–6, 6–1, 6–3. 4. Still in 1935, he tries to stop the speedy von Cramm at the net: result, 6–2, 6–4, 6–4. 5. He asks for new balls while changing court at Forest Hills in 1936. With his back turned is Don Budge, who is giving him a hard time. Result: 2–6, 6–2, 8–6, 1–6, 10–8. 2, 3. Two pictures of Bunny Austin, Perry's friend and inventor of shorts for court play and of a triangular-based racket that seemed to help his game, made up of accuracy and technique. The backhand rebound is no less admirable than the difficult volley. 6, 7. Two volleys by Perry, who uses his knees as if he were on a slalom ski course. 8. A balletlike movement by Pat Hughes, the doubles man of the English team, as he attacks a center ball ahead of Perry.

4

7

geous enough to make a tour of the German tennis world, still separated from the rest of the planet in 1926!

Directed by the veteran Roper Barrett, this brand-new team flattened all the competition and worried the Musketeers up to the very last match, when Cochet laid bare Perry's weak defense. In 1932 the team suffered the reversal of that ebullient success: the English lost to the Germans. The latter were aided by new talent, Gottfried von Cramm, and a Russian Jew, Daniel Prenn, who beat Perry and thus tipped the scales against the country that would accept him, once again a refugee, the following year.

Vines's dazzling tennis, Cochet's occasional good days, Crawford's mature sensibleness all conspired against Perry and Austin's ambitions. Patient, gifted with tenacity and wisdom, the two young men licked their wounds. Perry's naturally excellent health had improved even more due to his rigorous workouts with his friends at the Arsenal, under the guidance of Tom Whittaker. Fred was certainly no slower than Borotra at his best, and his wisely planned scheme of attack allowed him to play his last ball with the same lucidity that characterized his first. His forehand by this time had become so devastating that his opponents did their best to avoid it. The common belief that Fred could be beaten by forcing him into the left corner of the court did not avail them anything, but rather strengthened Perry's backhand, subject to their continual attack.

Bunny perfected a racket with a triangular handle which offered less resistance to the air. Totally broken up at being ridiculed for tinkering with the idea of a soccer team in long pants, he cut his own pants off above the knee, appearing in that comfortable attire at Forest Hills and even before the queen herself. As if by magic, the cramps that had always troubled him disappeared along with those two useless tubes of white flannel, and Bunny felt up to a match of five sets.

In 1933 Fred and Bunny snatched the Davis Cup away from the two worn-out Musketeers, and while Perry began his three-year reign as individual champion, Austin kept him company in team competition. Austin became more and more involved in pacifism, and was often tormented by a lack of understanding of his motives on the part of many people, including his wife, the actress Phyllis Konstam. But that apparently slight man still went on to win six out of his eight singles matches in the four Challenge Rounds. He lost to both Cochet and Quist, but he slowly wrested victory from

The wives of the two English champions were actresses. 1. From the theater, Phyllis Konstam (Mrs. Austin). 2. From the film industry, Helen Vinson (Mrs. Perry). 3. Perry turned professional at the end of 1936 and beat Ellie Vines and the aging Tilden (5) at Madison Square Garden. 4. Austin quickly dedicated himself to the cause of moral rearmament and became one of its leaders.

5

1

2

3

4

Wood and Shields, Wimbledon finalists in 1931; from Crawford, winner in 1933; and from Allison and Budge, American champions in 1935 and 1937. In the long, hard singles tourneys, Bunny lost his stamina and twice arrived worn out at the Wimbledon finals, facing vigorous opponents like Vines and Budge.

It became quite evident that Perry's difficulty was of a different sort. After he had interrupted poor Crawford's plans for the Grand Slam, Fred beat Gentleman Jack twice in a row, even pursuing him on his home courts. "I am as well trained athletically as the best of my adversaries," Fred often stated, with a smiling self-confidence that only his fans found agreeable. After the Davis Cup victory, with the triumphal arrival at Victoria Station, and the U.S. championship, the only thing he lacked was Wimbledon. At the beginning of the latter tournament, anyone else in his place would have thrown in the towel. Playing against de Stefani in Paris, he had twisted an ankle, and now the draw had opposed him once again to the ambidextrous Italian who had already frustrated Fred's defenses, beating him three times. Perry bandaged his ankle tightly and stated that the worst of his adversaries were on the other side of the draw. Then he waited until Lott had beaten de Stefani for him, until von Cramm caught a sore throat, and until a very attentive linesman called a foot fault, with Crawford serving to save the match point. "Perhaps," he wrote serenely, "some of the decisions and some of the net balls did help me in the semi-finals against Allison, but in a tournament like Wimbledon, luck and the draw also count for something."

With equal aplomb Perry glided effortlessly through twelve games in a row against an astonished Crawford, from one to three in the first. Such a feat must not have seemed too difficult to him compared to the other two finals won in the fifth set at Forest Hills in 1934 and in 1936: 8–6 in the fifth against Allison and 10–8 against Budge. His outstanding performance seemed due not only to a strong self-image but also to abundant courage.

At the beginning of the American finals in 1935, Fred slipped on the damp grass in one of his feverish sprints, and as he fell, the handle of his racket hit him in the lower back. He said nothing about it, played as usual, and lost the match. He still had enough strength left at eleven o'clock that night to look for a justice of the peace to marry him to actress Helen Vinson, one of the three wives that played a role in his stormy personal life. The accident to his back, which injured a kidney, turned out to be no less harmful than his nocturnal escapade.

In Paris the following year, Fred had not yet regained his strength, and von Cramm beat him only to fall himself in the Wimbledon finals. Perry won his third consecutive Wimbledon that year, his third Forest Hills, and his fourth Davis Cup. He was not a rich man, and temptations were many. Simpson of Piccadilly had offered him a percentage of six pennies on every pair of trousers sold that he advertised, but Fred had to decline. Paramount had proffered a contract, and he grudgingly said no. At Wimbledon the first prize was the Renshaw Cup, with a value of twenty guineas.

Tilden came up with a contract for sixty-one matches against Vines. Fred lost thirty-two of them, but received a large share of the proceeds at the box office, some $412,000 in all. He was seen more and more often tamping tobacco into his old pipe and producing clouds of smoke from within the bowl. He smiled often. He seemed content.

21 Helen, Queen of the Eight Wimbledons

The tennis goddess was certainly irreplaceable. Helen Wills, however, won as often as Suzanne, and all agree that she occupies second place in the ranks of the women tennis immortals.

The author, at this point, ought to state his methods of classification. They do not agree with the statistics of his friend Rino Tommasi, called Mr. Superstat by those Americans who consider him the Nobel of applied tennis mathematics.

First it should be stated that the typical coffeehouse discussions of the possible results of an imaginary match between Doherty and Tilden, or Watson and Lenglen, for example, have no place in this book. These tennis immortals played at different times with diverse equipment and apparel. Whalebone corsets, long pants, rackets stretched by hand on a workbench, rackets mass-produced by machine, balls inflated and covered with flannel or a synthetic fabric: these disparate elements prohibit any fair sort of direct comparison. The judgments reached by the champions themselves are more reliable, especially when players remain active for more than one era, like Baby Gore, Brookes, Tilden, von Cramm, Drobny, and Rosewall, whose careers were unusually long. The discovery of any system to correlate these statistics would rank in the same category as the uncovering of the philosopher's stone to turn base metals into gold.

Let us say that a champion wins a certain number of Wimbledons, of Forest Hills, of Davis matches, competitions which require top effort: Which of them is the best? There ought to be no doubt: this competitor is certainly stronger than another with an inferior record of events. However, two other elements enter that make it a more difficult consideration. In the first place, the speed of travel has increased enormously since the turn of the century. At that time to go from England to the United States required twenty days, and a journey from Australia to London lasted at least five weeks. It is therefore necessary to take into account how and how much the champions traveled and to assign a relative value to certain major tournaments often avoided by those who suffered either from laziness or from seasickness.

In the second place, from Tilden on, there is the additional problem of professionalism. It is not hard to imagine that people like Vines, Perry, and Budge would have improved their performance by remaining in the amateur field. The most glaring example of the inadequacy of pure statistics in this area is the case of Laver, the champion who won Wimbledon in 1961 and 1962, was excluded as a professional for five years, and then returned to win again in 1968 and 1969 when the event was declared open.

The reader who has followed me so far will continue to believe me as I frankly state the opinions that I have doggedly gleaned from hundreds of books and thousands of magazines. It would be a waste of space to offer examples in each case. I have already taken away too much space from the charming women champions of the 1930s.

The author never met Helen Wills. All the persons that he interviewed about her claimed not to like her. They had watched her play; they had spoken with her; they were able to recount anecdotes and tidbits of gossip; perhaps, however, they had not understood her. From its very title, *Fifteen-Thirty*, to the last page, Helen's autobiography reveals a witty and enchanting woman. The book is both surprising and fascinating, filled with understatement and the champion's humility, which someone described as "inflamed with chilly presumptiveness." In a volume published by Scribner's at the same time in New York City and in London, the introduction stresses the author's hope to present the public with an accurate picture of a sports woman of the twentieth century. In the last chapter, Helen expresses the doubt that her life and her memoirs can be of any interest to the reader.

This uncertainty is not at all the product of coquetry or mere rhetoric. Whether she was having supper with George Bernard Shaw or with the Duke of Gloucester, whether she was sporting in the snow on the Jungfrau or in the sea near Stockholm, Helen was always disarmingly simple and sincere. Called Poker Face by the reporters, this woman was capable of laughter when there was just cause. She was not frivolous, but endowed with a delightful sense of humor; she had no talent for acting, but when she appeared on the court, the only name that even her worst detractors could use on her behalf was "Queen Helen." She painted so well that she sold all she exhibited at the Grand Central Art Gallery in New York, but she confessed candidly that nothing pleased her so much as playing on Centre Court at Wimbledon. Helen came from wealth and married it in the person of Freddie Moody, but she quickly began to write for the United Press and the *Daily Mail* between matches, achieving excellent results that finally helped her decide to try her hand at a novel.

The legend of Helen's aloofness and of her indifference is perhaps the result of the needs of others, who wanted a champion of great complexity and simplicity all rolled into one. In Lenglen and Tilden, the public and the press had discovered personalities who gave of themselves freely. The audience and the media expected the same quality in Helen Wills.

Faced with Helen's reserve, a good reporter like Bill McGeehan hastens to assert in the *New York Herald*: "She is powerful, repressed, and imperturbable. She plays her tennis wrapped in a silent, deadly serious integrity, concentrating completely on her work. This is the way to win, but certainly not the way of a crowd pleaser. There is obviously no reason why an amateur athlete ought to try to curry favor with the public."

It was for this reason that American audiences never took to

1

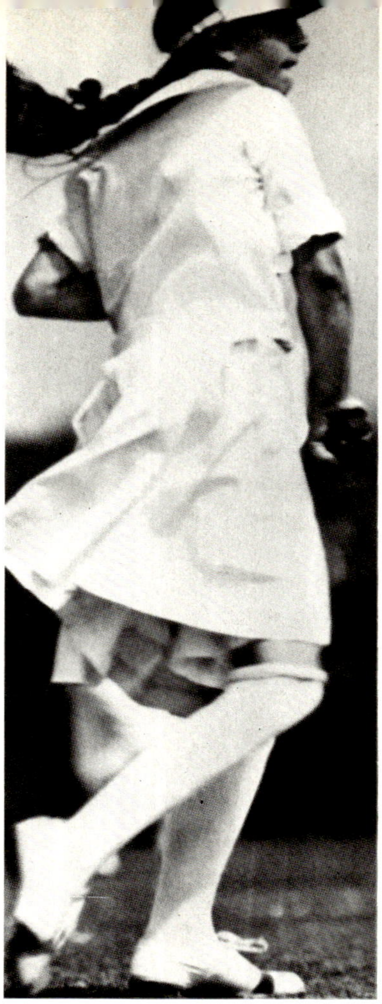

2

3

4

Helen Wills, called Queen Helen, won eight Wimbledons, and still found time to write and paint as a professional. 1. One of her paintings, depicting shoes and balls. 2, 5. Two childhood pictures showing her in the sailor-boy outfit and visor, one of her inventions she used on the court. 3. One of her first feuds with Helen Jacobs which she took 6–1, 6–2. 4. The only match that Wills lost against Jacobs, by forfeit, at Forest Hills in 1933. Wills unfortunately had to stay away from the game for more than a year. 6. Jacobs and Tilden, her adviser at Wimbledon in 1938, the year of the Queen's still unbeaten triumph.

Helen as did the English endowed with the same reserve that they in turn appreciated in their public figures. It is truly a shame that Helen's important and admirable biographers such as Paul Gallico have never seen a little poem that she wrote when she arrived on the Riviera for her match of the century against Suzanne Lenglen:

I'll set my house on the cliff edge
though the town lies down by the sea
and I'll build my wall just high enough
to shut the town from me.

Oh, mine the glory of wave and sky
of clouds and evening star,
white flashing breasts of wheeling gulls
and gleam of sails afar.

Oh, safe and glad on my cliff's edge
and only will I look down,
when the fairy lamps of night are lit
like stars in the hidden town.

It is not of the quality of her favorite Whitman, but there is enough substance there to give a keen insight into her personality.

Those who refused to understand her soon elected another Helen to spite her, a delightful girl with an urchin's whimsy, born a few yards down the street in the same Berkeley and a student of the same excellent coach. One day Pop Fullmer brought little Helen Jacobs to the court reserved for Helen Wills. The former was two years and ten months younger than her eighteen-year-old rival: the match lasted just one minute longer than the six games necessary for Helen the First to make an enemy for life.

The rivalry between the two, fomented and distorted by some reporters, was always of lively interest and reached the boiling point at the moment when Tilden also took sides against Queen Helen. Big Bill was always jealous of the other stars. Despite her more modern, net-oriented game, Jacobs never attained a forehand strong enough to face Wills's formidable one: a stroke which has probably never been equaled by any other woman champion. Helen the Second worked her whole life to improve her chop, and she finally achieved her goal and came very close to greatness. The world classifications, headed by Helen the First for nine years, saw Jacobs in first position only in 1936, thanks to the absence of the unfortunate queen.

In their frequent encounters, which numbered some fifteen, according to Wills, Helen the Second won only once. Circumstances kept her from a complete victory even then, though Queen Helen's detractors blamed her merciless nature for it. It was 1933. On the beach at their home, Helen had felt a sharp pain in her back while lifting a rock covered with shells. She refused to worry about it until after Wimbledon, but after she beat D. Round, she had to ask someone to untie her shoestrings. She could no longer bend over. She readied herself for Forest Hills by playing a few minutes each day and then lying down. Her back was in pain and assaulted by "a snowstorm of black spots" whenever she had to get up. Arriving at the final matches with a dislocated lumbar vertebra was an even more memorable occasion than her eight Wimbledon victories. The bad weather delayed the match, and Helen, waiting to recover, cried to herself and held her peace.

It stopped raining, and the poor queen gingerly placed her feet on the grass, which was still damp. "I couldn't bend over at all, and a strange stiffness had invaded my leg and back." She won the first set 8–6, lost the second 6–3, and when, at 0–3 in the third, it seemed to her that "the stadium was revolving in the air and that Jacobs was floating" she went over to the umpire's stand and wisely informed him that she could not go on. "I would have preferred to pass out on the court," she wrote later, in answer to

5

6

the gracious shower of invectives that greeted her departure. "It would have been a much more convincing end in the eyes of many. My decision, nevertheless, was instinctive rather than premeditated. Animals, and humans as well, often prefer to suffer in the dark. Had I been able to think a little more clearly, I would have decided to stay on the court." Turning to those who had accused her of not thinking of poor Helen Jacobs, who had nearly won when she left, Helen Wills confirmed that "being naturally egotistical, I thought only of myself."

Her career in tennis seemed over. She remained immobilized for four long months. It was her father, himself a doctor, who helped her for more than a year on the road to recovery, aided by patience and a pool. Once again she saw her beloved Centre Court, and faced Jacobs in the finals of 1935 at Wimbledon.

Shortly before the event, while she was having lunch, an elderly woman came over to the table. "I am Maud Watson, the first woman to win at Wimbledon," she smiled, her eyes bright and sparkling despite the wrinkles of age. After that success, she told Helen, the capsizing of a sailboat had dragged her under the water, bringing her close to drowning. Ill for three long years, she had never again been able to return to competition, and she still lamented that fact. "Especially for that reason," she concluded, "I want to let you know that I am thinking of you and wish you the best of luck."

Less imposing and slower than usual, Queen Helen found herself at 3–5 and 30–40, and stopped to look at her opponent, who had all the time she needed at the net to prepare a forehand volley, but inexplicably put this easy ball out by a hair's breadth. She suddenly felt an enormous inner faith surge through her and, one after the other, she scored the points she needed to win, ran to the net, and incredibly, threw her arms around the shoulders of her rival.

While she was walking off the court, the queen once again proved her detractors false by embracing and kissing that very pleased official, Herbert Wilberforce. At the age of seventeen, someone remembered, little Helen had repulsed the umpire who tried to plant a kiss on her cheek, after she had won the U.S. championship. The happy queen granted herself two years' respite with her painting and her journalism. She let her adversaries dispute her crown, as they had done during her illness, and to some extent in 1931.

It was the small German girl Cilly Aussem who took over at Roland Garros and at Wimbledon, in long, uneven matches, played stubbornly from the back of the court and punctuated with unexpected fits of nervousness. The victim of a mother as beautiful as she, Cilly was helped from the ranks of eternal childhood by Bill Tilden. When her mother asked him on the Riviera how she could transform Cilly into a champion, Bill replied simply, "Take the first train to Berlin." Surprisingly enough, Frau Aussem obeyed, and

1

2

3

4

5

6

7

1. Kay Stammers was the number one English player toward the end of the thirties, but a finals at Wimbledon lost in 1939 kept her from matching her elegant beauty with performance. 4. Stronger than she, the German superwoman Ilse Sperling was classified for ten years among the top world contenders, winning, for example, three consecutive French championships, 1935–1937. 5. Doubles companion of Lenglen, Bunny Ryan has a record of nineteen titles at Wimbledon in doubles and mixed play. 2, 3. Sketches by Wills that depict the tennis goddess's second doubles partner, Didi Vlasto, herself a magnificent woman, and Lili de Alvarez, a post-Lenglen marvel, courted by the king of Spain. 8. Lili played in red and gold, and neither jewels nor bracelets hindered her elegant and risk-fraught brand of tennis. She was a fine player, but lacked patience and humility needed for true greatness. 7. The Chilean Anita Lizana interrupted her Olympic climb for a sudden marriage after her victory at the 1937 U.S. championship. 6. Cilly Aussem, Tilden's delight, won Wimbledon from the base line in 1931.

Bill undertook with Cilly the strenuous regime of exercise and training that had failed with so many of his male students. Hardly had her instructor disappeared into the ranks of professionalism that the young Aussem went back to her former ways. She was sick on several occasions, finally married a nobleman from Verona, Count Murari della Corte, and retired.

Her natural adversary, Hilde Krahwinkel, who later married a Dane by the name of Sperling, held the field for a much longer time. Preferring tennis to the chance of becoming an Olympic athlete, Hilde was defeated by Aussem in finals play at Wimbledon in 1931, but on clay courts her game of clockwork precision and running won her three Roland Garros from 1934 to 1936. Dorothy Round, who seemed to have little of the qualities of a potential star, made the headlines for having left the Roland Garros Stadium on a Sunday in order to rest and pray.

Dorothy herself, who was a pleasant and pious Sunday school teacher, had her Pygmalion in the person of a Japanese, Ryuki Miki. He helped her gain a traditional style, induced her to perfect a devastating drop shot, and, after many hours of work, was able to crown his achievement on her behalf in the finals of the mixed doubles, 1934 edition, at Wimbledon. The brave young lady kindled the enthusiasm of her countrymen with two Wimbledon singles victories in 1934 and 1937. Like Helen the Second, she was gifted with the number one spot in the world championships in 1934, the year that saw Queen Helen taken ill.

In 1937, although helped by another of Helen Wills's absences, Dorothy Round, who had just married Dr. Little (whatever happened to Ryuki Miki?), fell to second place behind a diminutive Chilean by the name of Anita Lizana. Anita won Forest Hills that year against another girl who came, as did she, from a country poor in tennis, the Polish Jadwiga Jedrzejowska, who stayed among the top seven of the world for four years, firing out her admirable forehand shots.

Surprised at the grace and courageous telling power of Anita's strokes, the press discovered that her father, Don Roberto, was the extremely competent trainer of the Club Quinta Normal de Santiago, and decided that the tiny brunette had the backhand and the talent of the tennis goddess. This judgment was perhaps a bit premature, but nonetheless it circulated widely. At the age of twenty-two, Anita had just married Ronald Ellis, and had accompanied him to Scotland, when Queen Helen returned to establish order once again.

Her career, which was drawing to a close, needed one more crowning achievement to accompany the lovely tiara that had graced her forehead at Buckingham Palace: the record of an eighth victory at Wimbledon. For the last time the queen met Helen the Second in the finals. Helen the First allowed her only four games.

1

Top of the page: The legendary and violent forehand of Helen Wills. Notice the arc of preparation, not overly accentuated, and the shift of weight at the instant of impact. The ball is violently lifted. 1. A backhand with splendid follow-through in which the whole body participates. 2. A lateral step as the stroke is being prepared. Ms. Wills is especially fascinating due to her technical balance, which is quite fluid at the same time. 3. The arrival at Centre Court for the last match between the two Helens. Helen Wills is to the left, Helen Jacobs to the right. Result: 6–4 and 6–0.

2

3

22 Alice Seen through the Looking Glass

Far from informing its readers about the training regime of Helen Wills, who was practicing for her first victorious Wimbledon, the *San Francisco Examiner* opened its sports section with the following headline in its issue of 16 March 1927:

GIRL OF THIRTEEN PLAYS WITH THE STARS
OF THE PACIFIC COAST LEAGUE

With a half-serious tone, the reporter told of an urchin who jumped the fence of the baseball training camp at the invitation of her idol, Lefty O'Doule. The youngster identified herself as Alice (they had thought she was a boy!), became the mascot of the team, and finally earned the nickname of Little Queen of Swats.

Like Wills, Alice Marble came to town from the country, and like her, she was destined to be a world champion. Alice was as poor as Helen was rich. Alice's career was highlighted by moments of anguish that paralleled those of her namesake in Lewis Carroll's delightful whimsy, *Through the Looking Glass*. Her grandfather was a gold prospector and her father a woodsman, one of the few capable of climbing to the top of the sequoias, and they both had provided the Marble family with a tiny farm in a place called Dutch Flat.

It was hard for the little girl to leave that lovely green spot with its red plantings and to move into a run-down neighborhood in San Francisco, but life grew even more difficult after her father died and her mother had to get up at four every morning to feed her five children. At that time Alice began to realize that boys' clothes and rough male ways made her feel more protected. Quickly she graduated from "kick the can" to baseball and basketball, and once she was a little better known, she decided to become a gymnastics instructor.

Alice was fifteen, and, much to her surprise, she found that she had suddenly blossomed into a young woman, 1.7 meters (5 ft. 7 in.) in height and 70 kilograms (154 lbs.) in weight. Her big brother Dan offered her a racket, and told her frankly that baseball was no longer right for her and that it was time to start acting like a young lady. Alice cried, for she knew that it was impossible to win an argument with him, just as it was impossible to beat him at handball. Amid a chorus of derision from the neighborhood youngsters, she began to bat the tennis ball around on the asphalt and concrete surface of the Golden Gate Park Club, the public courts where both McLoughlin and Little Bill Johnston had begun their careers.

Alice seemed to be made for the sport. Even before she was able to execute a decent backhand and a dignified serve, her quick eye and natural athletic ability brought her some measure of success. Put on the school team, she beat her secret love Rudy, with tears in her eyes. He was a fine sportsman who played football for the school, but he never spoke to her again. Her brother Dan added more overtime hours to his already busy schedule to sign her up at the California Tennis Club, where Alice returned in vain every evening, without any of these elegant people having ever indicated that they even saw her.

She sought refuge in the public park where now even her old friends ignored her. They were good people of every race, who had immigrated from everywhere, and they were not used to sticking up their noses at anyone. Alice began to hit the ball again hour after hour, to win competitions of ever increasing difficulty, until the Association finally took notice of her and sent her to Vancouver to represent California. When she returned, she proudly showed her mother and Dan the $6.37 that she had saved. They quickly escorted her to the nearest post office so she could send the amount to the Association.

Once enrolled at the university, Alice found that she had to work hard, and wondered how she could improve her tennis technique at the same time, when she met Eleanor Tennant. Eleanor was a woman about thirty-five years old, with grey hair and huge eyes that gleamed with carefree madness. Moreover, she was an excellent coach, capable of giving a clinic to a thousand students or of suggesting a plan of attack to one champion.

Eleanor offered Alice a fleetfoot's job as her good right arm, secretary, and confidante. She had Alice sign a contract with Wilson's and took her personally to see Beese White, an architect in love with tennis, who, working with Tennant, would give her a greater range of shots. He had helped Helen Jacobs do likewise, and he saw no reason why he should not be able to teach Alice the same thing, especially since she was more talented. Beese had her buy quite a few books dealing with tennis and then study the problems they outlined. Eleanor, more direct in manners, gave Alice her own special indoctrination. She took her along when she visited her circle of tennis stars, her well-mannered students, and even the Hearst country estate at San Simeone.

The little country girl thus found herself one evening in the company of Charlie Chaplin and Paulette Goddard, Bing Crosby, and Constance Talmadge. She could hardly believe it! The following morning, Arthur Brisbane wrote in one of the newspapers owned by their host: "Quite a girl, that Alice Marble! She has all the attributes of the Venus di Milo, and in addition two beautifully bronzed and solid arms! Frederick MacMonnies ought to do a statue of her. She should marry the most intelligent young man in America and become the ideal mother, with twelve children, not only the best tennis player, which will soon happen anyway!" Her mother was scandalized when she read the report and telephoned her daughter to return home at once. Alice politely refused. She was to go to Europe. To Paris.

When Alice regained consciousness in a small room in the American hospital at Neuilly in France, she told Helen Jacobs in a weak voice that the last thing she remembered about her match against Sylvia Henrotin was a tennis ball that grew larger and larger until it looked as if it were about to crush her. Helen told Alice that she had fainted, and that her red blood count was so low that she was probably suffering from anemia. Helen returned to cheer her friend every day until the American team of the Wightman Cup had to leave for London. Alice remained alone to stare for hours on end at the six peaches that her friend had left her as a gift.

1

2

3

4

Alice Marble was the first woman to play a man's game, following the tenets of her teacher, Eleanor Teach Tennant. 1. At the net, she unconcernedly prepares to kill Sarah Palfrey's passing shot. 2. Alice finishes a serve, stepping into the court. 3, 5. She delivers two decisive volleys, with her arm, tense and rigid, held well in front. 4. She stands smiling next to her downcast foe, Helen Jacobs, having beat her at Forest Hills. She did this three times, in 1936, 1939, and 1940.

Weeks went by before Doctor Dax reached a final diagnosis. In a grave tone he informed her that her trouble was not just anemia or pleurisy. "My dear girl, the news is bad. You have tuberculosis, and you'll never be able to play tennis again." Two months later Alice got off the ship in New York City to find only two people waiting for her: Eleanor Tennant and Mr. Moss, the secretary of the U.S. Lawn Tennis Association. While Eleanor gave her a hug, the secretary repeated several times in a harsh voice that she ought to come with him into his office to make an official report of her expenses. Eleanor gave him a piece of her mind, bundled Alice into a taxi and, once at the hotel, got her quickly to bed.

A few days later Eleanor permitted Julian Myrick, the president of the committee for the Wightman Cup, to visit the patient. Both women soon realized that the aging official had not come to cheer Alice, but rather to have a doctor of his choosing confirm the diagnosis and to inform the girl that the Association did not intend to spend one cent more on her: she had cost them too much already.

Within the limits of propriety, Eleanor told Myrick what she thought of him in no uncertain terms. Alice's collapse, she felt, was in good measure due to Myrick's stubborn and ironclad moralism. The year before, Alice had gone to play at the Maidstone Club Tournament in East Hampton, Long Island. She had signed up for the singles events and was surprised to find herself paired with Helen Wills in the drawing for the doubles matches. When Alice complained to Myrick, he immediately took the initiative and replied coldly: "Mrs. Wills has offered you the honor of playing with her, and in order to be selected in Wightman Cup play, you ought to show yourself worthy in our eyes. We," he concluded, "are the judges in the matter." Alice could not refute what he had said. That terrible Sunday she had played five matches, eleven sets, from ten in the morning until seven in the evening, losing five kilograms (11 lbs.) under a scorching sun. That evening she had fainted in the arms of her hosts, and a few days later she had collapsed again after an encounter lost 5–1 and match point against Nuthall.

As soon as she had finished heaping insults on Myrick, Eleanor took charge of Alice and drove her to her home in Beverly Hills and then to Pottingers Sanatorium just outside the city. The weeks went by, and Alice did not improve at all while she was in a state of depression over having to give up the struggle. Eleanor kept her alive with her magnetic vitality. It was she who suggested to Carole Lombard, Alice's favorite actress, to write the invalid a letter of encouragement.

"I am also a student of Teach Tennant," Miss Lombard wrote, "and I found myself in a hospital bed for six months just like you. When the doctors said that I was finished, I thought there was nothing to lose anyway, and I put up the best fight I possibly could. I proved that they were all wrong, and I survived, and I continued my career. You can do the same thing, Alice."

As she read those words, Alice suddenly decided to face her illness like a tennis match. She started smoking, in secret, one cigarette each day, and slowly clawed her way back to health. After five months Alice was fed up with the indecision of the doctors, and she persuaded Eleanor to spirit her away without their knowledge. Miss Tennant accepted a job in Palm Springs and kept Alice with her, little by little giving her things to do to keep her mind off herself. She finally found the courage to insist that Alice have another thorough checkup.

Dr. Commons, a friend of Eleanor's, had Alice under his X-ray machine for an hour, auscultated her, questioned her, felt her carefully, and then declared with authority that she had never suffered from tuberculosis, but only from pleurisy aggravated by anemia. He concluded that there was absolutely no reason for her not to go back to tennis if she wanted to do so.

Alice began once again. She found the energy to build up her muscles and to refashion her strokes completely on the model of the great champions, and then underwent a four-day physical examination under the watchful eyes of Myrick and his worthy associates. They now refused to let her sign up for the championships, "to guard her compromised health." She felt Eleanor's bright and sparkling glance upon her, found her smile once again at the edge of the courts and later that evening when she returned home exhausted. At the end of the summer of 1936 she once again went out on the central court at Forest Hills to meet and take Helen Jacobs, four-time women's champion of the United States. What followed is carefully documented in all the record books.

23 Budge's Grand Slam and the Baron in Prison

Baron Gottfried von Cramm was the best runner-up of recorded history. Especially strong on clay courts, he won Paris in 1934 at the age of twenty-five. Although he did the same thing two years later in that event, he had to bow to Perry when the latter beat him at Wimbledon in 1935 and 1936. At the end of this last finals event, which was over in less than an hour with the devastating score of 6–1, 6–1, 6–0, the umpire, after having shaken his hand, made a sign to get the attention of the audience and announced: "Baron von Cramm begs your pardon for the quality of his game, due to a muscle pulled in the first game."

A game in which the score was tied ten times during Perry's first service, had indeed stretched a muscle in Gottfried's leg, and he continued only because one does not forfeit a tournament. When he was small and went riding bareback through their farm at Hildesheim, his father had taught him that in tournaments a player had to be worthy of his ancestors, splendid and brave gentlemen. During his baptism by fire at the Davis Cup, while he and Lund were close to defeating none less than Allison and Van Ryn, von Cramm had stopped the game to inform the umpire that their opponents' ball, before going out, had brushed against him: no one else on the court and in the whole stadium had noticed that fact. Once Perry had joined the professional ranks in 1936, the Germans were not alone in thinking that their beloved Gottfried would become world champion.

But the position of this blond giant of the tennis world was not so enviable as the public might imagine. An aristocratic tradition, coupled with a Rousseauistic education among farm workers, horses, and flocks of sheep, had quickly brought von Cramm into open disagreement with Hitler and his regime. Paradoxically, since Gottfried was the perfect model of those Nordic types so much fawned over by Rosenberg, the hierarchy put up with his unbelievably freewheeling audacity, hoping to be able to make use of him one way or the other. Early in 1937, to show him their strength, they forced him not to register for the French championships, with the excuse that they could thereby show their faith in the number two man, Henkel. He, good Aryan that he was, clicked his heels and stretched out his arm in the proper salute at the end of the match. They permitted Gottfried to train with Tilden, however, and let it be known in a friendly way that the fatherland could not do without a good showing in the Davis Cup competitions.

With Vines lost to them, the Americans, in the meantime, had found a brand-new and very young champion at home. His curly red hair, his bright red cheeks, and his sky-blue eyes gave him the look of a Modigliani portrait. When someone told him that to his face, the only reason he did not react to this unknown word was his shyness. Donald was the son of a Scot who had left the frigid lochs for better weather, after having suffered a lung disorder on the playing field of his soccer team, the Glasgow Rangers. Arriving in Oakland, California, the enterprising man set up a laundry, married, raised a family, and was able to state with something more than pride that the youngest of his children had very much taken after him. Donald was extremely good in baseball and even better in basketball, but rather than turn the ball loose he would

have allowed himself to be trampled to death.

Mr. Budge thus began a prudent outflanking maneuver, supported by the eldest son, Lloyd, who was wild over tennis. The day of his fifteenth birthday, Don finally let himself be talked into signing up for the California boy's championships, and in a week of arduous training, he learned enough to take the event. That success suddenly raised him, as if by magic, far above the neighborhood arguments about tennis. His brother Lloyd, who quickly became his well-informed coach, had to admit that if football had

23 Budge's Grand Slam and the Baron in Prison

Baron Gottfried von Cramm was the best runner-up of recorded history. Especially strong on clay courts, he won Paris in 1934 at the age of twenty-five. Although he did the same thing two years later in that event, he had to bow to Perry when the latter beat him at Wimbledon in 1935 and 1936. At the end of this last finals event, which was over in less than an hour with the devastating score of 6–1, 6–1, 6–0, the umpire, after having shaken his hand, made a sign to get the attention of the audience and announced: "Baron von Cramm begs your pardon for the quality of his game, due to a muscle pulled in the first game."

A game in which the score was tied ten times during Perry's first service, had indeed stretched a muscle in Gottfried's leg, and he continued only because one does not forfeit a tournament. When he was small and went riding bareback through their farm at Hildesheim, his father had taught him that in tournaments a player had to be worthy of his ancestors, splendid and brave gentlemen. During his baptism by fire at the Davis Cup, while he and Lund were close to defeating none less than Allison and Van Ryn, von Cramm had stopped the game to inform the umpire that their opponents' ball, before going out, had brushed against him: no one else on the court and in the whole stadium had noticed that fact. Once Perry had joined the professional ranks in 1936, the Germans were not alone in thinking that their beloved Gottfried would become world champion.

But the position of this blond giant of the tennis world was not so enviable as the public might imagine. An aristocratic tradition, coupled with a Rousseauistic education among farm workers, horses, and flocks of sheep, had quickly brought von Cramm into open disagreement with Hitler and his regime. Paradoxically, since Gottfried was the perfect model of those Nordic types so much fawned over by Rosenberg, the hierarchy put up with his unbelievably freewheeling audacity, hoping to be able to make use of him one way or the other. Early in 1937, to show him their strength, they forced him not to register for the French championships, with the excuse that they could thereby show their faith in the number two man, Henkel. He, good Aryan that he was, clicked his heels and stretched out his arm in the proper salute at the end of the match. They permitted Gottfried to train with Tilden, however, and let it be known in a friendly way that the fatherland could not do without a good showing in the Davis Cup competitions.

With Vines lost to them, the Americans, in the meantime, had found a brand-new and very young champion at home. His curly red hair, his bright red cheeks, and his sky-blue eyes gave him the look of a Modigliani portrait. When someone told him that to his face, the only reason he did not react to this unknown word was his shyness. Donald was the son of a Scot who had left the frigid lochs for better weather, after having suffered a lung disorder on the playing field of his soccer team, the Glasgow Rangers. Arriving in Oakland, California, the enterprising man set up a laundry, married, raised a family, and was able to state with something more than pride that the youngest of his children had very much taken after him. Donald was extremely good in baseball and even better in basketball, but rather than turn the ball loose he would have allowed himself to be trampled to death.

Mr. Budge thus began a prudent outflanking maneuver, supported by the eldest son, Lloyd, who was wild over tennis. The day of his fifteenth birthday, Don finally let himself be talked into signing up for the California boy's championships, and in a week of arduous training, he learned enough to take the event. That success suddenly raised him, as if by magic, far above the neighborhood arguments about tennis. His brother Lloyd, who quickly became his well-informed coach, had to admit that if football had

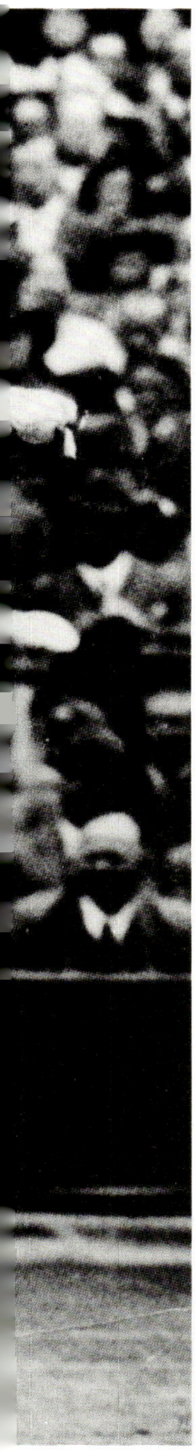

To the left: A lateral volley, well forward, showing Don Budge's tight wrist control of his backhand. To the right: One of Gottfried von Cramm's smashes that seems hit softly from the relaxed body position.

endowed Don with blind courage, at least baseball had given him a backhand unrivaled anywhere. Don had always batted as a left-hander, grasping the bat near the handle with his right hand: it seemed natural for him to use the same technique in tennis, without frills or adornments and with a much reduced arc, while striking the ball with the wrist and arm held rigid, as if he were going to drive it out of the park. His shorter opponents, who rushed the net after they served, were inevitably passed, one after the other, including Gene Mako, the child prodigy of that day.

For his tender years, Gene must have been a truly remarkable young man, for, as soon as he lost the finals of the junior championships at Culver, he recognized the victor's superior talent, and proposed to him that they collaborate in doubles play. So Budge and Mako began their grand tennis adventure together in a happy, studentlike revelry, punctuated with practical jokes and music: both being jazz fans, they refused to travel without their phonograph, records, and recorder; from early in the morning when they got up to shave, the music of Benny Goodman and Tommy Dorsey filled their room.

Mako's friendship not only helped polish Don's social graces, but also empowered him to overcome a natural timidity that became almost chronic outside the close circle of his university friends and associates. Among all the examples of his awkwardness, the episode of the queen is the most famous. During his first Wimbledon in 1935, Queen Mary entered her box while Budge was totally intent on his attack on Austin. Faced with all those people suddenly on their feet, Don was surprised, gave a hitch to his trousers, and turning in his tracks, lifted his racket in what to many looked like a salute. Then, when he saw Austin bowing deeply, he dropped his arms and tried his best to imitate his friend. Two years later, on the same court, Budge bowed with the effortless ease of a member of the court, and then heard the regal spectator say laughingly: "Dear Mr. Budge, I confess to you that some time ago, I did not notice that you greeted me with your hand. Had I seen you do so, I assure you that I would have responded in the same fashion."

This short and friendly regal audience had followed Don's success over Gottfried von Cramm. A few days later, Budge and von Cramm confronted each other on Centre Court once again. Since England had been weakened by Perry's turning professional, the United States and Germany were struggling bitterly in a decisive semifinals match. Walter Pate, the American captain who, at the beginning of his career, had fixed his sights on Budge, was responsible for a grave error in judgment, preferring tiny Bitsy Grant, known as the Atom, to Frank Parker. Grant had lost not only to von Cramm, but also to Henkel, and, at the beginning of the last match, the two teams stood tied.

That meeting, certainly important for Budge, represented a real baptism by fire for Gottfried von Cramm. If he were to emerge unscathed, the nimbus of victory would make him invulnerable and raise him to the stature of an unwilling model for the young people of the Third Reich. A defeat would provoke cruel criticisms and even suspicions of being a traitor, and his fate, similar to that of a defeated gladiator in ancient Rome, would depend on the good pleasure of the tyrant.

While the two adversaries were preparing to go out on the court, accompanied by Teddy Tinling, von Cramm was called into the office of the club by an urgent telephone message. Gottfried lifted the receiver, and his lips contracted as he pronounced three words: "*Ja, mein Führer.*" In a moment he rejoined Budge and Tinling, informing them quietly: "It was Hitler. He wanted to wish me good luck."

Faced by such a dramatic situation, with an enthusiastic and amused audience and an adversary totally intent on his work, Gott-

In the color plates on the following pages: 1. Politics raises its head in the encounter between Gottfried von Cramm of Nazi Germany and Donald Budge of the United States of America. An involuntary footman of Hitler, von Cramm will later become his victim. 2, 3. Wimbledon, capital of tennis. 4. Above: La musa metafisica (The Metaphysical Muse) *and* Il figlio del costruttore (The Son of the Construction Worker) *by Carlo Carrà. Below:* Two Girls Playing Badminton *by David Inshaw.*

fried played the best tennis of his entire life. Ahead two sets to zero, he paid for Budge's return in the third and had no luck in tripping him up in the fourth. But at the beginning of the fifth, he broke Budge's serve with two attacks on his forehand drive, and then surged ahead by a 4–1 that seemed decisive to all: Tilden himself, with doubtful taste, got up, and showed Henkel his index finger and thumb forming a tiny circle.

As he passed Walter Pate, with a dejected pall hanging over him, Budge had a sudden surge of pride: "We aren't finished yet, captain," he murmured. And then, as if to convince himself: "I am not tired. I feel very well indeed." From the base line, he pulled a love game out of the fire in a few violent serves, and taking advantage of a sudden weakness in von Cramm's serve, he anticipated his return at the net to repay him for the break. Von Cramm had two more break points for a five to three score, but Budge, by this time totally uncontrollable, wiped them out to surge ahead 7–6. That game must have been pure mental cruelty for Gottfried, but he bore it all bravely. After six deuces, having wiped out three match points, he crossed a tremendous forehand to Budge's right and followed it to the net. Don rushed to retrieve that angle shot with sheer desperation, slipped, and as he was falling, succeeded in placing a perfect drive that took the ball along the entire side line to drop in the corner, while von Cramm, diving after it in vain, watched it with desperate eyes.

Shaking Don's hand, Gottfried found the strength to smile: "This was the greatest match of my life. I am glad I lost it to a man like you." Later, in the dressing room, Tilden remarked that this had been "the most beautiful match of tennis ever played." After that encounter, and the following one lost by Gottfried at Forest Hills, the future seemed so clearly outlined that he no longer held back his disgust with the Nazis. When he returned home from Australia, he was accused of homosexuality, a maneuver often used by his enemies, then tried and imprisoned.

Without his only opposition, Donald Budge outdid himself. From July of that adventuresome 1937 until September 1938, he did not lose another match, winning the Australian and French championships as well as Wimbledon and Forest Hills. His record becomes even more fantastic if we note that only one of his opponents, the little known Yugoslavian left-hander Kukuljevic, ever succeeded in taking five sets from him in Paris, while at Wimbledon no one ever bested him in even one set! To assert his outright superiority even more, Don teamed up with Mako and Marble, and also won doubles and mixed at Forest Hills and at Wimbledon, which some humorist tried to rename Wimbledonald.

Behind these triumphant images of success are hidden the now forgotten pains, anguishes, and the small and yet sometimes shameful weaknesses. Before Budge began that incredible year, Jack Harris, the director of the professional troupe and a wise old owl that he was, did not fail to remind him that one slip, one small hole in the grass could cost him the $50,000 guarantee that was being offered him. "But then you might finish in a twinkling, with a fine silver cup to show your grandchildren." Don responded coldly that he was no longer a child: "If things go well for me, it will cost you a good deal more next year."

Vines tried to discourage him from making the trip to Australia, shortly before the departure. "Don't go," Ellie insisted, basing his comments on his own experience there. "With the chance of beating the world champion, and an American at that, the Australian players will do their utmost. You might very well win the Australian title for all of that, but later on you'll pay for it. Believe me, it's not worth the effort." Budge went nevertheless, accompanied by his buddy Mako, and took advantage of the crossing to build up a fine reserve of uncluttered and relaxing days, twenty-one in all.

Unconcernedly, he began to lose all his exhibition matches, looking upon them as exercises in futility. Shortly before the tournament began, he suddenly realized that he had lost his voice, and faced with the perplexity of the doctors, was afraid for a time that he might never recover it. He got it back the very day of the victory over Bromwich, just in time for the thank-you speech. Twenty-four hours later he was at sea. In the absence of von Cramm, what Budge feared most were the slow, dusty courts of Roland Garros. Don let himself get slightly run down before the event and had to struggle with a bout of dysentery before he ever got to his opponents. Pablo Casals was there to encourage him and promised him a private concert if he won. The night of the victory against Menzel, the great cellist played for two hours in a drawing room overlooking the Eiffel Tower, with the starry night for a backdrop.

When he arrived in London, Don won the Queens only to realize, halfway through Wimbledon, that his backhand, his most unfailing ally, was giving him trouble. He wandered alone along the hedges of red and blue hydrangea and stopped near an out-of-the-way court where two older women tennis enthusiasts were having a go at it. As he watched the ball being batted back and forth, he reflected on his lost stroke; suddenly, like an image brought into focus, the backhand of one of the two ladies caught his attention. She struck the ball as he did, with her arm held stiff, the movement executed from below with a slight lift. He ran madly to the dressing room and prevailed on Bitsy Grant, who had just put on his street clothes, to change and go out to court with him.

C.CARRÀ

C. CARRÀ 917-921

1

1. Lifted serve by von Cramm. He used this weapon, extremely effective in clay-court competition, on the green at Wimbledon as well, where this sequence was snapped by Arthur Cole. Von Cramm would alternate this spin with the cannonball, and would assume an aggressive stance, ready to rush the net. 2. The finals matches at Forest Hills in 1939, won by Budge over von Cramm 6–1, 7–9, 6–1, 3–6, 6–1. 3, 4. These drawings from Sports Illustrated *show the analogy that can be drawn between Budge's blow with a bat, begun with the left hand, and his famous backhand. 5. In this photo sequence, the legendary backhand is prepared well in advance, with effortless grace. It was probably the best backhand in the annals of tennis.*

2

3

4

5

1

Ten balls or so struck with precision and his accustomed speed restored his stroke to him, as if by magic, and made certain the winning of Wimbledon as well.

After the three transoceanic victories and the defense of the Davis Cup, the home tournament at Forest Hills seemed an easy event to the critics. During the Cup competition, a bad case of influenza and a terrible toothache had upset Budge a great deal more than Quist and Bromwich. He lost his voice once again, but was lucky enough to find a dentist who extracted the tooth that had been poisoning him from the beginning of the season. With that obstacle out of the way, despite the anxiety that always precedes the finishing touches, Budge felt sure of victory, so much so that he suggested to the most dangerous of his adversaries, Gene Mako, that they have a nightcap together. "When I ran to the net to shake his hand," commented Budge, "the man who congratulated me was the only one in the world who really knew what my accomplishment meant to me."

On November ninth of the same year, 1938, Walter Pate called a press conference to announce the addition of Donald Budge to the ranks of professionals, and, for the first time, none of the American officials refused to be present and not one sound of indignant protest was heard. "I do not believe that I have fully discharged my debt of gratitude toward the American Association," Budge stated generously, "but I must think of the future." He lost his opening match against Vines on the boards of Madison Square Garden, but then went on to best his adversary twenty-one matches to eighteen, beating Perry as well, with eighteen victories to eleven. The tour garnered him $100,000.

From his prison cell, von Cramm followed the victories of his fortunate rival. Budge seemed to be one of the very few who even remembered him. To show his support of his friend, Budge refused to play in Germany, and himself composed a letter of protest which he circulated for signature among twenty-five famous American sports figures. Gottfried also had another friend in Great Britain, John Olliff. As soon as he was released, von Cramm sent his registration to the tournament at Queens Club, which precedes Wimbledon. In a stormy session of the executive committee, Olliff managed to secure approval for von Cramm's admission, twelve votes to eleven. His courageous action ran aground, however, of the gentlemen at Wimbledon. Whether or not the accusation against von Cramm came by order of Himmler, whether or not it was even true, it was too infamous to admit the German into those hallowed halls.

These gentlemen cast out the black sheep, thus throwing their weight behind a bureaucracy that not too many months later would bomb London and ancient Centre Court itself. Von Cramm reached the finals of the Queens Club and there ran across Bobby Riggs, the American who had taken Budge's place. Von Cramm beat Riggs 6–1 and 6–0. Two weeks later Riggs would easily win the three Wimbledon titles.

1. The principals in the match: Budge, Mako, von Cramm, and Henkel. 2. A backhand volley by Henkel. 3. The German attack, after a smash by von Cramm. 4. One of Budge's smashes. To his left is Gene Mako. 5. Von Cramm, an anti-Nazi suspected of plotting against the Third Reich, bows before Adolf Hitler. Germany's most popular sports figure will be wished good luck by the Führer himself a few moments before the decisive match against Budge played at Wimbledon in 1937.

2

3

4

5

6

7

Up four to one in the fifth set, von Cramm was not able to stem the tide of the inspired play of the American at that point, thereby falling from grace with the Nazi overlords. 6. Going on the court for the decisive match. 7. Tension seen on the faces of von Cramm and his captain Kleinschroth. 8. von Cramm seen leaving the court, broken in spirit, after the game. What a contrast to (6)!

8

1

2

3

4

against Cooke (6), but beaten at the Queens Club tourney by von Cramm, just released from prison. 5. Austin without Perry will not succeed in defending the Davis Cup for the U.S. in 1938. With him is Parker.

1. Donald Budge, with Mako to his left, receives the U.S. Champion's Cup at Forest Hills, thereby winning the Grand Slam, first in the history of the sport to do so. 2. He will defeat Vines 6–1, 6–3, 6–0 in his debut as a professional at Madison Square Garden. 4. Bobby Riggs replaces him, winning Wimbledon in 1939

5

6

24 Tennis with a Stiff Upper Lip

By the time the war began the golden age of modern British tennis – the great years of Perry, Austin and the domination of the Davis Cup – had already ended. Britain's last appearance in the challenge-round had been in 1937. Then, without Perry and Hughes, they won only one rubber from the United States.

Austin reached the final at Wimbledon in 1938, but did not play in the Davis Cup. The team was being rebuilt and for the old rulers of Europe the process of reconstruction was proving difficult. With Ronald Shayes, Frank Wilde, Donald Butler and the painstaking C. M. Jones, they narrowly defeated Rumania in the first round at Harrogate and then failed to win a rubber from Yugoslavia at Zagreb. Dragutin Mitic and Franjo Puncec lost only one set between them. Charles Hare, who played singles in 1937, returned in 1939 and there were signs of improvement, but in the fourth round Germany – even without von Cramm – beat them 5–0 in Berlin, while at Wimbledon every title went to the United States.

The Americans at least were able to continue their national competitions during the war. Between 1939 and 1945, tennis stood still in Britain. Bombs fell at Wimbledon and sheep grazed on the outside courts. The indomitable Norah Gordon Cleather, acting as secretary and general factotum, kept the All-England flag flying. There were some charity matches, exhibitions in aid of the Red Cross, but after five years without tennis the game in Britain was never quite the same again. Those upper-middle-class young men, who had so much time to play in the tournaments of the 1930s, scarcely existed in the post-war age of austerity. The Americans and Australians returned. The Europeans, particularly the French, proved unexpectedly resilient – Yvon Petra surprised the world when Wimbledon resumed in 1946 – and the Championships became a tournament where the hosts did no more than offer great players from abroad opportunities to demonstrate their skills, and cheered furiously when a British man survived the first Tuesday.

It was a grey picture. The British were the most enthusiastic tennis spectators in the world ("They are Wimbledon mad, but not tennis mad," Arthur Ashe was to remark 30 years later), but their own troops had been scattered and no one had had time to train reserves. Tournaments declined – there had been more than 300 events of some quality in the 1930s, but 20 years later there were only 100; small tennis clubs, a special feature of pre-war social life, disappeared; golf, governed with more forethought and liveliness, became more fashionable than tennis; and the standard of play in Britain dropped sadly. The tennis court in the family garden became a rarity. The Vicar was too busy to invite us for tea and mixed doubles.

The game still had a broad base (where else were so many schoolgirls taught to play as a part of their education?), but there was no one at the top of the pyramid, no one with Perry's confidence or buccaneering arrogance to inspire the new generation. Matters might have been different if Britain had begun the peace with a strong Davis Cup team or even with a single national hero.

Instead Perry was a professional, living in America; Austin had exchanged tennis for Moral Rearmament; Hughes and Raymond Tuckey had retired; Hare was living in the United States; and the talent of their pre-war replacements had never been allowed to flower. For Britain's first (and only) match in the 1946 Davis Cup,

the Lawn Tennis Association almost found themselves in the position of looking for volunteers to play against France in Paris.

They found Donald MacPhail, a quarter-finalist in singles and doubles at Wimbledon in 1938, and Derek Barton – neither of whom won a set – for the singles, and an experienced doubles pair, Henry Billington, a Wiltshire farmer with a fine agricultural-looking forehand, and the talented, bulky John Olliff, Wallis Myers's successor as lawn tennis correspondent of the *Daily Telegraph*. Billington and Olliff had won the British Hard Court title at Bournemouth in 1939, but now Billington was 36 and Olliff 37. Even so, they played the only rubber which saved Britain's face in Paris, taking Marcel Bernard – who was to win the French singles later that year – and Bernard Destremau to 13–11, 4–6, 7–5, 6–1. One set in five rubbers! Britain's last visit to Paris had been for the dramatic triumph of the 1933 challenge-round when Roper-Barrett's team won 3–2. That match seemed to belong to another world of lawn tennis.

The glimmerings of improvement were seen the following year. There were two newcomers in the 1947 team – Tony Mottram, who had played in three minor international matches in 1939 and then won the DFC during the war, and Geoffrey Paish, a bespectacled civil servant from Croydon, persistent and industrious, who had attracted attention by a good performance at Bournemouth the previous year. Mottram, a handsome player in every sense of the word, a good volleyer and the possessor of an elegant backhand, was beginning his career as a serious tournament player at the age of 25.

Mottram is one of the might-have-beens of British tennis. A fine Davis Cup player, he won two-thirds of the 56 rubbers that he played for Britain, between 1947 and 1955; he reached the doubles final at Wimbledon with the Australian, Bill Sidwell, in 1947, and the following year beat Drobny to become Britain's first post-war men's singles quarter-finalist there. But what would he have achieved if it had not been for the gap of the war years? Would he have been a much better player? In tournament play he was inconsistent. Peaks of performance were followed by blank anti-climaxes. The victory over Drobny was followed by a disappointing match against Lennart Bergelin.

2

3

But in the Davis Cup he was more relaxed and more consistent. He could always astonish the Continentals by his coolness in the crises of international tennis. This was that famous English cold blood that they had heard about. Certainly, his decision to devote himself to the game was important. Here at last was a top player who looked like a top player. "Typically British," said everyone as Mottram appeared, immaculate, disciplined and detached, the embodiment of the stiff upper lip in tennis. There hasn't been anyone quite like him since then. He turned professional in 1955, became Britain's national coach 15 years later and then took over the direction of what the LTA calls "national development". He married Joy Gannon, a member of five Wightman Cup teams, and of their three children two have won all the British national junior titles and then represented Britain internationally.

With Mottram to lead, Paish, the civil servant from Croydon, the part-time player who found himself in the firing-line, was a more effective competitor. They carried Britain's Davis Cup burden for eight years. Paish, the admirable second man, a doubles player of considerable ability but also useful in singles, took part in 38 rubbers, and might have had an even better record if he had played in more of the dead rubbers in matches that were already won.

Their opening match in Warsaw in 1947 marked Poland's reappearance in the Davis Cup. The city was in ruins and the Poles were dismayed that the British had not brought with them two leading Polish players, Czeslaw Spychala and Ignacy Tloczynski, who had stayed in England after the war. The Poles said that they had been selected and expected them to play and the British had to say firmly that they had no control over the absent players. There was an awkward confrontation with the Polish press, and against a background of Polish bitterness Mottram won two singles and Paish partnered Butler, returning to the team at 37 after an absence of nine years, successfully in the doubles. South Africa (Eric Sturgess and Eustace Fannin) ended Britain's progress in the next round at Scarborough, but at least the first steps towards the rebuilding of the team had been taken.

1948 was the best of the Mottram-Paish years. There was an agonizing beginning against India at Harrogate. Howard Walton, bespectacled and unorthodox, a self-taught player from Birmingham, was chosen for the second singles. He suffered from stomach trouble and was beaten twice, but Mottram won both his singles and took the doubles with Paish. Thereafter Paish was entrusted with the second singles and Britain beat Norway and the Netherlands before falling to Sweden by 4–1 in Stockholm.

4

1

Czechoslovakia, who won 4–1 at Wimbledon, ended the 1949 campaign. There had been hopes of a British victory after Mottram's success against Drobny in the Championships the previous year, but this time no one could take a set from him in singles or doubles. Britain's consolation was Mottram's 6–2, 6–4, 6–4 victory over Vladimir Cernik. In 1950 it was Giovanni Cucelli's turn to frustrate the British. He won all three rubbers in Italy's 3–2 victory at Eastbourne. Paish, in his finest singles, nearly saved the match before going down by 1–6, 6–2, 4–6, 6–4, 8–6.

1951 was notable for revenge against France (3–2 in London) and another failure against Sweden. The following year began with a remarkable away victory, a captain's triumph, in Belgrade. Roger Becker, a pugnacious 18-year-old from Surrey, had travelled as a reserve, but in his opening rubber Paish injured an ankle against Josip Palada. The score was 1–1 and Paish was clearly unfit for the doubles. Colin Gregory, the captain, runner-up at Wimbledon with Ian Collins in 1929, decided that it would be safer if he took Paish's place and partnered Mottram instead of the inexperienced Becker. The gamble succeeded. They beat Palada and Laszlo 6–4, 1–6, 9–11, 6–2, 6–2. Mottram won both his singles and Britain were through by the odd rubber. Becker, making his first appearance, took Vladimir Petrovic to five sets.

5

6

7

8

Italy beat Gregory's team 4–1 in the third round at Bologna that year and, for the British, with the dislike of slow clay and heat, that was by no means a discreditable performance against a side which reached the inter-zone final. Mottram and Paish beat Cucelli and Mario del Bello in the doubles and Mottram had led Fausto Gardini, also so difficult to play in the Davis Cup in Italy, by two sets before losing 4–6, 4–6, 6–3, 6–1, 6–0. In both 1953 and 1954 Britain were Belgium's victims in the third round.

By then everyone knew that the time for change had come. Herman David had taken over as captain when Gregory was elected chairman of the All-England Club. Dan Maskell, who had coached Britain's teams since the 1930s, had now become the LTA's training-manager and the search for a successor had narrowed to George Worthington, a notable doubles player and a graduate of Harry Hopman's Australian Davis Cup academy. And a new group of young players were ready to take over. It was a time for optimism and new faces.

Becker had been given his initiation at Belgrade, and in 1955 he replaced Paish in the singles against Austria at Vienna, losing to the acrobatic Freddi Huber, a bewildering opponent for anyone playing a first "live" rubber, and beating Franz Saiko. Mottram won both his singles, defeating Huber 6–3, 5–7, 2–6, 6–4, 6–4 after trailing 2–4 in the final set. Against India at Manchester, Becker took command. Mottram lost to the promising Ramanathan Krishnan and then he and Paish fell in their last doubles to Krishnan and Naresh Kumar. India led 2–1 at the end of the second day, but Becker won both his singles and after losing the first two sets of an agonizing, protracted rubber, Mottram struggled home by 6–3 in the fifth against Kumar.

That was his last battle. He and Paish retired honorably and the

1. The Davis Cup begins again. Britain (Billington, Olliff, MacPhail and Barton) played their first post-war match in Paris in 1946. France (Petra, Pelizza, Destremau and Barnard) beat them 5–0. 2. Dan Maskell, left, as coach to the All-England Club, trained Britain's successful pre-war teams and contributed to the revival of the game after the war by touring with Fred Perry. In 1955 Maskell became the LTA's training-manager. George Worthington, an Australian, succeeded him at Wimbledon (3). 4. Watched by Tony Mottram, Geoff Paish smashes in the doubles against France in 1951. Together, they restored Britain's Davis Cup reputation. The Wightman Cup story was dismal in the immediate post-war years. 5, 6. Jean Bostock was the only player to capture a set in 1947 and 1958. 7. Angela Buxton was Britain's first post-war singles finalist. Shirley Fry beat her 6–3, 6–1 in 1956, but she won the doubles with Althea Gibson. 8. Roger Becker, the first of the new post-war generation of British Davis Cup players, was picked, aged 18, to play against Yugoslavia in 1952.

1

2

3

4

younger generation were given the task of meeting Italy in the zone semi-final at Edgbaston. Mottram was 35 and Paish 33. The average age of Herman David's new team was 20. Becker at 21, was the senior member. The others were Billy Knight, a left-hander from Northamptonshire, who had won the Australian junior title in 1953 and who was to become the first of Britain's post-war clay court specialists; Bobby Wilson, Knight's junior by ten days (November, 1935, was a good month for British tennis, just as November, 1934, had been a vintage time in Australia), a stylist from suburbia, possessing a grass-court game of infinite promise; and – the most interesting of the newcomers – Michael Davies from Swansea.

Davies broke the pattern. The others had risen with the help of the lawn tennis establishment. Becker and Wilson came from Surrey and Middlesex, the most fashionable and powerful counties in the LTA, and Surrey and Middlesex, geographically close to Queen's Club, the training-centre for British tennis, and politically always at the heart of the LTA's policy-making and selection processes, always look after their own bright juniors. Knight's family were prominent in Northamptonshire tennis. His sister, Jean, had been a determined competitor at Junior Wimbledon and the LTA had watched his progress since he was a small boy.

But in the early 1960s South Wales was a backwoods area in British tennis and Davies's struggle for a place in the Davis Cup team was more difficult. Becker and Wilson could live at home in Croydon and Finchley and, since the game was concentrated on London, travel easily to most of the important tournaments, but it was an expensive journey from Swansea to the Cumberland Club at Hampstead – where the tournament in April was regarded as an unofficial Davis Cup trial with the selectors meeting in a house near the courts as soon as the men's final ended – or Roehampton.

Davies may have been short of money, but never of ambition, determination or ingenuity. The showbiz streak showed itself early. He dressed flamboyantly (like a promising actor in a good rep, whereas Knight could have been mistaken for a budding country auctioneer, Wilson for a bank clerk and Becker for a boxer) and even when he grew fatter and headed the ranking-list regularly, he never forgot that he had been a hungry fighter. He admired American attitudes, but he was very much a European player, moody, artistic and apt to sink into dark Celtic swamps of frustration. American competitors aren't usually as complicated as that. The truth was that he had considerable talent and intelligence and an ambitious conception of the way that tennis should be played, but he wasn't quite athletic enough to carry out his imaginative designs. When he didn't satisfy himself, he receded into a kind of Celtic twilight, a sulky night of the soul.

The LTA found him full of grievances. He called his autobiography *Tennis Rebel* and it throws useful sidelights on the game in the days before open tennis. Herman David, for whom he played nobly, could bring the best from him and he was close to George Worthington, with his poker-faced jokes and Australian ironies, but mostly gulfs of non-communication yawned between Davies, the most articulate of the new men and a shrewd, passionate thinker about the game, and the rulers of British tennis. Twenty years later many of them were still expressing surprise that Davies had become the executive director and chief impressario of World Championship Tennis, the largest of the international professional touring groups.

In that tie in 1955 against Italy he partnered Wilson and they lost 4–6, 11–9, 8–6, 6–3 to Pietrangeli and Sirola. For a combination of opposites, totally different in temperament and attitudes to life, Wilson and Davies worked together remarkably successfully, reaching the Wimbledon final in 1960, winning Bournemouth in 1958 and a number of difficult Davis Cup rubbers. Italy took that match, at 5–0, as had been expected, but none of the rubbers were easy and Knight, who seemed to embody the new spirit, bursting with effort, attacking ferociously, forced the stylish, confident Pietrangeli to five sets.

With Becker and Knight in the singles and an assortment of doubles partnerships, they were semi-finalists again in 1956, losing to Sweden in Stockholm and they fell at the same stage to Belgium – Washer and Brichant, the tormentors of Mottram and Paish, again – in a damp tie at Brussels the following year. Davies and Wilson, who had beaten France in the previous round (Davies defeated Robert Haillet after losing the first two sets in the deciding rubber), had taken over and Britain led 2–1 at the end of the second day. This time it was Davies's turn to lose a crucial two-set lead. Washer overtook him to win 1–6, 4–6, 6–3, 6–4, 6–2.

But the real year of frustration, when the stiffest upper lips trembled with disappointment, was 1958, Herman David's last season as captain before he was elected chairman of the All-England Club. Brazil, West Germany and France were dismissed without the loss of a rubber and in the zone final Britain met Italy, the source of so many frustrations in this decade, at Milan. The odds were against victory. The sun was fierce; Wilson, who was ill, stayed behind in the team's hotel; and the crowd was noisily hostile and blatantly attempting to influence the line-judges. But in the opening match Davies, in the best of his 38 rubbers for Britain, defeated Pietrangeli 6–4, 6–3, 6–1. Sirola made it 1–1 by beating Knight in three sets. If Britain were to win, they had to beat the strongest pair in Europe in the doubles. Davies and Knight took Pietrangeli and Sirola to 6–3, 5–7,

6

7

The Davis Cup team that Herman David and George Worthington built – Bobby Wilson (1), Billy Knight (2), Mike Davies (3) and Roger Becker (4). They were European zone finalists in 1958, losing to Italy at Milan, and semi-finalists in five other years before Davies turned professional.
5. Australia-bound. Dennis Coombe (center) managed an LTA tour which was part of the tennis education of Mark Cox (left), Roger Taylor, Stanley Matthews and Graham Stilwell.
6. Angela Mortimer and Ann Shilcock won Britain's first post-war title at Wimbledon. In an all-British final they beat Shirley Bloomer (10) and Pat Ward.

5

6–4, 4–6, 9–7 and that was all they could do. The next day the Italians won the last two singles and Britain's chance in their first post-war European zone final had gone.

The following year there was a narrow victory over Chile at Eastbourne and an equally narrow failure against Spain in a semi-final at Barcelona. Knight beat Manuel Santana, who had not then appeared often outside Spain, on the first day; Davies and Wilson made it 2–1 by winning the doubles and in the deciding singles Davies led Santana by two sets to one. After the 10 minute interval the Spaniard, who had seemed to be flagging, returned to hit squences of audacious winners. Davies, who won only one game in the last two sets, watched disconsolately as the cheering crowd carried Santana around the court. "It was some of the greatest tennis I've ever seen," wrote Davies ruefully. It had been a devastating finish – an early glimpse of the skill and brilliance which was to bring Santana so many of the game's great titles.

In a way, that match marked the end of Davies's leadership of the team. He had been No. 1 on the ranking-list for three years, but Herman David had gone; he found the LTA increasingly unsympathetic; and by 1960 he was being tempted to turn professional. He was only 23, but he had just married and he was conscious of "a gradual dimming of his talent". He beat Knight in the final at Bournemouth to win the second national title of his career, but he did not play in Paris and at Wimbledon he lost badly in the second round to Gardnar Mulloy, who was then 45. That was hardly the kind of form that bred optimism. Britain's first two Davis Cup rounds were comfortable. Neither Holland nor Belgium won a rubber, but Italy, the old enemy, waited for them in the semi-finals at Wimbledon. The British mood was funereal, but Pietrangeli and Sirola enjoyed themselves by appearing at the ground in bowler hats, city suits and rolled umbrellas. In his last Davis Cup match Davies did not win a rubber

8

9

10

7, 8. Angela Mortimer, who later married John Barrett, a Davis Cup player, was Britain's most consistent woman player at Wimbledon in the 1950s. Runner-up to Althea Gibson in 1958, she won the title by beating Christine Truman in 1961. Like Angela Mortimer, Joan Curry (9) learnt tennis from Arthur Roberts at the Palace Hotel, Torquay. She won the British Hard Court title in 1949 and 1950 and the British Covered Court title in 1949.

1

2

3

and the British were unfortunately beaten 5–0 on their own grass.

Five years earlier at Edgbaston, when the LTA thought that at last they had built a team to conquer Europe, the margin of failure had been the same against the same two Italian players. Full-circle, and now Davies, who had achieved more than anyone else, was leaving. What went wrong? Why had the British never quite seemed to play to their potential? Most countries regard themselves as lucky if they find two players of Davis Cup quality at a time. Back in 1955 the LTA seemed to have four men – Becker, Knight, Wilson and Davies, with Alan Mills and Tony Pickard in reserve – to carry the burden and a shrewd respected captain in Herman David, and yet by 1960 it was clear that they had failed again. They had reached the zone final once, but otherwise they had merely been regular semi-finalists.

To some extent, they had been unlucky. Like all British teams, their basic training had been on fast courts – on grass because the LTA, rightly or wrongly, regarded success at Wimbledon as more important than victory in the Davis Cup and in winter at Queen's

4

Club on wood, a surface antiquated even by the standards of 1960, because the LTA did not recognize the need to replace it with a slower flooring. Queen's, built in 1887, was the last major tennis club in Europe with wooden courts. Borotra and Austin may have played spectacular matches there, but that did not help those who wanted to prepare international contests on slow red shale.

On grass David's team might have earned the success they so often seemed to deserve, but from 1956 to 1959 they were always drawn to play the best teams in Europe on clay. They lost in Brussels, Stockholm, Milan and Barcelona. The most successful post-war British teams – Duncan Macaulay's 1963 sides which reached the inter-zone semi-final and Headley Baxter's 1969 inter-zone finalists – were luckier in their programs. Both played one easy away match and then met their more difficult opponents at home.

The British are always at a disadvantage on European clay. Their own clay courts are faster, with a more erratic bounce, than most Continental courts. A cold wind usually blows through their Spring tournaments and hardly encourages the young British player to attempt the perfect touch of a Santana or a Pietrangeli. The psychological and tactical atmosphere is different. Continental coaches instill basic, patient control into the pupils because on good clay courts little can be achieved without soundness of technique. Fast court play is simpler. When service and volley dominate, sharp reflexes can cover a multitude of technical sins.

But there are no such short cuts on clay. In long tests of endurance and technique on slow courts, small weaknesses become glaring faults. Wilson, four times a Wimbledon quarter-finalist, beat Budge Patty and Neale Fraser there and threatened Ashley Cooper in his championship year, but he never learned the secret of clay court play. For all his bustle, Becker's shots always looked light and vulnerable the moment he crossed the Channel, and Knight – like Roger Taylor later – struggled to protect a backhand which every European knew to be far weaker than his forehand. He won the German title in 1959 and, taking 27 rubbers out of 43, played some brave matches for Britain. No one tried harder, but his most important ties were full of fourth and fifth sets which he didn't quite win.

When Davies joined the professionals, he was replaced by Michael Sangster, who appeared first in a dead rubber in Holland in 1960. Coached by Arthur Roberts, who also guided Angela Mortimer, the 1961 women's champion at Wimbledon, and Susan, at the Palace Hotel, Torquay, he had won the Junior Covered Court title in 1956 and 1957. He had possessed a remarkable service then. It became faster, heavier and more formidable – it was once measured at 154 mph – and in 1963 it played a major part in Britain's first post-war matches of the European zone.

Unlike Davies and Mottram, who were more effective in Davis Cup play than in individual tournaments, Sangster, severe, methodical and immaculate, achieved considerable personal success. In 1961

1, 2. Mike Sangster, whose service was once timed at 154 mph, reached the semi-finals at Wimbledon in 1961, the first British player to reach that stage since 1938. He was also a semi-finalist in Paris in 1963. He played in 65 Davis Cup rubbers in nine years – a British record. 3. Roger Taylor's Davis Cup career was interrupted in 1967 when he turned professional. He reached the semi-finals at Wimbledon in 1967, 1970 and 1973. 4. Graham Stilwell and Mark Cox in action in the doubles of the Davis Cup inter-zone final against Rumania in 1969. They were beaten by Nastase and Tiriac, which cost Britain a place in the challenge round.

5

6

he became the first British singles semi-finalist at Wimbledon for 23 years. Chuck McKinley beat him 6–4, 6–4, 8–6, but two months later he also reached the semi-finals at Forest Hills where he took Laver to 13–11, 7–5, 6–4. In 1963 he confounded those who thought that he lacked the flexibility to do well on clay by reaching the semi-finals in Paris – a rare position for an Englishman. Emerson beat him 8–6, 6–3, 6–4.

Britain lost in the semi-finals, in Sweden and in Italy, in 1961 and 1962, but the following year was full of home ties. They beat Belgium 5–0 in Brussels, allowed Russia only one rubber at Eastbourne, defeated Spain 4–1 – one of Britain's best post-war wins – at Bristol, and then Sweden 3–2 in the zone final at Wimbledon.

That was Sangster's match. Wilson lost twice, but Sangster beat Jan-Erik Lundquist 3–6, 6–2, 4–6, 12–10, 9–7 and, in the deciding rubber, Ulf Schmidt by 7–5, 6–2, 9–11, 3–6, 6–3. He and Wilson took the doubles 22–20, 6–4, 6–3 and it was the first time that a Wimbledon crowd had been heard to cheer as they might have done at a football match. The United States had to come to Bournemouth for the inter-zone semi-final. Knight, who had won the British Hard Court title there three times, was picked for the singles, but he lost by 4–6, 8–6, 6–4, 6–4 to Frank Froehling in a rubber which the British had expected to win and McKinley, the Wimbledon champion, completed the British discomfiture.

The US won 5–0 and if that defeat was a disappointment, the failure against France at Bristol in 1964 was bewildering. Knight was preferred to Wilson, who had won an anxious deciding rubber against Yugoslavia, but lost in five sets to Pierre Darmon on the first day. Wilson and Sangster made it 2–1 by winning the doubles. Sangster led Darmon by two sets to love, only to lose concentration fatally and Darmon won 8–10, 3–6, 6–4, 8–6, 6–2. Pierre Barthes gave France victory with a 6–4, 6–4, 6–1 victory over Knight. That was Knight's last match and a warning that Sangster was losing fire and confidence.

At the end of the year George Worthington, whom everyone had liked and admired so much, died after a long illness.

Sangster began the 1965 campaign by failing in a strange rubber to Eleazar Davidman of Israel at Hampstead and he was beaten in both his singles when Britain lost in a quarter-final to South Africa at Eastbourne. It was time for another change of heroes. Taylor, a powerful Yorkshireman, might have borne the main burden. He was stubborn and competitive, surprisingly fast for such a big man, and by the time Britain played Hungary at Budapest in 1966 he had established himself as dominating member of the side. Sangster had a depressing match there, but he and Wilson won the doubles again and Taylor took two singles, finishing with a remarkable five-set victory over the persistent Istvan Gulyas, the runner-up in the French Championships two weeks later. In the semi-finals West Germany won everything but the doubles and a dead rubber which they surrendered to Taylor after a thunderstorm.

In 1967 Mark Cox played for the first time – in a 6–0, 6–0, 6–0 doubles with Wilson against Bulgaria; Britain lost by 3–2 to Spain at Eastbourne after Santana had saved himself at match-point against Sangster; and Taylor, a semi-finalist at Wimbledon (a distinction he achieved again in 1970 when he beat Laver), joined World Championship Tennis and wasn't able to play in the Davis Cup again until 1973 when the rules were changed.

Taylor left temporarily and Sangster, underpraised, perhaps, because the end of his career had markedly less success than its beginning, took part in one last tie against Finland at Queen's Club in 1968 and retired to a sports shop in Torquay. In nine years he had played in 65 rubbers – a British record. He had won 29 singles out of 48 and 14 doubles out of 17 (11 out of 14 with Wilson). Wilson outlasted him by one tie – a depressing semi-final in Spain. Since 1955 he had appeared in 63 rubbers, winning 16 singles and 25 of his 33 doubles. Sometimes brilliant, sometimes irritating and brittle, he might have achieved much, much more if the LTA had handled him with more understanding at the start.

5, 6. Ann Jones, a patient, accurate left-hander, gained her first major successes on clay. She was runner-up at Forest Hills in 1961 and 1967 and won the Wimbledon title in 1969. 7. Angela Barrett led Britain to their third post-war Wightman Cup victory at Wimbledon in 1969, with Virginia Wade, Christine Janes, Nell Truman, Winnie Shaw and Joyce Williams. 8. Gerald Battrick took over as leader of Britain's Davis Cup team in 1970. His greatest success was in 1971 at Bournemouth, when he beat Zeljko Franulovic in the British Hard Court final.

7

8

1

2

3

1. The first indoor Wightman Cup match was played at Deeside, North Wales, in 1974. Led by Virginia Wade, Britain won 6–1 – their best victory since 1924. 2. Paul Hutchins, who was appointed as Britain's first professional team manager in 1974, here partners Bobby Wilson against Finland in the 1968 Davis Cup campaign. 3. Mark Cox at Forest Hills.

Lawn tennis can be a family affair. Buster and Linda Mottram (4 and 6), whose father, Tony, played Davis Cup and whose mother was a member of the 1947–48 Wightman Cup teams, won all the British national junior titles. David and John Lloyd (5) played against Egypt at Cairo in the 1974 Davis Cup. They were the first brothers to represent Britain since the Dohertys.

1969 did not seem to be a year of great promise. It became one because of the sudden emergence of Graham Stilwell, at 23, as a major Davis Cup player. He had been Junior Champion in 1963 and, always seeming to have considerable but under-employed talent, he became a perpetual travelling reserve. "Too plump and too lazy to achieve anything," was a popular LTA judgment on him, but in 1969 he trained with a diligence that astonished his friends, went to Catania where he beat Gulyas in the final, to Rome where Santana and Stolle were his victims, and to Wimbledon where he took Ashe to 12–10 in the fifth set.

Supported by Cox, a heavy server and volleyer from Leicestershire, and forceful but erratic Peter Curtis, his Davis Cup record was even more astonishing in this wonderful year when his talent burst out into such spectacular flower. Britain beat Switzerland, West Germany (a match in which he and Cox beat Bungert and Christian Kuhnke in 95 games, Europe's longest Davis Cup doubles), South Africa and Brazil before falling to Rumania in the inter-zone final, the last hurdle before the challenge-round, at Wimbledon. Stilwell beat both Nastase and Tiriac, but under the pressure of this last test Cox had grown increasingly tense and the Stilwell–Curtis doubles pair had been (mistakenly?) split.

For years afterwards there was nothing but anti-climax. Cox and Stilwell were immediately signed by WCT and lost to the team. The reserves were weak. In 1970 Austria upset a denuded team at Edinburgh. Then came disasters against Yugoslavia and – after Baxter, the captain since 1968, had resigned because the LTA had disciplined Gerald Battrick, his leading player – France.

Even when Cox and Taylor, who had come straight from the American indoor circuit, returned in 1973 against West Germany, they looked woefully unaccustomed to clay and Britain lost 4–1 at Munich. Team Tennis took them and the promising Buster Mottram away in 1974 and Egypt beat Britain 5–0 in Cairo. It wasn't until the September of that year, when the 1975 Davis Cup began early for the "weaker nations", among whom Britain was now classified, that the sequence of failure was broken with a 5–0 victory over Iran at Queen's Club. Taylor was back again for that match and, with Mottram and John Lloyd, he also led them to a comfortable away win against Austria – revenge in Vienna for that defeat at Edinburgh – and to a dramatic near-miss in Spain. At Barcelona he reached match-point against Manuel Orantes in the deciding rubber. Orantes frustrated him with a desperate backhand passing-shot and escaped to win.

That was another British failure, but honorable enough to suggest that the years of famine might be over. The early 1970s had been Britain's worst Davis Cup period and there is little consolation in the thought that if the American promoters had not lured away the top players – or if the LTA had been as successful as some of their Continental rivals in finding alternative inducements for the men they needed – Britain might have kept a place among the leading Davis Cup nations for the whole of that time.

4

5

6

25 The War Years

For a second time war broke out while the Australian team was playing Davis competition in Philadelphia in the United States. For the second time, this event of limited historical significance concluded with a 3–2 score in favor of the team whose homeland was immediately involved in the conflict. The Australian participants in the match, Quist and Bromwich, were twenty-six and twenty-one years of age; the two American singles men, Riggs and Parker, were twenty-one and twenty-three; whereas Hunt and Kramer, whom the Americans, with excessive confidence, sent into battle in doubles play, were twenty and eighteen. The war, which cost poor Hunt his life, damaged the careers of all the others beyond repair with the exception of Jack Kramer.

The American audience warmly accepted the Australians, but no one thought that Bromwich and Quist could carry the day against Bobby Riggs and Frank Parker. Parker, a champion built with great care by the great coach Mercer Beasley, was a terrible taskmaster to himself, and he would only have needed to perfect his forehand in order to become a truly unassailable player.

Underrated by the directors during the reign of Budge, Riggs was taking one return match after another, both on the home court and elsewhere. Tiny, weaving back and forth like a boxer, Bobby played his strokes perfectly, but it was his careful selection of maneuvers, his timing, and his craftiness, more than anything else, that made him a dangerous adversary. Truly calculating, he never failed to bet large sums of money on himself, at odds that were staggering. At Wimbledon he had almost bankrupted an important bookmaker by betting on his own triple victory.

In John Bromwich the Australians had an educated fighter, a man who played an excellent game on grass with a curious repertory of strokes. As many children do, Bromwich had grasped a racket too heavy for him with both hands, and he had never lost the habit. He would execute an orthodox left-handed forehand, but he used the right hand for the serve, a habit that remained from the days when he had served the ball grasping the racket with both hands. That serve and his smash, both of which remained a bit rough, were the handicap of a game that was admirable in all other regards. Even more than Brugnon, Bromwich was capable of playing a double without missing a return.

Adrian Quist knew how to take advantage of this quality of Bromwich's game. Quist was a small, solidly built, and yet very quick man who had taken the great Crawford as his model of technique and had come close to equaling him in this respect. Quist didn't even have to look toward Bromwich, for the sound of the impact of the racket against the ball was enough for him to throw himself into the middle of the court to intercept the ascending volley that his opponent had played. With the strength of the two Australians to look forward to in the doubles, it seemed a good idea to give Riggs some rest, so the Americans risked, at 2–0, the junior champion Kramer together with Hunt. The boys hammered away like blacksmiths, won a set, but then, little by little, Bromwich hypnotized them and Quist tore them to shreds.

Walter Pate said to himself with confidence that between Riggs and Parker, at least one point would be won. "If you beat Riggs," Bromwich promised Quist, "I'll beat Parker for you." Opening the court with fantastic cross-court shots and attacking the ball like Cochet, Quist played the match of his life and won it in the fifth. Against the very regular Parker, Bromwich faced the first point from the backcourt, and after a rally of more than twenty strokes, drove a ball to the line. He finished the first set 6–0, and left his unfortunate rival four games in all. The Cup safely under lock and key in a New York bank, the winners took the first steamship. Once home, sand-colored uniforms, broad-brimmed hats, and spiked shoes awaited them.

Like leaves, the tennis players were quickly carried along by the wind of war, and the important tennis centers began to close their white shutters. While Wimbledon was turned into a civil defense center, and the secretary, Nora Gordon Cleather, raised chickens in

the shade of the Centre Court, Roland Garros became a concentration camp, as Arthur Koestler, who was a prisoner there, recounts. Nevertheless, the game did not die completely. With France divided into two zones, the free zone soon became a meeting ground for tennis activities, and the Parisian tennis players went there for exhibitions, returning home with suitcases filled with flour and a few sandwiches stuck into the racket covers. The *Tournois de France*, a sort of national championship, witnessed the first official encounter between a professional and an amateur in 1941: Destremau won out over Professor Ramillon in four sets.

Mysteriously requalified as an amateur, Cochet began to beat players twenty years younger than he, not the last of these Yvon Petra, just set free from concentration camp. Borotra accepted the position of minister of sport for the Pétain government, but when he resigned from the post in 1942, he was arrested while trying to escape to North Africa. While he was a prisoner in the Castle of Itter, the protective hand of Gustav V of Sweden, the king of tennis, was extended to him. Von Cramm himself, sent to Russia as a raw recruit to be wounded and win the Iron Cross, probably

2

On the preceding page: Centre Court at Wimbledon after a bombing raid. As in 1914, the Australians beat the United States in Cup competition, with the war already under way. The decisive point is Bromwich's against Parker (1), with the Australian at the net. 5. Bromwich again playing his two-handed lefty backhand. 3.

1

3

4

Gathered around the Cup, the Australian team is made up of Quist, Crawford, Bromwich, Hopman, and the aging, ever-present Brookes. Other than Parker among the Americans, Bobby Riggs played singles (4) and the very young Kramer and Hunt debuted in doubles. 2. They chat with Captain Walter Pate, one of the architects of the defeat. While the war was raging, the American

5

7

8

women played cheerfully on. 6. Dating from September 1943, this photograph shows the best U.S. women players: from the left, Betz, Hart, Brough, Scofield, and Osborne. 7, 8. Joe Hunt, U.S. champion in 1943, and the German Henkel. Hunt (9) dies in his plane in 1945, and Henkel (10) will disappear at Stalingrad.

11. Gustav V, king of Sweden, will protect von Cramm from suspicions by the Nazis.

6

owes his life to his royal friend: to escape unscathed three questioning sessions by the Gestapo, one of which took place after the assassination plot against Hitler, was not a fate reserved to many anti-Nazis.

In the countries of the Axis and in a few occupied by the Germans, tennis continued with some regularity until 1942. The Yugoslavian players appeared on the court with the colors of Croatia, the Austrians and the Czechoslovak Menzel wore the insignia with the swastika upon it. Among the Hungarians the slim and elegant figure of Asboth stood out. He was the strongest European player of that time, pressed hard by the Italians Romanoni and Kucel, whom the Fascists had rebaptized Cucelli.

It was in the United States, the only country with its tennis population still intact, that the game continued to develop in an atmosphere of calm. Riggs became a professional in 1941 and was determined to make inroads into Budge's invincible game. However, first Schroeder and then Hunt became champions after Riggs. Then Hunt himself disappeared in his plane, just as on the other side of the barricades Henkel fell to his death in Russia. From 1943 on, everyone was in uniform, and the number of exhibitions increased dramatically so as to entertain the injured. At the same time the steady pace of Frank Parker's game won out over Billy Talbert, who was the first tennis player to conquer diabetes.

In Europe, with the cities ravaged and starving, tennis became more and more difficult. Players looked wistfully at Switzerland and at Sweden where Lennart Bergelin was preparing himself to become a champion. The war ended when the gods willed it. Just like the time before, the defeated were kept in vile quarantine, far from the courts, to pay for wrongs that they had not committed. When Hans Redl, the Austrian who had lost an arm in the conflict, finally returned to Wimbledon, and lifted the ball with his racket so as to serve it, the game was stopped by the applause of his former enemies. This was a sign that peace had really begun.

11

9

10

CONTEMPORA
JET TENNIS

**The Big Bang Theory in Tennis. Kramer. Women and Superwomen.
Little Mo and the Grand Slam at the Age of Nineteen.
Pancho Gonzales, Mexican-American. The Magic Twins
from Down Under, Hoad and Rosewall.
Rod Laver, the Rockhampton Rocket.
The Italians, Challengers in the Davis Cup.
A Rain of Dollar Bills. Women's Lob. Nastase and the Robots.**

RY

Maureen Connolly (in oval above). Left to right below: Jack Kramer, Pancho Gonzales, Rod Laver and Ken Rosewall, immortals among the contemporary players.

26 Professionals and Professional Amateurs. Kramer

The great tournaments lost participants to professional play. Tilden's troupe had taken proven champions like Perry and Vines, fading immortals like Cochet, and players on their way up, like Stoefen and Lott. At the height of his success in 1947, Jack Kramer decided to transform tennis into a respectable show. If one is to believe the annals of that day, such a project was becoming more and more difficult. Without Jack's decision, Bob Falkenburg would never have succeeded in winning in London in 1948. Patty and Savitt would probably not have snatched Wimbledon from an amateur Gonzales in 1950 and 1951, Trabert would not have prevailed against the professionals Sedgman and McGregor in 1954 and 1955, and dear old Drobny would not have won the Centre Court complex at the end of his career. From 1957 to 1961, Davidson, Pietrangeli, and Santana would have had greater trouble than they did in taking the Roland Garros from Rosewall, Hoad, and Segura, not to speak of Cooper, Olmedo, and Fraser, who would have been eliminated quickly by the pros on the grass. Nor would Emerson have been able to collect four Australian championships from 1963 to 1967, competing against his fellow Aussies who were in Kramer's camp. And last but not least, the Italians would not have beaten the American professional team in the Davis Cup finals of 1960 and 1961.

The traditional objections that were voiced, that amateurs were not playing for money and that they were training less, were groundless, or actually put forward in bad faith. At the beginning of the thirties, when Pierre Gillou promised Henri Cochet 200,000 francs a year, plus a percent of the receipts at the new Roland Garros Stadium, traditional amateur status began to change in definition. Nor is it true that it was the manager and the player who were responsible for this *amateurisme marron*, as the French called it, or "shamateurism" as the English would have it, a kind of shameful amateur status. To put it simply, poor people had begun to arrive in the tennis world, and when a poor person played better than a rich one, there was always a sponsor, glaring paternalism, and bombastic national anthems somewhere near.

The important players who did not turn professional after 1950 can almost be counted on the fingers of one hand: Schroeder, Savitt, Mulloy, Talbert, Davidson, McKinley, Fraser, . . . and all American university graduates or wellborn individuals in rich countries. Their amateur status was not the same as that of De Coubertin: hidden as an invitation for a partner, a transoceanic steamer ticket, the reimbursement of some money, dollars always managed to cross hands in some way or another. For other champions like Drobny or Pietrangeli, Santana or Lundquist, amateur status was so profitable that it induced them to refuse going pro, where life was harder, the opponents more difficult, and taxation terrible to put up with. In 1968 the British Association and a group of other countries decided to put an end to the hypocrisy of a paradoxical situation, and the first open tournaments were played. From that time on, all of the fans have once again been able to find out who is the strongest player in the world, despite the chaos of regulations, the open warfare among organizations, and the first strike of tennis players at Wimbledon in 1973.

Before continuing with our saga of the four cantons of tennis—Wimbledon, Forest Hills, Roland Garros, and the Davis Cup, it will be a good idea to bring out the opinions of the players themselves. From 1946 to 1954, Jack Kramer was the strongest player in the world, from 1954 to the early sixties, Pancho Gonzales, followed by Ken Rosewall and soon by Rod Laver. Among these tennis greats, Kramer won only once at Wimbledon, Gonzales not even once, and Rosewall, an inexperienced and overage finalist, lost the decisive match four times.

The story now becomes much more personal: gone is the tedious scholar of the first part of the book, as well as the zealous and often indiscreet reporter of the second and third sections. This section of the history is the most defective for several reasons. In the first place, it lacks that blissful ignorance listed by Strachey as indispensable for any truly good biography. Since the story is now told by the winners themselves, the historical perspective is absent. The author is, on the contrary, one of the most often beaten tennis players, and one of the weakest listed in the records. If he is to compare himself to anyone, the best example might be the poor comedian who came on the stage in a tiny Spanish hamlet where the writer had gone for a tournament and where the bullfight was very popular. He came down to the footlights, slightly hesitant but smiling, trying to make the audience like him. He too, he announced, had once been a matador. A moment of silence followed. Then a rain of harsh words and other things began to come down on him. The poor young man lowered his eyes and let the storm subside. Then he had an inspiration and asserted with unexpected pride: "*Si, yo era un matador muy malo. Pero lo fui.* (Yes, I was a matador, a very bad one. But at least I was one.)" His historic words would suit us here.

In my active years I met four Wimbledon winners and invariably lost. I also had the honor, yes, the great honor, of playing at Wimbledon twice, on one occasion against the doubles champions on Court Number One. My name will perhaps be best remembered in the history of that tournament as the name of an individual who obtained permission from the umpire and two linesmen to take a nap in the locker room at the end of a painful third set, and in this I am probably unique. It was then the year of our Lord 1954. In 1955 I finally called a halt to my clumsy attempts at greatness and dedicated myself to the profession of spectator. From that vantage point I have seen them all, great and small.

Kramer and Modern Times

Industrialism, statistics, and finally managerial activity and labor unions make their appearance in the tennis world with Jack Kramer. The Doherty brothers, Cochet, and Tilden had entered tennis by vocation. At the age of ten, like so many other boys born

2. Jack Kramer, at the net, confronts with ease a volley from Tom Brown, during the Wimbledon finals, 1947: Jack goes on to win 6–1, 6–3, 6–2. 3. Together with his adversary, he is congratulated by the Queen and King George VI, who himself played Wimbledon in doubles. 4. At Los Angeles Tennis Club, Jack and his wife Gloria give their firstborn baby a bath in the Davis Cup. 1. Jack's legendary forehand. It is a very wide

1

2

in 1921, Jack dreamed of Joe Di Maggio and had seven baseball uniforms, a catcher's mask, and a half dozen bats and balls. He already had the mentality of an autocrat, and one day when he could not choose the teams and select the batting order, he made such a row that his father had to intervene and explain to him that there were other people than he in the world. Little Jack did not seem to understand the admonition too well, and soon he discovered a way to break his nose. It was then that his mother decided that even a secondhand racket would be less dangerous for her budding athlete.

Jack accepted the setback reluctantly, but wanted to have no one spread the word around the neighborhood that he was playing a sissy game. The racket indeed seemed better suited to his hand than the bat, however, for at the age of thirteen he was already U.S. boys' champion. From that time on he was always highly ranked, and only unfortunate circumstances (appendicitis, a pulled muscle, indigestion) kept him from winning national titles. His excellent education as a well-rounded player is first of all due to the efforts of Dick Skeen, an instructor well qualified in basic technique. The family of the thirteen-year-old Jack had just moved from Las Vegas to San Bernardino, California; he had just bought his secondhand racket; and now he had to save five dollars a month from his allowance to learn fundamentals. Jack won the National Boys' Championships at Culver, and was quickly drawn into the institute of tennis planning of the Los Angeles Tennis Club, encouraged by the great Ellsworth Vines.

However, Jack's decisive meeting occurred with Cliff Roche, an automotive engineer. Jack was quickly convinced that the game

5

movement, describing an ample arc, with an especially fine and anticipated impact. The ball is hit almost flat and the shift in weight well executed. 5. Kramer's serve is also excellent, here followed to the net in the film of Kermadec although the maneuver takes place at Roland Garros. The leverage created at the beginning of the serve allows Jack to make good use of his height and of his exceptional strength: it is truly a cannonball!

3

4

ought to be made up of a well-controlled series of strokes, the whole scheme planned in advance like a line of fabricated models. Roche had worked in Detroit as a designer of items for mass production: it was the needs of the market rather than the demand of the individual that conditioned production, and this fact could very easily be applied to tennis. A forehand attack along the sideline could be executed, leaving out of consideration the position of the opponent and his defensive mechanism. After a period of intensive repeated training, this stroke was the easiest to place, according to the statistics.

Jack was a bright young man who was attentive to his surroundings, and it did not take him long to absorb these simple and efficient principles. "I hit all my forehand shots along the sideline," he said later, "unless I am given an easy cross-court shot. When I follow my attack to the net, my opponent will place a backhand passing shot along the line or else will have to attempt the most difficult shot in tennis, the crosscourt backhand that only Don Budge and Frank Kovacs know how to maneuver with safety. The majority of my adversaries will do the best they can, making twenty percent of the passing shots and missing the rest: the percentages are in my favor."

When he arrived in London in 1946, Jack was already specialized in these systems of "tennis by percentages." He was able to apply them with the same calculated coolness as in the South Pacific during the war. He took the Davis Cup final in stride, as he had done with military maneuvers, and Wimbledon would be as easy as accepting medals. In all his planning, he had failed to foresee, however, that the blisters on his right hand would deepen until they finally became painful sores. In the encounter with Jaroslav Drobny, a boy from Prague with a talent that showed clearly in his service and his drive, it took all of Jack's courage to keep his racket in his hand to the end of the match, and to be a good enough sport to state that the Czechoslovak had played an excellent game. His hand, he added, had nothing to do with his defeat. In fact, it was in such bad shape that Kramer missed all the following tournaments until Forest Hills, with the exception of a doubles attempt at Seabright. Once the wounds had healed, he easily swept away both of his rivals, Falkenburg in the semifinals and Tom Brown in the finals.

It was at that time that Big Game and Power Tennis began to be spoken of, creating confusion in the minds of the fans. Jack and his friend Schroeder were not the first to hit a ball across the net at the speed of 110 m.p.h. when serving, or fifty to sixty m.p.h. on a rebound, allowing their bewildered opponents barely a half second to a second to retrieve it. Vines and Budge had stroked just as rapidly and with the same cruelty. What Jack did, other than automate the sport, was to transform tennis into a vertical game, based on the service and on the volley. Even this technique was not new, for it had been used by Jean Borotra, but he had approached the net,

1

Pictures of the first Davis competitions after the war, where Kramer and Schroeder took the Cup back in Australia. 1. Schroeder is poaching , anticipating Kramer, who had already planned his shot. 2. Defeated Bromwich and Quist, shaking the Yanks' hands. 3. Kramer receives the U.S. International Champion's Cup at Forest Hills in 1947: next to him is the defeated Tom Brown. 4. Kramer in a lateral backhand volley, on June 28, 1946: that day, his first at Wimbledon, he was defeated both by Drobny and by the sores on his hands. 6. With the impresario Harris to his right, and his next opponent Riggs to the left, Jack is signing the papers to turn pro. 7. Kramer to the left of Riggs and Donald Budge. 5. A winning forehand volley against the 1939 world champion Budge. 8. A much more difficult

2

7

3

4

5

6

stretching volley against Bobby Riggs. 9. The terrible two-hand backhand and the grin of Pancho Segura, opponent and friend of Kramer, for many years in first rank among the pros.

following placed balls that described a careful arc and were pushed rather than hit forcefully. Kramer the Marine landed at the net preceded by an enormously powerful serve or by a cannonade forehand that exploded no more than two feet from the base line or three feet from the sideline.

In 1947 Jack won in such a landslide at Wimbledon that the victory seemed almost stale: more than a victory, it seemed the destruction of unarmed enemies. He defeated Cucelli 6–0, 6–2, 6–0; Johanson 7–5, 6–2, 6–3; Geoff Brown 6–0, 6–1, 6–3; Pails 6–1, 3–6, 6–1, 6–0; Tom Brown 6–1, 6–3, 6–2. Not even Dinny Pails could give me an account of the set Jack lost: "He missed everything by a hair for a quarter of an hour," he remembered years later, still surprised at what happened. Someone quipped that Jack had set his sights one millimeter off for that set. He returned to the United States, won Forest Hills once again and destroyed the poor Australians in Davis Cup competition, leaving them twelve games in six sets. Before the end of the year and after sixteen months of an unbeaten record in the important tourney play, Kramer decided to accept Jack Harris's offer to turn professional.

The evening of his debut against Riggs at Madison Square Garden, a terrible snowstorm hit New York City and covered it with snow, completely blocking traffic. "I felt like an Arctic explorer

9

8

1. *Marcel Bernard, in the foreground, and Yvon Petra, watching him, surprised the critics by winning respectively, the Roland Garros and Wimbledon in 1946.* 2. *Possessor of a very strong serve, Petra knocked down the net at Wimbledon, rusted after being inoperative for seven years.* 3. *Bob Falkenburg won Wimbledon in 1948, putting Bromwich into the category of the great unlucky Wimbledon players, together with Austin, von Cramm, and then Rosewall.*

1

2

3

when I came out of the hotel," Jack remembered, adding that his greatest worry was the reduction in box-office receipts. Despite the weather, 15,114 were on hand with $248,000 to applaud the victory of little Bobby Riggs, who was much better adapted to the artificial lights and the wooden floor. At the end of their tour, Jack had nevertheless surpassed Bobby 69–20 and then made the following statement: "Professional tennis is all serves and volleys. If you don't get to the net, even on the second serve, your opponent will anticipate you at the net and force you to a fault. The only defense that Riggs had was to push me to backcourt tennis, which I did not know. He forced me to lob, and he himself made his best showing in serves and volleys."

A real businessman, Riggs understood that he would do a great deal better as Jack's manager than as his opponent on the court. He replaced Harris, and in 1950, matched Kramer with Pancho Gonzales, the U.S. champion in 1948 and 1949. It was another massacre. Jack won the tour 96–27. Once at La Jolla, one of Riggs's men casually remarked that his repeated successes were emptying the stadiums and Jack threw him out. In 1951 Kramer's superiority discouraged the organizing efforts of Riggs, and from that time on, Jack himself assumed the management of professional tennis. He was seen less and less on the court in his white T-shirt.

By 1960 Kramer had earned enough, and had also garnered enough hatred from the amateur officials to step aside, convinced that without him the new professional association would have greater liberty of action. He loved the game too much, certainly a great deal more than he did the money, to get away from it altogether; he could still be seen in the company of tennis players as referee in Los Angeles, with top television commentators at Wimbledon, and finally, after the inauguration of the open, in the company of his old enemies from the International Lawn Tennis Federation (ILTF). He was very apt at projecting the outcome of the Grand Prix, in opposition to the World Championship Tennis (WCT) sponsored by the Texan Lamar Hunt. At the present time Jack has become the guiding spirit behind the new Association of Tennis Professionals (ATP), and his influence on tennis is always quite noticeable. He still wishes, perhaps through egotism, perhaps to repay what the game has done for him, to return to the number-one position, to be again in the limelight that intoxicates much more than mere money. He, like the majority of others, fends off death in his own way by refusing to grow old.

And what were the others doing during Kramer's reign? Were they all being good little children, allowing themselves to be beaten? In the United States, Jack's greatest rivals were Frank Parker, the very steady player who drowned him in the fifth set at Forest Hills in 1947, and Schroeder, who was his best friend. Together with Jack, Falkenburg won Wimbledon in 1947, and snatched the singles in 1948 from the famous John Bromwich. The Australian got to match point, had a sudden fear of finally taking the tournament, and was punished by Falkenburg. In 1945 Marcel Bernard signed up for the Roland Garros to practice in anticipation of the doubles. He got the magic combination of playing a casual game and finished by beating Drobny in the finals! The same year another Frenchman astounded the refined precincts with serves whose speed ripped the old worn-out Wimbledon net. Yvon Petra had been able to practice despite the discomforts of the war, and won three national championships from 1943 to 1945.

He disappeared quickly at the same time as Pancho Segura came up too rapidly from the amateur ranks. Segura's two-handed forehand was the match of Kramer's and has kept him, together with his flare for tactics, at the top of the professional ratings. He is a man of slight build, with a dark complexion, his feet turned in, and his eyes sparkling with amused wit. Joseph Asboth, a very slight Hungarian with excellent control of the backcourt, barely had time to win the Roland Garros in 1947 before he began to decline. For him, as for others, the war had been too long.

27 Queens of the Court

To the young Europeans who considered fascism not only hateful but also in bad taste, the first GIs seemed handsome and elegant; the first tennis players were no less fascinating, and we Italians fell in love with the first women players of the game. They enchanted us with their sweet scent of soap and water, the simple taste of their cycling trousers or shorts, their loose shirts, the graceful movement of their heavy rackets, and the way they dashed on beautifully muscled legs after the most unretrievable balls. They never gave up, always struggling and retaining a radiant smile even in defeat. This made us love them, and, throwing caution to the winds, we played mixed doubles with them, only to find out incredulously, that these foreigners might be men in women's clothing, or at least warlike amazons.

The first to admit this fact and to write about it freely was Teddy Tinling, the man who knew these women best. He chaperoned them into the sanctuary of the Centre Court, and he was the fashion designer who decided to dress them in more refined and, above all, more feminine garb. In his delightful memoirs Tinling divides our charming doubles companions into two categories: the girls and the amazons. Only Bueno and Goolagong were not consigned to be the subjects of Penthesilea, the legendary queen of the Amazons. As far as tennis was concerned, Tinling had the same values as did Ezra Pound in the thinking of the young Hemingway. As has been aptly said, he was always right, but when he was wrong, he was really in deep water.

The first great woman tennis star from the United States to appear in Europe had hair the color of wheat, gray eyes like those of a Tiepolo painting, a bust held gingerly in place by a shirt of fine wool, and two long flannel shorts that left a good deal of the length of her beautiful limbs in view. Her nose was straight, and her mouth had more an intelligent than sensual quality; she had fine skin and slender, yet deceptively strong hands. We soon realized that Pauline Betz not only had a dazzling offensive backhand, but also a fine arts degree, a consuming passion for bridge, and a flair for self-criticism unknown among most of our women companions: instead of whining when her balls failed to connect, you could hear her mutter to herself, "My dear Pauline, do you really think this rot you are playing is tennis?"

Not that she was a pusher, poacher, or devil-may-care, or not conscientious; she had her fears like the rest of us, and Teddy Tinling himself recounts that, the day of the Wimbledon final match, he had to scour half of London to find her a couple of fresh eggs, which at that time were still rationed. Nervousness had tightened up her throat muscles. Pauline won all the same, just as she had done everywhere in America during the war years. She was only beaten at Roland Garros because she spent too much time enjoying Paris. They used a kind of inquisition to disqualify her. The husband of her friend Sarah Palfrey Cooke had begun preliminary investigation on how the two women could join professional ranks, and the Association got wind of it. That in itself was enough for them to disbar her. Pauline stayed with the sport as a professional, but we hear nothing further from her.

The U.S. team was made up of some truly tall and powerful women and was quick to take the upper hand in competition. Rarely had such hotly-contested semifinals been seen, characterized by such masculine roughness. The most outstanding record in singles play may be Louise Brough's with three consecutive Wimbledons but her doubles partner Margaret Osborne-Dupont won three Forest Hills at the same time and was acclaimed both in Paris and in Australia. Margaret was a more positive and stable player, worked harder with the ball, and never seemed tired, upset, or nervous. If the referee at Wimbledon sent her out on the court number seventeen, she followed his instructions gladly. Little did she care that Suzanne Lenglen would have been terrorized by such a prospect and that Helen Wills would have stayed rooted to the sidelines at the mere suggestion of it.

Margaret spent her childhood at the Golden Gate Park in San Francisco, the school of tennis of Alice Marble. Margaret had learned there that the game itself was a prize, and that one can be friends, even very good friends, with one's opponents. Louise, who was devoured by her nervousness, even missing the ball altogether when serving, found a tender nurse in Margaret, and was able, little by little, to calm herself and find a balance for her style of play. Louise Brough was certainly the direct descendant of Alice Marble, but it is difficult to separate her merits from those of her friend, who lost to her most of the time when they played each other. In doubles play, the patient Margaret demonstrated fully her steady strength, with a record that was only surpassed by Bunny Ryan, the legendary partner of Suzanne Lenglen: twenty-two victories at Wimbledon, Forest Hills, and Paris! In many ways Doris Hart and Shirley Fry are similar to Margaret and Louise and only slightly weaker than they in doubles play. They, too, were born in the same month, a few days apart, and, like Brough and Osborne, often found themselves spending sleepless nights in the same room before important finals events. Doris, like Margaret, took the lead in direct confrontations, with a superiority more mental than technical.

Shirley was as muscular and untiring as a farm girl. Doris could not do much more than move with a strange dancing gait, which was not exactly limping, but not running either. Her right knee, which had been infected by a virus, was terribly deformed, and her unstylishly long skirts succeeded in keeping this hidden. Doris had grown up in a good, courageous family, whose members had helped her not to feel different and had encouraged her to measure herself with life, even in areas where her so-called shortcoming was clearly underlined. Her career had been very difficult, punctuated by initial reverses, by hopes that were quickly dashed, and by outright failures.

1.The Duchess of Kent congratulates the members of one of the strongest teams ever formed in Wightman Cup play. From the left, Osborne, Betz, Brough, Hart, and, half hidden by the donor, Mrs. Todd, "Miss Legs" at that time. 2. A service by Pauline Betz, so graceful that it seems posed (which it isn't). 3. Good friends Louise Brough and Margaret Osborne, after one of their five Wimbledon successes. These strong queens of the court also won the U.S. championships from 1942

1

2

3

4

5

6

to 1950 and again from 1955 to 1957!
4. Brough, always free and easy, has put a pair of colored socks on over her shoes to reduce the chance of slipping on the drenched grass. 5. A letter-perfect backhand return by Osborne. 6. Shirley Fry. 7. Her friend Doris Hart, the greatest lame tennis player of all time. Shirley is reaching for a stupendous forehand, while Doris has tried to stop a passing shot.

7

2

1. With Gussy Moran, called Gorgeous Gussy, the glamor of the musical comedy comes on the tennis scene. Gussy dazzled the spectators with her short shorts woven with gold or cut from leopard skin, mortified the poor princesses of the Egyptian court, and scandalized the royal box at Wimbledon.
2. On June 22, 1949, she descends on Centre Court, with smiling self-confidence, the target of flash cameras, accompanied by her opponent, Gem Hoahing, English born of Chinese descent.

1

3

4

3. Gussy streaks by showing her devastating lace and a smile. 4. A little more inhibited, she concentrates on a difficult forehand. 5. Gem, with an intense look on her face, goes on the counterattack. 6. Gussy tries in vain to make a return. A falling star.

6

Doris's very pure style, her strokes played with an elegant air and with magical precision, made up for her handicap and allowed her to compete on the same level as stronger, more solid, and quicker athletes. I have often asked myself, observing her command of the game with such an intent attitude, what would have become of her if she had been able to run, let alone leap, sprint, and jump in normal fashion. Counting, as she did, only on her strokes and on her almost superhuman intuition, Doris won a Wimbledon, two Forest Hills, two Paris titles, and the second Roman title against Connolly, the terrible, unbeatable, and ferocious Little Mo. It is Doris's just due that she be assigned a spot among the tennis immortals on the Olympus of the sport.

7, 8. Everyone rooted for Beverly Baker in the 1955 finals at Wimbledon. She played one forehand to the left and one to the right, and that unusual technique had doubtless contributed to the balanced development of her lovely arms. She lost 7–5, 8–6 to Brough, and the following year, when she was favored, she withdrew from the quarter finals, for she was expecting a child. 9. Gloria Butler, daughter of the donor of the famous doubles trophy, is remembered in the history of tennis for having organized and acted as master of ceremonies for the annual Monte Carlo tennis show. 10. Among the girls of Gloria's show, the Italian Lea Pericoli, called "la Divina," and the American Karol Fageros, the Golden Goddess.

7

8

5

9

10

28 The Short and Happy Life of Maureen Connolly

"Miss Connolly," the reporter asked, "what was your most amusing experience in the sport?" "I have never had one," Miss Connolly replied.

In 1951, Maureen Connolly won Forest Hills when she was only sixteen, won Wimbledon in 1952, and then, the first to do so in the annals of the sport, won the Grand Slam in 1953. In 1954, while she was mounting the horse given her by her hometown, an accident deformed her leg and ruined her career as an athlete. She later died of cancer at the age of thirty-five.

Maureen's father, a sailor, deserted the family when she was only three years old. Her mother's hands were too short for her to become a concert pianist, and she began again as organist in a church in San Diego. Abandoning all hopes of personal fulfillment, she concentrated all her dreams on her chubby, stubborn, and willful little daughter. Maureen's mother unwisely pushed her into ballet and then directed her into singing. When a badly performed tonsillectomy ruined her chances in that direction, her mother encouraged her to write, to draw, and in general to act like a child prodigy. The small girl really had no special talent and did not hold her own in these endeavors. She spent hours on end dreaming of a horse, for horseback riding was her real interest. The family's modest means denied her the chance to succeed as a horsewoman, however.

The three Connollys, mother, aunt, and daughter, lived very near to three cement courts. One day Maureen stopped short to see playing there, not the usual unfriendly neighborhood children or elderly couples, but Gene Garret, a tennis player gifted with a rigorous style. Tennis suddenly seemed to her the perfect substitute for riding, and she became ball girl for the teacher Wilbur Folsom, who hobbled around on a wooden leg. Maureen wrote with her left hand, but Folsom was aware that there had never been a truly successful left-handed woman player and encouraged her to hold the racket with her right hand. For once, using her right hand did not seem to bother her.

Thanks to the good offices of a dancing teacher, she quickly found herself in the presence of Teach Tennant, the enthusiast who had transformed Alice Marble. Teach had parted company with her first protégée after some stormy sessions, and Pauline Betz had slipped away from her authority too quickly. Teach must have realized that she was in the presence of greatness, but she made no indication of it to the girl. She said simply: "Well, let's see what you can do. Go ahead and play!" Maureen, who was then twelve years old, quickly decided that she wanted Teach Tennant to give her lessons more than anything else in the world. Teach did, and along with the instruction came the gradual rise to success that her mother had longed for so fervently.

At first, Teach could not imagine that a future world champion could be different from Alice Marble, who, though ungrateful to her, had still been greater than any of the others, including Wills and Lenglen. Although Maureen was totally unsuited for it, her teacher made her try the big game, rushing the net, thereby abandoning the backcourt where her real strength and potential lay. "I was upset by her authoritarian voice, by her dominating ways," Maureen wrote. Only after crying in secret on many occasions and many sleepless nights, did she dare confess that the nightmare of another smash hitting her, as had happened on the first days of play, paralyzed her every time she ventured to the net. Maureen played for hours on end, studied and breathed tennis. She had over Alice the advantage of excellent physical health and an iron will. Teach was content and spent her time modifying her student's strokes and her thoughts, selecting her food and her clothing. "I adored her. Her opinions were commands, and her dislikes controlled mine as well," Maureen wrote.

Teach had always been the teacher preferred by the stars. When she saw that Maureen was becoming interested in John Garfield and Cornell Wilde, she told her never to play with them, so as not to ruin her own game. Maureen refused to obey the order and was caught red-handed rallying with Gilbert Roland. An implacable Teach sent her home. "My world fell in pieces," Maureen wrote. She was also upset because her mother had remarried. She begged Teach to take her to live with her, but her Pygmalion refused to do so and socialized with her only on the court.

At the age of thirteen, Maureen went on her first tour and collected her first victories as well as a defeat. The public, which attended her match with Laura Lou Jahn in a jovial and unattentive mood, seemed a court of tyrannical judges. "They hate me now because I lost," she said. "If I had won, they would love me." One of the newspapermen called her "the killer in curls," alluding to her rigid, tight-lipped stance as she attacked her unknown opponents with ferocious tenacity. "Teach thinks that you can't be friends with your opponents. You have to stay alone," she commented sadly. Before every match, that girl, who "needed to hate, to detest each of her opponents," sought asylum for hours in the churches of these unknown cities where she was playing.

A close friend of Bishop Charles Buddy of San Diego, Maureen must have paraphrased him in her thoughtful observation that "tennis is a gift of God." "Losing therefore is an offense, a sign of ingratitude," the poor child reasoned, clutching with her chubby fingers her ring, upon which two dragons guarded a tennis ball. Without that talisman, without her devotions, Maureen was not only in no condition to win, but not even to go out on the court. Once she refused to compete for a half hour until an out-of-breath referee finally turned up her ring for her.

At the age of fourteen, the youngest to do so in the history of

2

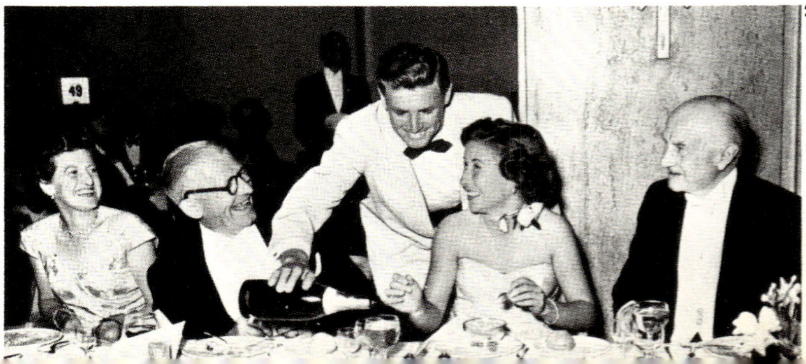

Little Mo Connolly, the first woman to win the Grand Slam, and at the age of nineteen at that! Mo won the U.S. championships at sixteen, and in the four following seasons of her brief career she was beaten only four times. She never lost at Wimbledon. 1. She lands in London with Eleanor Tennant. 2. She celebrates the 1952 victory with the other champion, Sedgman. 3. She returns in triumph to San Diego. 4. She blocks a well-placed high forehand volley. 5. With excellent balance, she finishes the follow-through to a strong backhand stroke. 6. She prepares to stroke a forehand that will in no way miss its mark.

3

4

5

6

U.S. tennis, Maureen won the junior championships, and both Tilden and Kramer came to congratulate her, unaware that, according to her own words, "no fame or immortality could compensate for the price that I paid for the victory." At the age of sixteen, she confronted Forest Hills for the second time, filled with anguish over the thought of survival on the court. Teach was far away trying to save the life of her dear sister Gwen, her only living relative. Perhaps Maureen was not aware of that fact, or perhaps she did not think that Gwen's drama was any more terrible than her own. She insisted on help, and Teach finally left Gwen to sustain her pupil as far as the semifinals with Doris Hart.

Doris was a delightful person and the year before in the same stadium she had done all she could to praise and encourage the young girl during the breaks in their match. Teach confided to Sophie Fisher that Doris really disliked Maureen, had called her a little brat and was only waiting for the chance to teach her a lesson on the court. Sophie told Maureen the lie, and she in turn rushed for confirmation to Teach, who played the role of Iago very well. The little dervish vented her rage on Doris, inflicting a 6–0 victory in the first set and beating her in a truly impressive second. Mervyn Rose said that he had never seen such an expression on a player's face, and everyone agreed with Nelson Fisher, the San Diego reporter, when he baptized her "Little Mo," from the name of the battleship bristling with cannons, the famous *Missouri*.

Maureen still had to defeat Shirley Fry, Doris's dearest friend. Shirley came out on the court ready for anything, and when she returned to the dressing room for the rest period before the decisive set, she was not the only one to believe that she might actually take the match. Little Mo felt terribly worn and incapable of willpower, but Teach was there to hold her up and to communicate her great drive. "You have to win this set, even if you kill yourself doing so," she said slowly, looking at the girl with her enormous burning eyes. Maureen suddenly got up, like one possessed. "I'll take care of her," she promised.

Not since the days of the tennis goddess had such a crowd of photographers been on the scene as those who greeted Little Mo, her mother, and Teach, when they arrived in London in June 1952. The English reporters tried in vain to interview Maureen. They were able to observe her practice sessions and finally got her to talk to them. Was this quiet, submissive young lady really the student of the greatest coach in the world? they asked themselves in amazement. Not only did Little Mo treat her mother like a simpleton, but she lost no opportunity to go against the wishes of Teach as well, and even made fun of her on occasion.

The misunderstandings and the arguments among the three women reached colossal proportions during the Queens Club Tournament. When Little Mo suddenly suffered a terrible pain in her shoulder, Teach could think of nothing better than to seclude her in the dressing room and answered the curiosity of the public with a stony silence. A reporter thought that this might very well be an indication of Little Mo's withdrawing from Wimbledon, and began to telephone the story. He had barely had time to get the first sentence out, when Little Mo came dashing up, half dressed, to snatch the telephone out of his hand. She had heard him from within.

The story made the day for the newspapers, and the doubts of the fans over whether or not she would be able to play were so many that even bookmakers began to phone the women asking for information. Both Dr. Hugh Dempster and Teach were of the opinion that Mo had pulled a muscle. Her teacher furiously opposed her playing Wimbledon, fearful of compromising her entire career. Encouraged by the diagnosis of a second doctor, Little Mo refused to listen to her. On Monday, the opening day, Teach declared that Little Mo would be foolish to play.

On Tuesday Maureen defeated Mrs. Moeller by sheer grit and immediately announced a press conference. The reporters were amazed to hear her say in measured tones, as if she were reading a prepared statement, that Miss Tennant did not represent her, and that her decisions did not express the views of Little Mo, who was determined to finish the tournament. Perry Jones was called from Los Angeles to help Mo's confused and anxious mother decide whether or not her underage offspring could risk her health this way. He agreed with Mo's doctor and decided that the one procured by Teach had been in error.

Maureen Connolly felt fine. She had no trouble playing. Suddenly, incredibly, she seemed near defeat at the hands of the beautiful but very little known Susan Partridge. In the nightmare of an anguished third set, she looked for and failed to find the suntanned face and the sparkling eyes of her beloved Teach. Perhaps it was the call of encouragement from a young American sailor, in marked contrast to the English crowd, that saved her from defeat. That evening, all alone, beyond the wall that divided her from Teach's room, Maureen suddenly felt a tremendous surge of power and freedom. She would win Wimbledon, she would win Forest Hills, she would win everything. And then perhaps, one day, tennis would no longer loom in her mind as some sort of wild aggression that seemed to consume her very heart. Perhaps one day, she sighed wistfully, she would find peace.

Above: a series showing Connolly's legendary forehand, played on the run at the very end of the rebound, still flat and nonchalantly played. To the left: Mother and daughter in the saddle. An unfortunate accident on horseback will interrupt Maureen's career.

29 Soldier Schweik Wins His Last Battle. Drobny

At his first Wimbledon, Jack Kramer lost to Jaroslav Drobny, who had been a ballboy for Tilden in Prague before World War II and then, at 17, had taken Budge to five sets. Jack turned professional in 1947, and everyone thought that, for the first time, the crown of the world's champion would grace the brow of a Central European. The Czechoslovakians had always had a fine school and a sports mentality that grew out of their yearly *Spartachiadi*. One of their number, Karel Kozeluh, won the number-one title among the professionals.

Drobny, solid and sure to the point of boredom, with a devastating power in his left-handed serve and in his drive, had an admirable touch and a backhand limited to a slice. He was a born sportsman and had the advantage of being a member of a club where his father was custodian. In the wintertime, the courts were flooded and transformed into shining ice-skating rinks, and the tennis enthusiasts into hockey players. In the Saint Moritz Olympics of 1948, Drobny, the forward center, fought valiantly together with two other members of the Davis team, Zadrobsky and Matous. All of these athletes ended by disavowing the politics of their government and, armed with their rackets alone, sought asylum in the West to face life there. Jaroslav, who had the good nature and pleasant sweetness of the fabled soldier Schweik, saw his promising career flawed: with no house, family, or friends, he would travel hit or miss, trying to seek residence permits as best he could. Faiza, the sister of King Faruk, finally was able to get him an Egyptian passport. Drobny felt less out of place, but the feeling of isolation and the solitude still troubled him.

That subtle anguish made him lose some well-played matches that turned out to be real cliff-hangers until the very last minute: in the Paris finals in 1948, against that solid wall, Parker; at Wimbledon in 1949, 4–6 in the fifth set against Schroeder; and then in Paris in 1950, 5–7 in the fifth set against Budge Patty. Drobny, peaceful man that he was, seemed to panic not only when faced by great champions. As soon as the score was in doubt, all of his opponents, even the weakest ones, inspired in him a terrible sense of doubt. At the tournament in Cortina d'Ampezzo, later the site of the 1956 Winter Olympics, I took him on, beginning with a respectable serve. I was certain that I was going to lose. In the motionless air of a late morning and under a hot sun, we were at six all in the second set, when Drobny asked me if I was thirsty, as was he, and if I would care to order something to drink. It made me laugh to think that such a match could last so long and I made the mistake of telling him so. Two minutes later it was all over.

Drobny's anxieties were alleviated by his love of Rita, the English player who later became his wife. He won Roland Garros in 1951 and repeated his victory the next year. But at Wimbledon, Jaroslav's magic formula failed to work. 1952 seemed a good year for him; then Sedgman rode him to defeat. In 1953 Jaroslav faced Budge Patty in the fourth round.

Patty was a mystery man who had entered tennis with the aid of the movie stars Robert Taylor and Barbara Stanwyck. He also was a friend of Barbara Hutton. Women of all ages mobbed him outside his home in Paris just after he had been demobilized. On clay courts, he played an offensive American tennis, which was refined by a splendid touch and a disconcerting lob, a game that was made even tougher by his concentration. On the way home from Roland Garros, this author once had the chance to greet him three times as he got out of his taxi. But it was to no avail, for Patty was immersed in the match that had just been called off on account of darkness.

With a truly phenomenal percentage of successful serves and a sabrelike volley, Patty had won both Wimbledon and Paris in 1950. His intentions were of the best to do the same thing in London during the summer of 1953. The match began at five in the afternoon, and at nine o'clock in the evening we were still nailed to our seats around the court, shouting words of encouragement, while those two men, at the point of exhaustion, miraculously continued to exchange winning volleys. Patty was as contorted by cramps as a piece of wire, and Drobny hobbled, with a hand pressed against his lower back between serves. At the end of the match, he, too, had cramps for the first time in his life. In the darkening night, Patty arrived at match point seven times, and seven times Drobny wiped out the advantage. Drobny felt like a man "walking on the bottom of the sea," and on two occasions, at 8 all and at 10 all in the fifth set, he asked for time out to adjust his glasses.

Legg, the referee, finally announced that only two more games would be played. Jaroslav threw all he had into his forehand, broke Patty's serve, and won. It was 9:15. Along with many other fans, this author waited for the two champions. Toward ten that night, they appeared together at the door of the dressing room: they were so worn and bedraggled looking that, out of respect, I dared not even congratulate them. Drobny hobbled into the semifinals and gave the match to Nielsen. Only Rita continued to believe with blind faith that somehow her man would come through.

The following year the organizing committee deigned to assign Drobny the eleventh place in the seeding. Furious within, Jaroslav practiced in silence under the grim vault of the old Queens Club, making an empty box of balls the target of his shots. He had not signed up for the doubles, and after every win went fishing at the lake on his wife's property. He defeated Hoad because he was angry at Hopman; he defeated Patty because one of the organizers had used bad language with Rita. The day of the finals play, everyone was on his side, and young Ken Rosewall, in that stadium seething with sentiment, must have felt the sudden need of his mother. Rosewall delayed his attack on Drobny's backhand, and Drobny took control of the game from that point on. This author had never seen people so enthusiastic and elated, had never listened to such thunderous applause until sixteen years later, when Rosewall himself occupied the position of Drobny. Rosewall lost in the fifth set against the young Newcombe, his third unfortunate finals encounter.

1

2

3

One of the most famous and longest matches of Wimbledon was played on June 25, 1953 between Jaroslav Drobny and Budge Patty. 1. The opposing forces at the entrance to Centre Court, toward four o'clock on a sunny afternoon. 2. Drobny plays a long volley shot, cut well in front. 3. After three hours of play, Patty is worn out. The scoreboard shows a score of nine all in the

4

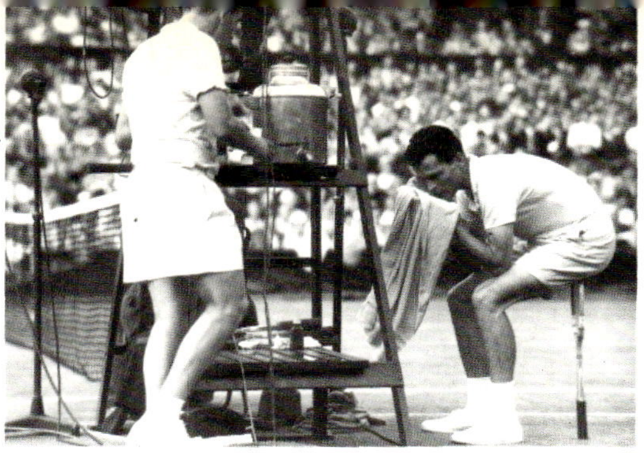

5

6

fifth set. 4. Patty leaning upon his racket to take advantage of a minute of repose. 5. Almost desperate with fatigue, he places a stretched volley. 6. It's all over, in the dusk, after a struggle of 4¼ hours. The two have enough energy left to smile at one another. Drobny the winner, 8–6, 16–18, 3–6, 8–6, 12–10, was too tired to profit from this victory and lost in the next round.

1

In this third attempt Drobny will succeed in carrying off the Wimbledon title. 1. He is at the net, facing the young Rosewall, who has just struck a razorlike backhand. 2. Drobny holding the cup between his opponent and Marina of Kent. 3. His wife Rita was nearby in the stands. 4. Between matches he relaxes fishing. 5. After years of waiting, he finally opens the Victors' Ball, dancing with Maureen Connolly. 6. The individualistic serve of Budge Patty. 7. Budge's smiling countenance in 1950, his great year that saw him victorious both at Roland Garros and at Wimbledon. 8. On Centre Court, Patty is on the offense against Sedgman, who has already prepared his backhand to pass him. 9. Dick Savitt, winner at Wimbledon in 1951, could not put up with the pace of the game and quickly gave it up. 10, 11. Lennart Bergelin and Kurt Nielsen, the two strongest Scandinavian players in the postwar period until the appearance of Davidson and Lundquist. Without being ranked, Nielsen got to the Wimbledon finals in 1953 and 1955. 12. The Austrian Fred Huber was also a goalkeeper in ice hockey, and he seems to be recalling those days in this dive for the turf at Wimbledon. The ball has been hit and looks as if it may win him a point!

2

3

4

5

6

7

8

9

12

10

11

30 Pancho Gonzales, Mexican-American

The feeble light that filtered through the dusty windowpanes brightened one corner of the room, casting the rest of it into dark and somber hues. Lost in a deep sleep under a coat, a naked man lay breathing. His long hand, with its slender and tapered fingers, had swept clean a tiny spot on the dusty floor as the sleeper unconsciously moved his arm. His long, dark hair was streaked with silver, and his thick, sensual lips signaled fatigue. They were the only visible features of the face, half hidden by a strong forearm. Standing out in the subdued mauve light, a scar on the right cheek grew ruddy as the blood coursed beneath it. The heartbeat rhythmically lifted the coat above the chest.

Richard Alonzo (Pancho) Gonzales was asleep. After the match against the Englishman Mark Cox, the first one lost by a professional to an amateur in history's first open tournament, the reporters had left Gonzales alone and were swarming around his blond rival in the packed clubhouse. It was April 1968 at Bournemouth. Pancho had collapsed on the soft cot and slept deeply as only the poor can or those for whom sleep is the only release from an immense grief. The walls of the old club, which protected the sleeper from the rainy gusts of wind, were no more worn than those of Arzy Kunz's store in Los Angeles. Pancho had once loved to call Arzy's place the "pad," and as a small Chicano boy he treasured that refuge where he could engage in the luxury of admiring the brand-new rackets. At the pad Pancho had learned to repair his first enormous, fourteen-ounce racket, worn and scraped by visits to the courts near the Los Angeles Coliseum. His mother, Carmen, would often come looking for him there, complaining loudly that this son of hers was always out in the street, always running around in bad company and managing to play tennis all day long, and that he would forget his supper when he got absorbed by the same Western film for hours on end.

In the Gonzalez household, meals were served with regularity to please the head of the family, Manuel, a decent man who had immigrated to Arizona from Chihuahua, the town famous for its lapdog and for its poverty. In Arizona, Manuel Gonzalez had married Carmen, and their arduous journey had come to an end in Los Angeles. Near Wrigley Field, the sports stadium, Richard came into this world on May 9, 1928, as the depression was gathering strength in the United States. Richard, and then Bertha, Margaret, Terry, Manuel, and Ralph had grown up in two rooms in that neighborhood, and in two others elsewhere when the family was pushed out by new waves of immigration and saddled with debts. The children were raised on spoonfuls of beans, omelettes with stewed tomatoes, and oatmeal patties. Not even the most optimistic prophet would have predicted that such a slow and awkward youngster as Pancho would one day be transformed into a prince on the tennis courts, a splendid warrior, 1.8 meters (5 feet 11 inches) in height, well armed with both serve and backhand, hard on the referees, the fans, and himself, but just and occasionally generous toward his enemies in the lists.

Even today the yellow ribbon still rests in a position of honor in his collection, next to a copy of the Davis Cup of 1949 and the rusty medal won for an oratory decathlon, together with other awards for paddle tennis, dice, chess, pool, basketball free throws, croquet, coin pitching, horseshoe pitching, and table tennis. Filled with pride, Pancho had run all the way home to give his mother the yellow ribbon, pinned to his torn sweater and awarded him for first place in the tennis tournament at Slauson Park. Carmen gave him a kiss and told him he was a fine boy, the best in the whole family. Encouraged by her praise, he quickly won two other events, and the *Los Angeles Times* devoted a few lines to him in the paper.

Pancho's dedication to the sport helped Frank Poulain to come to a decision. Like Arzy, Frank was interested in the boy's welfare. They would go to see Perry Jones, the tennis czar. Pancho immediately wanted to know if Jones was a great champion. Poulain said he was not. Pancho wondered why he was called a czar then. Poulain answered that Jones was an egotistical man. Not knowing what that meant, Pancho gingerly nodded in assent. Beyond a network of courts, meeting rooms, and dressing rooms swarming with attendants, Pancho found himself in the czar's office. Smiling

The immortal Pancho Gonzales at the age of twenty and at forty. Fatigue may leave its scars, the heart may beat its fierce tattoo, but the stern look, the long drive, the style, and the fierce will to win are unmistakable.

but also showing misgivings, Jones looked at the boy from behind the metal frames of his glasses which ringed his weak eyes and seemed connected to them. Poulain noticed his suspicions and attacked at once. "Here is the future champion of the United States," he said proudly.

Perry looked Pancho over with the eyes of a horse trader. "Perhaps," he murmured skeptically. Then with sudden enthusiasm, "That's a long road, a very long road."

"He'll make it," Poulain insisted.

"I've seen hundreds of them," Perry growled, angered at such a show of faith. "Almost none of them passed my easiest tests."

"Try him out."

Perry took off his glasses and began to clean them with a handkerchief embroidered with his initials and the emblem of a tennis racket. "The only positive proof," he muttered, "would be to take a dozen or so of them up on the roof and throw them off. A

couple would survive and the one with the best reflexes *might* become a champion."

Perry laughed wickedly, and while Poulain was doing his best to do likewise, Pancho jumped to his feet. "Let's go up on the roof, Mr. Czar!" he said determinedly.

"I'm not as bad as all that. Let's go out on the court," Jones answered. After ten minutes of volleys he turned angrily to Poulain: "Can't you see he's a cream puff? He doesn't have any drive. His metabolism must be off."

"His metabolism is better than mine," Poulain answered heatedly. "Richard is a fighter who shows his stuff when the chips are down. Send him East with your boys; you'll see what he can do." Jones shook his head. Gonzalez's high-school transcripts, he said, showed too poor a scholastic record. An educated man himself, Jones was not in the habit of aiding and abetting illiteracy. He was sorry, but he had already wasted enough time.

EXIT

R.LAVER
SETS
POINTS
15
SERVER
J.D.NEWCOMBE
3

Pancho saw Henrietta in the stands. She was leaning on the arm of Frank Shields, his only friend. Pancho smiled and then realized with a sudden shiver that she would soon begin to cry. His hand grazed his heart, forehead, and hair, an automatic gesture related to his Catholic upbringing.

Pancho made the sign of the cross and then tried, together with Henrietta, to erase from his mind all negative impressions from the past year. But his hatred for the rich and beautiful white society of the tennis world could not help but cross the net and engulf Ted, who had beaten him seven times to his one victory. Ted Schroeder stood there smiling like always and rallying with insulting indifference. He sent the balls back lightly or else suddenly with tremendous speed, keeping his opponent cold and unable to center his shots. Pancho answered with his serve and hit thirteen balls with increasing violence, while Schroeder stood his ground, keeping his legs wide apart as he eyed his opponent with irony. The umpire thought it opportune to end the warmup. "Play," he ordered simply.

Gonzales had not yet recovered from the shock of the first two sets having been lost and of the third set received almost as a gift from an absentminded Schroeder. He lifted his face toward the needles of the shower, and then Shields came to him, breaking the silence of the dressing room with his deep voice. "When Ted is a point ahead," the old champion repeated, "he always plays a slice instead of a cannonball." How could Pancho not have noticed that? Shields, however, did not give him time to reply before continuing: "You're staying too far back, and as a result you don't pick up that short ball of his. If you don't see what I mean, if you can't get it by yourself, pay attention to my hands. When he serves you a slice, I'll grip the railing."

When the game was resumed, Pancho cast a glance toward Shields, ready for his signal. He moved up two paces and suddenly there was the ball on his racket, ready to smash to bits. Before Schroeder could regain mid-court, the projectile had whizzed past him. Pancho continued to blindly follow his friend's signals, and, as if by magic, he got the break. From the fans a voice blurted out: "Put him on ice!" Schroeder lost his cool and requested silence. With a bellow, the crowd turned against him. Pancho ran off with the fourth set, 6–2. Schroeder was proud of his record as a winning player in fifth sets. Only Jack Kramer had managed to clobber him in a final set. He threw himself grimly into the game.

The game followed the serves up to four all. Pancho risked two anticipated shots and two forehand passing shots and made the break. A double fault and a net volley showed how nervous he was and cost him a 15–30 score. A volley on a ball possibly out put him in trouble, 30–40! Schroeder's lips rounded in a sneering grin. Pancho really drove the serve home twice and then closed with a volley. Match point. He kissed his racket and then served. Ted rushed the return with his forehand, and Pancho saved himself with a half-volley, while his opponent advanced to finish him with a drive. The ball flew out of reach near the line. The umpire raised his hand. "Out!" Pancho was the winner. Thirteen thousand fans got to their feet to applaud. Henrietta had begun to cry again, her head cradled on Shields's shoulder.

After his victory in the finals at Forest Hills, Pancho Gonzales joined Jack Kramer in the professional ranks. Bobby Riggs signed them up for a tour that was a financial success. After 96 matches lost in the long string of 123 challenge matches played against Kramer, Gonzales put $75,000 in the bank. But at the same time Pancho ruined his reputation as a tennis player. Listening to his wife's advice, he bought two small houses, gave one to his parents, and then bought himself a pair of red morocco leather slippers. His unfulfilled desire for competition and for danger soon drove him into playing poker and gambling for high stakes at an illegal establishment. After a couple of months he had lost everything

1

2

3

1. Ted Schroeder, in the finals match at Forest Hills in 1949, will be ridden to defeat by Gonzales, who will win 16–18, 2–6, 6–1, 6–2, 6–4.
2. A smiling Gonzales, clutching the U.S. Champion's Cup.
3. Some time later, Pancho, his face grim, goes into battle against a more fearful foe, Jack Kramer, world champion of the pro circuit.

1

3

1. *Pancho in a lateral backhand volley.* 2. *His devastating serve, backed up by 90 kilograms (198 lbs.) of muscle and grit.* 3. *One of his endless conversations with the fans, here English and highly pleased.* 4. *His lovely admirers, as numerous as his fallen foes on the court.* 5. *Pancho with his second wife Madelyn.* 6. *The unquenched self-assertion of the now mature champion as he intercepts a ball intended for Rosewall to score a point between Riessen and Okker.* 7. *Rapid repairs made to a recalcitrant racket.*

2

4

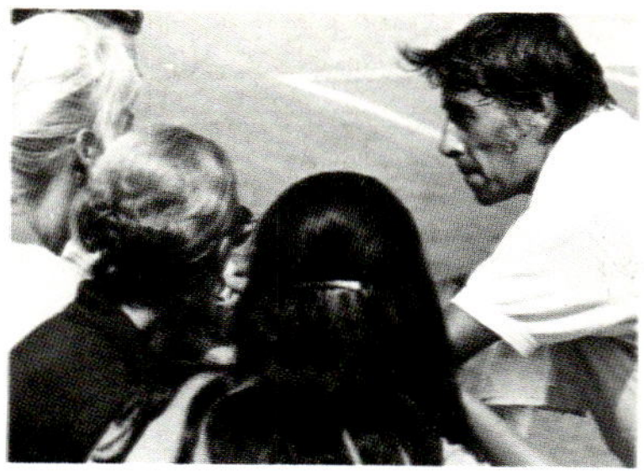

5

6

8. Perhaps his last great match, at Wimbledon in 1969, against Charlie Pasarell. Pancho wiped out seven match points and won 22–24, 1–6, 16–14, 6–3, and 11–9 after two afternoons of play, altogether five hours and twelve minutes.

7

8

and knocked on Riggs's door. The old champion was frank if cruel with him: "You're a drag on the market, Pancho, and your name isn't worth a red cent. Get in shape, start practicing, and bide your time. You've got to be patient." The insult was lost in the sound of the door being closed. After a long walk, as rambling and disjointed as his thoughts, Pancho found himself once again in front of Arzy Kunz's sporting goods store. "Don't you think you have worked here long enough?" he asked his friend. "Why don't you sell the store to me?" Kunz agreed.

After a few days Henrietta could see, tearfully, that it was impossible to transform Pancho into a small businessman. He would leave notes written on the windowpane, and off he would go to compete with the boys on the drag strip. In bowling he often scored 250, and in two week's training he played a round of golf in 75. Against his better judgment, he tried coaching in Hollywood, making Henrietta wrongfully jealous. When a starlet propositioned him, he threw her into a bed of tulips in her yard and shouted, "My tennis is not for sale!"

The few dollars Pancho was able to raise came from playing semipro basketball. He tried giving tennis lessons but had no success whatsoever. It was not his thing, and after a few attempts, he managed to alienate all the rich clients and found himself reduced to one student, Oscar Johnson, who would later climb to prominence as an Afro-American star. Angered by Riggs's indifference, Pancho finally rebelled and signed a contract with Jack Harris, which turned out to be a mistake. Within two years, Pancho was to win a pro championship of the United States which was boycotted by Riggs. At the end of 1953, Pancho was invited to visit Kramer in his new office.

Dressed in a dark suit, with a twenty-dollar tie around his suntanned neck, Jack encouraged him to sit down, then slumped into a comfortable revolving armchair. "Aren't you weary of being retired by now, Pancho?" he smiled. He had replaced Riggs, he explained quickly. It was a euphemism for what really had transpired, which was lost in Pancho's amazement. With his eyes glued to the contract that Jack was waving around like a fan to punctuate his elegant sales pitch, Pancho gritted his teeth, unable to hear a word of it.

At last, when he had finished his discourse, Kramer himself lost his customary calm just for a moment. "There is only one thing that keeps me from signing, Jack," Gonzales had observed. "I never carry a pen with me."

The tourney with Sedgman, McGregor, and Segura was not very profitable in the United States, but in Australia the crowds were staggering in proportion. In 1954 the Aussies were mildly intoxicated by the success of their own champions and identified themselves with their domination. The arrival of Pancho and his sixteen victories against nine for Sedgman, his fifteen triumphs that shut out McGregor showed to those with eyes that professional tennis was something more than a badly controlled amateur status. The strongest player in the world was a professional without a penny in the till.

In 1955 Gonzales became the victim of a curious phenomenon which had afflicted some other highly gifted professionals of the sporting world, like Joe Louis, Bobby Jones, or Willie Hoppe. Pancho was out of work because he was too strong for the competition. At the age of twenty-six, he played such an excellent game that Gardini and Merlo, Eleanor Tennant's guests, were able to take from him only one game in two successive singles matches of

On page 245: Lateral volley by Gonzales. The look of grim determination is typical.

two sets each! Another tour in Australia ended with forty-five victories for him against seven for his opponent Pails. Little by little the crowds began to dwindle. At the end of the tour Kramer invited him into his office, and, with a little more elegance, repeated Riggs's old argument. "I can't put you out on the court until I get Trabert, or Rosewall and Hoad."

Kramer tried in vain to get the Wimbledon and Forest Hills champion and the two young holders of the Davis Cup into professional tennis at the same time. His attempt to keep Pancho on the sidelines also failed, and he was forced to organize a challenge between the amateur champions and the professional stars. The large sum that he advanced to Trabert was a mistake: Gonzales would earn only $15,000 as opposed to $80,000 for his rival, whatever the outcome. Pancho certainly had no need of special provocation to dislike poor Tony Trabert. He grew so bitter that he refused a practice set before the tour began. "We will meet on the court one hundred and two times. Don't you think that's enough?"

Every evening, after his long and solitary car trip, Pancho would meet Tony and Jack in a new town. Under feeble lightbulbs, on treacherous canvas that covered a playing surface of wood or ice, in dancehall or circus tent, he unleashed himself against his adversary, pitting himself against his boss at the same time. At the end of the tour, with 75 victories to 27, Gonzales felt repaid for all the humiliations of the first tour and at the same time free of the hatred he had felt for the tall, good-looking, rosy Trabert. He was ready to discuss a seven-year contract with Kramer.

Up until 1960 Pancho would continue to match wits with the strongest opponents that the impresario could muster, the great Rosewall and Hoad. The ascent of Rosewall did not throw him out of the running, especially in the individual matches and in the tournaments: regular as clockwork, Pancho would combine the best tennis with the highest prizes. In 1966, at the age of thirty-eight, Gonzales would take Wembley, beating Rosewall in the semifinals 13–11 in the third, and Rod Laver in the fifth set of the final 10–8. His career was not yet over.

In April 1968, at Bournemouth, he had slept the sleep of the courageous in defeat. Beaten by Cox, Pancho would point an accusing finger at the balls, the playing surface which had been drenched by the spring rains, and the noise of the stands. "A tennis player is lifted by silence as if by a wave," he stated, raising his long brown arms. "It is difficult for me to get used again to this game and these crowds." He had indeed spent eighteen years on the professional circuit in nighttime arenas. He was now forty years old and the reporters counted him out altogether. Even a heart specialist recommended that he take it easy.

In a duel that lasted two days against an opponent like Pasarell, on Wimbledon's Centre Court, Pancho brought back the past with his racket and made everyone feel young again. He made up for two lost sets, scratched seven match points with six aces and a smash, and won 22–24, 1–6, 16–14, 6–3, and 11–9 in five hours and twelve minutes. In the stands, his wife was biting her nails, suppressing occasional shouts and holding on tight to a girl friend. Once she had just turned away when Pancho's eye caught her. She then sat primly in proper adoration of her lord and master, suffered those interminable match points with the rest of us, and, like us, rushed to wait outside the dressing rooms.

It took Pancho so long to appear that Mrs. Gonzales grew nervous once again and the fans began to grumble. For a moment I was hoping that Aphrodite or some intervention by Mercury would fix this event in time as being worthy of their action. The door finally opened and, radiant with his triumph and his agony on court, Pancho handed himself over to the adulation of the crowd, with his arms raised in victory and a large smile on his face gray with fatigue, which made his scar even more attractive.

Have I exaggerated? The story is too long, maybe a little rhetorical. Pancho's career was a long one, and many feel that he may well be the strongest of any of the tennis giants, including Tilden, Kramer, and even Laver. Gonzales's impressions of some of the strongest of his opponents are of interest:

"I would not want to meet Budge at one of his better moments. He had a fantastic backhand! Budge would have been hard for Laver to handle since Rod's left-handed service would always aim at his backhand.

"Jack Kramer was not a natural player. He was not very quick nor did he have good reflexes, but he knew how to win.

"Hoad was probably the best and the hardest when he felt like it. He was the only one to beat me in a head-to-head confrontation, fifteen matches to thirteen. But after the tour he never cared to try again.

"Sedgman was one of the strongest physically: he, Hoad, and Laver. He never tired in a long match. Not physically at any rate. Only two players beat him with consistency: Kramer and I.

"What Rosewall can do with his backhand, Segura did even better with his forehand. No one could beat him around 1954.

"What makes Laver great is his will and his ability in improving his game when the going gets rough. The fact that he is a left-hander gives him a five percent advantage, because right-handers rarely play against left-handers. He is so good on offense that he makes you forget how good a defensive game he has. His spins give trouble to many of his opponents, but Hoad would have been able to handle him.

"To finish up the survey, Segura and Jack had the best forehands, Budge and Rosewall the best backhands. With Rosewall on the left and Segura to the right, the best half-volleys. The best on the base line were Kramer, Segura, and Rosewall. Jack had a great serve. I really think the best, on serves, were the two of us."

In the two upper sequences we can admire two of the most famous and violent serves in the history of the sport, that of Gonzales and that of Court. The lower sequence shows Nastase's serve. All three are first service balls, followed to the net by Court and Nastase and by the ready position in the case of Gonzales. Both Gonzales and Court meet the ball above the right shoulder (8), with very little spin in order to increase its speed. Impact comes about 10 centimeters (about 4 in.) below the high point of the curve of the stroke (7, 8). Gonzales (his film is older), as he strokes, maintains contact with the ground with his pivot foot. The lateral displacement of his right leg (13) limits his foreward movement and keeps the player on the base line. Court and Nastase, on the other hand,

8 9 10 11 12 13

8 9 10 11 12 13 14

8 9 10 11 12 13 14

hit in flight, with both feet in the air. While the Australian keeps her tiny feet aligned (8–11), the Romanian uses a scissors. Nastase's sweep goes far beyond his side, as does Gonzales's, which is nonetheless more classic and free from any initial sway, with the head of the racket pointed straight down, reminiscent of the blow of a worker's hammer (1). The first phase of Court's movement (2–4) slides along her side in a semicircle vertical to the ground.

31 Tennis Goes Australian. Sedgman the Gymnast

The Australians had really won the Davis Cup only once, in 1939; the four previous victories, in the early part of the century, had gone to the mythical Australasia, the team that carried Brookes and the New Zealanders Wilding and Dunlop as well. Suddenly, from 1950 to 1967, an avalanche of fifteen Australian victories upset the Americans. What had happened? The Yanks' forces had been badly weakened by the loss of Kramer and Gonzales to the professional ranks. Sedgman and McGregor could easily have laid their hands on the Cup, but Jack brought things back into balance by spiriting these players away from the amateurs. The Australians had to try out Hoad and Rosewall, both a mere eighteen, only to have them quickly slip away, replaced by Cooper and Anderson, then Fraser and Laver, and lastly by Emerson and Stolle. That fantastic lode of talent was finally exhausted with Newcombe and Roche.

It is not true that the war hurt the Australians less than the Americans. Both countries did their part and had their dead, even if their geographic situation enabled them to escape the catastrophies of the Old World. Tennis had always been popular in Australia where it was one of the three major sports along with cricket and Australian football. The courts were numerous, and even in small towns and in the country one could find the familiar posts and nets, even if their proportions were somewhat sketchy. With that ideal climate, tennis was played all the year round as in California, the home of most of the U.S. champions. The improved life style and the lighted courts for night use were additional factors that brought to the game many of those who had never played it before. The sporting goods suppliers were faced with an increased demand and new competition. The country was rich in young people with a natural talent for athletics, the product of a background where sport received closer attention than culture per se. All it took was an announcement of a meet, and offers of participation poured in.

The provision of jobs for tennis players did not run counter to the Australians' definition of amateur status, as was the case in the United States. "I could not honestly state that I had used their racket, but I could say their racket had its place in the tournament I had just won," Frank Sedgman remarked, "for I would not have had the money for the tournaments if I had not worked for a sporting goods manufacturer." When later Sedgman and McGregor had won the Cup, a real thrill of pride and joy crossed that immense land with its ten million people. The Australians had never been first at anything, and now, suddenly, they were beating everyone, including the herculean Americans. That their enthusiasm did not degenerate into chauvinism was certainly due to their English heritage and to the sincere and lasting love for the sport in this newly fashioned but well-behaved nation.

The first to make a showing was Frank Sedgman, and the first to understand the implications of the accomplishment was Harry Hopman, called Hop. Hopman himself had once been a champion, outclassed in singles play by Crawford's talent and satisfied with his successes in doubles play and in mixed competition with Nelly Hall, who later became his wife. Hopman's job as a newspaperman on the *Melbourne Herald* gave him the time he needed to work for the sport he loved: he offered free courses for the young people, toured the country to excite interest in the tournaments, and enjoyed participating in them himself. When Frank Sedgman was twelve years old, Hopman placed a racket in his hands. He lost contact with the youngster during the war and ran into him again when the boy was eighteen. By this time Hop was about forty. Nelly had given him no children, and the conditions for the beginning of his triumphant career as the father figure to tennis could not have been more favorable.

Sedgman served far too lightly and had little muscular development. Hop got him into the routine of regular workouts at the gym, and Frank was able to double-time there in the evening, having just won a competition. Sedgman was sent to Wimbledon with money provided by the fans, where, paired with the aging Bromwich, he won the doubles by virtue of forceful serves, as well as jumps, reaches and athletic ability in general. Frolicking during his honeymoon, Sedgman appeared for the fans on the balcony of the Carlton Hotel in Cannes, clad only in his briefs. By 8 A.M. he already had his racket in hand and, in the cool morning air, was testing the movements that made up his admirable strokes.

During the same year, I had the good luck to play Sedgman at the Italian Internationals. The games went by and we stayed tied, much to my surprise. Totally at ease, I continued as if by magic to keep up with that rapid, flat ball, devoid of spin. Sedgman, I suddenly understood, was always playing the best shots and doing the most logical thing; for this reason I had been able to stay with him up to six games all. At the same moment I became aware that I would no longer be able to do so. First by one hundredth of a second, then by a tenth, first by a centimeter, then by a palm, I found myself incapable of connecting with those balls played strictly according to the rulebook. I lost the second set six love.

Harry Hopman's most important, fundamental, and very simple innovation had been to apply the principles of sports training to Jack Kramer's Big Game. His boys ran endless miles; they lifted weights; they practiced interval training with a simple series of basic repetitions, the first to do so. They slept a great deal; they did not smoke or drink; and when they broke training, they paid some stiff fines from their own pocket money. Hop was accused of driving them too hard, but, to the contrary, he always knew where to draw the line before they became stale from overtraining. He was accused of brainwashing as well, and in this area he probably did overdo it. Winning was the name of the game, and with his personality halfway between a military strategist and a drill sergeant, Harry did what he had to do: it was foolish to expect from him fine manners or to insist that he handle his men with kid gloves.

McGregor, for example, would most certainly have rather played football. Hop spoke with his father, an Australian football hero from the thirties, telling him that his son could not fail at tennis. They shook hands on the matter, and poor Macca McGregor was subjected to the big sell and for all practical purposes was drafted into a career that culminated with his victory against Schroeder, who had never lost in Davis competition. Taller, more solidly built, and stronger than Sedgman, McGregor was virtually impossible to

1

3

4

5

6

7

8

2

On page 248: Sedgman preparing a smash, alongside McGregor. The Australians won the first doubles Grand Slam in history in 1951. Two views of the doubles match between Sedgman and McGregor, and Schroeder and the beginner Trabert.

pass on a grass court, and he became known in doubles play as some sort of human barrier at the net. These two characters were the first to win the Grand Slam in 1951, the four important doubles championships. In 1952 they came very close to repeating the feat, not losing until the very end against Seixas and their fellow Australian Mervyn Rose. Having won the Cup for the third time in as many years, they finally accepted Kramer's offer. At the end of the tour, the most lucrative ever offered, McGregor set his racket aside and at last lovingly put on his football shoes.

The Americans had certainly not been watching patiently from the sidelines while the Australians won the Cup three times, Sedgman two Forest Hills and a Wimbledon, and McGregor an Australian championship. The United States had an eccentric player in Flam, a delightful madcap in Larsen, the perfect form in the aging Mulloy, and an aggressive fighter in Vic Seixas. The heir apparent of Kramer and Gonzales had not, we thought, made his appearance on the university courts. But when Talbert arrived in Europe with a new doubles partner and told us that this was he, the Lord's annointed one, we had little difficulty believing him.

Tony Trabert was the most American-looking individual that one could possibly imagine: hair close cropped like that of a Marine, a handsome, open face sprinkled with freckles, two enormous shoulders, and legs thick as pillars. The only hope that we smaller players had was that he might be a bit slow, but once we saw him in action on the court, we gave up that illusion and began to admire the man's great ability. Like his Australian adversaries, Tony seemed never to get off the courts. One evening, after three matches, I saw him politely ask a flabbergasted manager for some new balls in order to review a technical problem once more with Talbert.

Billy Talbert was a great technician and would demonstrate his craftsmanship as captain of the Davis Cup team and by writing three books which are tiny classics in their own right. He strove to prove to the public that, especially in singles play, he had been handicapped by the war and by diabetes. He was generous with his talents, and his students received invaluable daily suggestions and professional secrets known only to a few. In one year's time, that excellent training carried Tony from twelfth position to the Davis Cup team, and Frank Shields, according to Hopman, committed an error in using him only in doubles competition, and with Schroeder at that.

Trabert's stint in the Navy interrupted his rise to fame. It delayed the development of his overpowering serve as well as the strengthening of his tight backhand. His Navy time also slowed the perfection of his unrelenting attacks at the net. By the end of 1953 he saw himself number one in the world and also in first position in the eyes of Shauna Wood, who had done well in the Miss America Beauty Pageant. Kramer had taken Sedgman off his back, and the future seemed rosy. Suddenly, groomed in the wings by Hop, two unknowns made their appearance, two beardless young men with muscles still untried, their eyes filled with the surprise and determination of those destined to greatness.

9

10

1. Trabert ends up on the ground. 2. The Americans chase down a lob that escaped them. Sedgman's style was based on workouts and physical training. 3. Serve. 4. Anticipated attack. 5. Backhand with a tango rhythm. 6. Stretched volley. 7. High backhand volley. 8. Smash with scissors execution. 9. Sedgman's partner McGregor was hard to beat at the net, as witnessed by his long reach. 10. Tony Trabert, a great champion executing a great backhand. 11. The lifted forehand of Seixas, often beaten, always game. He took Wimbledon in 1953.

11

Surrounded by spectators, guards, fans, hats, and overwhelming affection, many of the great champions of Wimbledon are posing against the background of the Centre Court for the seventy-fifth anniversary of the tournament in 1961. Between Chattie Cooper Sterry, winner of the singles in 1895, and Dannis Ralston, doubles champion in 1960, there is an age span of seventy-two years. First row, from the left: Mudford, Holcroft-Watson,

Ryan, Round, Cooper Sterry, Marina of Kent, Boothby, McKane, Parton, Tuckey, Mathieu. Second row: Kramer, Perry, Buxston, Metaxa, James, Stammers, Shilcock, Mortimer, Borotra, Cochet, Décugis, Summers. Third row: Howe, von Cramm, Patty, Godfree, Woosnam, Brugnon, Tuckey, Hughes. Fourth row: Schmidt, Trabert, Laver, Drobny, Emerson, Fraser, Mulloy, Ralston.

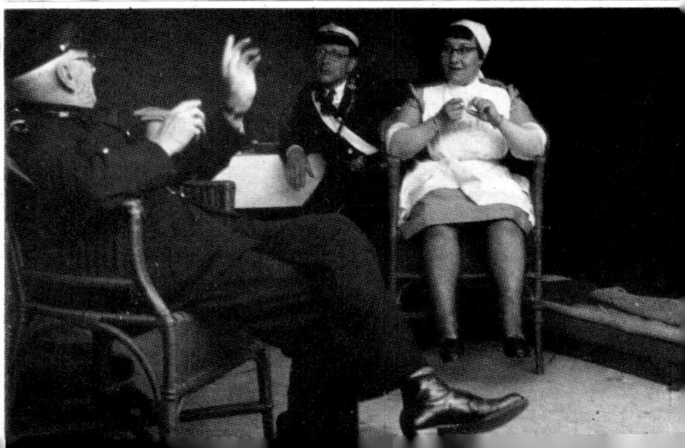

32 The Magic Twins: Hoad and Rosewall

1. Hoad and Rosewall with the Davis Cup in 1953.

Hero worshippers called them the Whiz Kids, the Sorcerer's Apprentices, or the Magic Twins, for they were born under the sign of Scorpio in November, only twenty-one days apart, as had been the case with Brookes and Crawford. Their features, the color of their hair, and their style of play were nevertheless as different as their personalities.

Towhead Lew Hoad soon grew into a giant of a man, with the wrists of a stonemason and a hand that completely engulfed the handle of his racket. On account of his slight build, Ken Rosewall was ironically called Muscles by George Worthington. Ken's unbeatable qualities were his speed, his shrewdness, and his technique. From a very young age, accustomed to peppering the side of his parents' garage with a barrage of tennis balls, Ken developed almost magical coordination and sensitivity. A left-hander by nature, he was taught to play with his right hand, which does not seem to have harmed his play except for his serve, which always remained studied, laborious, and awkward. Hoad also began his career practicing against a wall, thereby causing complaints from sleepy neighbors awakened from their slumbers by the dull thumping of tennis balls at daybreak. The first two matches he played against his brown-haired twin were a total disaster, and only in the third was he able to win a game.

Ken, according to those who saw him play as a child, even then never made a mistake and placed the ball squarely on the line. Lew relied on his strength to help himself, but he often found it of no use as he would obstinately go to the net only to watch a lob go whizzing by. It didn't take a great deal of foresight to predict a fine career for both of them. Their climb to the top was dizzying in its speed: a real blitz. I myself had the good fortune to witness their first European tour in 1952, both at Paris and at Wimbledon. Rosewall beat Fausto Gardini badly, who at his worst was still one of the best players in the world at that time in clay-court competition. In the end, Fausto fell back into a convenient chair, made the sign of the cross, and sighed: "It's lucky I ran into him now, when he's only seventeen!"

I had not seen Hoad at Roland Garros and I actually thought that Rosewall's equal didn't exist. Then at Wimbledon, while the spectators at the Centre Court were bursting with enthusiasm, I saw both Rosewall and Hoad easily defeat Mulloy and Savitt. It was a swift, incredible, and delightful encounter of the David and Goliath order. Mulloy was a superb athlete and Savitt a huge, good-natured, grizzly bear of a man. The two youngsters anticipated their every move, cheated them, and often, instead of playing crosscourts, hit directly and forcefully at the man at the net. With two additional months of experience, Rosewall beat Seixas, and Hoad trounced Larsen at Forest Hills.

The following year, old René Lacoste, his former ailments forgotten, burst into the dressing room at Roland Garros to give young Ken a bear hug and to kiss him on both cheeks, a typically French response to the youngest winner in that brutal tournament. The Parisians themselves, who have a fondness for taking players to their hearts, discovered that Ken had a backhand like Lacoste himself, the half-volley and anticipation of Cochet, and Borotra's speed on the court. Despite the accolades, the young man remained calm and smiling, demonstrating himself to be both of good upbringing and of few words, a fine combination. He was a serious sort, much more so than Hoad, and his only defect, if he had one, was this seriousness. Tennis was Ken's salvation. Those great backhand strokes were so razor-sharp and clean, so perfect in their execution that it made one gasp in amazement. Ken made up for his shy nature with his shots, which were executed with a precision that bathed his matches with a white light, a touch of geometric perfection reminiscent of a Mozart composition.

Hoad was the exact opposite. He stamped his feet, leaped into the air, snorted, his shirt occasionally hanging out of his shorts (something that never happened to Rosewall during the entire course of his career). Hoad was even known to argue with the linesmen or with the fans on occasion. He would give his all to win: he got in shape, he got out of shape, he raged when defeated and then just as quickly forgot all about it, for there was always some great jazz concert, or even better, a boxing match to take his mind off things afterwards. Later, when he reached his majority, a good bottle also became a boon companion. He loved his wife Jennifer deeply. She was of the same age as he and an excellent player. He married her unexpectedly at Wimbledon, to the consternation of Hopman and the delight of the British press.

There were weaknesses in Rosewall's game, and his forehand grew as strong as his backhand only by virtue of great effort. Hoad, on the other hand, on one of his good days, was the equal of any of tennis's hall of fame. He summed up the evolution of the game with its increasing speed by using only one grip, which was the opposite of Ken's and yet no less telling on the court. Hoad's greatest weakness was probably his rashness, his inability to understand that this pastime played in bright sunlight and in the presence of thousands of people had its precise rules of tactics so as not to make many mistakes. Large-boned as he was, Lew had to work hard to stay in shape. Since he didn't always feel in the mood, occasionally he lacked the necessary staying power that he needed. He played like a young god at the age of nineteen, and

2

2. *The two prodigies at a very tender age.*
3. *Their longtime opponents. Trabert is ready to smash, next to Seixas.*
4. *Rosewall and Hoad in doubles competition.*

3

4

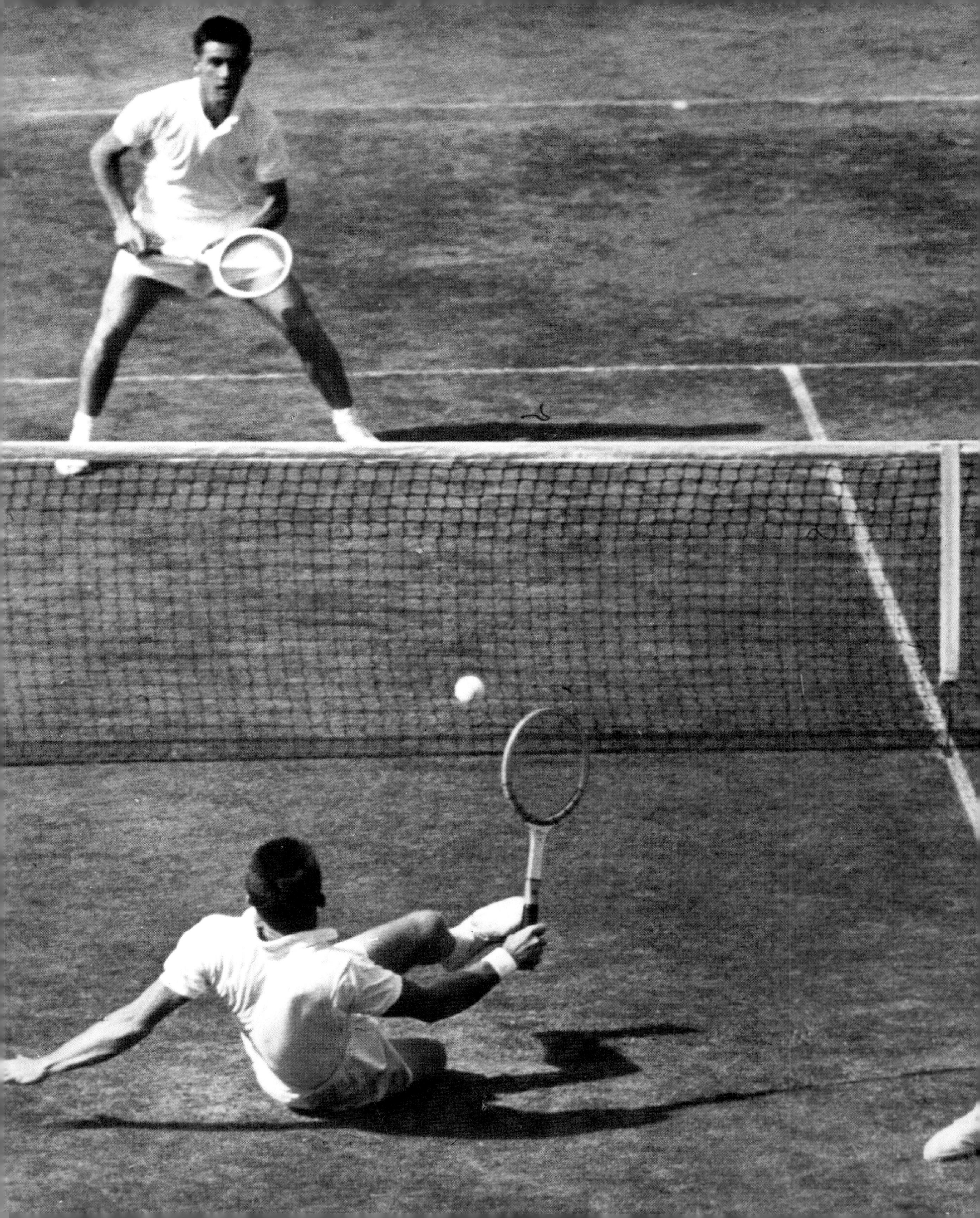

Rosewall, to the left, and Hoad are ready, despite the fact that Trabert is down, possibly trying to return a very different ball. Seixas instinctively goes to the aid of his friend. Beaten in 1953, the Americans claimed the rematch of the following year, but the Twins massacred them in 1955, 5–0!

some of Tony Trabert's remarks on the future of the Davis Cup did not sit well with him. It seemed, to listen to that braggart, that his only problem was how to crate the Cup for shipment after winning it.

The responsibilities of the Davis Cup competition upset Rosewall. He lost his drive, his berth in the doubles competition went to someone else due to poor judgment on the part of the selection committee, and his mother had to be brought to console him.

With the match standing two to one in favor of the Americans, Lew faced Trabert, led his opponent two sets to nothing, then slipped and fell on the rain-drenched turf in the fifth. Even mud-clogged spikes failed to slow Trabert down. The Australians talked of nothing else, and glued to their radios, roughly one million people held their breath as Hoad tripped and fell headlong at Hopman's feet. With a laugh, Hop got up and helped Lew to his feet, but as he threw him the towel, he couldn't refrain from muttering, "You clumsy oaf!" Lew got back to work with a grin. Suddenly the strings of his favorite racket broke, and he noticed with amazement that the new one he chose had more response. Overjoyed, he mustered one of his famous bursts of enthusiasm, won eight to six, and, incredulous, saw his huge adversary burst into tears.

Tied at two each, their play began again on the fourth day. Rosewall had regained his upper hand over Seixas and was never to lose it again. Of all his victims, Vic Seixas was both the most consistently fine player and yet the easiest for him to beat.

At Sidney, in 1954, the American finally had a chance at revenge, and he mustered the grace and good humor to state during their ninth match that Rosewall must be getting tired of beating him. For 1954 was the year when these two lads, who had been brought on the firing line a bit prematurely, buckled temporarily. Coached by Talbert, Trabert and Seixas had trained for two solid months, their one aim being to make good their challenge. And Hoad was head over heels in love with Jennifer at that time, while Rosewall was both angered and disappointed at the choice of Hartwig as Hoad's partner in doubles competition. In front of a record crowd of 27,500 people, the Americans finally recovered the Davis Cup with a hard-fought three to zero.

Trabert paid dearly for the overconfidence that often follows a great triumph, losing the Australian championships at the hand of Rosewall and thus the possibility of reaching the Grand Slam with its three successive great victories. 1955 proved to be Tony's year. He only returned empty-handed from the Davis Cup competition, where the Twins, gunning for revenge, were able to make good their previous defeat, with interest, running up five-to-zero. Tony was signed up by Kramer for a very high fee that made Gonzales furious. Pancho destroyed Trabert's reputation as amateur world champion.

Radiating peace, a picture of health, with his lovely wife Jennifer at his side, Hoad seemed ready for the laurels to be bestowed upon him. He faced and upset the whole field, racket poised, with a cool violence that only his smile and twinkling blue eyes made bearable. He had won three of the four titles for the Grand Slam, when he found himself face to face with Muscles at the

3

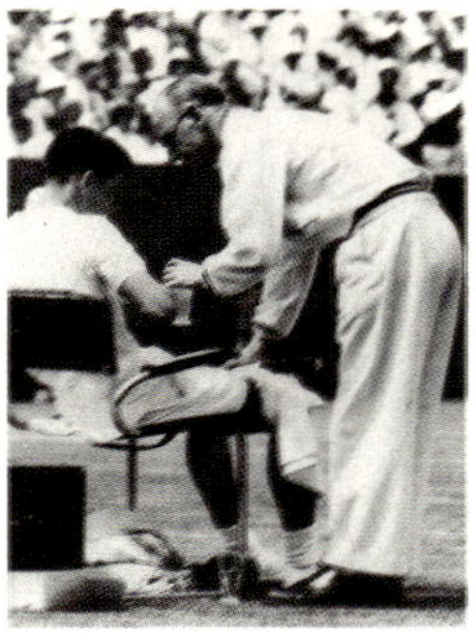

1. Challenge Round in 1953. Hoad passing with an exaggerated cross-court backhand, despite Seixas's volley. The Australian will win 6–4, 6–2, 6–3. 2. Harry Hopman giving advice to Hoad, during the first match of the Sydney tournament of 1954, in front of a record crowd of 25,578. Hoad lost to Trabert 6–4, 2–6, 12–10, 6–3. 3. Advice to Rosewall courtesy Hop. 4. In 1955 Tony Trabert showed the Twins off in Paris, at Wimbledon, and in New York. He lost in the Davis Cup. 5. Young Rosewall delights Paris with his backhand and (6) wins Roland Garros in 1953. 7. Rosewall has jumped the net to congratulate Seixas, his opponent in the finals.

1

2

end of the American championships. Fascinated by the prospect of the Slam, Lew became inhibited and, for once in his life, was as tense as a steel spring. Rosewall had his eye on the title and on Kramer's offer. A wit had said that for one thin dime Muscles could easily have slid under a low-slung car. Ken won out over his friend and was accepted before Hoad by Jack Kramer's troupe.

The Australians kindly kept Hoad on among their amateurs for one more season and for one more Davis competition. He won against Rosewall at Wimbledon in 1956, and the new Australian contender, Ashley Cooper, could do nothing against him in 1957. It was almost embarrassing to watch that blond destroyer scoring points with impossible shots and never making a mistake. What did stop him momentarily was a fly in his eye. A kind linesman removed it with the corner of his handkerchief, and Cooper's last hope vanished with it. In that forty-five-minute match, Cooper managed to scrape together less than thirty points.

There was no one left among the amateurs who could give Hoad any trouble, and he accepted the larger offer that Kramer made him. Hoad succeeded in beating out Gonzales in a locked-horns confrontation, but slowly a sharply increasing pain in his spine made it harder for him to train and extremely painful for him to unleash his cannonball serves. Having never been a fanatic about tennis, Hoad ended up by buying a small piece of land in Fuengirola, Spain, where he built a fine house and set up a tennis school.

Rosewall, on the other hand, is still going strong. Indefatigable, ever more precise, with greater technical perfection, he continued to fight his way and accumulate bullion. But once the barriers between the professionals and the amateurs were removed, he quickly won the French Open Championship in the festive, topsy-turvy atmosphere of Paris in May 1968, fifteen years after his first victory. Logic would dictate that this would be Muscles's swan song, for he played less well and we expected him to retire. But in 1970 there he was at Wimbledon, in the finals for the third time, sixteen years after losing at the hand of Drobny. The fifteen thousand fans at Centre Court were all playing right along with him, and his opponent Newcombe succumbed to the great rush of spirit for the surviving Magic Twin. The small and aging Whiz Kid got as far as the fifth set, but suddenly his magic forces failed him, and that evening the postmortems, the farewells, and the typeset tears began all over again.

Yet Rosewall was still to be reckoned with. He felt even better, got into his stride, and was twice able to win the year's richest prize: the $50,000 first place at the WCT. As I write these lines in 1974, Ken Rosewall has turned forty, and doesn't seem about to be slowed down by age.

After the Twins

When Hoad and Rosewall joined the ranks of the professionals, the sport lost a good deal of its fascination, and the important titles

4

more and more frequently went to excellent craftsmen, to perfect athletes, to virtuous fighters that no god would have seen fit to carry off to any Olympic hall of fame. The inexhaustable Australians held on tenaciously to the Cup, relying on Anderson, a new champion at Forest Hills, and Cooper, a roughhewn master craftsman. They also brought Rose back to doubles play, and his frightening left-handed serve and his volleys with their Borotra-like quality put both an aging Seixas and an unsteady MacKay out of commission.

These new defeats brought about a real crisis in the U.S. Lawn Tennis Association. After a small revolt within the ranks, old Perry Jones was selected to manage the team. Despite the Australian successes, the three grass tournaments of the Slam taken by Cooper, and the capture of Paris and Rome by Rose who was used to clay courts, Jones refused to call it quits and developed two brilliant cards.

He selected a Peruvian youngster, Alejandro Olmedo, who was studying at UCLA, as a leading player. Then Jones asked Jack Kramer to take charge of the team. Ready to sign a contract with Cooper and Anderson, Jack felt a conflict of interest, but his patriotic sentiments prevailed over his mercenary ones; he threw himself into the task of conditioning the American players to defeat his future stars.

The tense atmosphere of the team was ignited by the special treatment that Perry was giving Olmedo on Jack's orders. Richardson, who really felt himself victimized, raised the loudest hue and cry. Ham Richardson, the son of a family from the Deep South, had finished his studies at Oxford and had reached the number one place in the American ranking. Suddenly, with no warning or apparent justification, he was replaced by a foreigner, by a South American with dark skin! Both Perry and Jack came in for brickbats by the critics, but they defended themselves by reminding their detractors of Richardson's diabetes and of the right to use any foreign national in the service of a country in which he had resided for more than three years.

Olmedo himself answered all the critics by winning twice in singles competition and then in doubles play, where he was matched with Richardson himself. Ham, who never exchanged a word with his captain, played with furious brilliance, bouncing back from two sets and two match points down to win the longest doubles match in the history of the Davis Cup competition: 10–12, 3–6, 16–14, 6–3, and 7–5. But the taste of victory was sweet and Olmedo also won the Australian championships. They began to call him The Chief on account of his noble Aztec brow and curried favor with him. Kramer let it be known that if he won at Wimbledon, he could expect a bid. Olmedo mastered no out-of-the-ordinary strokes, but it was hard to beat him at the net. To win against him on grass, it took great power or a much more refined technique. He played a rushing game, he won at Wimbledon, and in the nick of time he got together with Kramer.

5

Hopman had already found the right opponents for him: Fraser had the powerful drive of a blacksmith, Laver and Emerson ran like gazelles and knew touch game at the same time. Fraser took Forest Hills in 1959, and all three Australians then retook the Davis Cup from MacKay and Buchholz. The Australians would continue their domination of the field until 1962. To give them more competition than the Americans could provide, two Southern Europeans, Pietrangeli and Santana, suddenly arrived on the scene.

6

7

1

2

3

4

1. With a moderately undercut slice, his wrist firm, Lew Hoad attacks the ball on the Center Court of Roland Garros in 1956. He will take the tournament as well as the Australian championships and Wimbledon. Rosewall himself will keep him from the Big Slam by beating him at Forest Hills. 2. Hoad beats Rosewall at Wimbledon in 1956: 6–2, 4–6, 7–5, and 6–4. 3. He devastates Cooper the following year in less than an hour's time. 4. He joins Rosewall, Sedgman, and Trabert among the pros. The same year, in 1958, Cooper, a less talented player, won three tournaments of the Grand Slam. It was a great injustice in sports with regard to professionals.

With a grim look on his face, the Wilson clutched in a Western grip of the old school, Tony Trabert eyes the ball he has just struck. He learned to play the game on cement courts. In his exceptional athletic prowess and in his backhand, Trabert found the qualities he needed to take Roland Garros in 1954 and 1955. In the postwar period, this was reserved to very few clay-court specialists like Parker, Drobny, Pietrangeli, and Kodes. The French loved Trabert for his good sportsmanship. The sequence above shows him rushing to aid Ham Richardson, who has fallen in a desperate run. Ham was later forced to retire.

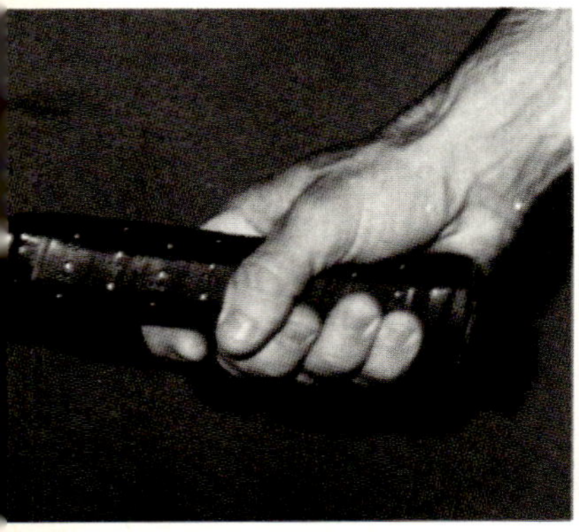

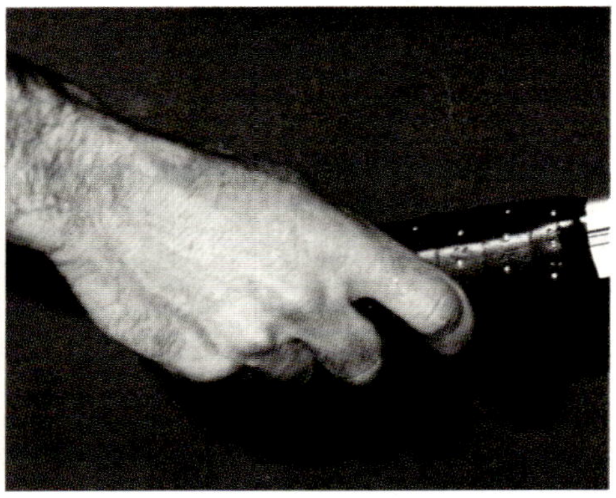

A A¹

In the twenty-nine pictures of this sequence we see an exchange between Gimeno, serving, and Rosewall, with his back to us. In photo A, a forehand grip by Rosewall, midway between Continental and Eastern, called Australian by many. In photo A1, Gimeno's forehand grip, which is more closed (Eastern), and in B and B1 their backhand grips, both unusual and Continental.
1. Gimeno is ready to hit a powerful first serve, which Rosewall senses (3) and rushes to return, preparing his stroke in advance (5, 6, 7, 8). Gimeno, who was slightly thrown off balance, appears surprised at that long backhand, and is forced to stroke during

6 7 8 9 10

16 17 18 19 20

26 27 28 29

another hasty sidestep (11, 12, 13). Always very fast, Rosewall attacks, taking advantage of the split second in which his opponent's eyes are fixed on the ball. 13, 14. He prepares his high volley (16, 17), plays it, sliced and cross-court, to the left of the Spaniard (18, 19, 20, 21), and then advances (22) and closes the angle while his opponent is hitting the backhand passing shot. Gimeno's ball is neither angled nor low enough. Rosewall suddenly readies himself (23, 24) and strokes (25) with such determination that Gimeno has no chance to retrieve.

B

B[1]

1

4

2

Moments from the glorious career of Ken Rosewall, born in Sydney on December 2, 1934. 1, 2, 3. The unfortunate Wimbledon finals matches in 1954, 1956, and 1970 against Drobny, Hoad, and Newcombe. Together with Gonzales and von Cramm, Rosewall is the only tennis immortal not to have won the Grand Tournament. 4. The finals match of the first Open Championships at Bournemouth in 1968: Laver striking at a sideline passing shot by Rosewall. The latter will win.

3

5

6

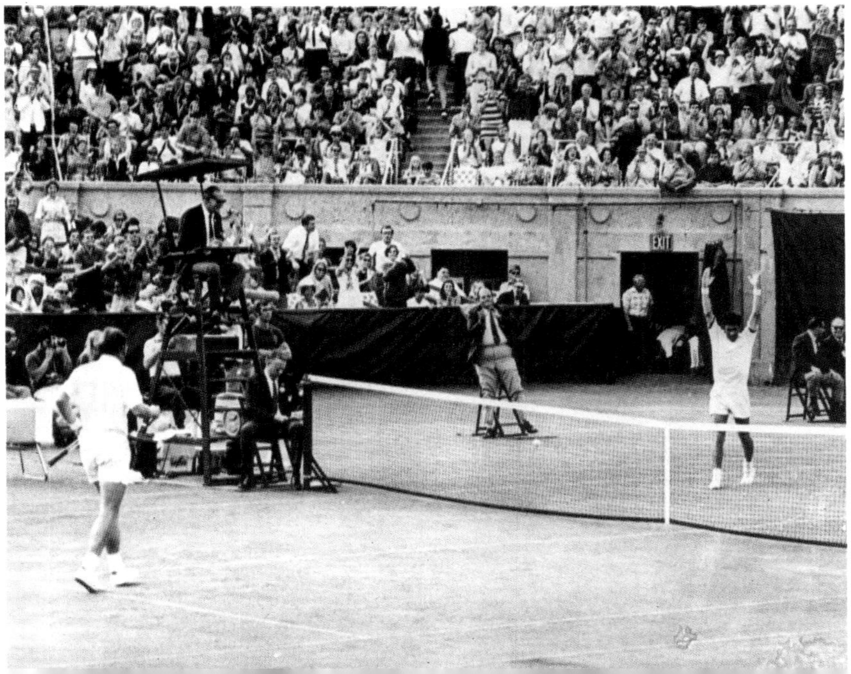

7

5. At Roland Garros in May, 1968, Rosewall seen at the net, ready to smash Laver's lob with a scissors. 6. One of the World Championship Tennis (WCT) finals in Texas, the $50,000 match, the richest of the year. Rosewall, always interested in improving his financial picture, beat Laver there in 1971 and 1972. 7. His arms thrown heavenward, Rosewall has just defeated Tony Roche, thereby repeating his first success at Forest Hills fourteen years earlier.

33 The Return of the European Virtuosos. Pietrangeli and Santana

Nicola Pietrangeli and Manolo Santana dominated continental European tennis as well as worldwide clay-court competition for almost ten years. The slower rebound on clay courts allowed them to accomplish feats of touch that have not been equaled to this day. The same factor enabled them to play an all-court game that reminded one of the virtuosos of the thirties. A fledgling player, even the young Fraser or Laver, would go into battle against them with the chances of a poorly equipped foot soldier against an experienced bowman.

Stronger on his backhand, Nicola was both a retriever and a counterattacking player, capable of excellent touch in the volley. Manolo's stronger forehand and his greater mobility allowed him to develop a game that was also admirably suited for lawn competition. He won both a Wimbledon and a Forest Hills; while Pietrangeli, faced with stiffer competition, never got past the semifinals. Their record in the Cup (Nicola's is first in world ratings for the number of matches played) took Italy and Spain to the Challenge Round at the expense of Americans weakened by Jack Kramer. The Australian grass and a lack of technical know-how and support kept Nicola and Manolo from achieving more.

Nicola Pietrangeli was born in Tunis, where his paternal grandfather had introduced the first railroad. His father Giulio was a tremendous athlete. His mother Anna, born in Russia, was a sweet woman who had all the characteristics of a spendthrift, which she passed on to Nicola. Until he reached his majority, Nicola had a choice between French and Italian citizenship. His preference for Rome over Paris probably caused irreparable damage to his career as a sportsman. A city where people sleep late, where work is looked down upon, where life is sweet, does not seem to be the best training ground for a potential world champion.

As a boy, Nicola demonstrated a decided preference for soccer to both tennis and going to school. When I played him the first time, his father had to drag him away from the nearby soccer field to the center court of the old Parioli. That chubby boy with his mischievous blue eyes subjected me to one of the most difficult and hard-fought matches of my entire career. As I followed my service to the net, I would ask the powers that be for aid in locating the ball, which his backhand would cleverly return in the most unexpected places, sometimes with a whistle and on other occasions with the softness of a feather. After almost two hours, my greater age and physical strength enabled me to get out of the scrape. With a kind and absentminded smile, the boy shook my hand and then darted away again toward his soccer game.

Nicola Pietrangeli had come from an affluent family; Manolo Santana was born into poverty. His story was similar to that of all the other boys who came to tennis not for mere pleasure but by virtue of hard work. At the Velázquez Tennis Club, thin little Manolo worked as a ball-boy for the rich Madrid society. Finally his natural intelligence and his winning ways brought him to the attention of a generous member of the club named Romero. Now Manolo could eat better and could play as much as the son of a rich man. After years of painful dedication, his efforts brought him to the stadium of Roland Garros. There his opponent was Nicola, who had won the title for the last two years.

At the end of a hard-fought match, which at one point saw him down 1–2, in the presence of an audience grief-stricken at the defeat of their adopted champion, Manolo endeared himself to the heart of all those present by doing two things with great spontaneity and candor. In memory of his former days as a ball-boy, he went under the net instead of leaping gracefully over it on his way to shake hands with his rival. As Nicola stretched out his hand, Manolo embraced him warmly, and, with his head turned toward his opponent's sweat-soaked back, burst into tears at the thought of his sudden freedom after so many years of adversity. Having been comforted by his defeated opponent, Manolo dashed off to the dressing room. There a middle-aged, dark-haired, elegant, and handsome man was waiting for him, his patron Romero. The young man called him father, as indeed he had become, and then offered him the victory as a pledge of honor.

From that day on, Manolo Santana took the place in the hearts of the Spanish people, previously occupied by Dominguin and Di Stefano. Once in Madrid an animated conversation with a passenger made Manolo forget to drive on when the light turned green. The shouts and invectives of a long line of motorists turned to applause as soon as the young tennis champion got out of his car and was recognized. Now he had won Forest Hills, and all the Spaniards who had not even known that tennis existed or much less had the means to play were suddenly projected into the role of faithful fans of the sport.

To the left: Manolo Santana bows to the Duchess of Kent. Below: He is surrounded by ball-boys after the Wimbledon victory in 1956. Facing page: Santana's most important weapon is his forehand with its very closed grip and its tremendous left-to-right snap. Other of his armaments are his speed, cleverness, his indifference to suffering, and above all, his hombría *(integrity and courage).*

3

1

2

Manolo lacked only Wimbledon. He brought a new style where, for years, there had been only splendid but boring aces. In the final, all the *idées reçues* of Ralston were shaken by this great craftsman who had begun to play with a poor wooden racket fifteen years earlier. The faces of the audience lighted up with happiness as they applauded Manolo, who, in a burst of enthusiasm, had tried to kiss Marina of Kent's gloved hand and then had bowed profusely by way of gestured excuse. His *hombría* (courage and integrity) and good sportsmanship were best expressed in his statement that he in no way felt superior to Emerson who had to withdraw due to an accident. "The moral victor of the tournament is certainly Emerson," Manolo asserted.

The Spanish officials, who were almost all from Catalonia, still thought highly of him, a *madrileño* (Madrilenian). But they committed a terrible mistake in allowing another excellent prospect from their native Barcelona to get away. Andrés Gimeno joined Kramer, who rapidly gauged his potential when the young man was only twenty-two. Gimeno always remained among the strongest in the professional ranks. When changes in the political climate of the sports world allowed him to do so, he succeeded in winning at Roland Garros and came close to taking his country into the final Davis Cup competition by knocking out Stan Smith.

Unfortunately, by this time Manolo had retired because of boredom and because of a feud with the president of his federation, who lost his job almost immediately afterwards. Manolo's return to Davis competition in 1973 was his last noble gesture toward close personal friends who had been thrown into a difficult situation by the disqualification of the most important members of the team, Orantes and Gimeno. Out of condition and worn down by fatigue, the great Santana was beaten in Turin by an upcoming young Italian player, Barazzutti. Despite the unpleasant circumstances, Manolo's bearing, his natural elegance, and cordiality were on a par with his days of glory in Paris and London.

4

5

6

Nicola Pietrangeli won the Roland Garros in 1959 and 1960, then passed the world title in clay-court competition to Manolo Santana. 1, 2. Santana goes under the net to embrace his defeated friend. 5. Another finals match between the two in 1964. 3, 6. Nicola's two finals victories, pictured during two almost identical backhand volleys, the first along the sideline to Ayala, the second cross-court to Vermaak's left. 4. Max Décugis, champion in the early part of this century, at the presentation of Coco Gentien's charming tennis book; behind the two is the twenty-year-old Clerici. 7. The great Spaniards of the postwar period. From the left: Orantes, Santana, and Gimeno and the wives of the latter two. 8. Santana beats Emerson in the Davis Cup competition, 1965: this will be the only victory for the Spaniards. 9. Victorious Santana at Forest Hills in 1965 with Bob Kennedy. 10. One of the nicest dividends that success brought to Manolo Orantes. 11. Andrés Gimeno, champion of France in 1972.

10

7

8

9

11

1

2

3

4

5

6

7

Other greats who were active between 1950 and 1960. 1. The Mexican Rafael Osuna, winner at Forest Hills in 1963; extremely speedy and gifted with a catlike lunge. 2. Tappy Larsen, a character both on and off the court; bold and deft in numerous feats and strokes similar to the one we see here. It is surprising that Larsen had the time and presence of mind needed to strike the lob that had passed over him. We do not recall having found another photograph of this type in all our research. 3. The Swede Jan Eric Lundquist, winner in Rome in 1964, in the midst of a difficult volley in tango time. 4. The great American MacKay, Italian international champion in 1960, in a desperate sprint to retrieve the set point of the first Davis Cup match against Anderson in 1957. MacKay was inconsistently great, an unbeatable player on his good days, totally incapable of pulling himself up on the bad ones. He served with the same vigor as did Kramer and Gonzales, but his double faults could be discouraging when he was not on all cylinders. 5. Sven Davidson, the most reliable among the great Swedes, salvaging a ball from the base line during his victorious Roland Garros in 1957. A tireless clay-court contender, Davidson achieved success in Paris after he lost the 1955 and 1956 finals to the great Trabert and the immortal Hoad. 6. The Australian Mervyn Rose knew how to adapt his attack plans to the slow rebounds on clay courts, and achieved the maximum continental success with twin victories at Rome and Paris in 1958. Thirty years later at Roland Garros, his volley seems a reincarnation of Borotra. 7. Cliff Drysdale continues the grand tradition of South African tennis. His two-handed backhand is one of the most lethal shots in the trade. On the opposite page: a smash by Maria Ester Bueno.

34 Black on White. Althea Gibson. Maria Bueno, Genius and Beauty Combined

Had she been born a boy as her father had hoped, Althea Gibson would have come out of Harlem as a boxer. He trained her nevertheless and dug the boxing glove deep into her skinny side. Only the fact that boxing between women was outlawed kept him from continuing with her education, and from that moment on, whenever she did something wrong, she was whipped instead. These beatings with a belt took place almost every day. She showed up at school only for basketball or softball practice, and spent the rest of her time on the sidewalks stealing fruit. In order to get to the Coney Island fair, she rented a bicycle, turned the corner where she sold it, and then took a taxi.

Althea enjoyed visiting her aunt and uncle. They manufactured moonshine in a homemade still. When she returned home drunk, her father would put two fingers in her throat to make her sick instead of the customary strapping. If she did something really bad, she would not go home at all, but would spend the night in the subway station between the Cortland Park and Lots Avenue exits.

At the age of eleven Althea realized that Social Services provided a dormitory with beds and real sheets. She went to live there, leaving the three rooms on 143rd Street where the family had migrated from South Carolina, driven off the land by three failures of cotton crops. Althea began to work and had a host of varied jobs: cashier, messenger girl, elevator operator, pieceworker in a button factory, and chicken plucker. She was too hungry to be disgruntled with the job of cleaning chickens. But she was discharged from this last and certainly the most profitable job because she did not ask permission and went to hear Sarah Vaughan sing in the neighborhood. Along with Sugar Ray Robinson, Sarah remained one of her lifelong idols. Sugar Ray and his wife Edna Mae actually became her friends, always helped her, and once bought her a saxophone.

Another prominent man, Buddy Walker, the director of the Harlem Society Orchestra, was the first one to see greatness in Althea as a tennis player by observing her play paddle ball. Not only did Buddy buy her a real tennis racket, but he also brought her to the Harlem River Tennis Court and paid Fred Johnson, a handicapped teacher, for her first lessons. From that day on, along the secret pathways of the humble Black mafia, Althea followed her desperate search for success, which turned out to be no less rigorous than her childhood and a good deal more humiliating.

Althea had to struggle for opportunities all her life. Two rich Blacks, Dr. Eaton and Dr. Johnson, who had clinics in the South, took an interest in her. She studied at the home of the former in Wilmington, North Carolina, and then traveled around Lynchburg, Virginia, in the summertime in the station wagon of the latter. The car would be full of young Black tennis players, but the name of Lynchburg was not very inspiring for a girl not used to the harsh discrimination in the South.

Daily discipline both at school and on the court brought Althea success in the championships of the American Tennis Association, the Black organization for the sport. Althea's victory in the event also earned her three lines of copy in *The New York Times*. She was admitted to two indoor tournaments in New York at the old Armory, and she finished twice among the first eight. After her

1. Maria Bueno seen in a tense moment at the net while behind her Darlene Hard hits a high forehand volley. It is 1960 and the two friends will win the title. 2, 3. Two grimaces of pain from Hard and Bueno, and a gesture of relief from Maria Ester (4).

sharing a room with Karol Fageros, a beautiful blonde who knew how to be her friend and taught her how to dress and how to better set her hair.

Althea's first important championship was Rome, the least racially conscious city in the world, then Paris, and then Wimbledon, the coldness of the audience there notwithstanding. She served with extreme vigor and began an offensive game against Darlene Hard, a strong, pink-cheeked, white American girl. Althea won in fifty minutes, made a delightful curtsy to Queen Mary, and then spoke with her in a friendly fashion. That evening Althea recited perfectly the acceptance speech that she had committed to memory, was cajoled into singing two songs with her almost professional voice, and then went out on the floor to dance. "It is a long road," she wrote, "between a ball with the Duke of Devonshire and being forced to leave a bowling alley in Jefferson City, Missouri, due to the color of one's skin."

Maria Ester Bueno

Althea won her second Wimbledon at the age of thirty. In the doubles, where it was never easy to find someone who could measure up to her, she was paired with a Brazilian girl who was not yet eighteen years old. Her name was Maria Ester Bueno, and she showed no less talent than her famous partner on the court. If it was true that Althea served like a man and showed herself to be of Olympic caliber at the net, Maria served like a young man, and as she served, the base line seemed to be scorched beneath her feet. The English spectators began gradually to take an interest in and then a liking to Maria, and a chorus of "Isn't she lovely?" and sighs of approval were exchanged in the stands. The women's fashion designer, Teddy Tinling, had no peace until he was assured that he would be able to dress her.

Dozens of Roman spectators were thinking about something quite different from my friend Teddy. Maria is a rather common name in the City of Saint Peter, but the office of birth registration had never before registered so many Maria Esters as after that happy 1961. The Foro Italico was duly lined with boisterous young men, all singing praises of the special abilities of Miss Bueno. Roman fans are real homebodies and do not like to root for out-of-towners. This cruel enthusiasm, this desire to see the defeat of one of the contestants even more than the victory of the other is called *tifo*, an attitude that is referred to as typhoid fever, a contagious disease, in Italian. The appearance of Maria Ester produced a real epidemic in her favor. The rave reviews garnered by her were the exception that proved the rule. She certainly had a graceful way about her, with a figure that was between slight and voluptuous where her severe lines suddenly went tender in all the proper places.

Her great charm lay in her talented strokes, her continual innovation, her touch, her curves and spirals: a neo-baroque tennis as proclaimed by Giorgio Bassani, the Italian novelist and connoisseur of the sport. Maria Ester lived from inspiration alone, and it was

1

2

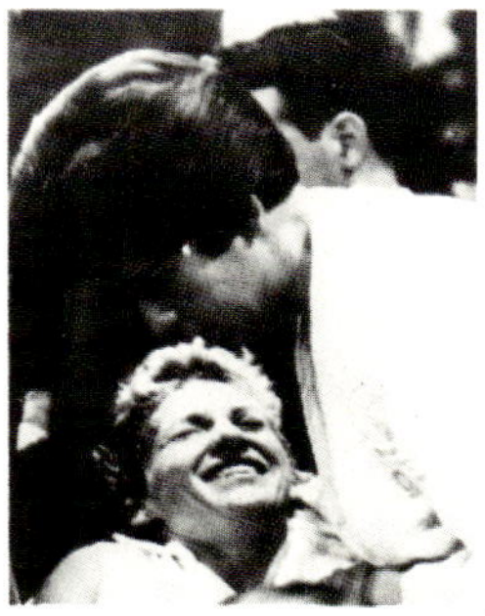

3

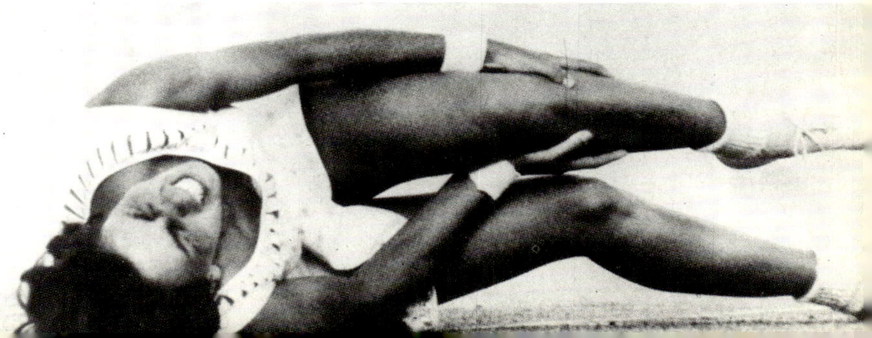

1

clear then that her career would never achieve the massive proportions of a Wills or a Court-Smith.

After the first two triumphant years, Maria fell victim to a series of accidents ranging from viral hepatitis to a torn double meniscus and from tennis elbow to repeated attacks of colic. These minor tragedies taken together were enough to curtail her success and then to exclude her from competition altogether. Could all of these misfortunes have been an inner defense against the inhuman wear and tear of daily performances, or could they have been a self-punishment inflicted by a strictly Catholic girl who was afraid of worldly success? From her hospital bed Maria once phoned Tinling to inquire how he could possibly have dressed her rival, Sandra Reynolds, in an orange dress—a fashion he had designed for her.

Darlene Hard, her doubles partner, was with her at the time. Darlene would never have been able to defeat her had not their friendship allowed her to know Maria Ester well and to find out about her weaknesses. Whatever these weaknesses may have been, misfortune conceded Miss Bueno only three Wimbledon crowns, four at Forest Hills, and three at Rome. The latter was a tournament that, starting with the fifties, began to rival those that took place in Australia.

Maria's fellow Brazilians, even more excitable than the Romans, erected an enormous statue of her at São Paulo, put her picture on a postage stamp, crowned her with a tiara of diamonds, and failed to dedicate a street in her honor only because Brazilian law does not permit this commemoration of a living person. Discounting Connolly, Bueno was the greatest talent of the postwar period. When Jimmy Jones asked her what her greatest ambition might be, she replied: "To make my game perfect." The same words that Jimmy had heard from the lips of Little Mo a few years earlier.

2

3

4

The English, who had no male champions worthy of Wimbledon after Perry, salvaged their sporting reputation with women players.
1. Angela Mortimer, victorious at Wimbledon in 1961 against her fellow Briton Christine Truman (2), 4–6, 6–4, 7–5.
3. Ann Haydon-Jones, the English girl with the most titles in the postwar period: Rome in 1960, Paris in 1961–1966, and Wimbledon in 1969.
4. Karen Susman prepares a chop on Wimbledon's Centre Court. She wins the event in 1962 against a truly difficult Bohemian woman, Vera Sukova.
On the opposite page: Roy Emerson follows his serve to the net.

35 Australia Über Alles

We have seen how the Australians dominated the Davis Cup competitions during the fifties. At the beginning of the sixties they began to meet and destroy opponents other than the old reliable Americans: Italians, Spaniards, and even Mexicans and Indians. In this comfortable garrison warfare, an American commando succeeded in getting through the lines in 1963 and landed a telling blow. McKinley and Ralston profited from Laver's defection to professional ranks. He had just repeated Budge's Grand Slam the year before. Ralston was better as a doubles player and had won Wimbledon as an outsider together with Osuna, but Chuck McKinley was the real power on the team: small, wrangling, always alive; all in all, a real Irish-American.

In the Adelaide Challenge Round, the Americans found an unwitting ally in old Harry Hopman. Harry had faith in Neale Fraser, a player with a bad leg, and insisted on using him in the doubles. In the singles, Hopman replaced Fraser with the young John Newcombe, to the detriment of Fred Stolle. Emerson's two victories only helped his personal record in the Challenge Rounds: his eleven winning matches out of twelve played (Emerson lost only to Santana), represent one of the most impressive collections of personal achievements in the sport. It was a success as glorious as the two Wimbledons, two Roland Garros, two Forest Hills, and the six Australian titles.

If one were to believe blindly in statistics, an essay on the parallel lives of Tilden and Emerson would be in order. Emmo's successes are rather a denouncement of the mediocrity of the sixties and of the foolish policies of the managers, who stubbornly refused to recognize that real tennis by this time was played by real professionals. Even Emerson and his colleagues were regularly paid under the table according to a custom established by the Italian Tennis Federation, whose president, Giorgio de Stefani, was the greatest advocate of the values of de Coubertin. The players themselves were less than diplomatic. Answering a reporter who asked what his opinion was on amateur status, Emerson replied candidly, "What's that?" Always smiling and good-natured, Emmo would be the last one to believe that he was the strongest tennis player in the world and made no bones about it. Before Emmo came on the scene, hadn't his partner Neale Fraser been seen winning a Wimbledon and two Forest Hills by pure stubbornness aided by aggressive serves? Fraser himself, a man as honest as he was clear-thinking, remembers that he achieved success after fourteen straight defeats against Hoad and thirteen against Ashley Cooper. Had they not turned professional, he would never have made the name for himself that he did.

According to Hopman, Emerson was the strongest, the most dependable, and the swiftest athlete of the whole Australian wave that followed Sedgman, Hoad, and Rosewall. Emmo burst into action behind his serve like a beast of prey and clawed his way to victory from the net almost at once. His persistence in a tennis devoid of the nuances of technique often succeeded in upsetting players of great talent. At the time of a Davis Cup tournament in Sweden, I saw him nail down a match that was in doubt by increasing the already dizzying pace of the exchanges. His opponent Lundquist first raced his motor and then stalled out altogether.

Montage of the champions of the sixties. 1. Neale Fraser, diving successfully after the ball. He won Wimbledon in 1960 and 1961, Forest Hills in 1960. 2. Stages in Tony Roche's serve. He won in Rome and Paris in 1966, and was the strongest foe of Laver in the Grand Slam of 1969. Repeated surgery on his elbow afterwards kept him from using fully his great talent. 3. Chuck McKinley, one of the few to remain an amateur, a constant fighter and court performer. He and Ralston won Wimbledon and the Davis Cup in 1963. 4. Mal Anderson, U.S. champion in 1957, and his brother-in-law Ashley Cooper. 5. In 1958 Cooper missed the Slam by only one tournament, the Roland Garros.

2

Emerson is also remembered as the leader of the first rebellion of Australian players against the establishment and the protectionist policy that prohibited them from playing abroad more than 210 days. Emerson, Stolle, Hewitt, Mulligan, and Fletcher were all disqualified. The last three eluded the system by establishing residence in South Africa, Italy, and Hong Kong, while Emerson and Stolle were pardoned *in extremis,* just in time to bring the Cup back to Australia. It had been vainly defended by Ralston and McKinley. The Cup remained down under until 1968, thanks to the presence

1

3

of Emerson and the rise to fame of Newcombe and Roche, one of the best doubles tandems in the annals of tennis.

That same year, which was of historic importance due to the recognition of open tournaments, the American team composed of Ashe, Graebner, Smith, and Lutz went to Australia to beat the weakest Aussie formation fielded in the postwar period. The admission of professionals was handled with discretion. The International Federation, fearful of a sudden rush, decided that only players who had been approved by their own organization should be admitted to Davis Cup tournaments. The Cup remained in the United States, and the following finals matches fell off in quality. Meanwhile, Laver, Rosewall, and Newcombe carried the day in individual tourneys. In 1969 Rod repeated his Grand Slam victory of 1962, becoming the first player ever to win it twice.

4

5

8

6. Emerson was certainly a legenday great in doubles. Here he succeeds in stroking a ball behind his back to the amazement of his partner Stolle. 7. Emerson again, in a lateral backward dive for the ball that looks good. Emmo won twelve Grand Slam events, six Australian championships among them, but the great professionals did not compete against him. 8. Stolle lifts his arms in disgust. The sad occasion is one of the three Wimbledons he lost in 1963, 1964, and 1965, a backward record indeed! 9. Alex Olmedo, the Peruvian who won the Cup in 1958 for the United States and Wimbledon in 1959 for his own country. 10. Another doubles immortal is Hewitt, an Australian who is now a naturalized South African. Bob won the Australian Championships in

9

10

6

7

1963 and 1964 with Stolle, the French Championships in 1972 with McMillan, and Wimbledon with Stolle in 1962–1964, and with McMillan in 1967–1972. Here, with a backhand volley, he precedes McMillan with his two-handed grip. 11. John Newcombe in a running lifted forehand. His record, which includes three Wimbledons, is certainly improving. In 1973 Newcombe was one of the two strongest in the world, the other being Nastase.

11

1

2

3

4

5

6

7

Photos of the Davis Cup competitions, handicapped by the absence of the pros. 1. The Peruvian Olmedo in a jubilant mood, having won the Cup in 1958 for the United States. 8. The U.S. team: Richardson, Olmedo, Captain Perry Jones, McKay, Bucholz. 2. Sirola and Pietrangeli together with their coach Drobny. The Italians made the finals in 1960 and 1961. 3. Osuna carried Mexico to the Challenge Round of 1962. 9. Laver and Osuna leave the courts after the doubles. Behind them, Captain Contreras and Emerson. 10. In 1963 the United States interrupted the Australian triumphs. Riessen, Froehling, Scott, Captain Kelleher, and the titleholders McKinley and Ralston after 3–2. 4. 1966. Krishnan, the strongest player born in India, leads his country to a dignified 1–4 against the Australian titleholders.

11. The Australian team of 1965: Captain Hopman, Emerson, Stolle, Newcombe, and Roche.

12. The participants in the Spain-Australia clash of 1965: Gisbert, Santana, Emerson, and Stolle. Santana beat Emerson and led two sets to love against Stolle.

13. 1968. The United States recaptures the Davis Cup from the Aussies, professional amateurs. After the 4–1, from the left, Smith, Graebner, Captain Dell, Ashe, Lutz, and Pasarell.

5, 7. Kuhnke and Bungert lead Germany to the finals in 1970.

6. The Romanians Tiriac and Nastase, three-time unlucky opponents of the United States in 1969, 1970, and 1972. Contrary to custom, the two American finals were not contested on grass, but on clay courts which were faster than the European ones. In the second of the finals matches, the United States was saved by a hair. The third finals match was played in the year of the elimination of the Challenge Round, and the Americans, with typical good sportsmanship, accepted the challenge to play at Bucharest. In order to reciprocate, the Romanians tried to rob them, and only Stan Smith's remarkable performance frustrated a partisan crowd.

8

9

10

11

12

13

36 Rod Laver, Queensland Cowboy

He was a young cowboy, but not of the Texas variety. His homeland was farther away, more rugged and more barren than the Lone Star state. As a boy he and his friends had gone kangaroo hunting. The Laver family came originally from a place called Gipsland in the Australian province of Victoria. Rod's grandmother Alice was ninety in 1967, and a few days before she passed away, she was still able to ride horseback. His father Roy grew up in the saddle and then married a girl name Melba, a namesake of the singer Nellie Melba, the only Australian famous in the world at large in the first quarter of the twentieth century.

Together with his eleven brothers and cousins, Roy played cricket on a team that was unbeaten in their zone. His uncle Frank became captain of the national team. Roy Laver's estate was called Langdale, comprising a total of twenty-three acres of land above Brisbane. From there the family moved to Marlborough, a small town not far from the tropic of Capricorn. Meat was never lacking, for Roy had become a butcher. When Rod was eleven, the family put down roots once more, this time in Rockhampton, a town of 30,000 inhabitants. In that region the heat at Christmas time is enough to make a Northerner pass out. The three Laver brothers and their sister quickly decided to build a tennis court on the place, similar to the one they had in the country. Their parents often played in mixed competition, and the children were fanatical about the game. They also decided to illuminate their court and added the luxury of five 1500-watt floodlights. At Rockhampton the family had all the advantages and comforts of civilization.

There was also a tennis teacher, Charles Hollis, and to judge by the success of his student Rod, and by what his student has to say about it, he must have been the very best anywhere. "The young one," he said to Rod's father, "is not hot-blooded like you and his brothers. He is calm like his mother. If I can get the killer instinct into him, he'll be perfect." Rod had red hair, a sad face alive with freckles, and gangling arms and bowlegs. The first thing that Hollis taught him was that he should always win 6–0, 6–0, and that he should never leave the ball, even if the rebound had topped the highest tree around. Rod promised to follow his advice, and Hollis spent his time on his student's shots, especially the backhand. Hollis, this Chiron of Queensland, knew very well that for some strange reason which no anatomist has yet explained, left-handers have the habit of slicing their backhand strokes. Rosewall, Connolly, and Court, all natural left-handers, had been taught to play right-handed by instructors who were afraid of this eventuality. Hollis could see that Rod would not grow to be very tall, and he could not run the risk of training him to use an unnatural serve, which was the biggest handicap of both Little Mo and Rosewall. Hollis decided to help Rod develop a slice and a backhand stroked from below and turned over.

The tennis coach also programmed the development of a strong wrist. To this end he insisted that Rod carry an old tennis ball with him and mash it in his fist from time to time. Years later someone had the bright idea of measuring the forearm of that man, who weighed 68 kilograms (150 lbs.). They discovered that it measured twelve inches, the same as Rocky Marciano's. Rod's wrist had a circumference of seven inches, one inch larger than Floyd Patterson's. It is clear, then, where Rod got the strength for those extraordinary lift shots, even when the speed of the rebound did not give him time for a proper backswing. This new type of tennis, a sort of glorified Ping-Pong, was pleasant work, with only one grip on the racket and an increasingly important role for the wrist. Jet tennis was still ten years away.

The Chiron not only taught his student strokes and tactics, but, like his centaur forefather, also prepared Rod for entry into the social life of Wimbledon and into the lore of tennis. "How will you get along at Wimbledon, if you hold your fork that way? Do you know where the Roland Garros Stadium is? Who was Crawford, and why did they call him Gentleman Jack?"

In 1956 a young Laver, fearful but not unprepared, crossed the seas. He discovered that the grass at Wimbledon was the best in the world and that at Forest Hills the turf was far less appealing. Rod quickly learned that the public is quite capable of selecting a whipping boy instead of a favorite among the players. He also found out that, on clay, tennis is something else again, each point resembling a small war, with the contestant emerging as muddy as if he had fallen into a pothole.

Rod attended the victories of his hero, Lew Hoad, and witnessed his defeat by Rosewall at Forest Hills, a match that was decisive for the Grand Slam. And while Rod was at the barricades, sitting quietly alone, as usual, and watching, it occurred to him that perhaps one day he, too, might be able . . . a secret thought that made him blush and brought his freckles all the more into evidence, when he noticed that Hopman was looking at him: "Hey, Rocket. Do you want to bat the ball around for a while?" Hop had given him that nickname the first time they met. Rod seemed so slim and so shy that Hop had the inspiration of calling him that, to the general hilarity of the other boys.

A few years later the nickname turned out to be prophetic as hundreds and thousands of newspapermen beat on the typewriter keys, shouted into microphones, and repeated mindlessly the name of Rockhampton Rocket, while Rockhampton was now known to all as the hometown of the champ. Laver won the first Grand Slam in 1962 at the age of twenty-four. He had reached the Wimbledon finals at twenty when he was beaten by Olmedo in 1959;

Mulligan, in the Wimbledon finals of 1962, has just played a backhand volley, from right to left, that would make the best player tremble. Rod Laver, the Rocket, is sprinting toward it, and, in front of the astonished eyes of the linesman, is about to connect with the ball and perhaps score a point. Rod will win 6–2, 6–2, 6–1.

he had lost to Fraser in 1960, and then devoured McKinley in 1961. Up to that time, the Slam had been won by Don Budge in 1938 and by Little Mo in 1953. The idea of that four-part world championship had been born quite casually. It was first mentioned in 1933, when Crawford came as close as one set to accomplishing the feat himself.

Actually, the Australian Internationals were always the least important of the competitions, due to the reluctance of the players to make the long and costly trip. Also the Slam seemed weighted in favor of offensive players, in view of three events being played on grass. In his first important competition, Rod was aided by the absence of Hoad, Rosewall, and Gonzales, who were at that time superior to him, a fact he readily admitted as soon as he himself had joined professional ranks and was beaten. These considerations set the record straight and do little, if anything, to diminish the stature of Laver's accomplishments.

The problems of the Slam are similar to those of a harrowing initiation test; before worrying about his adversaries, the participant must keep himself free of temptations and inner weaknesses; in a word, he must become free of himself. En route from the hot Australian winter to the mild Parisian spring, from the unsteady briskness of London at the end of June to the stifling humidity of New York at the beginning of September, the man of destiny didn't have time for a moment's peace or recreation.

It has been theorized that the Australian National Championships are the least difficult of the four, but there are many treacherous pitfalls and eager tennis unknowns waiting to strike down the unsuspecting champion. In Sydney an unknown by the name of Geoff Pares had Laver on the mat for more than three hours in 1962, forcing him to defend himself with every trick available in his magic box. Rod won 10–8, 18–16, 7–9, 7–5. Once the first of the Four Horsemen of the Apocalypse had been defeated, Laver had to move to the shifting red, sandy clay that was the worst possible background for his game of gentle violence.

"I had to relearn everything from the beginning," Rod admitted. "Only those players win on clay who know how to control the ball and their natural impulse to hit it too hard. In Europe the player has to know how to play touch tennis, to find new angles, to postpone the attack, and then, when one does attack, to use a deep approach shot. Much patience is required. A great deal of patience. Sometimes it is a good idea to bring lunch along." Rod's reasoning was perfect, but all of his good intentions were of no use against Martin Mulligan, an Australian who had liked Europe so much that he had decided to stay there.

Martin fought with two violent, yet routine drives, his legs sometimes being in such rapid motion that they resembled those of a bicycle rider. Faced with such a flexible wall, Rod found himself two sets down, 4–5 and 30–40: match point. Luckily it was his serve, and he decided to place an excellent shot at three-quarter speed to Mulligan's backhand, and then to lunge quickly to the service line, where Martin had almost always fired his passing shots. Mulligan played his stroke precisely there, Rod sliced a winning cross-court volley, and, at eight all, one of the linesmen came to the champion's aid by deciding a doubtful ball against Martin. En-

1

2

Seven splendid examples of Laver's style. Photo (4) is not a reverse impression of the same negative as photo (3). It shows a high volley by Hoad (4) that is remarkably like that of Laver (3). Hoad was the model of Laver in his years of apprenticeship. 1, 2. Both dives by Laver are to the right with the balls caught as if by magic and transformed into dangerous side-line volleys. 5. A serve, excellent both for control and shift. 6. At the very end of a run, a backhand that will become a passing shot. 7. A forehand passing shot in progress. 8. The Rocket regains solid ground at the end of a high jump to execute an extremely effective smash.

3

raged, the young man began a long, involved argument, and when he finally decided to come back to the game, his concentration was gone.

That was the hardest moment of the Slam, but certainly not the only one. Still in Paris, at the finals, Rod found himself two sets down, and then 0–3 in the fourth against Emerson, another cowboy, his partner and very good friend. "I was so absorbed in keeping my eye on the ball and on playing the point that I almost didn't notice the score. I played the net more, and, fortunately, Emmo isn't a guy who lobs a great deal. When I won the last point, it was hard for me to believe that I had actually done so."

At Wimbledon, Rod had his most difficult time with Manolo Santana, who was really in top form as they got underway. Manolo did not play one shot like another, and he lifted even more than Rod. He won a first set that was worthy of being recorded for posterity 16–14, got to 5–1 in the second, then at 5 to 4, with Laver serving, Manolo climbed to love 30. The author copied faithfully from an old notebook what follows:

Laver serves, goes to the net, and Manolo passes him with a lifted lob. Rod twists to the side, his shoulders facing the net, catches the ball with the wood of his racket and miraculously makes the point, 15–30. Rod serves again and Manolo moves to the side, dishing up a long forehand drive that skims the sideline. Rod dives for it and again manages to catch it with the head of the racket after it has passed, returning a scoring half-volley. It's 30 all. Santana lets go with two or three *madonnas,* then a brilliant passing shot, and advances to set point. Rally. Santana is at the net and hits a volley which seems beyond human reach. Rod sprints for it, with a desperately lifted forehand on the run, returns it to the astonished Manolo, who connects with but misdirects the volley. End of match, 9–7, 6–2, 6–2.

In the semis and in the finals Rod once again defeated Fraser and Mulligan, his victims from Roland Garros, without leaving them one set. The green carpet cared for by Mr. Twynam, the groundkeeper, must have seemed much more pleasant to him than the powdered French brick nicely smoothed by Monsieur Le Goffe.

Forest Hills was still left. By this time Rod must have dreaded the sleepless nights, the worn-down sensation, and the tension of the last matches even more than he did his opponents. With a generosity that often characterizes people of greatness, Don Budge came to help him, the man who would lose the income from his Grand Slam title if Rod were to win. Budge trained with him, stated that he couldn't lose, and took Rod to the country on the eve of the finals matches, one of the few vacation days he had in that year of dedication. With a man like that in his corner, Rod's future was no longer in doubt, and he lost only two sets in the whole tournament.

Gonzales sent a challenge to the champion of the world of the amateurs, and also included a sizeable check for a face-to-face encounter. Hoad and Rosewall told him that they needed him in the new International Professional Tennis Association (IPTA) which had replaced Jack Kramer. Things were not going well, and they themselves would guarantee the $110,000 that the organization would pledge him. Rod chose the smaller amount of money and his friends. The first match saw him beaten by Hoad, then he defeated Rosewall, but the average of the first twelve encounters rose rapidly to ten defeats against two victories: 0–6 Hoad and 2–4 Rosewall. The professionals drew a sigh of relief: they had shown that they were still the stronger. After a spate of newspaper gossip, the establishment regained control, and their names disappeared from the headlines. But they played on, trying to draw blood, even when they didn't earn one additional cent, to prove to each other which was the stronger, with the pride of mad knights errant.

"All it would have taken was money, and we would have played barefoot on broken glass. We were Gypsies, and Gypsies don't care where they put on their show at night. We made a tour in America in two station wagons, playing in sixty cities in eighty days. Once, for one thousand dollars, four of us went to Khartoum, where we found a revolution in progress. The organizer telephoned some friends, these friends called some other friends, and, before long, about one thousand fans arrived amid the soldiers and the barbed wire. We played on a grass court and then moved to a cement court with artificial lights. So many gnats, moths, and mosquitoes came to bother us that at one point we were forced to quit. The spectators applauded and then drifted away as the sound of firing drew closer."

Laver and his friends dragged the trailer around until 1967, when Dave Dixon, a golfing enthusiast who needed to fill up the new stadium in New Orleans, took notice of them. Dixon went

4

5

6

to Lamar Hunt, an oil tycoon, the owner of several teams, and the brother-in-law of a good tennis player, Al Hill. Hunt became interested in tennis and put eight players under contract: three former associates of Laver—Bucholz, Ralston, and Barthès; as well as five former amateurs—Newcombe, Roche, Drysdale, Tylor, and Pilic. In three months Lamar lost $100,000, but when a reporter asked old man Hunt what would happen as a result, he responded: "If we go on like that, we'll be broke in a little more than a century."

In competition with Hunt, another group was formed, the National Tennis League, directed by George McCall, captain of the U.S. team in Davis play from 1965 to 1967. The new association was composed of Laver, Rosewall, Gonzales, Gimeno, Emerson, and Stolle. The action of these two commandos and of the board of directors at Wimbledon, who had decided to open the championship even if they were disqualified for doing so, brought on the avalanche of open tournaments, voted in April 1968, in Paris.

When the first open tournament began at Bournemouth, we shook hands all around with a joy that we had experienced only in 1945, surprised and happy to find everyone around the courts

7

8

once again. Laver was trounced by the immortal Ken Rosewall. A few days later, the Little Master (as Ken was nicknamed sometimes) repeated the same finale at the Roland Garros Stadium. Rosewall had won his first French championship in 1953. Rod calculated that he would have to wait for 1977 to do something similar. It would be wiser to think of another Slam, he said.

The whole group was assembled this time, and Rod's intentions were quickly interpreted as a challenge, however discreetly he might try to hide them. His elbow was giving him difficulty, and Rod had an unusual preparation for fighting off the pain: a piece of sponge dipped in boiling water and then covered momentarily with ice. If the packs didn't do the trick, he would inject cortisone, and, most effective of all, just grit his teeth.

Opposed to professionalism, the directors created a model of poor organization in the Australian National Championships. Rod played there anyway, contending for prizes that were a mere pittance. His first vicitim was an unknown Italian, Di Domenico. But in the semifinals Rod found himself faced with some stiff competition, Tony Roche, a left-handed country boy whose father was a butcher; a young Laver who was fifteen kilograms (33 lbs.) heavier. Rod had taken him easily in the Wimbledon finals of the preceding year. Roche, in his simple way, had said, "I was looking for a stone to hide under to get away from the eyes of those 15,000 English fans."

Roche's spins were always difficult for Laver. During 1969, the younger Australian beat him five times out of eight and their Australian semifinal went to five sets. Rocket won the first two 7–5 and 22–20, and then Roche took two. Under a broiling sun with the temperature at 38 degrees Centigrade (100 degrees Fahrenheit), the two went at it hammer and tongs to 4–3 in Rod's favor, without taking a break. At 15–30 Roche served down the middle, right at Rod's chest. Rod in turn blocked and sliced the ball from beneath. Roche saw it rise and let it go as he caught his breath. The ball landed near the line, and the baseline judge said nothing. Roche started over toward him, and the linesman held out his hands parallel to the ground, indicating that he called it good. Roche was beside himself with anger. He returned to the base line, unleashed his serve, and Rod's passing shot went right by him before he could do anything about it.

Laver beat Gimeno in the finals and arrived in Paris, pleased with

2

3

1

8

The discrimination practiced against the professional kept Laver from Wimbledon for five years in a row, from 1962 to 1968. Despite this, Rod got to the finals six times and won four. 1. With inspired play in evidence, the followthrough of a forehand volley on the famous Centre Court. 8. He lifts the Cup with its engraved legend "Championship of the World." 6. 1959. The first finals competition lost, at twenty-one, against Olmedo, 6–4, 6–3, 6–4. From mid-court, Rod watches the Peruvian's backhand volley. 7. 1960. Second defeat, at the hands of Fraser, 6–4, 3–6, 9–7, 7–5. 4. 1961. The Rocket takes off, 6–3, 6–1, 6–4, against McKinley. 5. 1962. Another knockout, this time Mulligan is the victim, 6–2, 6–2, 6–1. At the net, Laver counters his opponent's volley with his own backhand volley. 2. 1968. First Open Finals. Laver returns to his lucky court to beat Tony Roche 6–3, 6–4, 6–2. 3. 1969. Perhaps the last victory.

7

6

4

5

Laver is at the net against Newcombe, and has played one of his incredibly short, cross-court volleys. He will win 6–4, 5–7, 6–4, and 6–4.

1 2 3 4 5 6 7

1 2 3 4 5 6

the memory of his seven previous tourney victories and ready to face "the two hardest weeks of the year." He tried to figure out whom he would end up with in the final matches, and then only too soon found himself down 2–0 against a stalwart 1.95 meters (6 feet 6 inches) in height, Dick Crealy, an Australian that he knew by sight only. He won the third set, and then a storm interrupted his attempt to fight back. The following morning he tied the match two all to empty stands. As soon as a few fans were stirring, Crealy came to life again, and hammering away like a blacksmith, got to four all, 40–30. He put in a devastating service which Rod just managed to send back. He tore into the return which was long by a hair. Rod drew a sigh of relief. He breathed even more easily when Rosewall, his old nemesis, took Roche off his back altogether. "The only way for me to beat Muscles," Rod said, "is to have a really super day." He did.

Even at Wimbledon the traps were sprung early, during the second round, against the Indian Premjit Lall, who played well but won little. After an hour Premjit was up two sets and three all in the third, and Laver was really fighting for his life. They were on the fourth court, which is surrounded by trellises of roses and hydrangea, and has no stands. Some British spectators walked on the flowers to see Premjit hold a point to lead 4–3 and then miss an easy smash. Fully recovered, Rod took eleven games in a row from him. Rod got as far as Smith. Stan Smith of Pasadena, who is taller than anyone else, hits harder than anyone else, and thinks that God is on his side. Fortunately for Rod, Stan's backhand was variable, and he did not bend enough to hit his passing shots. In the fifth set of that duel with rackets, Rod wildly defended his service to save the match.

Next to take him on was Arthur Ashe, who had won Forest Hills the year before and who had dared to speak of the era "after Laver." Rod let Arthur's initial storming pass because it was too

1 2 3 4 5 6

8 9 10 11 12 13 14

7 8 9 10 11 12 13 14

In the upper sequence, Adriano Panatta rushes toward the ball (1, 2, 3), either deciding to attack it or unaware of the depth of the opponent's stroke. He suddenly holds back (4), decides on a waiting game, and begins the swing with the head of the racket held high, due to the very Continental grip (6). The fact that the left leg is kept stationary hinders free movement and keeps the player from getting his weight behind the ball. In the bottom sequence, as far as the sixth frame, Ilie Nastase executes a stroke which is similar to Panatta's. The Romanian, however, has positioned himself in the corner of the court (the singles sideline and the alley can be seen in photos 1, 2, 3) and about four feet closer to the net. From photo (7) on, Nastase's movements assume greater determination, and the transfer of weight to the left leg is clearly evident to the end of the swing (12). In the center sequence, Rod Laver, different in this respect from both Panatta and Nastase, strokes upward. As a result, the ball has a forward spin. Rod's appraisal of the depth and speed of the ball is perfect, and hence he is able to afford it a lengthy trajectory. The impetus of his execution and the swing of the racket allow him to hit the ball the instant his feet leave the ground (7). The right leg describes a perfect scissors (7–11), which retards the forward movement and allows Rod to remain in the backcourt as he completes the swing. In the insert to the left, Gil de Kermadec, now the national director of the French Tennis Federation, is seen holding his movie camera.

7 8 9 10 11 12

violent to last very long. Rod came back from one set down, 2–4 in the second, and, at the end of third, was even able to increase the rapid pace that Arthur had established. Ashe left the match visibly shaken.

John Newcombe was left. He is the most intelligent of the serious tennis players, and, at the time of this writing, he has the best record of those born after Laver. But I am afraid that in a few years the author of another book like this will not be able to rank John among the immortals of tennis. He is a real champion due to his tremendous serve and his forehand, his clearheaded and lucid knowledge of tactics, and his good sportsmanship that allows him to laugh at himself when the going gets rough.

But John will never make a shot like the one that Laver punished him with at just the right moment, during one deuce set, then 4–2, and with Laver's serve to him. At 0–15 Newcombe hit a forehand shot that crossed to Rod's right, followed it to the net, positioning himself to intercept the probable longline. "I decided to change my game, and I used my wrist in a kind of karate-chop style on the ball. It was a real slice, hit at an impossible angle, and there was no way that it could cross the net and stay in the court. It took off, almost parallel to the net, then glided far from Newcombe's racket to come down along the opposite line. Newc was completely flabbergasted."

I will never be able to erase from my mind the angle of that ball, and I know people who have tried to measure it with calipers and goniometers and are still unable to explain it successfully. Rod did not fail on the third leg of the Slam and was thereby able to bring his nonstop match victories in four Wimbledons to the impressive total of twenty-eight, beating Fred Perry who had only twenty-one. Rod is a humble sort of guy. Yet on the day of the finals he asserted that he felt confident of beating anyone, even Tilden's ghost, if he had had the nerve to show up!

After that win, Rod lost no further matches or tournaments until he hit the finals at Forest Hills. The greatest trouble that he and his American wife Mary had was the concern over her pregnancy when she was expecting a child seventeen years after having the first three. Rod assures us that he would gladly have returned to Florida to cook and swap stories in their new house at Corona del Mar. But what could he do about the fact that, as soon as he got on a court, something inside himself brought back that old yearning to win? Forest Hills was flooded by violent electrical storms and the grass was in terrible shape. Rod began to use his spins and a twist serve, American style, that would have been suicide at Wimbledon.

He stayed with his friend John McDonald, listened to records, adjusted the handles on his rackets, and was seen only at the courts. The longest match took place during the fourth round against Dennis Ralston, a player who was not noted for decisive victories. Rod played his hardest match against his friend Emmo, who may have been cheated by an umpire's decision on a ball that would have carried him to twelve all in the third set. Then came Ashe and finally Tony Roche once again. Fortunately, Rod Laver has never been troubled by insomnia. He had learned no superstitions at Hollis's knee. Rod bounded out on the court to play this match after a good night's sleep, a fine steak, and a bottle of beer. At the first rain shower, he asked to put on his spikes and after one game felt at home in them. Heavyset, like a barrel on ice, Roche slipped and fell, cursing and making mistakes.

It was a massacre. Rod suddenly found himself leaping the net. It was the first time since he beat Flam when Rod's youthful enthusiasm made him trip and fall over the net. Rod had promised himself then and there in 1957 that he would never again be "one of those damned exhibitionists who cannot control their own emotions." Ashamed, he said to Roche he was sorry. Roche tried to smile. "I feel very humble when I beat someone," Rod had once said.

37 The Women's Lob. Court and King. The Latest Darlings

Margaret Court, *née* Smith, was born in Albery, New South Wales, on July 16, 1942. In 1970 she repeated Maureen Connolly's feat by winning the four titles of the Big Slam. In twelve seasons of competitions, she won twenty-four of the four great championships, a record that is without precedent. She was champion of Australia from 1960 to 1966, 1969 to 1971 and in 1973. She held the same position in France in 1962, 1964, 1969, 1970, and 1973; at Wimbledon in 1963, 1965, and 1970; and in the United States in 1962, 1965, 1969, 1970, and 1973. After the Forest Hills finals match that brought Margaret to the Big Slam in 1970, her opponent Rosie Casals said of her: "She seems all arms and legs, and she really makes you fearful when you look at her across the net. You can't put a ball out of reach of her drive." In 1974 Margaret Smith Court left competitive tennis to give birth to a baby, but she was not planning to make that "retirement" permanent.

Billie Jean King and Women's Liberation

In the early rounds at Wimbledon, 1962, top-seeded Margaret Smith came up against an unseeded and virtually unknown Californian named Billie Jean Moffitt. As an astonished audience looked on, the determined newcomer came back twice from almost certain defeat to eliminate Smith from the tourney. Suddenly tennis fans everywhere knew who Billie Jean was—an "upstart" on the courts in 1962 (though she didn't win Wimbledon that year) and an upstart off the courts ever since.

She grew up in Long Beach, California, the daughter of a fireman. Two childhood experiences at the Los Angeles Tennis Club stayed with her into adulthood as she became the most political of tennis stars. She remembered the day she was not allowed to have her picture taken with others in her tennis program because she did not have a white tennis dress. She also remembered how travel money was given to the promising boys, but not to her. The tennis establishment, she later concluded, was both "snooty" and sexist.

Meanwhile, Billie Jean Moffitt had become Billie Jean King, queen of the courts. She won Wimbledon in 1966, 1967, 1968, 1972, and 1973, and took the Forest Hills championship in 1967, 1971, 1972, and 1974.

"Money is what people respect, and when you are a professional athlete, they want to know how much you have made. They judge you on that." Billie Jean King expresses herself like a perfect American parvenu. In 1971 she became the first woman in the history of tennis to have earnings over $100,000, doubling this figure the following year. Her career, which was never an easy one, interrupted by torn muscles, is a classic example for those booklets that teach how to succeed in life by virtue of much elbowing. It would have been impossible for the path that Billie Jean trod in the early years of the seventies not to cross with the feminist movement, women's lib, or women's lob (as Tinling cunningly rebaptized it).

Women had always been kept to one side in the important tournaments. With the exception of a starring role for three or four of the tennis greats, women were forced to accept a minor role, often related solely to their good looks. This discrimination was not altogether illogical. Aside from Wimbledon, most of the paying public was composed of men. These poor sports seemed to get bored to death when confronted with the serious volleying of the women. Women also suffered the insult of earning a fraction of what the male players did. At the Pacific Southwest Open in 1970, for example, the men's champion got $12,500 while the women's took home just $1,500!

That same year, Gladys Heldman, by a stroke of genius, made the lucky discovery that feminist ideas could be brought to bear in a commercial contest as highly organized as tennis. Not for nothing was Gladys raised in the loving atmosphere of a Jewish home, with its emphasis on culture; nor was it unimportant for her success that she published *World Tennis* magazine, and that her husband held the post of manager with Shell. Gladys turned to Joe Cullman, the owner of the Philip Morris tobacco company, and a real tennis enthusiast, who immediately found a sponsor for her, Virginia Slims, a cigarette manufacturing company that had made use of women's lib in its advertising slogans. This action created conflicts between Mrs. Gladys Heldman and the U.S. Lawn Tennis Association when Billie Jean, Rosie Casals, and other women began playing in Slims tournaments that conflicted with USLTA events. In 1971 the USLTA organized a counter-tour starring the two newest darlings of the tennis circuit, Chris Evert and Evonne Goolagong. But it didn't discourage the women who were disenchanted with life on the regular tournament tour. In fact, the uproar publicized the tournaments, the Slims tour was successful, and Billie Jean pocketed her checks. By 1974 Evert and Goolagong had joined up too. Peace was declared.

Billie Jean King's moment of greatest public attention did not result from her wonderful victories at Wimbledon and elsewhere, but from a comic charade enacted by Bobby Riggs and her in September 1973. Bobby was the world champion in 1939 and one of the most dedicated gamblers ever seen. Fifty-five years old, Riggs worked hard to create the image of the male chauvinist and dragged poor Margaret Court into battle on Mother's Day of that year. She was totally dedicated to home and church and had little interest in feminism. He taunted her, defeated her, and then quickly passed the challenge to Billie Jean, who had been waiting for her chance. The encounter between the suffragette and the chubby-cheeked old male took place at the Houston Astrodome, in front of a crowd of 31,000 fans and a huge television audience. Riggs had worked hard to create a circuslike atmosphere for the match, which he hoped would break King down psychologically. It didn't work. Billie Jean played well as always and ended the match with her usual irrepressible enthusiasm, and a winning score of 6–4, 6–3, 6–3. Afterwards she declared, "This is a culmination of a lifetime in the sport. Tennis has always been reserved for the rich, the white, the males—and I've always been pledged to change all that. There's still a lot to be done, but this is certainly a great high point." No male chauvinist was on hand to try to heckle her. She had many qualities in addition to the technical mastery of her game.

Billie Jean played her role not only because she enjoyed acting in front of audiences. Her feelings of resentment against the establish-

1

2

3

4

1, 2, 3. The prodigy Margaret. Her jumping serve, her backhand and forehand attacks give an idea of Margaret Court's strength and determination. 5. A split second of relaxation, before gathering together all her force to send back a serve and then once again, as always, to go on the attack. 4. The grimmest of Margaret's successors, Chris Evert, in her two-hand backhand. 6. Another of Margaret's opponents, Rosie Casals, being lectured by Mike Gibson, referee at Wimbledon, about her clothing, which carries a women's liberation emblem.

5

6

ment went back beyond the time when she joined forces with Rosie Casals and the others on the Slims circuit, back beyond the free lessons she offered to ghetto youngsters with her husband, Larry King, a well-known attorney. Billie Jean was never able to take in the unwholesome air of snobbism that choked American tennis for years. She was often heard to repeat that "the future of the game is in the arenas and with the sporting public, not with those damned tennis clubs." At least Billie Jean's actions are consistent with her own viewpoints.

At the present time she is involved in the most revolutionary experiment since the days of good old Major Wingfield: the organization of intercity tennis of the WTT League, made up of sixteen teams, each composed of three men and three women. They play one mixed doubles and two singles matches, with the possibility of changing players during the match. The organization is also armed with well-documented rules, easy to understand even for the rankest recruit among tennis audiences. For the first time in the history of the sport, a women's event takes on the same importance as a men's tourney, thereby making a mixed competition decisive.

In 1971 it seemed that the triumphant and turbulent reign of Mrs. Court and Mrs. King was about to come to a close at the hand of a young brown-skinned girl, an unusual sort of woman tennis player who took delight in playing the most unheard-of shots, blissfully unaware of percentage tennis and other such dogmas. Evonne Goolagong is an Australian aborigine, the daughter of a sheepshearer. She was discovered by a trainer, Vic Edwards, who later adopted her. So that she wouldn't feel in his debt, he quickly began to charge for interviews when fame came her way. Fascinated by Evonne, Wimbledon quickly took the charming young woman to its heart in 1971. Crusty old reporters, who usually limited their pleasures to statistical revelations, threw themselves wholeheartedly into flights of rapture and romanticism, all in deplorably bad taste. There was good reason for the hurrahs, however, for Evonne, after winning the Roland Garros, took both King and Court at Wimbledon, without leaving them one single set, with an ease that was almost infuriating in view of her radiant smiles.

On a bad day Goolagong might suffer from "walkabouts," periods in which she lost her concentration. Or it might become apparent that she lacked the sort of killer instinct that usually marks the play of a champion. In the summer of 1971, though, Evonne didn't have many of those days. She was quick, she could improvise better than any player in the sport, and she found the ball as if guided by radar.

A month after Evonne's breakthrough at the age of nineteen, another girl, only sixteen, was mobbed at Forest Hills by photographers, reporters, and thrill seekers overwrought with enthusiasm. Young enchantress that she was, Chris Evert reached the semifinals, proudly shaking her ribbons, and swaying her hips with an innocent air, a nosegay held primly in her hand. Ready to do anything rather than become outmoded, Billie Jean was able to stop her. But Chris had won 46 straight matches that year before meeting Billie Jean, and she wasn't going to be stopped for long. In the Wightman Cup tourney that same season, it took her just 40 minutes to de-

1

2

3

4

5

1, 2, 3. Margaret Court's enemy number one as well as the major competitor of the poor males, Billie Jean King, seen in two volleys that show her temperament and heaving a sigh of relief after a bad moment. With her five Wimbledon crowns, Ms. King ranks third among modern women greats, after Wills and Lenglen. Her game is less graceful and natural than the style played by Evonne Goolagong, the lovely Australian aborigine who beat her and Court at Wimbledon in 1971. 4. Here we see Alexandra of Kent making the presentation to Evonne. 5. A backhand on a high rebound in the corner of the court. 6. Billie Jean King plays a high backhand volley against Evonne Goolagong at Wimbledon, a shot executed with complete control.

stroy Virginia Wade 6–1, 6–1. Two years later at the venerable age of 18, Chris Evert turned pro.

1974 was her year. She took Wimbledon, plus seven of the twelve Slims contests she entered, and won five of the big European clay tournaments. Her trademarks were consistency and coolness. "She never even sweats," some fans reported. That year it paid off to the tune of $261,460. Evert was just 19 years old.

Her off-court romance with Jimmy Connors also made headlines. When both of them won at Wimbledon in 1974, the press, predictably enough, billed it as a "love match." But their engagement had been temporarily broken by the end of the year. Neither had much room in life at that point for anything but tennis.

Evert's only misfortunes on the courts in 1974 were dealt her by Evonne Goolagong. At Forest Hills, Goolagong beat Evert before losing to Billie Jean in the final. Then, at the third annual Virginia Slims Championships, Goolagong upset Billie Jean 6–2, 4–6, 6–3, and trounced Evert in the final 6–3, 6–4. The young Australian walked off with a check for $32,000, the biggest purse in the history of women's sports.

6

38 After Laver. A Rain of Dollars. Nastase and the Robots.

This amateur historian, small in stature, is suddenly struck with amazement that these five centuries in the saga of tennis should end with one final burst of speed from the Rockhampton Rocket. Even using "After Laver" as part of the chapter title seems a weak ploy. At the end of 1973, during the last match of the first truly open Davis Cup, Rod became the hero once again when, with Newcombe, he inflicted a 5–0 defeat on the Americans.

Some people would say that when the score reaches three–love in a match, such play automatically becomes an exhibition. Rod did something more than this against Stan Smith, who had himself dominated the opening of 1973 by winning the WCT (World Championship Tennis) title. Rod's performance was a hurricane, complete with lightning bolts, which utterly devastated his hulking opponent. There is no need to write an epitaph, unless it be for a tennis world that is changing greatly from the one that we have observed up to the present time

The way things are today, it is very difficult for anyone to achieve the laurels of the tennis greats of the past. The gods have fled the scene of battle on the courts. In 1968, together with the enactment of open tourney play, the International Federation unfortunately failed to make the move that would have allowed it to regulate the sport: within its own sphere of influence, this organization did not create a professional arm in which the players themselves could participate. The economic interests that had brought about a conflict between the federation and the professional amateurs, on the one hand, and the managers and the professionals, on the other hand, remained in confrontation. Skirmishes and brushfire warfare soon turned into large-scale hostilities.

Inspired by Jack Kramer, the International Lawn Tennis Federation (ILTF) promoted the Grand Prix in 1970. This prize competition involved a vast network that linked the best tournaments the world over, with point evaluation based on their importance, and with a prize scheme that had the backing of a $1,600,000 kitty from one sponsor. The Grand Prix had its final, which was called the Masters, a decisive tourney that took place among the highest ranking eight players and quickly attained great prominence. The Texas group of the WCT organized a series of twenty tournaments, peopled by the thirty-two best players selected by the press, with the finals in Dallas among the top eight players. One million dollars was offered as prize money, and the last finals match itself brought fifty thousand dollars to the lucky winner.

The rivalry between the two organizations became acute when the WCT tried to infiltrate into the important tournaments, and the ILTF countered with the exclusion of the Texas players from their tournaments. From January to August of 1972, the tennis players were once again divided, and the technical level of the Roland Garros and Wimbledon was halved at the very least. The armistice led to a contract with the WCT for the first four months of each year. Contrariwise, the Texas group would be limited to organization and would no longer be able to renew contracts with individual players.

The players finally realized their own importance and strengthened their union, the Association of Tennis Professionals (ATP), electing Cliff Drysdale as their president and Jack Kramer as their executive director. The ATP was quickly involved in the disqualification of one of its associates, Nicola Pilic, by the Yugoslavian Federation, since he refused to play in the first elimination matches at the Davis Cup. The International Federation thought it was backing up its affiliate, and the ATP tried to take away its authority by defending the case in the Queen's Bench Division in London. The judge declared himself incompetent to adjudicate the matter. The ATP stiffened its position, deciding at the last to boycott that Vatican of tennis, Wimbledon. It was a serious step to take, which, of course, did nothing to turn away the throngs that the tournament attracted, but it aided in reducing the quality of the men's competition. Jan Kodes of Czechoslovakia beat USSR's Alex Metreveli there in a lackluster final.

As we make reference to these struggles of interest, we must not forget that other elements go together to change the Great Tradition as well. The massive coverage of television and the constant spin-off of new tournaments tend to reduce the playing time possible. At Wimbledon in 1877, the set would end peacefully after the eleventh game, but the service at that time was a matter of opening the game, nothing more. The advantage of two games needed to win a set would not be introduced until the finals of 1878 and would become mandatory in the eighties. This rule led to matches that seemed to go on forever, like the one between Gonzales and Pasarell in 1969, which lasted for more than five hours. When the tie break was inaugurated, the clock was turned back to the beginning, with a playoff at six all, adopted at Forest Hills in 1970 and perfected at Wimbledon in 1971. Other attempts have been made, especially by Jim Van Allen, to introduce the scoring of Ping-Pong, and to change the sequence 15–30–40 to 1–2–3, abolishing deuce and the two add points and making the fourth point decisive, and so forth.

The adaptation of metal and synthetic fibers in racket construction has also sped up the game, if at the same time reducing accuracy. Since the construction of the ball is also subject to regimentation, the game, played on surfaces that have little arresting quality, is often reduced to a frenzied series of brutal serves.

These rapid-fire observations may have suggested the picture of a tennis player harried to the border of exhaustion by the expansion of the game. Any reader who cares to do so, may consult the records at the end of the book, and will note there that over the past several years the career of each champion has been strictly tied to this or that series of competitions. It would be foolhardy to try to attack any one season and carry off all the laurels. The breakdowns, the defeat of champions at the hands of players less gifted than they, are becoming more and more frequent. When muscular development is there in fine supply, attention span fails, or motivation itself seems to be lacking.

At the end of each year the experts at classification wonder whether they ought to follow their intuition or introduce their perforated record cards into the impersonal mind of a computer. Do the Big Four, the tournaments of the Grand Slam, often avoided or boycotted, have the same importance as the money-making Masters finals or the finals of the WCT? Or are the routine matches more important? Following the rule of conformity or not, the highest

1 2 3 4 5 6 7

1 2 3 4 5 6

1 2 3 4 5 6 7

In the upper montage of photos, Rosewall is faced by such a deep and angular ball that he has to dash to one side to make contact with it. His position, within the base line, is rather unusual for a magician of the art of anticipation. Ken pivots on his left foot (2) and (3) springs into action. After another step (4) he begins his preparation, balancing himself with his left hand as he brings the racket back. After one step more to the left (5, 6), the preparation is complete, and the champion opens his stance, his eye on the ball, which has now appeared in the film clip. Rosewall makes contact and follows through (8, 9), the ball angling off in the direction opposite to his rush. His speed has inclined his body backward, but the compensation of his right leg and arm brings him back into balance and allows him to shift his weight to his left foot (12) and, with a pivot (13), to return to the right half of the court. The second tier of photos shows an interesting technical detail of an offensive backhand by Gonzales, the "tango step." A moment before impact (4), Gonzales's left foot begins to move toward the one bearing his weight, the right, and he ends the maneuver far in front of it (8). The right leg is extended slightly, allowing the player to save time and to execute a more fluid movement. In the lower montage of photos, Adriano Panatta hits a backhand, the racket under the ball and the wrist less blocked than in the case of Rosewall and Gonzales, with the back more rounded. Panatta's is a waiting stroke.

8 9 10 11 12 13 14

8 9 10 11 12 13

8 9 10 11 12 13 14

laurels in 1973 had to go to Newcombe and Smith, or the aging Laver and Rosewall, or even the tireless, madcap, extremely able Ilie Nastase from Bucharest.

Nastase is called Nasty by the English speakers, and also dubbed the king of the Gypsies by the speakers of some other languages. Quite a few years ago he arrived as a pilgrim in Italy. A lawyer from Ancona by the name of Brunetti had offered the Romanian player, Tiriac, five hundred dollars to exhibit his prowess along the Adriatic coast. Tiriac was a surly looking type, with his hair crew cut. He attracted attention with his craftsmanlike play and his friendship with Ceausescu. Brunetti thought highly of him, seeing the potential of his vast talent, and did not have the courage to reject his proposal to raise the fee to six hundred dollars. In return, Tiriac was to bring from Bucharest a young man of twenty, highly gifted, by the name of Ilie Nastase.

I had the good fortune to see both of them during their first visit. Tiriac always walked a few paces ahead, with the look of someone ready to whip a pistol out of his holster and shoot down anyone who might block his path. Nastase walked behind him, very good, very dark-haired, very thin, carrying rackets, bags, packages, and clothes tied together with string. Someone said that he collected plastic bags to take them home. Tiriac and Nastase were then playing a brand of tennis which was different not only from all the Westerners, but even from the richest Communist nations, like the

EXIT

40

Ilie Nastase, the king of the Gypsies, is in reality no Gypsy at all except for his continual traveling about and his snatching away of victories. He was born into a poor family in 1946 in Bucharest, in a tiny house facing the Progressul, the stadium that will later be reconstructed to welcome Tiriac and him. His earnings there make him the wealthiest man in his country, his talent the most pleasant player to watch, and his behavior provokes spectators and opponents to blows on occasion. In the large photo: a forehand drive hit at Wimbledon while walking on air. This tournament is the only major one that Ilie has not won, perhaps due to his nerves, or perhaps because of his natural shyness. In the series to the left: a most unusual recovery shot, a sudden stop before contact with the net, followed by a pantomime of savage joy. A scene taken from the victorious Forest Hills finals in 1972 against Arthur Ashe. In the small photo: the Texans Lamar Hunt and Al Hill, Jr., the owners of the World Championship Tennis, the organization that controls the first four months of the tennis season and has changed the sport into big business.

Russians and the Czechs. The strokes of these two players did not follow the canons of American technique, nor those of the Australians, and all things considered, not even those of the European style, adapted to clay courts, where the ball digs into the playing surface on contact, slowing its velocity and increasing the height of the parabola. Their movements were roughhewn and at the same time natural. Their serves reminded one of the simple, inspired gestures of certain saints shown on village icons from Bessarabia.

Whenever Tiriac had a match, there was Nastase sitting motionless and tense, ready to go out for something to drink, towels, or rackets, at a moment's notice. When it was his turn on the court, Tiriac would rise to his feet to shake his fist at his young friend. Under a shower of baleful glances, of imprecations, and occasionally of playful slaps on the rump, the young Achilles improved each time out, and the rough Chiron took his share, so they say, of his prize money, holding it out as his royalty. The two became wiser, their trips longer, and their purses grew fatter: when they had free time, they wisely preferred Italy to their far-off homeland. Tiriac imitated the Milanese accent, playing for Olona, and raking in millions of lire from the generous president of the association, the Marxist Giuseppe Stante. Nastase preferred Roman delights, bought his wardrobe at Piattelli. He learned how to distinguish the Rosati Café on the Piazza del Popolo from that on the Via Veneto after a date broken by a girl with high connections whose grandfather was a wealthy descendant of the Avignon popes.

1

2

Nastase had learned some of his mentor's court behavior, and certain tricks that had been in vogue in professional wrestling on the county-fair circuit toward the turn of the century. If the opponent managed to get in three or four points and things took a bad turn, this little trickster was quick to stop the game and protest over some imaginary disturbance, argue with the umpire, or trump up some kind of altercation with a linesman. Ilie was not so clever as his master and his tricks were more difficult to swallow. His amateur theatrics brought on the indignation of the fans and the players. In London his American opponent, Graebner, finally got him near the net. Threatened by a shiny metal racket, Nastase turned pale and could think of nothing better to do than pick up his Italian sweater and his English rackets and leave the court just a little bit hurriedly. His game benefited from this natural caution.

Ilie could run for hours on end, with the grace and speed of a young colt, inventing new strokes as he did so. His highly angular tennis, rather short in depth and totally unpredictable, was soon the only alternative to the strong and violent Anglo-Saxon variety. Nastase began to win more and more often, and Tiriac would punctuate his congratulations with a hearty pat on the back. Nastase knew that his friend was proud of his newly acquired moustache. To make fun of him, he showed up on Centre Court with a false growth of moustache firmly affixed to his upper lip. Tiriac was fuming inside, but he managed to maintain a calm exterior. His main aim in life was to win the Davis Cup.

The two friends had sought it in vain in competition against the Americans. Their performance had touched Ceausescu's heart, and Tiriac had presented his best wishes to President Nixon during the reception for the Romanian tennis players. By a curious coincidence, the American president was soon to fly to Bucharest. Ilie certainly had nothing to do with politics himself. He enjoyed life at a fast pace and led a worldly existence. When he won at Rome in 1970, it was impossible for me to reach him by phone. I learned from a weary telephone operator that the number of admiring women who flooded him with calls had gotten really out of hand.

Many successes were to follow. At Wimbledon in 1972, Ilie lost at the hands of Stan Smith due to a too tightly strung racket which put him in a bad mood. Before the match he vainly stood on the strings to try to relax the tension. A month later, the tables were turned, and he took every game in sight. In 1973 he began to make fun of his adversaries at the Roland Garros. The ease

5

Recent happenings and events in the history of the sport. 1. Newcombe and Laver, finally admitted to Davis Cup competition in 1973, thrash the United States at Cleveland and take the Cup back to Australia. Indoor play is possible for the first time. 2. At the Houston Astrodome, 30,472 spectators outdo the previous attendance record of 25,578 in Sydney in 1954. 4. 36 million TV fans attend the match of the century between the Women's Libber (Billie Jean King) and the Male Chauvinist Pig (Bobby Riggs) (5) The woman player wins easily as can be seen from the scoreboard (3) and pockets $200,000. 6. The symbols of the American intercity championships, with which team spirit revolutionizes what was previously an individual sport.

3

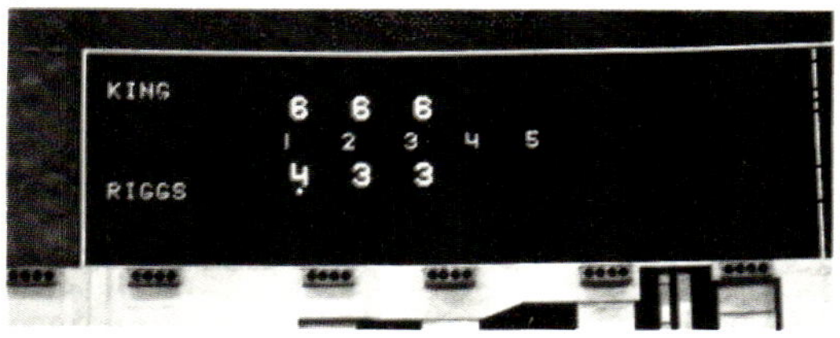

4

6

of his game and the rapidity of his recovery enabled him, after an especially fine stroke, to turn his attention for a moment to the French-Romanian journalist Judith Elian. "What did you think of that?" he asked in a devil-may-care fashion and then dashed back to return his opponent's riposte with dispatch. The following week Nastase won at Rome, and here he behaved even worse than the most uncivilized spectators. One of them threw a bottle at him, which fortunately missed its mark, and later on, in the locker room, a man overcome with wrath attacked him but without doing any bodily harm.

Nastase, who had come from a really poor background, did not only look for big successes, but was also on the weekend tourney circuit where his play was always well groomed and tight. Victorious on the Grand Prix circuit, he made the acquaintance of some Western bankers and began to scan the pages of the *Financial Times* every morning. By way of ending this exemplary novel of a rags-to-riches tale, I must also include the fact that Tiriac deserted his young friend, and that the latter married his own princess, the beauteous Dominique Gracia, daughter of a Belgian banker. I have myself seen Nastase in a Paris hotel toasting with his little finger raised, under the fascinated eyes of his wife's entire family, while she and he embraced lovingly. Conquered by the West, benefited by and yet the victim of consumerism, winner of the Grand Prix and of the 1973 Masters, Nastase is being wooed with astronomical figures by American business interests of the World Tennis Team, the organization that is trying to change tennis into a team sport.

Nastase's roots and his feelings still tie him strongly to his homeland, where he is second to none in popularity. The night of the match he lost to Smith, during the finals of the Davis Cup in 1972, Bucharest was in mourning and was then shocked by a wild rumor: Ilie had sold out for ten thousand dollars! The rumor was ridiculous for a man of his stature. It was an act of love on the part of people who could not believe that their idol could be defeated in the most important match in the annals of Romanian tennis.

Adieux la raquette sonore
Les crix anglais
Les gestes blancs.
Le seul jeu de ce jaune octobre
est de s'embrasser
sur les bancs.

Farewell to the singing racket
The English sighs
The white movements.
The only game of this yellow October
Is to kiss each other
On benches.

1

2

3

4

5

6

7

8

9

10

11

The first ten players in 1973, according to the computerized classifications of Rino Tommasi and his assistant Vittorio Selmi. Bowing to the anonymous power of the machine age, the author is in complete disagreement with these brave high priests of the world of statistics. 1. Ilie Nastase seems to be sitting down as he plays an unreal half-volley. 2. Jimmy Connors: a left-handed volley using both hands, a recent American habit, the result of the liberal education of the young tennis champion. 3. The earnest Rod Laver transforms the racket into a net to pick up the ball as it flutters to the ground. 4. Rosewall, the Little Master, here has hit one of his 100,000 flawless backhand shots, a maneuver that would have sent many of his competitors sprawling. 5. A forehand stroke caught on the move and in the air, executed by Stan Smith. 6. Tom Okker on all fours minus one, recovering the ball despite his fall. After Nastase, he is the best juggler of the new wave. 7. John Newcombe in a scissors serve. The author, who follows his whims and his uncertain memory, considers him second only to Nastase. 8. Orantes in a lateral volley. He is a good player but not a court genius. 9. Arthur Ashe in a stretched volley. More talented than Orantes, sometimes too kind on the court, unable to inflict punishment. 10. Jan Kodes. Aggressive, highly trained, very strong, he has the tendency of the Prague native to play the role of the underdog. 11. Our account nears an end as another young player becomes a force in the tennis world: Bjorn Borg, a new champion in 1974.

1

5

9

2

6

10

3

7

4

8

11

1 2 3 4 5

1 2 3 4 5

1 2 3 4 5

We observe here the important strokes of twenty of the tennis greats. In the upper tier of great forehand drives we see: 1. Laurie Doherty. 2. Brookes. 3. McLoughlin. 4. Tilden. 5. Cochet. 6. Perry. 7. Kramer. 8. Drobny. 9. Gimeno. 10. Laver. Laurie's running drive is incredibly modern, and it is interesting to compare it with Cochet's, played thirty years later. The most dated is doubtless the Western drive played by McLoughlin, while Brookes, although using a very closed grip, begins to lift no less than Drobny, or than his grandson Laver, who places a similar stroke sixty years later. Of great classic beauty and part of the same stylistic pattern are the forehand drives of Tilden, Kramer, and Gimeno, even though the photos were snapped at times when the tactical requirements for each were different. In the middle tier of great backhand drives: 1. Reggie Doherty. 2. Laurie Doherty. 3. Wilding. 4. Tilden. 5. Lacoste. 6. Budge. 7. Kramer. 8. Gonzales. 9. Hoad. 10. Rosewall. The diagonal backhand drive by the great Reggie is not so different from the one executed with a metal racket by Gonzales, and the exemplary flat stroke by Laurie can be easily set aside Kramer's backhand. Tilden's anticipation is unusual; observe Big Bill's burst of energy to meet the ball, then to follow to the net with the authority of a master. Donald Budge's stretch, despite the fact that it is slowed by his flannel trousers, is

6 7 8 9 10

6 7 8 9 10

6 7 8 9 10

like that of Lew Hoad, played, moreover, on the same Centre Court at Wimbledon. The movements of the forerunners are certainly more laborious, the preparation more graceful due to the slower speed of the ball: nevertheless, when they have time, certain contemporary players play great classical backhand drives like Rosewall's. In the bottom tier of great serves: 1. *Reggie Doherty.* 2. *Davis.* 3. *McLoughlin.* 4. *Tilden.* 5. *Vines.* 6. *Drobny.* 7. *Kramer.* 8. *Gonzales.* 9. *Hoad.* 10. *Newcombe. The very pure movements of Reggie and Big Bill Tilden are continued in Jack Kramer, even though the photo, snapped a fraction of a second later, may give us the idea only of this great similarity. With the increase of aggressive play and the permissiveness of the rule on the foot fault, the forward tilt is accentuated; nonetheless, Vines and even McLoughlin do not play very differently from Newcombe, though the Australian is permitted to lift both feet from the playing surface. Two other parallel strokes are those of Gonzales and Hoad. It is difficult to compare the two serves of the great left-handers, Davis and Drobny, since we have no photo of the twist serve of the donator of the Davis Cup.*

39 The Exploding Wimbledon

Wimbledon, which manages to be both the sacred temple of tennis and a highly profitable commercial enterprise, continues to break its own attendance-records. In 1975, 338,507 spectators paid to watch the Championships – 32,796 more than the previous record which had been set a year earlier. The sun shone all the time and the daily record, which had stood for 16 years, was broken twice. On the third day, 37,081 people were packed into the grounds of the All-England Club. Two days later the crowd reached 37,290. There was scarcely room to eat strawberries and cream. Wimbledon was bursting at its seams. Whatever would Major Wingfield have thought?

For two weeks the whole world seemed to be watching tennis – those who went to the matches and the eight million television viewers. Here was tangible evidence of the tennis boom. Tennis was in fashion across the Atlantic and on the Continent. 1975 was a record year for Rome and Paris as well as for Wimbledon, but this was the heart of the business. After five days the press-office, just behind the Centre Court, sent a small bulletin pointing out that already more people had paid to see this particular Wimbledon than had ever attended the 12 days of Forest Hills. The final total more than doubled the best figure achieved at the US Championships. As the fortnight progressed, All-England Club officials discussed the need for further extensions to the ground.

Bigger and bigger. When they moved from Worple Road to Church Road, there were those who thought that the new stadium was far too big. Now they were considering the possibility of building a second Centre Court. And yet by all the rules of sports promotion and show business, this expansion, this ever-increasing popularity ought to have been halted in the early 1970s. Open tennis had brought the great professionals back to Wimbledon in 1968. In 1972 and 1973, the tangled politics of the game's prosperity – so many dollars, so many sponsors, so many rival tournaments and so many people wanting pieces of the action – excluded them again. Could the play be acted without stars? Wimbledon proved that it was possible, surviving both the ban on players who had signed World Championship Tennis contracts and the boycott by the Association of Tennis Professionals a year later.

For the All-England Club, the gratifying part was that the crowds flocked in as they had always done. The record was 301,896, set in 1967, a year when the sun shone almost as much as it did in 1975, and the 1972 gate was only 800 below that – and might have beaten it if it hadn't rained on the second Saturday – and the attendance the following year was 1,724 short of the best. The standard of play was lower, even though the Smith–Nastase final in 1972 was full of character and drama, but in both years the British had closed ranks, so determined for Wimbledon to succeed that no one said too much about the quality of the Emperor's new clothes. The Championships conquered in the political battle.

There were similarities about both disputes. Both times Herman David, the chairman of the All-England Club, supported the International Lawn Tennis Federation, a body which he had not admired greatly up to then. Both times he felt that outside groups were threatening Wimbledon's sovereignty. It was an essential part of his creed that Wimbledon mattered more than anything else in tennis. When in 1967 he had felt that the ILTF's failure to introduce open tennis was damaging the Championships, he attacked them, and his description of their concept of "amateurism" as "a living lie" had done more than anything to break the old system. He demonstrated the power and prestige of Wimbledon to the Federation on that occasion. In the next two battles they asked him to use this strength in their support.

Through both ran the old thread of Anglo-American rivalry, which dates back to the beginning of the game. ATP might have had a broad international membership, a South African president in Cliff Drysdale and a British director, Mark Cox, but for David and the ILTF its accents, attitudes and most of its grievances were those of the American circuit. WCT, owned by Lamar Hunt, a Texas oil millionaire, was, to the British and the other Europeans, the embodiment of the American idea of show business tennis, neatly packaged for quick public entertainment and maximum profit.

David's support for the ILTF against WCT was made plain in public at a bitter confrontation with Hunt in the press-room at Wimbledon on the final Saturday of the 1971 Championships. WCT had made the mistake of suggesting to the All-England Club that they might pursue together new ways of increasing the revenue from the tournament. "It is a gold-mine which isn't being exploited properly. Other people are making high profits from concessions which are given to them too cheaply. That money ought to go to Wimbledon itself, the players and all the others who contribute to the success of the tournament," said Michael Davies, WCT's executive director.

David saw this as an attempt to interfere with Wimbledon. The ILTF, led by Allan Heyman, a Danish barrister who lived and practiced in London, took the view that WCT's "demands" to Wimbledon were part of an attempt to dominate the international game. Yesterday the WCT circuit, today Wimbledon, tomorrow the world. When WCT refused to accept their terms on the question of the international calendar and the rival jackpot competitions, their Grand Prix and Hunt's 20-city World Championship of Tennis, they banned WCT's contracted players from all their tournaments in 1972. Hunt

1

had become the new tennis ogre. "American tycoon wants to take over Wimbledon," was a typical London evening paper headline.

For the ILTF, there are always ogres and dragons. In the early 1960s the battle had been between the professionals and the ILTF's approved brand of amateurs, who could, it seemed, take all kinds of financial rewards as long as they also accepted the authority of their national association, and Jack Kramer, who led the professionals, was the dragon. Then, with open tennis, Kramer, as the initiator of the Grand Prix, which was designed to counter WCT's attractions and persuade the top players to appear in as many ILTF events as possible, was accepted into the establishment – albeit temporarily – and Hunt, a quiet, courteous man, who enjoyed a rich man's hobby of making sports teams and leagues run efficiently, replaced him as the ILTF's principal opponent. When Kramer became ATP's executive director and led the boycott, he returned to ogredom until the noisy dragon of World Team Tennis appeared in 1974.

All Hunt's previous experience – American football, soccer, basketball – had been in domestic sport in the United States. He had acquired his interest in tennis almost accidentally and learned about it by hard commercial experience. Dave Dixon, from New Orleans, WCT's first promoter, had seen it as a spectacular form of show business. "I went to this small town in New York State and there the pros were playing the most marvellous tennis and nobody was watching them. There was no presentation, no color, no attempt to catch the attention of the public and say: 'This is a great game'," he said. Colored shirts, audience participation, music, table tennis scoring.

1. Falling champion. Jan Kodes won Wimbledon in the non-vintage year, 1973. Connors beat him in five sets in the quarter-finals the following year. 2. Nikki Pilic, the left-handed Yugoslav, was at the center of the dispute which led to the boycott of the Championships by the Association of Tennis Professionals.

2

1

2

1. Coming to terms with Wimbledon. Connors was a quarter-finalist at Wimbledon in *1972* and *1973*. In *1974* he was the champion. *2.* The end of the *1973* final. Billie Jean King defeated Chris Evert 6–0, 7–5. It was Miss Evert's third failure in a major European final that year. Evonne Goolagong beat her in Rome and she lost narrowly to Margaret Court in Paris. *3.* Dianne Fromholtz, the brightest hope of Australian tennis, made her first appearance on the Centre Court against Virginia Wade in *1973*. *4.* Virginia Wade reached the quarter-finals at Wimbledon for the third time in *1973*. And yet again she lost to Mrs. King. *5.* Chris Evert avenged a defeat in the French final by beating Margaret Court at Wimbledon – the best grass-court performance of her career up to then.

3

5

4

6. One of the moments of high emotion of the 1973 Wimbledon. Nastase, who was playing in spite of the ATP, comes on to court to a tremendous ovation for his first match against Hans Plotz (West Germany). He was fined $5000 by the players' union for defying their instruction. 7. A low backhand volley from the champion. Mrs. King attacks on the way to the title.

7

6

Dixon's experiments hadn't worked in 1968 and WCT's Handsome Eight – Newcombe, Roche, Pilic, Taylor, Drysdale, Barthes, Buchholz and Ralston – did not exactly seem like the outriders of the tennis explosion.

Nothing could have been colder than their opening night in an ice-rink in the middle of the cattle-market in February, 1968, in Kansas City. As the chill of failure was descending, Hunt arrived and suggested diffidently that it might all be more exciting if the linesmen blew whistles when shots were out. The format changed as the tour stumbled from city to city. Ideas were tried and rejected. The tennis public preferred the conventional game and the new, untapped audiences didn't come.

Dixon retired, ahead of his time (look at all the color on court now and think how the Wimbledon crowd shouted encouragement to Connors and Ashe in 1975's final: "Come on, Connors." "I'm trying for Christ's sake."); the Handsome Eight laughed to keep themselves from weeping; and Hunt turned back to the concept of a conventional but properly organized tournament-circuit. It was the first modern pro tour. When Rosewall won the first WCT final in the grand climax at Dallas in 1971, he said that he felt that he had been lucky to have stayed in the game long enough to see pro tennis reach such a peak of organization.

Once Hunt had set his own tour in order, he began to look further afield. He had large contracts to meet. In their haste to sign players, WCT had made profitability difficult. When European tournaments were asked to pay "management fees" for the appearance of WCT

1

2

3

4

players, ILTF officials objected to having to pay for the pro group's extravagant indiscretions. Others, like the Italian Championships, made quite lucrative agreements for co-operation with them. But he was still under suspicion. Every advance he made seemed to be a blow at the Federation's traditional control of the game. This was the maze of international tennis politics ("There are many footprints at the cave of this mystery, none of them pointing outwards") and he must have wondered what kind of world he had entered. Life must have seemed so much easier back among the Kansas City Chiefs and the Dallas Cowboys.

Certainly, he was completely astonished by Wimbledon's flat rejection of what seemed to him to be a legitimate and sensible business approach. With so many formidable players at his command, he felt strong enough to talk to the All-England on equal terms. The Championships had been in existence since 1877, but who was to say whether they could use one or two new ideas? WCT was four years old, full of the effervescence of novelty, considering itself aggressive and progressive, and with little reverence for the old guard of the ILTF.

They underestimated the Federation. There had been a perceptible change in its leadership since open tennis and the new younger men were determined to keep the game alive in Europe. America was offering huge prize-money and Hunt, in spite of his operations in Europe, was regarded in Europe as a major force in the Americanization of the game. In particular, the French were bitter about the failure of WCT to keep to the agreement whereby they were to send a number of their leading men to the 1971 French Championships. Laver, Rosewall, Newcombe and Okker were among the notable absentees. WCT said that they had made every possible attempt to ask the players to compete, but that they could not compel them to play. "What is the use of trying to make an agreement with them?" asked the French.

In some ways that was the turning-point. The celebrated Hunt–David confrontation followed at Wimbledon and a week later at Stresa, WCT were given notice that they would be banned from all ILTF courts and tournaments from the following January. The next few months were full of heated bargaining. There was a seller's market for players. WCT and the national associations indulged in an expensive auction for loyalties. If it was going to be war, there were six months for recruitment. Pepsi-Cola, the original sponsors of the Grand Prix, withdrew, apparently under the impression that the ILTF

5

1. Three times a Wimbledon semi-finalist, Roger Taylor came closest to the title when he lost to Kodes in the fifth set in 1973. 2. Mrs. King under pressure. 3. Nastase volleying easily. 4. Margaret Court lost to Chris Evert in 1973, then broke the news that she was expecting her second child. 5. Jack Kramer, ATP's executive director, disappeared from Britain's TV screens after the boycott. 6. Taylor's presence saved the 1973 Championships for the All-England Club, providing national interest in the men's singles.

1

4

1. Virginia Wade reached the semi-finals at Wimbledon for the first time in 1974. Olga Morozova beat her 1–6, 7–5, 6–4 after the British No. 1 had led 4–2 in the final set. 2. Cliff Drysdale resigned the presidency of ATP to play Team Tennis for Miami. 3. Taylor takes a balanced view of a difficult situation.

2

3

could not win, and Heyman promptly replaced them with Commercial Union, the British insurance group, who shrewdly saw the competition as a way of publicizing themselves on the American market.

In the end the ILTF were saved by the refusals of Stan Smith, the leading American, and Nastase to accept WCT's terms. Smith had been runner-up to Newcombe at the 1971 Wimbledon and was to win it in 1972, but Nastase, the Commercial Union Master, the most brilliant entertainer in the game, was the man upon whom most depended. As long as he stayed with the ILTF, as long as he played at Wimbledon, WCT could sign any dozen less exciting players.

The Rumanian rejected a £100,000 three-year contract in January, 1972. "I guess he just doesn't want to sign for us and the amount of money just doesn't make any difference," said Mike Davies ruefully. Most of the best Europeans – Jan Kodes, Andres Gimeno, Manuel Orantes and Adriano Panatta – also elected to remain independent. They kept the European season alive and after four months of the ban, peace was signed in April – too late for the WCT players to compete in Paris or at Wimbledon because the terms had to be ratified by the ILTF's annual meeting at Helsinki, three days after Wimbledon ended. That was the official version of the situation. The general view was that the ILTF's leading officials wanted to show that they could stage both tournaments successfully without WCT. When they did that triumphantly and robbed the professional group of its important argument, they approved the peace terms. These gave WCT the right to operate in the period between mid-January and mid-May and left the rest of the year for the Grand Prix. It seemed a sensible compromise.

Exiled from Wimbledon, the old champions passed the time at a tournament in St Louis. There was considerable bitterness about the fact that the British had done nothing to speed the processes of the ILTF and make a place for them in the Championships. The resentment they felt then may well have been a factor in the action they

5

6

4. Kathy May, one of the new generation of Californians. 5. Connors takes off vertically in his semi-final against Dick Stockton (US). They had been rivals in American junior tennis and Connors won 4–6, 6–2, 6–3, 6–4. 6, 7. Bjorn Borg and his friends. "It is very comforting to know that they all like me and want me to win," he once remarked.

7

took a year later. At Forest Hills, in the September of 1972, ATP was formed and Kramer was asked to be its executive director. Here at last was the tennis equivalent of the Professional Golfers' Association.

The ILTF took two views of the new body. Most administrators held them simultaneously. Clearly, it was important that there should be a properly representative organization which put the players' points of view, but at the same time the Federation did not want to find a new third force complicating the game's power structure. They had just made peace with Hunt and WCT. Now Kramer, once their principal opponent, was reappearing as the principal spokesman for a players' union, which sought to promote tournaments – as the PGA did in golf – and to share in the decisions which the ILTF made on questions like discipline and the Grand Prix. Hunt had wanted nothing more than commercial co-existence. If the ILTF didn't interfere with him, he was happy to keep as far as possible from them. But ATP asked for something more – a share in the government of the game – and that meant, to some officials, a diminution of the Federation's powers.

The Pilic affair brought out the militancy of the players ("Why should amateurs whose livelihoods are not at stake take decisions which affect our jobs without consulting us?") and stirred the conservatism of Heyman's management-committee into direct opposition. Nikki Pilic was one of the circuit's senior members, a left-handed Yugoslav, much given to histrionics and self-justification. He had been an original member of the Handsome Eight and the first Iron Curtain player to become an officially approved circuit professional. Yugoslavia, apparently, had asked him to play for them – after an interval of five years – in the Davis Cup against New Zealand at Zagreb. He agreed, provided that Zeljko Franulovic, their second player, who suffered from a chronic arm injury, was fit. Then he reached the WCT doubles final at Montreal; Franulovic's arm seemed, according to his information, to be no better; it was a long way to Zagreb; he had had no chance to practice on clay, he did not feel that he would do himself justice; and so he did not go.

Franulovic played and Yugoslavia lost 3–2. The absent Pilic was blamed for the failure and suspended for a year by the Yugoslav Federation. ATP appealed immediately and Kramer and Donald Dell, their attorney, appeared for him at an ILTF tribunal at the end of the French Championships in Paris. They argued that there had been considerable confusion as to what exactly had been agreed between Pilic and the Yugoslavs – all the relevant documents were in Serbo-Croat – and that a player ought to be free to choose whether or not he represented his country.

That immediately became the principle at issue. The Pilic case offered ATP a martyr and a situation which affected every top-class player – and the Americans, who had a great habit of dropping out of USLTA events, more than anyone. Most countries are wise enough not to pick reluctant players. Most ranked Europeans expect to be asked to play and make arrangements with their national associations about the Davis Cup. Suspensions were rare, but Pilic had been suspended and the matter had been raised. Even when the tribunal reduced the suspension to one month, ATP weren't appeased.

Pilic reached the final of the French Championships and, as he left the court after losing to Nastase, the result of his appeal was announced. The suspension should have begun the following day but he went to Rome and presented himself at the Foro Italico for the Italian Championships. Cliff Drysdale, the ATP president, told the Italian Federation that if he was not allowed to play, the association's members would walk out. The Italians considered the possibility of a ruined tournament, sent a hasty cable to the ILTF saying that Pilic's suspension ought to date from the week after their tournament because the event had already begun by the time it had been announced. Pilic played, lost quickly to the Frenchman, Patrice Dominguez, and flew away.

1

2

3

4

That meant that Wimbledon, three weeks later, would have to take the responsibility of implementing the ILTF's decision. Herman David let it be known at once that Pilic's entry would be rejected and the ATP members in Rome met and agreed to carry out their threat to boycott the tournament if he didn't play. For several days that seemed unthinkable. ATP regarded Wimbledon as the prisoner of the Federation, but David had defied the Federation over open tennis so why, they asked, did he not use the All-England Club's power and influence to force a compromise now?

Pilic did not play in the John Player tournament at Nottingham. Instead he spent the week in the Queen's Bench Division of the High Court as ATP asked for an injunction to restrain the All-England Club from barring him from the Championships. After three days the judge ruled against them. "Now we shall know whether we have an association or not," said Kramer as he left the court.

The week that followed was full of long discussions in the daytime at Queen's Club, where the Rothmans London Championships were being played, and meetings lasting far into the night of the ATP board of directors at the Westbury Hotel in Mayfair. Two prominent members, Nastase and Roger Taylor, announced that they would break the boycott. Nastase said that he was under orders from the Rumanian Government. ATP skeptically fined him 5,000 dollars for obeying Bucharest.

Taylor argued that as Britain's No. 1 his duty to Wimbledon outweighed his obligation to ATP: "This is my national championship. It is easier for Australians and Americans to pull out. They don't live here." The atmosphere in the dressing-rooms grew strained. There were rumors of attempts by senior players to force younger men, who weren't union members, to join the strike. In the hope of peace the All-England Club postponed the draw from Wednesday to Friday and Eldon Griffiths, the Minister for Sport, attempted to mediate. But neither side moved. Those who thought that ATP would climb down if it came to a choice between Wimbledon and Pilic were mistaken.

Some compromises were suggested. The best seemed to be a plan by which Pilic, who had gone to Split, would withdraw voluntarily from the Championships provided that ILTF would agree to set up a joint disciplinary committee, with ATP representation, to deal with such cases in the future. The ILTF refused that on the Thursday before Wimbledon. Some months later – when that Wimbledon was a frustrating memory – they embraced the idea of a joint professional council with powers of that kind.

Ken Rosewall flew in from Sydney in time to attend the board's decisive meeting. Only Mark Cox, the British director, voted against the boycott. "We talked and argued for hours, restrained, remarkably civil, but always on edge, for we realized we were in the process of declaring war. The issue was simple: should an independent contractor have the right to decide when and where he is to play? If Nikki Pilic could be forced to play Davis Cup and denied entry to Wimbledon, then wouldn't a precedent be set where, say, I would be forced to play some rinky-dink tournament at the risk of being denied admittance to Forest Hills," wrote Arthur Ashe, who was to succeed Drysdale as ATP's president, in his diary, *Portrait in Motion*.

When at last the debate ended, there was another long and emo-

1. Tony Roche and John Newcombe won the men's doubles for the fifth time in 1974. They beat Stan Smith and Bob Lutz in the final. 2. Olga Morozova, the first Russian to reach the women's singles final, meets the Duke of Kent. 3. Victory for Pittsburgh Triangles. Evonne Goolagong and Peggy Michel, Team Tennis partners at Pittsburgh, took the women's doubles in 1974. 4. Jan Kodes, one of the game's great workers. 5. Bjorn Borg plays a high forehand volley against Graham Stilwell. 6. Manuel Orantes beat Tony Roche, but lost to Ishmael El-Shafei. 7. Wimbledon, 1974, ended in the fourth round for Nastase. Dick Stockton beat him 5–7, 6–4, 6–3, 9–8.

5

6

7

tional press-conference. Drysdale seemed near tears. Rosewall kept saying gloomily: "No Wimbledon. Can you beat that? We aren't going to play at Wimbledon. You wouldn't think it was possible." The draw was full of names that no one who hadn't toured the minor English tournaments could identify. Who was Karp? Who was Peebles? Myers? Stovovic? Or Buwalda? An hour before it was made Taylor telephoned the All-England Club to say that, after all, he had decided to withdraw. Ten minutes later he phoned again and asked to be reinstated. When Captain Gibson, the referee, announced that, the press applauded. Emotion was running deep. Everyone understood the extent of the Yorkshireman's dilemma.

On the Saturday before Wimbledon he had to play Nastase in the final at Queen's. In the clubhouse he was giving yet another press-conference. Suddenly he turned to a friend and said: "You believe I'm doing the right thing, don't you?" There had never been so much applause at a Queen's final as when Taylor and Nastase walked out to play. Nastase won 9–8, 6–3 but only after collapsing early in the match and complaining of a pain in his kidneys. Was it another Rumanian joke? If so, there was too much tension for anyone to laugh.

The first day of this depleted Wimbledon was full of the Dunkirk spirit. ATP and Pilic had made their protest and gone. Now the British were faced with the task of saving a national institution and it was all rather like the comradeship of the blitz. Defiance ("Who do you think you are kidding, Mr Kramer, if you think old England's done?") in sunshine – just like the summer of 1940. The Centre Court

1

2

3

4

5

6

7

1. 1974 was Ishmael El-Shafei's best Wimbledon. He beat Borg and Orantes. *2.* Jaroslav Drobny, the *1954* champion, played in the Veteran's doubles. *3.* Francoise Durr lost to Mrs. King in the singles and failed in the quarters of the doubles. *4.* Rosewall in triumph at the end of his semi-final against Smith. *5.* Wade in dejection, after falling to Morozova. *6.* Rosewall at the end. He rests in the third set of the final against Connors. *7.* Mark Farrell and Lesley Charles, the first British mixed finalists since *1939*, lost to Owen Davidson and Mrs. King in the final. *8, 9.* Chris Evert won her first important grass-court title without losing a set. *10.* Tom Okker, "The Flying Dutchman", tongue in cheek against Drysdale.

8

9

10

1

3

1. Raul Ramirez won Rome in 1975, but lost to Connors in the quarters at Wimbledon. 2. The end of the day in SW19. 3. Martina Navratilova, the promising left-handed Czech, lost to Margaret Court (6), who was beaten in the semi-finals by Evonne Cawley. 4. Ken Rosewall, playing in his ninth Wimbledon, fell to Tony Roche by 6–3, 6–8, 8–6, 6–4, after a disputed line-call in the crisis of the third set. 5. Nastase fell to Sherwood Stewart from Texas.

2

4

6

was packed, noisy, emotional and bloody well determined to enjoy itself; and the attendance was almost a record for the start of the Championships.

From standing-room to Royal Box (to which Morecambe and Wise had been invited in case the All-England Club needed to be cheered up) there was a tremendous unity. Taylor, Nastase, Borg . . . they were the heroes, and yet Jan Kodes, that industrious Czech, the sort of player that Samuel Smiles would have applauded, won the tournament. When Nastase came on with Hans Plotz, an energetic little German, to open the tournament, the applause must have been heard from Wandsworth to Kingston. "It was as though I had won Wimbledon," he said.

Everyone stood. Everyone cheered. And the welcome for Taylor was even more rapturous. Dark, shoulders broad and brow furrowed, he looked round the court. He might have been in Coventry in the dressing-room during the week at Queen's, but here he was among friends, who recognized that he had taken the decision that was going to save the tournament.

On that day, too, the Borg cult began. This was the 16-year-old

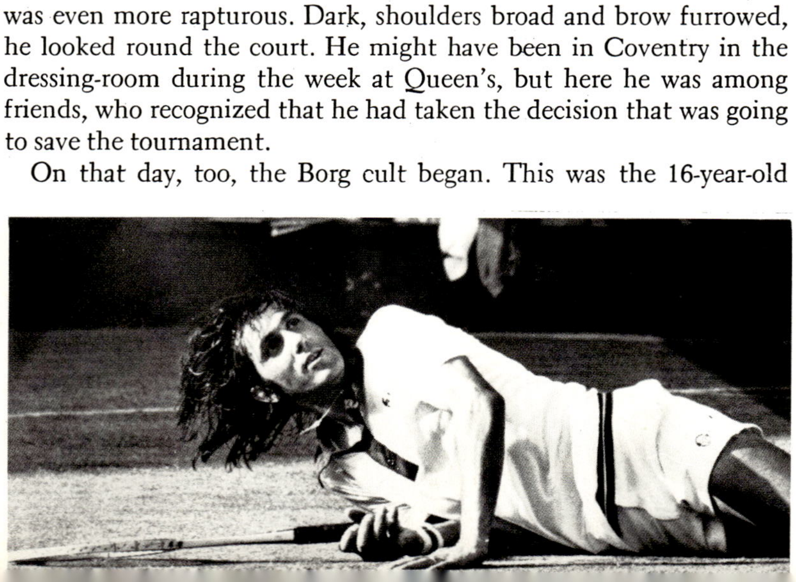

Swede's first appearance in the main event at Wimbledon and he marked it by winning a 20–18 tie-break to complete a 6–3, 6–4, 9–8 victory over Premjit Lall. Afterwards as he tried to cross the main concourse he had to be rescued by stewards from 200 schoolgirls, shrieking and thrusting autograph-books at him. He reached the quarter-finals where Taylor beat him 6–1, 6–8, 3–6, 6–3, 7–5 and all the time the fervor of this gymslip army was increasing. Policemen escorted him to his matches. Photographers followed everywhere. Heavy top-spin on both sides and double-handed backhands became such a fashion that they were almost orthodox style.

Nastase lost to Alex Mayer, a Hungarian-American, ranked eleventh in the US, and never served or returned with anything like the confidence and accuracy of his 1972 Wimbledon. Then, at Forest Hills two months later and in the 1974 Commercial Union Masters at Melbourne, he had looked as though he might become a great grass court player. His failure against Mayer was followed by a loss to Dick Stockton, another of the younger Americans, in 1974 and to the bearded Sherwood Stewart in 1975. By then he seemed to have lost the power to concentrate. The Championships were too large an event for him.

Taylor fell in his third semi-final – the others were 1967 when he lost to Bungert and 1970 when he fell to Rosewall after defeating Laver – to Kodes by 8–9, 9–7, 5–7, 6–4, 7–5. That was another of Wimbledon's damp days. The match started late and turned into a long, dour struggle. By the time they reached the fifth set it was almost dark. Taylor reached 5–4 and then it began to rain so heavily that they were forced to stop. When they resumed Kodes took the three games that he needed for a place in the final. In the Iron Curtain match, by

7

8
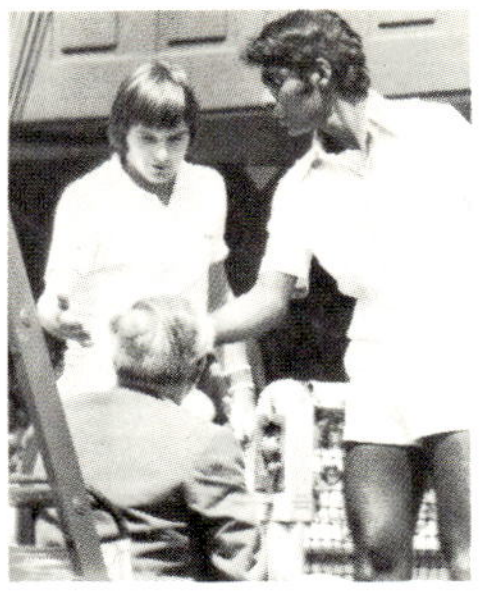

9

10

11

12

7. Virginia Wade stretches for a backhand against Evonne Cawley. 8. Sympathy for the net-cord judge. Connors and Vijay Amritraj commiserate with him after a shot from Connors hit him in the eye.
9. A backhand from Roche against Rosewall.
10. Roscoe Tanner at the net.
11. Betty Stove took a set from Chris Evert.
12. Ashe's hardest match. Tony Roche, who took him to five sets, serves in their semi-final.

no means Wimbledon's most sparkling final, Kodes beat Alex Metreveli 6–1, 9–8, 6–3. He had been seeded fifteenth in the original draw and was promoted to second when ATP left. His victory was a final proof that he had learned to play on grass. He won only one match in his first six appearances at Wimbledon. "I used to come and play only one match. This year I finally played seven," he said. Later he was runner-up for the second time in three years at Forest Hills, where he took Newcombe to five sets in the final – an achievement which firmly answered those who regarded him as a Wimbledon champion by default.

In the women's singles Billie Jean King, the president of the Women's Tennis Association, an organization which resisted the temptation to threaten to boycott Wimbledon until 1975 when they successfully negotiated an increase in prize-money, won her fifth title, defeating Chris Evert, who was to take her place as the ruler of the Virginia Slims circuit, 6–0, 7–5. She also took the doubles again with Rosemary Casals and the mixed with Owen Davidson.

The 1973 men's doubles went to Nastase and the precocious Jimmy Connors, a pupil of Segura and Gonzales, who was then 20. Shrewdly managed by Bill Riordan, the promoter of the Independent Players' Association tour, which rivalled the WCT circuit in the American Spring, Connors was plainly the most confident and aggressive young player in the US. Swift and strong, with a double-handed backhand and a number of jokes and mannerisms (some of them borrowed), he was an imitative player. He watched carefully, learned from all the best models and then mixed in his own talent to evolve a style. He wasn't one of the sophisticated new heroes – like Borg, Vilas or Panatta – and he wasn't popular with large sections of the crowd, but no one could deny the completeness of his victory in the 1974 Championships.

Until the final Saturday, 1974 had been a wonderfully nostalgic Wimbledon. ATP had returned and Rosewall, at thirty-nine, was making another of his last attempts on the title. Seeded ninth, he began with a quiet little match against Barry Phillips-Moore, an Australian only three years his junior, then he beat the respectful, talented Vijay Amritraj, the Swiss Kanderal, the forceful left-handed Roscoe Tanner, who had dismissed Ashe, Newcombe, the 1971 champion, and – after saving a match-point in third set – Smith, the winner in 1972, in the semi-finals.

Was it to be Rosewall's year at last? Connors had cut through the rest of the field, bouncing and exploding. Everything had been in contrast to Rosewall's careworn craftsmanship. It was the Australian's fourth final in twenty years and a classic sporting situation: the old hero, shrewd and subtle, with experience to compensate for waning power, and the brash boy, forceful, talented and athletic, without pressure from the years or the crowd. Until that last day it had been a wonderful fortnight for Rosewall. Unperturbed by winds and damp courts, his resilience and stamina had been astonishing.

Connors surprised him and almost everyone in the Centre Court crowd, that noble army of martyrs with Rosewall. The Australian won a long first game, then lost the next ten and went down dismally by 6–1, 6–1, 6–4. Only in the third set did he have even the smallest chance, then he held three points for a lead of 3–1. Fiercely Connors frustrated him, blasting all the life from his game. "I suppose it was tiredness," said Rosewall glumly. "But I don't want to take anything away from Jim. Everything he touched turned to gold." They met

1

again in the final at Forest Hills. The match was almost identical. Connors won 6–1, 6–0, 6–1.

Chris Evert took the women's title with equal severity, defeating Olga Morozova, the first Russian woman to reach a singles final, 6–0, 6–4. "When I got to the semi-finals and saw who was left in I thought I could win," said the new champion briskly. Miss Morozova had lobbed and volleyed Mrs. King into subjection in the quarter-finals and then had counter-attacked from 2–4 in the final set to beat Virginia Wade. Newcombe and Roche won the men's doubles for the fifth time; Miss Goolagong and Peggy Michel were the women's champions; and Mark Farrell, a left-hander from Liverpool, and Lesley Charles, from Worcester, became the first all-British pair to reach the mixed final for 35 years. They were beaten 6–3, 9–7 by Davidson and Mrs. King.

For most of the 1975 Wimbledon, Connors seemed completely in command. In 1974 Phil Dent had tested him and Kodes had taken him to five sets, but this time he reached the final without losing a set. He had come to England early and had lost to Bernie Mitton, a South African Davis Cup player, at Chichester and to Tanner at Nottingham. But those were preliminary bouts. He regained all his accuracy and ferocity for the Championships. John Lloyd, Vijay Amritraj, Cox, Dent again, Raul Ramirez, and eventually – outpacing the paceman – Tanner were his victims.

He was the hottest favorite for years. Newcombe had beaten him in the Australian final, but he had avenged that defeat in a challenge match at Las Vegas and an injured leg had forced the Australian to withdraw from Wimbledon. Rosewall, who had played only occasionally, had been seeded second; Borg, who had retained Paris after surrendering Rome, was third and Vilas, the winner of the Grand Prix, fourth. The one player who seemed under-seeded was Ashe, who, having ended a long blank spell by winning the WCT title in Dallas, was in sixth place. He had taken Forest Hills in 1968 and Australia

2

3

4

1975 – an American year at Wimbledon and two unseeded pairs won doubles titles. 1. The art of the double-handed backhand: Jimmy Connors reaches for a wide ball. 2. Arthur Ashe, the 1975 champion, at the moment of triumph. 3, 4. Evonne Cawley, on the way to victory against Virginia Wade, and at the end of a final in which she won only one game from Billie Jean King.

5

5. Ashe, grimly concentrating, moves into his third set against Connors. 6. Vitas Gerulaitis from New York and Alex Mayer from New Jersey won the men's doubles. 7. Kazuko Sawamatsu, partnering Ann Kiyomura, a Japanese Californian, was Japan's first Wimbledon champion since 1934. 8. Billie Jean's sixth singles title. Staying back, she watches the progress of a backhand. She won her first Wimbledon event – the doubles with Karen Hantze – in 1962 at the age of 18.

6

7

in 1970, but those were his only major championships. He prepared methodically for this Wimbledon. Instead of playing in Paris, he chose to have an extra week of match-play on grass in the Robertsons tournament at Beckenham, where he beat Tanner. Most of his opponents tested him at Wimbledon – Hewitt, Stilwell and Borg, who had an injured leg, took sets from him and Roche, more effective in singles than he had been for years, took him to 5–7, 6–4, 7–5, 8–9, 6–4.

That proved to be a closer match than the final. Connors had beaten Ashe in their three previous contests – twice in South African finals and once at Boston. The black American had failed in the battles of pace. This time he deliberately reduced the pace, chipping, lobbing and denying Connors the angles that he liked and, for all his power and ferocity, Connors could not escape from this tactical cobweb. He won only two games in the first two sets, took the third after Ashe had broken to lead 3–2, then faltered after leading 3–0 in the fourth. Ashe, sitting in his chair, closing his eyes and relaxing at every change-over, quietly regained his rhythm and overtook him to win 6–1, 6–1, 5–7, 6–4. It was an admirably disciplined and thoughtful performance and the most surprising result in a Wimbledon final for years.

The women's final was also remarkable. Mrs. King allowed Evonne Goolagong Cawley, the 1971 champion, only one game – the eleventh of the second set. It was her sixth singles title and it enabled her to equal Elizabeth Ryan's Wimbledon record of 19. Mrs. Cawley had beaten Virginia Wade and Margaret Court in the semi-finals, but she was utterly dominated by Mrs. King, who scarcely made an error, in the last match. The women's doubles went to an unseeded pair, Kazuko Sawamatsu, the leading Japanese, and Ann Kiyomura, a Japanese-Californian; the men's doubles, equally unexpectedly, went to Alex Mayer and Vitas Gerulaitis (United States), and the mixed to the old partnership of Marty Riessen and Mrs. Court.

8

Winners of the Great Tournaments through 1975

The following tables list the players who have won the singles competition in at least two of the four classic events of the international calendar: The Australian Championships (AUS), the French National Championships (R/G), Wimbledon (WIM), and Forest Hills (F/H).

Men

Name	*Nationality*	*Born on*	*AUS*	*R/G*	*WIM*	*F/H*	*Total*
Roy Emerson	Australia	11 3 1936	6	2	2	2	12
Rod Laver	Australia	8 9 1938	3	2	4	2	11
William Tilden	United States	2 10 1893	—	—	3	7	10
Fred Perry	Great Britain	5 18 1909	1	1	3	3	8
Ken Rosewall	Australia	11 2 1934	4	2	—	2	8
Henry Cochet	France	12 14 1901	—	4	2	1	7
René Lacoste	France	7 2 1905	—	3	2	2	7
John Newcombe	Australia	5 23 1944	2	—	3	2	7
Donald Budge	United States	6 13 1916	1	1	2	2	6
John Crawford	Australia	3 22 1908	4	1	1	—	6
Laurie Doherty	Great Britain	10 8 1876	—	—	5	1	6
Anthony Wilding	New Zealand	10 31 1883	2	—	4	—	6
Frank Sedgman	Australia	10 29 1927	2	—	1	2	5
Tony Trabert	United States	8 16 1930	—	2	1	2	5
Jean Borotra	France	8 13 1898	1	1	2	—	4
Ashley Cooper	Australia	9 15 1936	2	—	1	1	4
Lewis Hoad	Australia	11 23 1934	1	1	2	—	4
Frank Parker	United States	1 31 1916	—	2	—	2	4
Manolo Santana	Spain	5 10 1938	—	2	1	1	4
Norman Brookes	Australia	11 14 1887	1	—	2	—	3
Jimmy Connors	United States	1952	1	—	1	1	3
Jaroslav Drobny	Czechoslovakia	10 12 1921	—	2	1	—	3
Neale Fraser	Australia	10 3 1933	—	—	1	2	3
William Johnston	United States	11 2 1894	—	—	1	2	3
Jan Kodes	Czechoslovakia	3 1 1946	—	2	1	—	3
Jack Kramer	United States	8 5 1921	—	—	1	2	3
Gerald Patterson	Australia	12 17 1895	1	—	2	—	3
Bobby Riggs	United States	2 25 1918	—	—	1	2	3
Ellsworth Vines	United States	12 29 1911	—	—	1	2	3
Arthur Ashe	United States	7 10 1943	1	—	1	1	3
Don McNeill	United States	4 30 1918	—	1	—	1	2
Ilie Nastase	Romania	7 19 1946	—	1	—	1	2
Alex Olmedo	Peru	3 24 1936	1	—	1	—	2
Budge Patty	United States	2 11 1924	—	1	1	—	2
Mervyn Rose	Australia	1 23 1930	1	1	—	—	2
Dick Savitt	United States	3 4 1927	1	—	1	—	2
Ted Schroeder	United States	7 20 1921	—	—	1	1	2
Vic Seixas	United States	8 30 1923	—	—	1	1	2
Stanley Smith	United States	12 19 1946	—	—	1	1	2
Fred Stolle	Australia	10 8 1938	—	1	—	1	2
Bjorn Borg	Sweden	6 6 1956	—	2	—	—	2

Women

Name	*Nationality*	*Born on*	*AUS*	*R/G*	*WIM*	*F/H*	*Total*
Margaret Smith Court	Australia	7 16 1942	11	5	3	5	24
Helen Wills Moody	United States	10 6 1905	—	4	8	7	19
Billie Jean Moffitt King	United States	11 22 1943	1	1	6	4	12
Maureen Connolly	United States	9 17 1934	1	2	3	3	9
Suzanne Lenglen	France	5 24 1899	—	2	6	—	8
Maria Ester Bueno	Brazil	10 11 1939	—	—	3	4	7
Louise Brough	United States	3 11 1923	1	—	4	1	6
Margaret Osborne Dupont	United States	3 4 1918	—	2	1	3	6
Doris Hart	United States	6 20 1925	1	2	1	2	6
Pauline Betz	United States	8 6 1919	—	—	1	4	5
Althea Gibson	United States	8 25 1927	—	1	2	2	5
Helen Jacobs	United States	8 6 1908	—	—	1	4	5
Alice Marble	United States	9 28 1913	—	—	1	4	5
Shirley Fry	United States	6 30 1927	1	1	1	1	4
Evonne Goolagong Cawley	Australia	7 31 1951	2	1	1	—	4
Chris Evert	United States	12 21 1954	—	2	1	1	4
Darlene Hard	United States	1 6 1936	—	1	—	2	3
Ann Haydon Jones	Great Britain	10 17 1938	—	2	1	—	3
Angela Mortimer	Great Britain	4 21 1932	1	1	1	—	3
Dorothy Round	Great Britain	7 13 1909	1	—	2	—	3
May Sutton Bundy	United States	9 25 1887	—	—	2	1	3
Cilly Aussem	Germany	1 4 1909	—	1	1	—	2
Nancy Gunter Richey	United States	8 23 1942	1	1	—	—	2
Virginia Wade	Great Britain	7 10 1945	1	—	—	1	2

Men's Singles

Big Slam

The Big Slam is the winning by one player of the four most important tourneys in the same year. In the history of tennis, this feat has been accomplished by:

1938 Don Budge (United States)
1962 Rod Laver (Australia)
1969 Rod Laver (Australia)

¾ Slam

Seven players missed a Big Slam by only one tournament. They are listed below along with the tournament they lost:

1933	Jack Crawford (Australia)	lost Forest Hills
1934	Fred Perry (Great Britain)	lost Roland Garros
1955	Tony Trabert (United States)	lost the Australian Championship
1956	Lewis Hoad (Australia)	lost Forest Hills
1958	John Cooper (Australia)	lost Roland Garros
1964	Roy Emerson (Australia)	lost Roland Garros
1974	Jimmy Connors (United States)	barred from Roland Garros

Women's Singles

Big Slam

1953 Maureen Connolly (United States)
1970 Margaret Court (Australia)

¾ Slam

1928	Helen Wills (United States)	lost the Australian Championship
1929	Helen Wills (United States)	lost the Australian Championship
1962	Margaret Smith (Australia)	lost Wimbledon
1965	Margaret Smith (Australia)	lost Roland Garros
1969	Margaret Court (Australia)	lost Wimbledon
1972	Billie Jean King (United States)	lost the Australian Championship
1973	Margaret Court (Australia)	lost Wimbledon

Men's Doubles

Big Slam

1951 Ken McGregor — Frank Sedgman (Australia)

¾ Slam

1952	Ken McGregor — Frank Sedgman (Australia)	lost Forest Hills
1953	Lewis Hoad — Ken Rosewall (Australia)	lost Forest Hills
1956	Lewis Hoad — Ken Rosewall (Australia)	lost Roland Garros
1967	John Newcombe — Tony Roche (Australia)	lost Wimbledon

Mixed Doubles

Big Slam

1963 Margaret Smith and Ken Fletcher (Australia)
1965 Margaret Smith (with different partners)
1967 Owen Davidson (with different partners)

¾ Slam

1951	Doris Hart (United States) and Frank Sedgman (Australia)	lost the Australian Championship
1952	Doris Hart (United States) and Frank Sedgman (Australia)	lost the Australian Championship
1953	Doris Hart and Vic Seixas (United States)	lost the Australian Championship
1963	Billie Jean King (United States) and Owen Davidson (Australia)	lost the Australian Championship

Women's Doubles

Big Slam

1960 Maria Bueno (Brazil) (with different partners)

¾ Slam

1946	Louise Brough and Margaret Osborne (United States)	lost the Australian Championship
1947	Louise Brough and Margaret Dupont (United States)	lost the Australian Championship
1951	Doris Hart and Shirley Fry (United States)	lost the Australian Championship
1952	Doris Hart and Shirley Fry (United States)	lost the Australian Championship
1953	Doris Hart and Shirley Fry (United States)	lost the Australian Championship
1960	Maria Bueno (Brazil) and Darlene Hard (United States)	lost the Australian Championship
1973	Margaret Court (Australia) and Virginia Wade (Great Britain)	lost Wimbledon

Men's Singles

Australian Championship	*Roland Garros*	*Year*	*Wimbledon*	*Forest Hills*
		1877	S. W. Gore	
		1878	P. F. Hadow	
		1879	J. T. Hartley	
		1880	J. T. Hartley	
		1881	W. Renshaw	R. D. Sears
		1882	W. Renshaw	R. D. Sears
		1883	W. Renshaw	R. D. Sears
		1884	W. Renshaw	R. D. Sears
		1885	W. Renshaw	R. D. Sears
		1886	W. Renshaw	R D. Sears
		1887	H. F. Lawford	R. D. Sears
		1888	E. Renshaw	H. W. Slocum
		1889	W. Renshaw	H. W. Slocum
		1890	W. J. Hamilton	O. S. Campbell
		1891	W. Baddeley	O. S. Campbell
		1892	W. Baddeley	O. S. Campbell
		1893	J. Pim	R. D. Wrenn
		1894	J. Pim	R. D. Wrenn
		1895	W. Baddeley	F. H. Hovey
		1896	H. S. Mahony	R. D. Wrenn
		1897	R. F. Doherty	R. D. Wrenn
		1898	R. F. Doherty	M. D. Whitman
		1899	R. F. Doherty	M. D. Whitman
		1900	R. F. Doherty	M. D. Whitman
		1901	A. W. Gore	W. A. Larned
		1902	H. L. Doherty	W. A. Larned
		1903	H. L. Doherty	H. L. Doherty
		1904	H. L. Doherty	H. Ward
R. W. Heath		1905	H. L. Doherty	B. C. Wright
A. F. Wilding		1906	H. L. Doherty	W. J. Clothier
H. M. Rice		1907	N. E. Brookes	W. A. Larned
F. B. Alexander		1908	A. W. Gore	W. A. Larned
A. F. Wilding		1909	A. W. Gore	W. A. Larned
R. W. Heath		1910	A. F. Wilding	W. A. Larned
N. E. Brookes		1911	A. F. Wilding	W. A. Larned
J. C. Parke		1912	A. F. Wilding	M. E. McLoughlin
E. F. Parker		1913	A. F. Wilding	M. E. McLoughlin
P. O'Hara Wood		1914	N. E. Brookes	R. N. Williams
F. G. Lowe		1915		W. M. Johnston
		1916		R. N. Williams
		1917		R. L. Murray
		1918		R. L. Murray
A. R. F. Kingscote		1919	G. L. Patterson	W. M. Johnston
P. O'Hara Wood		1920	W. T. Tilden	W. T. Tilden
R. H. Gemmell		1921	W. T. Tilden	W. T. Tilden
J. O. Anderson		1922	G. L. Patterson	W. T. Tilden
P. O'Hara Wood		1923	W. M. Johnston	W. T. Tilden
J. O. Anderson		1924	J. Borotra	W. T. Tilden
J. O. Anderson	R. Lacoste	1925	R. Lacoste	W. T. Tilden
J. B. Hawkes	H. Cochet	1926	J. Borotra	R. Lacoste
G. L. Patterson	R. Lacoste	1927	H. Cochet	R. Lacoste
J. Borotra	H. Cochet	1928	R. Lacoste	H. Cochet
J. C. Gregory	R. Lacoste	1929	H. Cochet	W. T. Tilden
E. F. Moon	H. Cochet	1930	W. T. Tilden	J. Doeg
J. H. Crawford	J. Borotra	1931	S. B. Wood	H. E. Vines
J. H. Crawford	H. Cochet	1932	H. E. Vines	H. E. Vines
J. H. Crawford	J. H. Crawford	1933	J. H. Crawford	F. J. Perry
F. J. Perry	G. von Cramm	1934	F. J. Perry	F. J. Perry
J. H. Crawford	F. J. Perry	1935	F. J. Perry	W. Allison
A. K. Quist	G. von Cramm	1936	F. J. Perry	F. J. Perry
V. B. McGrath	H. Henkel	1937	J. D. Budge	J. D. Budge
J. D. Budge	J. D. Budge	1938	J. D. Budge	J. D. Budge
J. E. Bromwich	W. D. McNeill	1939	R. L. Riggs	R. L. Riggs
A. K. Quist		1940		W. D. McNeill
		1941		R. L. Riggs
		1942		F. R. Schroeder
		1943		J. R. Hunt
		1944		F. Parker
		1945		F. Parker
J. E. Bromwich	M. Bernard	1946	Y. Petra	J. A. Kramer
D. Pails	J. Asboth	1947	J. A. Kramer	J. A. Kramer
A. K. Quist	F. Parker	1948	R. Falkenburg	R. A. Gonzales
F. A. Sedgman	F. Parker	1949	F. R. Schroeder	R. A. Gonzales
F. A. Sedgman	B. Patty	1950	J. E. Patty	A. Larsen
R. Savitt	J. Drobny	1951	R. Savitt	F. A. Sedgman
K. McGregor	J. Drobny	1952	F. A. Sedgman	F. A. Sedgman
K. R. Rosewall	K. R. Rosewall	1953	E. V. Seixas	M. A. Trabert
M. G. Rose	M. A. Trabert	1954	J. Drobny	E. V. Seixas
K. R. Rosewall	M. A. Trabert	1955	M. A. Trabert	M. A. Trabert
L. A. Hoad	L. A. Hoad	1956	L. A. Hoad	K. R. Rosewall
A. J. Cooper	S. Davidson	1957	L. A. Hoad	M. J. Anderson
A. J. Cooper	M. G Rose	1958	A. J. Cooper	A. J. Cooper
A. Olmedo	N. Pietrangeli	1959	A. Olmedo	N. A. Fraser
R. G. Laver	N. Pietrangeli	1960	N. A. Fraser	N. A. Fraser
R. Emerson	M. Santana	1961	R. G. Laver	R. Emerson
R. G. Laver	R. G. Laver	1962	R. G. Laver	R. G. Laver
R. Emerson	R. Emerson	1963	C. R. McKinley	R. H. Osuna
R. Emerson	M. Santana	1964	R. Emerson	R. Emerson
R. Emerson	F. S. Stolle	1965	R. Emerson	M. Santana
R. Emerson	A. D. Roche	1966	M. Santana	F. S. Stolle
R. Emerson	R. Emerson	1967	J. D. Newcombe	J. D. Newcombe
W. W. Bowrey	K. R. Rosewall	1968	R. G. Laver	A. R. Ashe
R. G. Laver	R. G. Laver	1969	R. G. Laver	R. G. Laver
A. R. Ashe	J. Kodes	1970	J. D. Newcombe	K. R. Rosewall
K. R. Rosewall	J. Kodes	1971	J. D. Newcombe	S. R. Smith
K. R. Rosewall	A. Gimeno	1972	S. R. Smith	I. Nastase
J. D. Newcombe	I. Nastase	1973	J. Kodes	J. D. Newcombe
J. Connors	B. Borg	1974	J. Connors	J. Connors
J. D. Newcombe	B. Borg	1975	A. R. Ashe	M. Orantes

Women's Singles

Australian Championship	*Roland Garros*	*Year*	*Wimbledon*	*Forest Hills*
		1884	M. Watson	
		1885	M. Watson	
		1886	B. Bingley	
		1887	L. Dod	E. Hansell
		1888	L. Dod	B. Towsend
		1889	G. W. Hillyard	B. Towsend
		1890	L. Rice	E. C. Roosevelt
		1891	L. Dod	M. E. Cahill
		1892	L. Dod	M. E. Cahill
		1893	L. Dod	A. M. Terry
		1894	G. W. Hillyard	H. R. Helwig
		1895	C. Cooper	J. P. Atkinson
		1896	C. Cooper	E. H. Moore
		1897	G. W. Hillyard	J. P. Atkinson
		1898	C. Cooper	J. P. Atkinson
		1899	G. W. Hillyard	M. Jones
		1900	G. W. Hillyard	M. McAteer
		1901	A. Sterry	E. H. Moore
		1902	M. E. Robb	M. Jones
		1903	D. K. Douglass	E. H. Moore
		1904	D. K. Douglass	M. Sutton
		1905	M. Sutton	E. H. Moore
		1906	D. K. Douglass	H. Homans
		1907	M. Sutton	E. Sears
		1908	A. Sterry	M. Bargar-Wallach
		1909	D. Boothby	H. Hotchkiss
		1910	Lambert Chambers	H. Hotchkiss
		1911	Lambert Chambers	H. Hotchkiss
		1912	D. R. Larcombe	M. K. Browne
		1913	Lambert Chambers	M. K. Browne
		1914	Lambert Chambers	M. K. Browne
		1915		M. Bjurstedt
		1916		M. Bjurstedt
		1917		M. Bjurstedt
		1918		M. Bjurstedt
		1919	S. Lenglen	G. W. Wightman
		1920	S. Lenglen	F. Mallory
		1921	S. Lenglen	F. Mallory
B. H. Molesworth		1922	S. Lenglen	F. Mallory
B. H. Molesworth		1923	S. Lenglen	H. Wills
S. Lance		1924	K. McKane	H. Wills
D. Akhurst	S. Lenglen	1925	S. Lenglen	H. Wills
D. Akhurst	S. Lenglen	1926	L. A. Godfree	F. Mallory

Australian Championship	*Roland Garros*	*Year*	*Wimbledon*	*Forest Hills*
E. Boyd	K. Bouman	1927	H. Wills	H. Wills
D. Akhurst	H. Wills	1928	H. Wills	H. Wills
D. Akhurst	H. Wills	1929	H. Wills	H. Wills
D. Akhurst	H. W. Moody	1930	H. W. Moody	B. Nuthall
C. Buttsworth	C. Aussem	1931	C. Aussem	H. W. Moody
C. Buttsworth	H. W. Moody	1932	H. W. Moody	H. H. Jacobs
J. Hartigan	M. C. Scriven	1933	H. W. Moody	H. H. Jacobs
J. Hartigan	M. C. Scriven	1934	D. E. Round	H. H. Jacobs
D. E. Round	H. K. Sperling	1935	H. W. Moody	H. H. Jacobs
J. Hartigan	H. K. Sperling	1936	H. H. Jacobs	A. Marble
N. Wynne	H. K. Sperling	1937	D. E. Round	A. Lizana
D. M. Bundy	R. Mathieu	1938	H. W. Moody	A. Marble
V. Westacott	R. Mathieu	1939	A. Marble	A. Marble
N. Bolton		1940		A. Marble
		1941		E. T. Cooke
		1942		P. M. Betz
		1943		P. M. Betz
		1944		P. M. Betz
		1945		E. T. Cooke
N. Bolton	M. Osborne	1946	P. M. Betz	P. M. Betz
N. Bolton	P. C. Todd	1947	M. E. Osborne	L. Brough
N. Bolton	N. Landry	1948	L. Brough	W. D. Dupont
D. J. Hart	W. D. Dupont	1949	L. Brough	W. D. Dupont
L. Brough	D. J. Hart	1950	L. Brough	W. D. Dupont
N. Bolton	S. J. Fry	1951	D. J. Hart	M. Connolly
T. D. Long	D. J. Hart	1952	M. Connolly	M. Connolly
M. Connolly	M. Connolly	1953	M. Connolly	M. Connolly
T. D. Long	M. Connolly	1954	M. Connolly	D. J. Hart
B. Penrose	A. Mortimer	1955	L. Brough	D. J. Hart
M. Carter	A. Gibson	1956	S. J. Fry	S. J. Fry
S. J. Fry	S. J. Bloomer	1957	A. Gibson	A. Gibson
A. Mortimer	S. Kormoczy	1958	A. Gibson	A. Gibson
S. J. Reitano	C. C. Truman	1959	M. E. Bueno	M. E. Bueno
M. Smith	D. R. Hard	1960	M. E. Bueno	D. R. Hard
M. Smith	A. S. Haydon	1961	A. Mortimer	D. R. Hard
M. Smith	M. Smith	1962	J. R. Susman	M. Smith
M. Smith	L. R. Turner	1963	M. Smith	M. E. Bueno
M. Smith	M. Smith	1964	M. E. Bueno	M. E. Bueno
M. Smith	L. R. Turner	1965	M. Smith	M. Smith
M. Smith	P. F. Jones	1966	B. J. King	M. E. Bueno
N. Richey	F. Durr	1967	B. J. King	B. J. King
B. J. King	N. Richey	1968	B. J. King	S. V. Wade
M. S. Court	M. S. Court	1969	P. F. Jones	M. S. Court
M. S. Court	M. S. Court	1970	M. S. Court	M. S. Court
M. S. Court	E. Goolagong	1971	E. Goolagong	B. J. King
S. V. Wade	B. J. King	1972	B. J. King	B. J. King
M. S. Court	M. S. Court	1973	B. J. King	M. S. Court
E. Goolagong	C. Evert	1974	C. Evert	B. J. King
E. Goolagong	C. Evert	1975	B. J. King	C. Evert

Men's Doubles

Australian Championship	*Roland Garros*	*Year*	*Wimbledon*	*Forest Hills*
		1879	Erskine-Lawford	
		1880	Renshaw-Renshaw	
		1881	Renshaw-Renshaw	Clark-Taylor
		1882	Hartley-Richardson	Dwight-Sears
		1883	Grinstead-Welldon	Dwight-Sears
		1884	Renshaw-Renshaw	Dwight-Sears
		1885	Renshaw-Renshaw	Clark-Sears
		1886	Renshaw-Renshaw	Dwight-Sears
		1887	Lyon-Wilberforce	Dwight-Sears
		1888	Renshaw-Renshaw	Campbell-Hall
		1889	Renshaw-Renshaw	Slocum-Taylor
		1890	Pim-Stoker	Hall-Hobart
		1891	Baddeley-Baddeley	Campbell-Huntington
		1892	Barlow-Lewis	Campbell-Huntington
		1893	Pim-Stoker	Hobart-Hovey
		1894	Baddeley-Baddeley	Hobart-Hovey
		1895	Baddeley-Baddeley	Chace-Wren
		1896	Baddeley-Baddeley	Neel-Neel
		1897	Doherty-Doherty	Sheldon-Ware
		1898	Doherty-Doherty	Sheldon-Ware
		1899	Doherty-Doherty	Davis-Ward
		1900	Doherty-Doherty	Davis-Ward
		1901	Doherty-Doherty	Davis-Ward
		1902	Riseley-Smith	Doherty-Doherty
		1903	Doherty-Doherty	Doherty-Doherty
		1904	Doherty-Doherty	Ward-Wright
Lycett-Tachell		1905	Doherty-Doherty	Ward-Wright
Heath-Wilding		1906	Riseley-Smith	Ward-Wright
Begg-Parker		1907	Brookes-Wilding	Alexander-Hackett
Alexander-Dunlop		1908	Ritchie-Wilding	Alexander-Hackett
Keane-Parker		1909	Barrett-Gore	Alexander-Hackett
Campbell-Rice		1910	Ritchie-Wilding	Alexander-Hackett
Heath-Lycett		1911	Decugis-Gobert	Little-Touchard
Dixon-Parke		1912	Barrett-Dixon	Bundy-McLoughlin
Hedemann-Parker		1913	Barrett-Dixon	Bundy-McLoughlin
Campbell-Patterson		1914	Brookes-Wilding	Bundy-McLoughlin
Rice-Todd		1915		Griffin-Johnston
		1916		Griffin-Johnston
		1917		Alexander-Trockmorton
		1918		Richards-Tilden
P. O'Hara Wood-Thomas		1919	P. O'Hara Wood-Thomas	Brookes-Patterson
P. O'Hara Wood-Thomas		1920	Garland-Williams	Griffin-Johnston
Eaton-Gemmell		1921	Lycett-Woosnam	Richards-Tilden
Hawkes-Patterson		1922	Anderson-Lycett	Richards-Tilden
P. O'Hara Wood-St. John		1923	Godfree-Lycett	Norton-Tilden
Anderson-Brookes		1924	Hunter-Richards	Kinsey-Kinsey
P. O'Hara Wcod-Patterson	Borotra-Lacoste	1925	Borotra-Lacoste	Richards-Williams
Hawkes-Patterson	Kinsey-Richards	1926	Brugnon-Cochet	Richards-Williams
Hawkes-Patterson	Brugnon-Cochet	1927	Hunter-Tilden	Hunter-Tilden
Borotra-Brugnon	Borotra-Brugnon	1928	Brugnon-Cochet	Hennessey-Lott
Crawford-Hopman	Borotra-Lacoste	1929	Allison-Van Ryn	Doeg-Lott
Crawford-Hopman	Brugnon-Cochet	1930	Allison-Van Ryn	Doeg-Lott
Donohoe-Dunlop	Lott-Van Ryn	1931	Lott-Van Ryn	Allison-Van Ryn
Crawford-Moon	Brugnon-Cochet	1932	Borotra-Brugnon	Gledhill-Vines
Gledhill-Vines	Hughes-Perry	1933	Borotra-Brugnon	Lott-Stoefen
Hughes-Perry	Borotra-Brugnon	1934	Lott-Stoefen	Lott-Stoefen
Crawford-McGrath	Crawford-Quist	1935	Crawford-Quist	Allison-Van Ryn
Quist-Turnbull	Bernard-Borotra	1936	Hughes-Tuckey	Budge-Mako
Quist-Turnbull	Henkel-Von Cramm	1937	Budge-Mako	Henkel-Von Cramm
Bromwich-Quist	Destremau-Petra	1938	Budge-Mako	Budge-Mako
Bromwich-Quist	Harris-McNeill	1939	Cooke-Riggs	Bromwich-Quist
Bromwich-Quist		1940		Kramer-Schroeder
		1941		Kramer-Schroeder
		1942		Mulloy-Talbert
		1943		Kramer-Parker
		1944		Falkenburg-McNeill

Australian Championship	*Roland Garros*	*Year*	*Wimbledon*	*Forest Hills*
		1945		Mulloy-Talbert
Bromwich-Quist	Bernard-Petra	1946	Brown-Kramer	Mulloy-Talbert
Bromwich-Quist	Fannin-Sturgess	1947	Falkenburg-Kramer	Kramer-Schroeder
Bromwich-Quist	Bergelin-Drobny	1948	Bromwich-Sedgman	Mulloy-Talbert
Bromwich-Quist	Gonzales-Parker	1949	Gonzales-Parker	Bromwich-Sidwell
Bromwich-Quist	Talbert-Trabert	1950	Bromwich-Quist	Bromwich-Sedgman
McGregor-Sedgman	McGregor-Sedgman	1951	McGregor-Sedgman	McGregor-Sedgman
McGregor-Sedgman	McGregor-Sedgman	1952	McGregor-Sedgman	Rose-Seixas
Hoad-Rosewall	Hoad-Rosewall	1953	Hoad-Rosewall	Hartwig-Rose
Hartwig-Rose	Seixas-Trabert	1954	Hartwig-Rose	Seixas-Trabert
Seixas-Trabert	Seixas-Trabert	1955	Hartwig-Hoad	Kamo-Miyagi
Hoad-Rosewall	Candy-Perry	1956	Hoad-Rosewall	Hoad-Rosewall
Fraser-Hoad	Anderson-Cooper	1957	Mulloy-Patty	Cooper-Fraser
Cooper-Fraser	Cooper-Fraser	1958	Davidson-Schmidt	Olmedo-Richardson
Laver-Mark	Pietrangeli-Sirola	1959	Emerson-Fraser	Emerson-Fraser
Laver-Mark	Emerson-Fraser	1960	Osuna-Ralston	Emerson-Fraser
Laver-Mark	Emerson-Laver	1961	Emerson-Fraser	McKinley-Ralston
Emerson-Fraser	Emerson-Fraser	1962	Hewitt-Stolle	Osuna-Palafox
Hewitt-Stolle	Emerson-Santana	1963	Osuna-Palafox	McKinley-Ralston
Hewitt-Stolle	Emerson-Fletcher	1964	Hewitt-Stolle	McKinley-Ralston
Newcombe-Roche	Emerson-Stolle	1965	Newcomber-Roche	Emerson-Stolle
Emerson-Stolle	Graebner-Ralston	1966	Fletcher-Newcombe	Emerson-Stolle
Newcombe-Roche	Newcombe-Roche	1967	Hewitt-McMillan	Newcombe-Roche
Crealy-Stone	Rosewall-Stolle	1968	Newcombe-Roche	Lutz-Smith
Emerson-Laver	Newcombe-Roche	1969	Newcombe-Roche	Rosewall-Stolle
Lutz-Smith	Nastase-Tiriac	1970	Newcombe-Roche	Barthes-Pilic
Newcombe-Roche	Ashe-Riessen	1971	Emerson-Laver	Newcombe-Taylor
Davidson-Rosewall	Hewitt-McMillan	1972	Hewitt-McMillan	Drysdale-Taylor
Anderson-Newcombe	Newcombe-Okker	1973	Connors-Nastase	Davidson-Newcombe
Case-Masters	Crealy-Parrun	1974	Newcombe-Roche	Lutz-Smith
Alexander-Dent	Gottfried-Ramirez	1975	Gerulaitis-Mayer	Connors-Nastase

Women's Doubles

Australian Championship	*Roland Garros*	*Year*	*Wimbledon*	*Forest Hills*
		1890		Roosevelt-Roosevelt
		1891		Cahill-Fellowes Morgan
		1892		Cahill-McKinley
		1893		Butler-Terry
		1894		Atkinson-Helwig
		1895		Atkinson-Helwig
		1896		Atkinson-Moore
		1897		Atkinson-Atkinson
		1898		Atkinson-Atkinson
		1899		Craven-McAteer
		1900		Champlin-Parker
		1901		Atkinson-McAteer
		1902		Atkinson-Jones
		1903		Moore-Neely
		1904		Hall-Sutton
		1905		Homans-Neely
		1906		Coe-Platt
		1907		Neely-Weimer
		1908		Curtis-Sears
		1909		Hotchkiss-Rotch
		1910		Hotchkiss-Rotch
		1911		Hotchkiss-Sears
		1912		Browne-Green
		1913	Boothby-McNair	Browne-Williams
		1914	Morton-Ryan	Browne-Williams
		1915		Sears-Wightman
		1916		Bjurstedt-Sears
		1917		Bjurstedt-Sears
		1918		Goss-Zinderstein
		1919	Lenglen-Ryan	Goss-Zinderstein
		1920	Lenglen-Ryan	Goss-Zinderstein
		1921	Lenglen-Ryan	Browne-Williams
Boyd-Mountain		1922	Lenglen-Ryan	Jessup-Wills
Boyd-Lance		1923	Lenglen-Ryan	Covell-McKane
Akhurst-Lance		1924	Wightman-Wills	Wightman-Wills
Akhurst-Harper	Lenglen-Vlasto	1925	Lenglen-Ryan	Browne-Wills
Boyd-P. O'Hara Wood	Lenglen-Vlasto	1926	Browne-Ryan	Goss-Ryan
Bickerton-P. O'Hara Wood	Heine-Peacock	1927	Wills-Ryan	Godfree-Harvey
Akhurst-Boyd	Bennett-Watson	1928	Saunders-Watson	Wightman-Wills
Akhurst-Bickerton	Bouman-De Alvarez	1929	Michell-Watson	Michell-Watson
Hood-Molesworth	Moody-Ryan	1930	Moody-Ryan	Nuthall-Palfrey
Bickerton-Cozens	Nuthall-Whittingstall	1931	Sheperd Barron-Mudford	Nuthall-Whittingstall
Buttsworth-Crawford	Moody-Ryan	1932	Metaxa-Sigart	Jacobs-Palfrey
Molesworth-Westacott	Mathieu-Ryan	1933	Mathieu-Ryan	James-Nuthall
Molesworth-Westacott	Mathieu-Ryan	1934	Mathieu-Ryan	Jacobs-Palfrey
Dearman-Lyle	Scriven-Stammers	1935	James-Stammers	Fabyan-Jacobs
Coyne-Wynne	Mathieu-Yorke	1936	James-Stammers	Babcock-Van Ryn
Coyne-Wynne	Mathieu-Yorke	1937	Mathieu-Yorke	Fabyan-Marble
Coyne-Wynne	Mathieu-Yorke	1938	Fabyan-Marble	Fabyan-Marble
Coyne-Wynne	Mathieu-Jedrzejowska	1939	Fabyan-Marble	Fabyan-Marble
Coyne-Wynne		1940		Fabyan-Marble
		1941		Cooke-Osborne
		1942		Brough-Osborne
		1943		Brough-Osborne
		1944		Brough-Osborne
		1945		Brough-Osborne
Bevis-Fitch	Brough-Osborne	1946	Brough-Osborne	Brough-Osborne
Long-Bolton	Brough-Osborne	1947	Hart-Todd	Brough-Osborne
Long-Bolton	Hart-Todd	1948	Brough-Dupont	Brough-Dupont
Long-Bolton	Brough-Dupont	1949	Brough-Dupont	Brough-Dupont
Brough-Hart	Hart-Fry	1950	Brough-Dupont	Brough-Dupont
Long-Bolton	Hart-Fry	1951	Hart-Fry	Hart-Fry
Long-Bolton	Fry-Hart	1952	Fry-Hart	Fry-Hart
Connolly-Sampson	Fry-Hart	1953	Fry-Hart	Fry-Hart
Hawton-Penrose	Connolly-Hopman	1954	Brough-Dupont	Fry-Hart
Hawton-Penrose	Fleitz-Hard	1955	Mortimer-Shilcock	Brough-Dupont
Hawton-Long	Buxton-Gibson	1956	Buxton-Gibson	Brough-Dupont
Fry-Gibson	Bloomer-Hard	1957	Gibson-Hard	Brough-Dupont
Hawton-Long	Ramirez-Reyes	1958	Bueno-Gibson	Arth-Hard
Reynolds-Schuurman	Reynolds-Schuurman	1959	Arth-Hard	Arth-Hard
Bueno-Truman	Bueno-Hard	1960	Bueno-Hard	Bueno-Hard
Reitano-Smith	Reynolds-Schuurman	1961	Hantze-Moffitt	Hard-Turner
Ebbern-Smith	Reynolds-Schuurman	1962	Moffitt-Susman	Bueno-Hard
Ebbern-Smith	Jones-Schuurman	1963	Bueno-Hard	Ebbern-Smith
Tegart-Turner	Smith-Turner	1964	Smith-Turner	Moffitt-Susman
Smith-Turner	Smith-Turner	1965	Bueno-Moffitt	Graebner-Richey
Graebner-Richey	Smith-Tegart	1966	Bueno-Richey	Bueno-Richey
Tegart-Turner	Durr-Sherriff	1967	Casals-King	Casals-King
Krantzcke-Melville	Durr-Jones	1968	Casals-King	Bueno-Court
Court-Tegart	Durr-Jones	1969	Court-Tegart	Durr-Hard
Court-Dalton	Durr-Chanfreau	1970	Casals-King	Dalton-Court
Court-Goolagong	Durr-Chanfreau	1971	Casals-King	Dalton-Casals
Gourlay-Harris	King-Stove	1972	King-Stove	Durr-Stove
Court-Wade	Court-Wade	1973	Casals-King	Court-Wade
Goolagong-Michel	Evert-Morozova	1974	Goolagong-Michel	King-Casals
Goolagong-Michel	Evert-Navratilova	1975	Sawamatsu-Kiyomura	Court-Wade

Mixed Doubles

Australian Championship	Roland Garros	Year	Wimbledon	Forest Hills
		1892		Cahill-Hobart
		1893		Roosevelt-Hobart
		1894		Atkinson-Fischer
		1895		Atkinson-Fischer
		1896		Atkinson-Fischer
		1897		Henson-Magruder
		1898		Neely-Fischer
		1899		Rastall-Hoskins
		1900		Codman
		1901		Jones-Little
		1902		Moore-Grant
		1903		Chapman-Allen
		1904		Moore-Grant
		1905		Hobart-Hobart
		1906		Coffin-Dewhurst
		1907		Sayres-Johnson
		1908		Rotch-Niles
		1909		Hotchkiss-Johnson
		1910		Hotchkiss-Carpenter
		1911		Hotchkiss-Johnson
		1912		Browne-Williams
		1913	Tuckey-Crisp	Browne-Tilden
		1914	Larcombe-Parke	Browne-Tilden
		1915		Wightman-Johnson
		1916		Sears-Davis
		1917		Bjurstedt-Wright
		1918		Wightman-Wright
		1919	Ryan-Lycett	Zinderstein-Richards
		1920	Lenglen-Patterson	Wightman-Johnson
		1921	Ryan-Lycett	Browne-Johnston
Boyd-Hawkes		1922	Lenglen-P. O'Hara Wood	Mallory-Tilden
Lance-Rice		1923	Ryan-Lycett	Mallory-Tilden
Akhurst-Willard		1924	McKane-Gilbert	Wills-Richards
Akhurst-Willard	Lenglen-Brugnon	1925	Lenglen-Borotra	McKane-Hawkes
Boyd-Hawkes	Lenglen-Brugnon	1926	Godfree-Godfree	Ryan-Borotra
Boyd-Hawkes	Bordes-Borotra	1927	Ryan-Hunter	Bennett-Cochet
Akhurst-Borotra	Bennett-Cochet	1928	Ryan-Spence	Wills-Hawkes
Akhurst-Moon	Bennett-Cochet	1929	Wills-Hunter	Nuthall-Lott
Hall-Hopman	Aussem-Tilden	1930	Ryan-Crawford	Cross-Allison
Crawford-Crawford	Nuthall-Spence	1931	Harper-Lott	Nuthall-Lott
Crawford-Crawford	Nuthall-Perry	1932	Ryan-Maier	Palfrey-Perry
Crawford-Crawford	Scriven-Crawford	1933	Krahwinkel-Von Cramm	Ryan-Vines
Hartigan-Moon	Rosambert-Borotra	1934	Round-Miki	Jacobs-Lott
Bickerton-Boussus	Payot-Bernard	1935	Round-Perry	Fabyan-Maier
Hopman-Hopman	Yorke-Bernard	1936	Round-Perry	Marble-Mako
Hopman-Hopman	Mathieu-Petra	1937	Marble-Budge	Fabyan-Budge
Wilson-Bromwich	Mathieu-Mitic	1938	Marble-Budge	Marble-Budge
Hopman-Hopman	Fabyan-Cooke	1939	Marble-Riggs	Marble-Hopman
Wynne-Long		1940		Marble-Riggs
		1941		Cooke-Kramer
		1942		Brough-Schroeder
		1943		Osborne-Talbert
		1944		Osborne-Talbert
		1945		Osborne-Talbert
Bolton-Long	Betz-Patty	1946	Brough-Brown	Osborne-Talbert
Bolton-Long	Summers-Sturgess	1947	Brough-Bromwich	Brough-Bromwich
Bolton-Long	Todd-Drobny	1948	Brough-Bromwich	Brough-Brown
Hart-Sedgman	Summers-Sturgess	1949	Summers-Sturgess	Brough-Sturgess
Hart-Sedgman	Scofield-Morea	1950	Brough-Sturgess	Dupont-McGregor
Long-Worthington	Hart-Sedgman	1951	Hart-Sedgman	Hart-Sedgman
Long-Worthington	Hart-Sedgman	1952	Hart-Sedgman	Hart-Sedgman
Sampson-Hartwig	Hart-Seixas	1953	Hart-Seixas	Hart-Seixas
Long-Hartwig	Connolly-Hoad	1954	Hart-Seixas	Hart-Seixas
Long-Worthington	Hard-Forbes	1955	Hart-Seixas	Hart-Seixas
Penrose-Fraser	Long-Ayala	1956	Fry-Seixas	Dupont-Rosewall
Muller-Anderson	Puzejova-Javorsky	1957	Hard-Rose	Gibson-Nielsen
Hawton-Howe	Bloomer-Pietrangeli	1958	Coghlan-Howe	Dupont-Fraser
Reynolds-Mark	Ramirez-Knight	1959	Hard-Laver	Dupont-Fraser
Lehane-Fancutt	Bueno-Howe	1960	Hard-Laver	Dupont-Fraser
Lehane-Hewitt	Hard-Laver	1961	Turner-Stolle	Smith-Mark
Turner-Stolle	Schuurman-Howe	1962	Dupont-Fraser	Smith-Stolle
Smith-Fletcher	Smith-Fletcher	1963	Smith-Fletcher	Smith-Fletcher
Smith-Fletcher	Smith-Fletcher	1964	Turner-Stolle	Smith-Newcombe
Smith-Newcombe	Smith-Fletcher	1965	Smith-Fletcher	Smith-Stolle
Tegart-Roche	Van Zyl-McMillan	1966	Smith-Fletcher	Fales-Davidson
Turner-Davidson	King-Davidson	1967	King-Davidson	King-Davidson
King-Crealy	Durr-Barclay	1968	Court-Fletcher	Ejsel-Curtis
	Court-Riessen	1969	Jones-Stolle	Court-Riessen
	King-Hewitt	1970	Casals-Nastase	Court-Riessen
	Durr-Barclay	1971	King-Davidson	King-Davidson
	Goolagong-Warwick	1972	Casals-Nastase	Court-Riessen
	Durr-Barclay	1973	King-Davidson	King-Davidson
	Navratilova-Molina	1974	King-Davidson	Teeguarden-Masters
	Bonicelli-Koch	1975	Court-Riessen	Casals-Stockton

Davis Cup

Year	Location	Winner	Loser	Results
1900	Boston	United States	British Isles	3-0
1902	New York	United States	British Isles	3-2
1903*	Boston	British Isles	United States	4-1
1904	Wimbledon	British Isles	Belgium	5-0
1905	Wimbledon	British Isles	United States	5-0
1906	Wimbledon	British Isles	United States	5-0
1907*	Wimbledon	Australasia	British Isles	3-2
1908	Melbourne	Australasia	United States	3-2
1909	Sydney	Australasia	United States	5-0
1911	Christchurch, New Zealand	Australasia	United States	5-0
1912*	Melbourne	British Isles	Australasia	3-2
1913*	Wimbledon	United States	British Isles	3-2
1914*	New York	Australasia	United States	3-2
1915-1918	Not played			
1919	Sydney	Australasia	British Isles	4-1
1920*	Auckland, New Zealand	United States	Australasia	5-0
1921	New York	United States	Japan	5-0
1922	New York	United States	Australasia	4-1
1923	New York	United States	Australasia	4-1
1924	Philadelphia	United States	Australia	5-0
1925	Philadelphia	United States	France	5-0
1926	Philadelphia	United States	France	4-1
1927*	Philadelphia	France	United States	3-2
1928	Paris	France	United States	4-1
1929	Paris	France	United States	4-1
1930	Paris	France	United States	3-2
1931	Paris	France	Great Britain	3-2
1932	Paris	France	United States	3-2
1933*	Paris	Great Britain	France	3-2
1934	Wimbledon	Great Britain	United States	4-1
1935	Wimbledon	Great Britain	United States	5-0
1936	Wimbledon	Great Britain	Australia	3-2
1937*	Wimbledon	United States	Great Britain	4-1
1938	Philadelphia	United States	Australia	3-2
1939*	Philadelphia	Australia	United States	3-2
1940-1945	Not played			
1946*	Melbourne	United States	Australia	5-0
1947	New York	United States	Australia	4-1
1948	New York	United States	Australia	5-0
1949	New York	United States	Australia	4-1
1950*	New York	Australia	United States	4-1
1951	Sydney	Australia	United States	3-2
1952	Adelaide	Australia	United States	4-1
1953	Melbourne	Australia	United States	3-2
1954*	Sydney	United States	Australia	3-2
1955*	Adelaide	Australia	United States	5-0
1956	New York	Australia	United States	5-0
1957	Melbourne	Australia	United States	3-2
1958*	Brisbane	United States	Australia	3-2
1959*	New York	Australia	United States	3-2
1960	Sydney	Australia	Italy	4-1
1961	Melbourne	Australia	Italy	5-0
1962	Brisbane	Australia	Mexico	5-0
1963*	Adelaide	United States	Australia	3-2
1964	Cleveland, Ohio	Australia	United States	3-2
1965	Sydney	Australia	Spain	4-1
1966	Melbourne	Australia	India	4-1
1967	Brisbane	Australia	Spain	4-1
1968*	Adelaide	United States	Australia	4-1
1969	Cleveland, Ohio	United States	Romania	5-0
1970	Cleveland, Ohio	United States	West Germany	3-2
1971	Charlotte, N. C.	United States	Romania	3-2
1972	Bucharest	United States	Romania	3-2
1973	Cleveland, Ohio	Australia	United States	5-0
1974	—	South Africa	India	default

*Cup changed hands

First round

Player	Player	Match	Winner
William Tilden United States	Vincent Richards United States	FH - 25 SF	**Tilden 68 64 64 61**
Gerald Patterson Australia	James O. Anderson Australia	W - 22 SF	Patterson 61 36 79 61 63
Jean Borotra France	George Loft United States	Davis 30	Borotra 57 63 26 62 86
Wilmer Allison United States	Gene Mako United States	FH - 35 4° round	Allison 62 60 75
Laurie Doherty Great Britain	Arthur W. Gore Great Britain	W - 1900 SF	A. W. Gore 46 86 86 61
Anthony Wilding New Zealand	Cecil Parke Great Britain	W - 10 SF	Wilding 75 61 62
Norman Brookes Australia	Beals Wright United States	Davis 1911	Brookes 64 26 63 63
Maurice McLoughlin United States	William Clothier United States	FH - 12 SF	McLoughlin 86 62 36 64
Henry Cochet France	Giorgio De Stefani Italy	RG - 33 F	**Cochet 60 64 46 63**
William Johnston United States	John Hawkes Australia	Davis 23	Johnston 60 62 61
René Lacoste France	Norris Williams United States	FH - 26 QF	Lacoste 60 63 86
Colin Gregory Great Britain	Hubert De Morpurgo Italy	Davis 28	De Morpurgo 60 61 62
Donald Budge United States	Harry Hopman Australia	FH - 38 QF	**Budge 63 61 63**
Fred Perry Great Britain	Frank Shields United States	Davis 34	Perry 64 46 62 15 13
Jack Crawford United States	Sidney Wood United States	FH 28 1° round	Crawford 97 79 12 10 64
Ellsworth Vines United States	Bunny Austin Great Britain	W - 32 F	Vines 64 62 60
Adrian Quist Australia	Frank Parker United States	Davis 39	Parker 63 64 16 75
Eric Sturgess South Africa	Ted Schroeder United States	W - 49 SF	Schroeder 36 75 57 61 62
Ken McGregor Australia	Frank Sedgman Australia	Aus. - 50 F	Sedgman 63 64 46 61
Arthur Ashe United States	**Pancho Gonzales United States**	Las Vegas - 69 F	**Gonzales 60 62 64**
Bobby Riggs United States	Gottfried Von Cramm Germany	FH - 37 SF	Von Cramm 06 86 68 63 62
Budge Patty United States	Jaroslav Drobny Czechoslovakia	W - 53 3° round	Drobny 86 16 18 36 86 12 10
John Bromwich Australia	Bob Falkenburg United States	W - 48 F	Falkenburg 75 06 62 36 75
Don McNeill United States	**Jack Kramer United States**	FH - 46 QF	**Kramer 63 62 16 62**
Sven Davidson Sweden	Tony Trabert United States	RG - 55 F	Trabert 64 75 61
Ashley Cooper Australia	Lewis Hoad Australia	W - 57 F	Hoad 62 61 62
Mervyn Rose Australia	Vic Seixas United States	W - 53 SF	Seixas 64 10 12 9 11 64 63
Roy Emerson Australia	**Ken Rosewall Australia**	Aus. - 71 QF	**Rosewall 64 64 63**
Ilie Nastase Romania	Stanley Smith United States	W - 72 F	Smith 46 63 63 46 75
Jan Kodes Czechoslovakia	John Newcombe Australia	FH - 73 F	Newcombe 64 16 46 62 63
Neale Fraser Australia	Nicola Pietrangeli Italy	Davis 60	Pietrangeli 11 9 63 16 62
Manolo Santana Spain	**Rod Laver Australia**	W - 62 QF	**Laver 14 16 97 62 62**

Second round

Match	Winner
W - 20 F	**Tilden 26 63 62 64**
Davis 32	Borotra 16 36 64 62 75
W - 12 F	Wilding 64 64 46 64
Davis 1911	Brookes 86 62 36 64
Davis 27	**Cochet 64 46 62 64**
Davis 27	Lacoste 26 60 62 06 61
FH - 36 F	Perry 26 62 86 16 10 8
W - 33 F	Crawford 46 11 9 62 26 64
FH - 42 F	Schroeder 86 75 36 46 62
Davis 49	**Gonzales 86 64 97**
Hmb - 50 F	Drobny 63 64 64
FH - 46 SF	**Kramer 60 64 64**
Davis 55	Hoad 46 63 63 86
Davis 53	**Rosewall 62 26 63 64**
W - 71 F	Newcombe 63 57 26 64 64
W - 60 SF	**Laver 46 63 8 10 62 64**

Third round

Match	Winner
Davis 25	**Tilden 46 60 26 97 64**
W - 14 F	Brookes 64 64 75
RG 28 F	**Cochet 57 63 61 63**
W - 34 F	Perry 63 60 75
FH - 49 F	**Gonzales 16 18 26 61 62 64**
FH - 47 SF	**Kramer 36 63 60 61**
FH - 56 F	**Rosewall 46 62 63 63**
W - 69 F	**Laver 64 63 64**

Fourth round

Match	Winner
Davis 1920	**Tilden 108 64 16 64**
Davis 31	**Cochet 64 16 97 63**
Phil. - 50 F	**Gonzales 75 63 64**
RG - 69 F	**Laver 64 57 64 64**

Semifinals

Match	Winner
Davis 27	**Tilden 64 26 62 86**
MSG 67 F	**Laver 75 14 16 75 62**

Final match not played

Aus. = Australian Championship
Davis = Davis Cup
FH = Forest Hills
Hmb. = Hamburg
MSG = Madison Square Garden
Phil. = Philadelphia
RG = Roland Garros
W = Wimbledon
WC = Wightman Cup
QF = Quarterfinals
SF = Semifinals
F = Finals
1° = 1st round
3° = 3rd round
4° = 4th round

Suzanne Lenglen France
W - 23 F
Kitty McKane Great Britain
Lenglen 62 62

Dorothea Lambert Chambers Great Britain
W - 14 F
Ethel Larcombe Great Britain
Lambert Chambers 75 64

W - 19 F
Lenglen 10 8 46 97

Molla Mallory Norway
FH - 26 F
Elisabeth Ryan United States
Mallory 46 64 97

Mary Browne United States
FH - 12 F
E. Sears United States
Browne 64 62

FH - 21 F
Mallory 46 64 62

W - 22 F
Lenglen 62 60

Helen Wills Moody United States
W - 27 F
Lilly De Alvarez Spain
Wills 62 63

Joan Hartigan Australia
Aus. - 34 F
B. H. Molesworth Australia
Hartigan 61 64

W - 35 SF
Wills 63 63

Dorothy Round Great Britain
W - 36 1° round
Betty Nuthall Great Britain
Round 97 63

Simone Mathieu France
RG - 38 F
N. Landry France
Mathieu 60 63

W - 34 SF
Round 64 57 62

W - 33 F
Wills 64 68 63

Helen Jacobs United States
W - 36 F
Hilda Sperling Germany
Jacobs 62 46 75

Alice Marble United States
WC - 37
Mary Hardwick Great Britain
Marble 46 62 64

W - 38 SF
Jacobs 64 64

Sarah Palfrey United States
W - 34 4° round
Jedrzejowska Poland
Palfrey 62 62

Margaret Scriven Great Britain
W - 37 4° round
Kay Stammers Menzies
Scriven

WC - 33
Palfrey 63 61

FH - 34 F
Jacobs 61 64

Wills 63 36 75

Cannes 1926
Lenglen 63 86

Final match not played

Pauline Betz United States
FH - 43 F
Nancye Bolton Australia
Betz 60 63

Margaret Dupont United States
WC - 48
Betty Hilton Harrison Great Britain
Dupont 75 62

RG - 46 F
Dupont 16 86 75

Shirley Bloomer Great Britain
RG - 57 F
Dorothy Knade Head United States
Bloomer 61 63

Jean Bostock Micoll Great Britain
WC - 48
Louise Brough United States
Brough 62 46 75

WC - 55
Brough 62 64

FH - 60 F
Brough 108 16 108

Christine Truman Great Britain
WC - 58
Althea Gibson United States
Truman 26 63 64

Ann Jones Great Britain
FH - 61 F
Doris Hard United States
Hard 63 64

WC - 62
Hard 62 62

Margaret Court Australia
Aus. - 71 F
Evonne Goolagong Australia
Court 26 76 75

Maria Bueno Brazil
W - 65 SF
Billie Jean King United States
Bueno 64 57 63

W - 64 F
Bueno 64 79 63

FH - 60 F
Hard 64 10 12 64

W - 55 SF
Brough 63 86

Susan Partridge Great Britain
WC - 52
Shirley Fry United States
Fry 60 86

Pat Todd United States
RG - 50 F
Doris Hart United States
Hart 64 46 62

W - 51 F
Hart 61 60

Sandra Reynolds South Africa
W - 61 SF
Angela Mortimer Great Britain
Mortimer 11 9 63

Jean Walker Smith Great Britain
WC - 52
Maureen Connolly United States
Connolly 36 61 75

WC - 53
Connolly 61 61

W - 53 F
Connolly 86 75

W - 52 F
Connolly 75 63

These tables show the competitions (both men's and women's) regularly played in a "world's series" of tennis. The finals never took place, due to the fact that the older greats are no longer with us.

Bibliography

Part One

Plautus, T. M., *Curculio* (193-189 B.C.).
—, *Prisoners.*
Horace, Q., *Satires* (35-30 B.C.).
Propertius, *Elegies* (30-16 B.C.).
Ovid, P., *Ars amatoria* (1 B.C.).
Seneca, L. A., *On Benefits* (ca. A.D. 40).
Petronius, T., *Satyricon* (A.D. 1 cen.).
Martial, *Epigrams* (ca. A.D. 102).
Pliny the Younger, *Letters* (ca. A.D. 62-113).
Plutarch, *Life of Alexander* (A.D. 110-115).
Pollux, J., *Onomasticon* (A.D. 166-176).
Galen, *Letter to Epigenes* (ca. A.D. 180).
Athenaeus, *The Deipnosophists* (A.D. 2-3 cen.).
Sidonius Appollinaris, *The Letters of Sidonius* (A.D. 461).
Saint Isidore of Seville, *Etimologiae* (A.D. 633).
Messaoudi, *Prairies d'Or* (ca. 930).
Avicenna, *Canon medicinae* (ca. 1000).
Comnena, A., *The Alexiad of the Princess Anna Comnena* (1118).
Cinammus, J., *De rebus gestis* (1160).
Anonymous, *Libro de Apollonio (The Book of Apollonius)* (1230-1250).
Joinville, J. de, *The History of St. Louis* (1250).
Alfonso the Wise, *El fuero real de España* (1255).
—, *Cantigas de Santa Maria* (1255).
Geoffroi de Paris, *Chronique rimée* (1316).
Velluti, D., *Cronica di Firenze dall'anno 1300 c. fino al 1370* (1324).
Petrarch, F., *De remediis utriusque fortunae* (1354-1356).
Chaucer, G., The *Book of Troilus and Criseyde* (1373-1385).
Gower, J., *Balads and Other Poems* (1400).
Otterbourne, T., *Liber de vita et miraculis Henrici VI ti* (1415).
Charles, Duke of Orléans, *J'ai tant joué avecques Aage e la paulme* (1439).
Anonymous, *Secunda pastorum* (1450).
Lydgate, J., *Harleian Ms 656* (15 cen.).
Van den Berghe, Jan, *Kaetspel ghemoralizeert* (1477).
Vives, J. L., *Scenes of School and College Life in Latin Dialogues* (1492-1550).
Erasmus, D., *The Colloquies of Desiderius Erasmus* (1518).
Castiglione, B., *The Book of the Courtier* (1528).
Rabelais, F., *Gargantua and Pantagruel* (1534-1552).
Frissart, R., *Carmen de ludo pilae reticulo* (1541).
Cellini, B., *Autobiography* (1545-1569).
Hall, W. E., *Chronicle* (1548-1550).
Scaino, A., *Trattato del gioco della Palla* (1555).
Perlin, E., *Description des Royaulmes d' Angleterre et d'Escosse* (1558).
Anguillara, G. A. dell', *P. Ovidii Nasonis metamorphoseon libri XV* (1561).
Sambucus, J., *Emblemata* (1564).
Mercurialis, H., *De arte gymnastica* (1573).
Holinshed, R., *The Chronicles of Englande, Scotlande, and Irelande* (1573-1578).
Gosselin, J., *Declaration de deux doubtes qui se trouvent en comptant le Jeu de la Paume* (1579).
Brantôme, P. de Bourdeille de, *Mémoires* (1584).
Montaigne, M. de, *Essays* (1588).
Shakespeare, W., *Henry V* (1596).
—, *Much Ado About Nothing* (1598).
Pasquier, E., *Les Recherches de la France* (1596).
Bon, F. A., *Relazione di Spagna* (1602).
Giacomo, I., *Basilicon Doron* (1603).
Minsheu, J., Ἡγεμῶν εἰς τὰς γλῶσσας *Ductor in Linguas, The Guide into the Tongues* (1617).
Chiabrera, G., *Ode a Cintio Venanzi* (1619).
Galileo, G., *Dialogo dei massimi sistemi* (1624).
Hulpeau, C., *Le Jeu royal de la Paume* (1632).
Comenius, J. A., *Orbis sensualium pictus* (1664).
Courtils de Sandras, G. de, *Mémoires de Monsieur le Marquis de Montbrun* (1713).
Bernoulli, J., *De ludo pilae reticularis* (1713).
Quadrio, F. S., *Lettera intorno alla sferistica* (1751).
Rousseau, J.-J., *Emile* (1762).
Garsault, F. A., *Art du Paumier Raquetier* (1767).
Carli, G. R., *Le lettere americane* (1781).
Manivieux, M., *Traité sur la connaissance du royal jeu de Paume* (1783).
Santillana, I. L., *Carta critica sobre las noticias y modo de jugar a la pelota* (1786).
Chénier, A. M., *Le jeu de Paume* (1791).
Strutt, J., *The Sports and Pastimes of the People of England* (1801).
Leopardi, G., *A Carlo Didimi (Dialogo di Ercole e Atlante)* (1821).
Lukin, R., *A Treatise on Tennis* (1822).
Goethe, J. W. von, *Goethe's Travels in Italy* (1828).
Dickens, C., *The Pickwick Papers* (1836).
Dumas, A., *Three Musketeers* (1844).
Premoli, P., *Cenni sulla sferistica* (1857).
Rador y Delgado, *Historia de la Villa y Corte de Madrid* (1860-1884).
Becq de Fouquières, *Les Jeux des Anciens* (1873).
Travers, S. S., *A Treatise on Tennis* (1875).
Marshall, J., *Annals of Tennis* (1878).
Cochard, Abbé T., *Le Jeu de paume á Orléans* (1888).
Nanteuil, E. de, Saint-Clair, G. de, Delahaye, *La paume et le lawn-tennis* (1898).
Jusserand, J.-J., *Les Sports et jeux d'exercises dans l'ancienne France* (1901).
Allemagne, H. R. d', *Sports et jeux d' adresse* (1903).
Noel, E. B. and Clark, J. O. M., *A History of Tennis* (1924).
Antiquarius, "The Field" (November 1927).
Whitman, M. D., *Tennis Origins and Mysteries* (1932).
Paoli, U. E., *Vita romana.*
Huizinga, J., *Homo ludens* (1938).
Carcopino, J., *La vie quotidienne à Rome* (1939).
Trevelyan, G. M., *English Social History* (1942).
Santoro, C., *Giuochi e Passatempi nei secoli passati* (1957).
Bouet, M., *Signification du sport* (1968).
Piernavieja, M., *Deporte 2000, dic.* (1970).
Kalma, I. J., *Kaatsen in Friesland* (1972).
Mussi Giannuzzi Manzo, *100 anni di pallone elastico.*
Trulok, J., *Pelota valenciana* (1973).

Part Two

Wingfield, W. C., *Sphairistiké, or Lawn Tennis* (1873).
—, *Letters patent N. 685* (1874).
Marylebone Cricket Club, *Laws of Lawn Tennis, revised by the M.C.C.* (1875).
Jones, H., (Cavendish), *The Game of Lawn Tennis* (1876).
Marshall, J., *Lawn Tennis* (1878).
Crawley, R., *Lawn Tennis* (1879).
Punch's Pocket Book (1880).
Dodgson, C. L., *Lawn Tennis Tournaments. The True Method of Assigning Prizes* (1883).
Marshall, J., *Tennis Cuts and Quips* (1884).
Dwight, J., *Lawn Tennis* (1886).
Heathcote, J. M. and C. G., Bouverie, and Ainger, *Tennis, Lawn Tennis, Rackets, Fives* (1890).
Guillaume, A., *Le Tennis à travers les ages* (1890).
Slocum, H. H., *Lawn Tennis in Our Own Country* (1890).
Heredia, J. M., *Les Trophées* (1893).
Baddeley, W., *Lawn Tennis* (1895).
Wilberforce, H. W. W., *Lawn Tennis* (1895).
Foster, F. W., *A Bibliography of Lawn Tennis (1874-1897)* (1897).
Myers, A. W., ed., *Lawn Tennis at Home and Abroad* (1903).
Paret, J. P., *How to Play Lawn Tennis* (1903).
Doherty, R. F. and H. L., *On Lawn Tennis* (1903).
Vaile, P. A., *Modern Lawn Tennis* (1904).
Paret, J. P., *Lawn Tennis, Its Past, Present, and Future* (1904).
Beldam, G. W. and Vaile, P. A., *Great Lawn Tennis Players, Their Methods Illustrated* (1905).
Myers, A. W., *The Complete Lawn Tennis Player* (1908).
St. Clair, G. de, *Lawn Tennis* (1909).
Lambert-Chambers, D. K., *Lawn Tennis for Ladies* (1910).
Allard, R., *Poésies légères* (1911).
Wilding, A. F., *On the Court and Off* (1912).
Myers, A. W., *The Story of the Davis Cup* (1913).
Décugis, M., *Manual de Tennis* (1914).
Lichtenberger, A., *Le Tennis* (1914).
Bonacossa, A., and Lambertenghi, G. P., *Il Tennis* (1914).
McLoughlin, M. E., *Tennis As I Play It* (1915).
Paret, J. P., *Methods and Players of Modern Lawn Tennis* (1915).
Myers, A. W., *Captain Anthony Wilding* (1916).

Part Three

Crawley, A. E., *Lawn Tennis* (1919).
Tilden, W. T., *The Art of Lawn Tennis* (1920).
Lenglen, S., *Le Tennis* (1920).
Gobert, A., *Le Tennis* (1921).
Myers, A. W., *Twenty Years of Lawn Tennis* (1921).
Tilden, W. T., *It's All in the Game* (1922).
—, *Singles and Doubles* (1923).
Crawley, A. E., *The Technique of Lawn Tennis Demonstrated by Cinematography* (1923).
Hillyard, G. W., *Forty Years of First-Class Lawn Tennis* (1924).
Tilden, W. T., *The Phantom Drive and Other Tennis Stories* (1924).
—, *Match Play and the Spin of the Ball* (1925).
Lichtenberger, A. and Micard, *Leur 400 Coups* (1925).
Myers, A. W., *Fifty Years of Wimbledon* (1926).
Anet, C., *Suzanne Lenglen* (1927).

Merrihew, S. W., *The Quest of the Davis Cup* (1928).
Lacoste, J. R., *Le Tennis* (1928).
—, *Lacoste on Tennis* (1928).
Brugnon, *Le Tour du monde en jouant au tennis* (1928).
Tunis, J. R., *American Girl* (1930).
Albarran, P. and Saillard, R., *Le Tennis* (1930).
Austin, H. W., *Lawn Tennis Bits and Pieces* (1930).
Torquet, C., *Championne de Tennis* (1930).
Redelsperger, N., *Le Tennis* (1930).
USLTA, *50 Years of Tennis in the U.S.* (1931).
Myers, A. W., *Memory's Parade* (1932).
Topping, T., *Coupe Davis, 1900-1932* (1933).
Perry, F. J., *Perry on Tennis* (1936).
Hawk, P. B., *Off the Racket* (1937).
Wills, H., *Fifteen-Thirty* (1937).
Budge, J. D., *Budge on Tennis* (1939).

Part Four

Hughes, G. P., *Improving Your Tennis* (1947).
Marble, A., *The Road to Wimbledon* (1947).
Gordon Cleather, N., *Wimbledon Story* (1947).
Jacobs, H., *Gallery of Champions* (1949).
Riggs, B., *Tennis Is My Racket* (1949).
Ollif, J., *Romance of Wimbledon* (1949).
Kramer, J., *How to Win at Tennis* (1949).
Gentien, C., *Les aventures d'un joueur de tennis* (1953).
Samazehuil, J., *Champion et voyages* (1953).
Smyth, J. G., *Lawn Tennis* (1953).
Cutler, N., *Inside Tennis* (1954).
Prouteau, G., *Balle de match* (1954).
Drobny, J., *Champion in Exile* (1955).
Sedgman, F., *Winning Tennis* (1955).
Talbert, W. F. and Old, B. S., *The Game of Doubles in Tennis* (1956).
Hopman, H., *Aces and Places* (1957).
Connolly, M., *Forehand Drive* (1957).
Mottram, T., *Modern Lawn Tennis* (1957).
Hoad, L., *My Game* (1958).
Brady, M., *The Encyclopaedia of Lawn Tennis* (1958).
Gonzales, P., *Man with a Racket* (1959).
Gibson, A., *I Always Wanted to Be Somebody* (1959).
Mulloy, G., *The Will to Win* (1959).
Albarran, P. and Cochet, H., *Histoire du Tennis* (1959).
Talbert, W. F. and Old, B. S., *The Game of Singles in Tennis* (1962).
Fraser, N., *Power Tennis* (1962).
Mortimer, A., *My Waiting Game* (1962).
Wilder, R., *Friend of Tennis* (1962).
Davies, M., *Tennis Rebel* (1962).
Potter, E., *Kings of the Court* (1963).
Tinling, T., *White Ladies* (1963).
Pollard, J., *Lawn Tennis Australian Way* (1963).
Lalanne, D., *Le Tennis* (1963).
The Professionals (1964).
Wilson, B., *My Side of the Net* (1964).
Talbert, B., *Tennis Observed* (1965).
Smith Court, M., *The Margaret Smith Story* (1965).
Macaulay, A. D. C. and Smyth, J., *Behind the Scenes at Wimbledon* (1965).
De Laborderie, R., *Histoires de Tennis* (1966).
Metzler, P., *Tennis Style and Stylists* (1969).
McPhee, J., *Levels of the Game* (1969).
Austin, H. W. and Konstam, P., *A Mixed Double* (1969).
Budge, D., *A Tennis Memoir* (1969).
Potter, E., *The Davis Cup* (1969).
Davidson, O. and Jones, C. M., *Lawn Tennis: The Great Ones* (1970).
Petra, Y., *Bon pour le service* (1970).
Talbert, W. F. and Old, B. S., *Stroke Production in the Game of Tennis* (1971)
Davidson, O. and Jones, C. M., *Great Women Tennis Players* (1971).
Laver, R. G. and Collins, B., *The Education of a Tennis Player* (1971).
Jones, J., *Match Winning Tennis* (1971).
Bellamy, R., *The Tennis Set* (1972).
Grimsley, W. and Heldman, J. D., *Tennis: Its History, People, and Events; Styles of the Greats* (1971).
Revie, A., *Wonderful Wimbledon* (1972).
McPhee, J., *Wimbledon* (1972).
USLTA *Encyclopaedia* (1972).
Danzig, A. and Schwed, P., *The Fireside Book of Tennis* (1972).
Tingay, L., *History of Lawn Tennis in Pictures* (1973).
Scott, E., *Tennis Game of Motion* (1973).
Riessen, M. and Evans, R., *Match Point: A Candid View of Life on the International Tennis Circuit* (1973).
Clerici, G., *I gesti bianchi* (1974).
Bassani, G., *Epitaffio* (1974).

Index

Roman numbers indicate references in the text.
Italicized numbers indicate references in captions.

The publishers gratefully acknowledge the use of photographs for chapters 24 and 39 from the following sources: Mrs Henry Billington; Camera Press Ltd; The Guardian; Keystone Press Agency Ltd; London News Service; Popperfoto; Slazengers Ltd; Sport and General Press Agency and Tennis World magazine.

The photograph on the front jacket, of Jimmy Connors at Wimbledon (1975), is by courtesy of Gerry Cranham. Tennis World magazine supplied the back jacket photographs of: Margaret Court, Billie Jean King, Suzanne Lenglen, Fred Perry and Ken Rosewall.

Chronological Table

500 B.C.	Bas-reliefs on the Wall of Themistocles.
340-330 B.C.	Monument for Alexander's trainer, Aristonicos.
Ca. 193 B.C.	Plautus, *Curculio*, servers and returners.
Ca. 1 B.C.	Ovid, *Ars Amatoria*, the racket is mentioned.
Ca. A.D. 102	Martial's *Epigrams*.
Ca. A.D. 180	Galen, *Letter to Epigenes*.
2nd Century	Frescoes on the Via Portuense.
A.D. 461	Sidonius Apollinaris, *Letters to Euripius*.
633	Saint Isidore of Seville, *Etymologiae*.
809	Harun al-Rashid plays Ciogan.
Ca. 1000	Avicenna's canons of medicine.
1230-1250	*Libro de Apollonio* (Book of Apollonius).
1255	Alfonso the Wise.
1292	Philip the Fair. Edict against *paume*. Twelve tennis courts on the Parisian tax rolls.
Ca. 14th Century	Miniature of the history of Lancelot.
1316	King Louis the Quarrelsome dies playing tennis at Vincennes.
1325	Donato Velluti cites the word "tenes."
1373	Chaucer cites the word "racket."
1427	Margot, the first woman champion of the game.
1439	Charles of Orléans, first poem about tennis.
1470	Galeazzo Maria Sforza beats Lodovico Moro.
1477	The Flemish *Game of Chases*.
1505	Philip of Austria gives a handicap of fifteen to the Marquis of Dorset.
1522	Henry VIII and Charles V together in doubles play.
1552	Charles IX holds a racket at the age of two.
Ca. 1540	Lucas Gassel, painter of *David and Bathsheba*.
1555	Scaino, *Trattato del Gioco della Palla*.
1573	Mercurialis, *De Arte Gymnastica*.
1579	Gosselin, *Déclaration de deux doutes*.
1600	Caravaggio kills Ranuccio Tommasoni.
1612	Contract issued to Pierre Gentil, tennis master of Louis XIII.
1624	Galileo, *Dialogo sopra i due massimi sistemi del mondo*.
1632	Hulpeau, *Le jeu royal de la paume*.
1701	Courtilz de Sandras, *Mémoires du Marquis de Montbrun*. The first novel dealing with tennis.
1767	Garsault, *Art du Paumier Raquetier*.
1793	"Field tennis" mentioned in *Sport Magazine*.
1815	Marchisio beats Cox in London for the real (or royal) tennis world championship.
1872	Major Gem and Pereira.
Dec., 1873	First rules of lawn tennis set by Major Wingfield.
Feb., 1874	Request for patent by the same Major Wingfield.
Dec., 1874	J. M. Heathcote introduces the covered ball.
1874	Lawn tennis in the United States, perhaps in France and Germany as well.
1877	Wimbledon tournament. Court dimensions set at their present proportions.
1878	Lawn tennis at Bordighera on the Italian Riviera.
1880	Era of the Renshaw brothers in Great Britain. Beginning.
1883	The Clark brothers (United States) at Wimbledon. Net placed at current height.
1897	Era of the Doherty brothers in Great Britain. Beginning.
1900	Davis Cup. United States beats Great Britain 3-0.
1903	The Davis Cup in Great Britain. Laurie Doherty—U.S. champion. (Feet behind the service line.) Great Britain defeats the United States 3-2.
1905	May Sutton (United States) wins Wimbledon.
1907	Norman Brooks (Australia) wins Wimbledon. Davis Cup in Australasia.
1910-1913	Tony Wilding wins Wimbledon.
1911	Décugis-Gobert (France) win in Wimbledon doubles.
1913	Foundation of the International Lawn Tennis Federation (ILTF).
1913	Davis Cup in the United States. United States beats Great Britain 3-2.
1914	Davis Cup in Australia. Australia beats the United States 3-2.
1919	Abstention of the United States from Davis competition in homage to the fallen heroes in Great Britain and Australia.
1919	Era of Suzanne Lenglen (France), the Superstar.
1920	Era of Big Bill Tilden from the United States. Beginning.
1921	Japan in the Challenge Round of the Davis Cup.
1922	Abolition of the Challenge Round at Wimbledon.
1923	New Wimbledon and the present-day Centre Court.
1923	Establishment of the Wightman Cup for women. United States beats Great Britain 7-0.
1924	Norman Brookes, at the age of forty-six, among the first eight at Wimbledon.
1925	Twenty-five teams enrolled for Davis Cup play.
1926	Era of Helen Wills (United States), the Queen.
1927	Davis Cup in France. France beats the United States 3-2.
1927	Era of the Musketeers—Cochet, Lacoste, Borotra, Brugnon. Beginning.
1930	Tilden wins Wimbledon ten years later at thirty-seven.
1931-1932	Vines, champion of the United States.
1933	Davis Cup in Great Britain. Great Britain beats France 3-2.
1933	Era of Perry in Great Britain. Beginning.
1934	Bunny Ryan (United States) wins her nineteenth women's doubles title at Wimbledon.
1937	Davis Cup in the United States. United States beats Great Britain 4-1.
1938	Don Budge (United States) wins the Big Slam.
1938	Helen Wills's eighth victory at Wimbledon.
1939	Riggs (United States) takes three titles at Wimbledon.
1939	Alice Marble (United States) garners three titles at Wimbledon.
1946	Davis Cup in the United States. United States beats Australia 5-0.
1947	Jack Kramer, champion of the United States and of Wimbledon.
1947	Era of Kramer among the Pros. Beginning.
1948-1949	Gonzales, champion of the United States.
1948-1950	Louise Brough wins three Wimbledon titles.
1950	Australian era in Davis Cup play.
1950	Inauguration of the Galea Cup for under 21. Italy beats France 4-1.
1951	Big Slam in doubles, Sedgman-McGregor (Australia).
1952	Era of Maureen Connolly (United States). Beginning.
1953	Connolly wins the Big Slam.
1953	Rosewall (Australia) wins the French Internationals at the age of nineteen.
1954	Era of Gonzales among the professionals. Beginning.
1956-1957	Lew Hoad (Australia) wins Wimbledon.
1957	Olmedo, from Peru, wins the Davis Cup for the United States. America beats Australia 3-2.
1957-1958	Althea Gibson, first Black winner of the Wimbledon and U.S. crowns.
1959-1960	Maria Bueno (Brazil) wins Wimbledon.
1960	Era of Rosewall among the Pros. Beginning.
1960-1961	Italy in the Challenge Round of Davis Cup.
1962	Rod Laver (Australia) wins the Big Slam.
1963	Mexico in the Challenge Round of Davis Cup.
1963	Inauguration of the Women's Federation Cup. United States beats Australia 2-1.
1965	Spain in the Challenge Round of Davis Cup.
1965	Era of Laver among the Pros. Beginning.
1966	India in the Challenge Round of the Davis Cup.
1968	First Open Tournament at Bournemouth. Rosewall beats Laver.
1968	Rosewall, fifteen years late, wins the first French Open Championship. Laver wins the first Wimbledon Open. Ashe wins the first U.S. Open Championship. Davis Cup in the United States. United States beats Australia 4-1.
1969	Rod Laver wins the second Big Slam.
1970	Margaret Court Smith (Australia) wins the Big Slam. Inauguration of the Grand Prix, won by Richey, and the Masters, won by Smith.
1971	Inauguration of the WCT Circuit, won by Laver. Finals won by Rosewall.
1972	Organization of the Association of Tennis Professionals (ATP).
1972	Abolition of the Challenge Round in Davis play. United States beats Romania 3-2.
1973	Boycott of Wimbledon by the ATP.
1973	Davis Cup Open. Australia beats United States 5-0.
1974	Intercity WTT Championships in the United States.
1975	Billie Jean King equals Elizabeth Ryan's 19 Wimbledon titles.